England
in the 1690s

A History of Early Modern England
General Editor: John Morrill

This new series will provide a detailed history of early modern
England. Its distinctiveness lies in the fact that it aims to capture the
spirit of the time from the point of view of the people living
through it. Each volume will be broad in scope covering the political,
religious, social and cultural dimensions of the period.

Published
The Birth of the Elizabethan Age
England in the 1560s
Norman Jones

England in the 1690s
Revolution, Religion and War
Craig Rose

The Birth of Britain
A New Nation 1700–1710
W. A. Speck

In preparation
The Birth of the Jacobean Age
England 1601–1612
Pauline Croft

England in the 1590s
David Dean

The Rule of Charles I
England in the 1630s
Kenneth Fincham

England in the 1650s
Ann Hughes

England
in the 1690s

Revolution, Religion and War

Craig Rose

First published 1999

2 4 6 8 10 9 7 5 3 1

Blackwell Publishers Ltd
108 Cowley Road
Oxford OX4 1JF
UK

Blackwell Publishers Inc.
350 Main Street
Malden, Massachusetts 02148
USA

British Library Cataloguing in Publication Data

A CIP catalogue record for this book is available from the British Library.

Library of Congress Cataloging-in-Publication Data

Rose, Craig.
    England in the 1690s : revolution, religion, and war / Craig Rose.
      p.   cm. — (History of early modern England)
    Includes bibliographical references and index.
    ISBN 0–631–17545–8 (acid-free paper). — ISBN 0–631–20936–0
    (pbk. : acid-free paper)
    1. Great Britain—History—William and Mary, 1689–1702. 2. Great
    Britain—History—Revolution of 1688—Influence. 3. Great Britain—
    History, Military—17th century. 4. England—Church history—17th
    century. 5. England—Civilization—17th century. I. Title. II. Series.
    DA460.R67 1999
    942.06'8—dc21   98-39045
                                                            CIP

Typeset in Baskerville
by Grahame & Grahame Editorial, Brighton
Printed in Great Britain by TJ International, Padstow, Cornwall

This book is printed on acid-free paper

To Francine
and
My Parents

'. . . History is my beloved Study, with it I would (if I had it in my
power) grow old and die.'

Edmund Bohun, *The Character of Queen Elizabeth* (1693), preface

Contents

Illustrations

Picture researcher: Thelma Gilbert

Preface and Acknowledgements

It is often said that the 1690s are an under-researched decade. This is misleading. Over the last 30 years, our understanding of the period – based for so long on Lord Macaulay's magisterial but one-sided political narrative – has been enriched by some outstanding specialist studies. Without the work of Henry Horwitz and David Hayton on politics, Paul Hopkins on Jacobitism, G.V. Bennett on the Church, A.G. Craig and Tony Claydon on reformation of manners, P.G.M. Dickson and John Brewer on finance, and D.W. Jones on the war economy – to name but a few – this book could never have been written. I am deeply indebted to these authors and to the many other scholars whose works are cited in the notes.

Nevertheless, there are two obvious deficiencies in the historiography of the 1690s. The first is the lack of a single-volume general account of the period to supersede David Ogg's *England in the Reigns of James II and William III*, first published in 1955. I became aware of the problems this creates when teaching early modern British history at Cambridge between 1988 and 1992. Although William III's reign was the period with which I was most familiar, I found it the most difficult era to teach. Undergraduates attempting essays on the 1690s tended to flounder, usually through no fault of their own. Their reading lists would contain specialist studies and text-book chapters, but precious little in between. Those brave souls who tackled the specialist articles and monographs were unable to see the wood for the trees. The pragmatists who relied on textbook chapters produced essays lacking in depth or any sense of chronology.

The second weakness in the historiography is a certain lack of imagination and perspective. Over the last 25 years, imaginative scholarship has transformed our understanding of the first half of the seventeenth century. Historians of the early Stuart period no longer write with the lofty detachment born of centuries of hindsight. Of course, they remain devoted to discovering the 'truth' and destroying myths. They are just as interested, however, in investigating contemporary perceptions of the truth. This has led them to explore the mental world and the language of the men and women who lived through Charles I's reign. In the last 10 years or so the lead of the early Stuart historians has been followed by scholars of the Restoration period such as Mark Goldie, Tim Harris and Jonathan Scott. But with one or two exceptions – notably David Hayton's work on political mentalities and Tony Claydon's on 'courtly reformation' – the Williamite era remains a largely barren area for the history of mentalities and perceptions. As a result, the 1690s have a different historiographical feel from the previous decades. They are treated as the beginning of a 'long eighteenth century' rather than as part and parcel of the seventeenth. Indicative of this approach is Professor Horwitz's comment that recent publications on Restoration politics do not have 'as direct a significance for the 1690s as does eighteenth-century historiography'.[1] This historiographical iron curtain has had some unfortunate consequences. Too much attention has been paid to the structure of politics, theoretical justifications of the revolution and the emergence of 'constitutional monarchy': not enough to the political and religious gut issues.

This study seeks to fill the first of these gaps in the historiography – the lack of a student-friendly general book on the period – and go some way towards filling the second, the dearth of studies of the 1690s rooted in the perceptions of contemporaries. Although each chapter has a strong narrative thread, the approach is thematic. Students can therefore dip into individual chapters without having to wade through the whole book. But those who do read it from cover to cover will, I hope, find it more than the sum of its parts. By drawing on a wide range of primary sources – correspondence, diaries, memoirs, parliamentary speeches, pamphlets, sermons, poems, ballads and plays – the book seeks to reconstruct King William's reign through the eyes, and in the words, of those who lived through it. Not only does this give a new flavour to the 1690s – a seventeenth-century flavour – it also tells us much about the impact of the Williamite revolution.

It is fashionable these days for historians to stress the conservatism of the revolution. 'The Revolution', writes one, 'secured the hegemony of the (Anglican) aristocracy and gentry against the threat perceived to be posed by a (Roman Catholic) monarchical bureaucracy: in that sense, 1688 only preserved what 1660 was supposed to have re-established, and establishment theorists consistently laboured to minimise the extent to which 1688 represented a fundamental discontinuity.'[2] If we view the revolution from the perspective of 1760 – a moment of conservative whig consensus – there is much to be said for this view. It all seemed very different, however, to those conservatives who actually lived through the revolution and its aftermath – the tories and High Churchmen of the 1690s. By the middle of the decade at the latest, it was plain to tories that the revolution had brought change, and change for the worse. When they looked to the Continent, they saw English men and money being frittered away on a war to defend Dutch Calvinists. When they looked to Scotland, they saw episcopacy demolished and presbyterianism rampant. When they looked to Whitehall and Westminster, they saw the nation's affairs being directed by whig 'roundheads'. When they looked to the parishes, they saw 'fanatick' meeting houses sprouting up daily. When they looked to the episcopal bench, they saw a group of men ready to 'sell' the Church to the 'fanaticks'. And when the tories looked to the throne, they saw a King profoundly unsympathetic to the Church state which they had fashioned during the early 1680s. The world had not been turned upside down, but it was listing dangerously. The tories would spend the latter part of King William's reign and the whole of Anne's trying to correct the tilt.

I have incurred numerous debts while working on this book. Most of the research was done between 1989 and 1992 when I was the Adrian Research Fellow at Darwin College, Cambridge. I am grateful to the Master and Fellows of Darwin College for giving me the opportunity to engage in post-doctoral research and for providing me with a home during my years as a research fellow.

My principal academic creditor is John Morrill. He first suggested that I should write this book, and read most of it in draft. A letter I received from him in February 1995 convinced me that it was all worthwhile after all. I am also grateful to Mark Goldie and Bill Speck for their comments on draft chapters.

I have gleaned much from conversations with other scholars working in the field, notably Tony Claydon, David Hayton, Steve Pincus, Martin Greig, Peter Le Fevre, Stuart Handley, Andrew Hanham, Andrew Barclay, John Spurr, Mark Taylor, Jonathan Scott, Stephen Taylor and Jeremy Gregory. My friend and colleague Gordon McBain proofed the typescript, spotted internal inconsistencies and corrected the infelicities of my prose.

During the research on this book, I consulted materials at Cambridge University Library, the Bodleian Library, Christ Church Library, Oxford, the British Library, the British Museum, the Public Record Office, the Institute of Historical Research, Dr Williams's Library, Lambeth Palace Library, the Centre for Kentish History, the Hertfordshire Records Office and Trinity College Library, Dublin. I am deeply obliged to the staffs of all these institutions.

Chapter 6 is a modified version of my essay 'Providence, Protestant Union and Godly Reformation in the 1690s', published in the *Transactions of the Royal Historical Society* for 1993. I am grateful to the Royal Historical Society for allowing me to reproduce it here.

My biggest 'thank you' is reserved for my publishers whose patience must have been sorely tried over the last few years. When they commissioned this book in the Summer of 1989, I promised to deliver the manuscript by October 1993. Although that was always a little optimistic, the book was well on course for completion by September 1992 – perhaps another six to nine months research and then writing-up. But in that month my research fellowship came to an end. Instead of finishing the book, I found myself learning the law, grappling with such thrilling concepts as the doctrine of equitable estoppel, non-charitable purpose trusts and the duty of care in tort. Research into primary sources came to an end. Writing was confined to weekends and holidays.

The book has suffered as a result. Scotland and Ireland, the principal victims of King William's revolution, also came out the worse from my personal upheaval. I originally intended to write separate chapters on the Celtic realms. The chapter on Scotland would have included a section on high politics, and there would also have been a much fuller account of the Scottish and Irish revolutions and the subsequent revolutionary war. But this would have required a good deal more research, and after September 1992 there was no time to do it. Faced with a choice between no book and a flawed book, I opted for the latter. It remains for others to judge whether I made the right choice.

During the last six years, there were many times when I despaired of finishing this book. Its completion owes everything to the love and support of the three people to whom it is dedicated.

Craig Rose
June 1998

Abbreviations

BL	British Library
Bod	Bodleian Library, Oxford
CSPD	*Calendar of State Papers Domestic*
CCL	Christ Church Library, Oxford
Cobbett, *Parliamentary History*	William Cobbett, ed., *The Parliamentary History of England* (36 vols, 1806–20)
CUL	Cambridge University Library
DNB	*Dictionary of National Biography*
DWL	Doctor Williams's Library
EHR	*English Historical Review*
Grey, *Debates*	Anchitell Grey, *Debates of the House of Commons, From the Year 1667 to the Year 1694* (10 vols, 1763)
Hatton Correspondence	*Correspondence of the Family of Hatton being chiefly letters addressed to Christopher First Viscount Hatton* AD *1601–1704*, ed. Edward Maude Thompson (2 vols, Camden Soc, ns 22–3, 1878)
HJ	*Historical Journal*
HMC	*Historical Manuscripts Commission Reports*
IHS	*Irish Historical Studies*
JBS	*Journal of British Studies*
Locke Correspondence	*The Correspondence of John Locke*, ed. E.S. De Beer (8 vols, Oxford, 1976–89)
LPL	Lambeth Palace Library
Pepys Ballads	*The Pepys Ballads*, ed. H.E. Rollins (8 vols, Cambridge, Massachusetts, 1929–32)
POAS	*Poems on Affairs of State*, ed. George deForest Lord et al. (7 vols, New Haven, Connecticut, 1963–75)

PP	*Past and Present*
PRO	Public Record Office
SHR	*Scottish Historical Review*
Somers Tracts	*A Collection of Scarce and Valuable Tracts . . . selected from libraries, particularly that of the late Lord Somers,* ed. Sir Walter Scott (13 vols, 1809–1815)
State Tracts	*A Collection of State Tracts, publish'd on occasion of the late revolution in 1688, and during the reign of King William III* (3 vols, 1705–7)
TCD	Trinity College Library, Dublin
TRHS	*Transactions of the Royal Historical Society*
Vernon Correspondence	*Letters Illustrative of the reign of William III from 1696 to 1708 addressed to the Duke of Shrewsbury by James Vernon, Esq,* ed. G.P.R. James (3 vols, 1841)

Note to the Reader

During the 1690s, the Julian (Old Style) Calendar used in the British Kingdoms was ten days behind the Gregorian (New Style) Calendar used on the Continent. This discrepancy grew by a further day after 1700. When referring to events in the British Isles, all dates are in Old Style, save that the year is taken to begin on 1 January rather than 25 March. Both Old and New Style dates are given when referring to events on the Continent.

Original spelling has been retained, but I have usually extended contemporary contractions and sometimes added punctuation.

Unless otherwise stated, London is the place of publication of all works cited in the notes.

1

William the Conqueror

On 5 November 1688 a Dutch army invaded England. Six weeks later, it occupied London, expelling the Catholic King, James II, from his capital. By mid-February, its commander, Prince William of Orange, had been proclaimed King of England, the last monarch to attain the crown by force of arms.

The events which had led to the Dutch invasion were no less astonishing than the invasion itself.[1] From the day he had succeeded his brother, Charles II, in February 1685, King James had been a driven man. Not for him the shuffling pragmatism and deceitful compromises which had characterized his brother's reign. Instead, a single unwavering objective: the reversal of the Protestant Reformation in the three British Kingdoms.

The King did not intend to impose Catholicism upon his subjects. No need for anything quite so crude. As one who had himself seen the light – he had converted to Catholicism in the early 1670s – King James was convinced that only fear and expediency prevented Englishmen from embracing the Church of Rome. Fear was induced by the savage laws against Catholic worship: expediency by the statutes excluding Catholics from office. Scrap those laws, and before long the people of England – or at least those among them who mattered – would come flooding back to the one true and universal church. King James therefore neutered all anti-Catholic legislation, and proceeded to advance the Catholic religion by every means in his power. The results were plain for all to see, and thoroughly uncomfortable viewing they made from a Protestant perspective: Catholic aristocrats and a Jesuit in the Privy Council; Catholic gentlemen sitting on the county benches; Catholic officers in the army; Catholic priests openly celebrating the mass; Catholic missionaries on the streets of London; even Catholic fellows in the Oxbridge colleges.

All this had been achieved through lavish use of the dispensing power: the Crown's right, confirmed by the judges in 1686, to grant individual exemptions from the penal laws. Securing parliamentary repeal of the

offending legislation – the King's ultimate objective – would be more difficult. The parliament elected on King James's succession was dominated
by the tory, or Church, party. The tories had been instrumental in securing
the King's accession, having successfully opposed an agitation to bar him
from the succession during the 'exclusion crisis' of 1679–81.[2] But the tories
had not backed the then Duke of York because they loved his religion.
Rather they had stood firm against exclusion because they saw its proponents – the so-called whigs – as latter-day roundheads: 'fanaticks' intent
upon destroying the Crown and Church of England. When the Crown
turned against the Church, the tories stood by the Church.

King James responded with a bold stratagem. In the Summer of 1687
he dissolved parliament – which had in fact not sat since November 1685 –
and began to make preparations for a fresh parliament. This would require
new allies. There were simply too few English Catholics – they formed less
than two percent of the population – to rule entirely through them. So the
King turned to his erstwhile enemies, the whigs, party of pan-Protestantism
and militant anti-popery. After the final defeat of exclusion in 1681, King
Charles had launched a ruthless campaign against the whigs. Some were
executed, others fled into exile, the rest were driven from public life. King
James now offered to rehabilitate the whigs in return for supporting
repeal of the anti-Catholic laws. Moreover, the benefits of toleration and
civil equality would be extended to Protestant dissenters – the most clearly
identifiable element of whiggery – who had been remorselessly persecuted
since 1681. To this end, in April 1687 the King issued a Declaration of
Indulgence suspending the operation of the penal laws and the sacramental
tests for office.

It was a policy which met with some success. True, whig exiles continued
to plot against the King from their Dutch sanctuary. But in England many
whigs and dissenters were won over, actively supporting King James's
preparations for the new parliament, scheduled to meet in the Autumn of
1688.[3] Others simply accepted the benefits of the Indulgence, and kept
their heads down.

In contrast, the Church of England defied the King at every turn,
resisting him not by force – this remained anathema to a Church which
prided itself on its loyalty to the Crown – but through a campaign of civil
disobedience.[4] The climax came in the Spring of 1688 when King James
reissued the Declaration of Indulgence, and ordered the clergy to read it
from their pulpits. In May seven of the bishops, led by Archbishop

*Figure 1 A plan of St James's Palace, 1688. When the Prince of Wales was born in June
1688, many Protestants forced themselves to believe that he was a 'suppositious' babe, smuggled into the Queen's bed in a warming-pan. The dotted line purports to trace the route taken
by the mythical warming-pan through St James's Palace.*

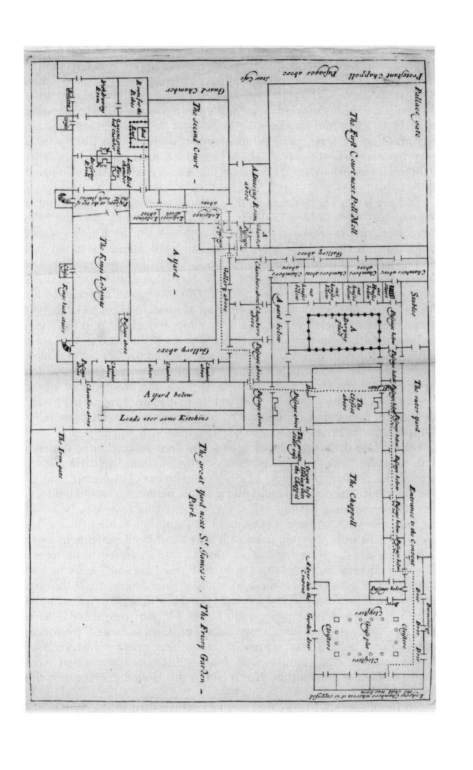

Sancroft of Canterbury, petitioned the King to withdraw his order. King James's reaction – charging the bishops with seditious libel and imprisoning them in the Tower – brought about a rare degree of Protestant unity. The whigs had no reason to love Archbishop Sancroft and his minions. Not only had the bishops led the opposition to exclusion in the parliaments of 1679–81, they had also been at the heart of the subsequent campaign against the dissenters. But the imprisonment of the 'Seven Bishops' was seen by many whigs as an attack on Protestantism in general, inevitably evoking memories of the Protestant bishops martyred by Mary Tudor in the 1550s.

To King James's consternation, the bishops were acquitted at the end of June amidst scenes of wild rejoicing. But a shadow hung over the celebrations. Until the Summer of 1688, time had been the King's greatest enemy. He would be 55 in 1688, an old man by the standards of the day, and he lacked an heir to continue his work. The two daughters of his first marriage, the Princesses Mary and Anne, had been raised as Protestants and were married to Protestant princes. Fifteen years of marriage to his second wife, the Catholic princess Mary of Modena, had been childless. It seemed certain, therefore, that Catholic hopes would die with the King, a reassuring thought for all Protestants. But on 10 June came shattering news: the Queen had given birth to a son, James Francis Edward, supplanting the two princesses in the line of succession. Gone was the prospect of a Protestant succession. In its place, the likelihood of a long line of Catholic monarchs. Small wonder that many Protestants forced themselves to believe that the new Prince was not the Queen's son, but a 'suppositious' babe smuggled into her bed in a warming-pan.

On the face of things, very little could be done to ameliorate this dire state of affairs. True, King James's electoral preparations – in particular his remodelling of parliamentary corporations in favour of dissenters – might fail to produce the desired results. But a hostile parliament would hold few terrors for the King. Thanks to the Crown's buoyant revenues, he could happily rule without parliament should its composition not prove to his liking. There had, after all, been only one short-lived parliament since 1681. Nor did the King have any reason to fear an armed insurrection. Since his succession, King James had transformed the small army he had inherited from his brother into a formidable force, some 40,000 strong. An army of fewer than 10,000 men had proved sufficient to deal with the rebellion launched by his nephew, the Duke of Monmouth, in 1685. What price a rising against a force more than four times as large? Not much, unless the rebellion was supported by foreign military intervention. Unbeknown to King James, plans for just such an intervention were already being laid across the North Sea in the United Provinces of the Netherlands.

No European ruler had closer ties to England than Prince William of

Orange, 37 year-old captain-general of the Dutch Republic and Stadholder (governor) of five of its seven provinces.[5] A blood nephew of King James, the Prince had been third in line to the throne in his own right until the birth of the Prince of Wales. The first in line had been his wife of 11 years, Princess Mary. Her hopes of the succession had been destroyed by the Prince's birth, and she was convinced that her so-called brother was in reality a monstrous fraud. Whether Prince William thought likewise remains uncertain. What is clear is that the Prince's interest in English affairs was strategic as well as dynastic. True, news of the Queen's pregnancy in December 1687 appears to have prompted his decision to intervene in England. But the Prince was motivated less by the obligation to protect his wife's interests, important though that was, than by the need to defend his beloved homeland.[6]

The security of the state had been Prince William's obsession ever since his elevation to the Stadholderate during the great French invasion of 1672. Called upon to save the Republic from Louis XIV, he had done just that. But the peace of 1678 had done nothing to reduce the power or ambitions of the King of France. By the end of 1687 Franco-Dutch tensions were again reaching dangerous levels, stoked up by the French King's decision to impose draconian restrictions on Dutch trade with France.[7]

Faced with a massively superior foe, Prince William sought to redress the balance by forging a grand coalition against King Louis. The King of Spain, the Emperor Leopold and the German princes – threatened by the French King in Flanders and along the Rhine – were generally responsive. The King of England was not. He had no quarrel with the King of France. Quite the contrary. Like his brother before him, King James happily accepted financial *douceurs* from the French King. Nor did the prospect of military glory seem overly attractive to a king who prized his financial independence above all else. A European war would require taxes, taxes meant parliaments and parliaments with financial clout were potentially unruly beasts. So King James had no intention of committing himself to an anti-French alliance. He had a spanking new army, to be sure. But it was designed for use only against domestic enemies.

This was immeasurably frustrating to Prince William. But he was not a man to take no for an answer, especially when the fate of his country was at stake. If King James would not willingly join the anti-French camp, he would have to be compelled to do so. To this end, the Prince hatched an audacious plan. He would bring an army to England, ostensibly to restore the nation's liberties. The English army, suborned by Dutch agents before the landing, would desert its master. 'Spontaneous' uprisings, planned to coincide with the Dutch landing, would do the rest. Abandoned by both people and army, King James would have no option but to bow to the Prince's will. Prince William would control the destiny of England, bringing her into the struggle against King Louis.

In April 1688 Prince William disclosed his intentions to sympathisers in England, and at the end of June seven of them – the so-called 'Immortal Seven' – asked him to intervene. Their 'invitation' was given without a shred of legal authority, but it would help to sustain the fiction that the Prince was simply responding to the cries of the English people.

Far more important from a practical point of view – indeed wholly indispensable – was the support, at first tacit but eventually formal, of the Dutch ruling elite and its representative institutions. The various assemblies – especially the provincial assembly of the most powerful state, Holland, and the council of its richest city, Amsterdam – had traditionally been wary of supporting any venture which smacked of Orange military adventurism and dynastic aggrandizement. But the French assault on Dutch trade – culminating at the end of September in the arrest of all Dutch ships in France – coupled with fears that King Louis was on the verge of dominating the strategically-important lower Rhine, won over the reluctant burghers of Amsterdam and the other Holland towns. Realising that the Prince's cause was also their own, they agreed to provide him with the men and money required for the invasion of England. Waverers in the other provinces were brought into line by claims that King James was conspiring with King Louis to attack the United Provinces – a bare-faced lie, but one lent credence by the events of 1672 when England had indeed joined France in assailing the Dutch.[8]

Through the Summer and into the Autumn of 1688, a massive armament – 53 men of war, 10 fire-ships, 400 transport vessels, 21,000 soldiers and the Republic's powerful artillery train – was prepared in the Dutch ports.[9] An enterprise on this scale – the largest combined operation in European waters until the Second World War – could not long remain undetected. By mid-August, reports of the Dutch preparations had reached both Versailles and Whitehall. The King of France responded by threatening the Dutch with war: the King of England, by putting his head in the sand. Despite all the evidence to the contrary, King James simply refused to believe that the Prince of Orange – his own flesh and blood – was about to invade his realm. When the scales finally fell from his eyes towards the end of September, King James panicked, scrapping the planned elections and turning for help to his old friends, the tories.

The King's efforts to patch up relations with the tories met with only limited success. Their faith in King James had been shattered over the previous three years, and few were prepared to take his side against a Prince whose aims appeared to be limited.[10] In his *Declaration*, published at the end of September, Prince William made no mention of any designs on the Crown. He was coming merely to deliver King James from the 'evil counsellors' who had led him astray, to preserve the Protestant religion, and to ensure that the King called a 'free' parliament to redress the nation's grievances. Nothing objectionable in that to the average tory.

By mid-October only adverse winds were holding the Dutch back. To protect the Republic while its army was in England, the States General – the federal body of the United Provinces – hired 14,000 soldiers from friendly German princes. These mercenaries took up position on the frontiers, ready to deal with any attack by King Louis. Yet for all his bellicose noises, the French King was in no position to interfere with Prince William's plans. His navy was in the Mediterranean, ready for a move against the Papal States. Then in September King Louis committed his army to an offensive against the Emperor on the middle Rhine, nearly 200 miles from the borders of the Dutch Republic. King James would face the Dutch alone.

Among those waiting impatiently for the winds to change was the Anglo-Scots cleric, Gilbert Burnet. A political exile in the Netherlands since 1686, Burnet was due to accompany the Dutch expedition as one of Prince William's chaplains. He could hardly contain his excitement. 'The Designe is as just as it is great,' he wrote in the chronicle which was to form the basis of his celebrated *History of My Own Time*,

> and the Prince as far as it is possible to see into a Mans heart goes into it with great and noble intentions; and he seems to be marked-out by providence for the doing of wonders: And as his first Essay was the saving of this State, when it was almost quite over-run by the French, so he seems to be now led by Providence to a much nobler undertaking, In which if God bless him with success, and if he manage the English Nation as dexterously as he hath hitherto done the Dutch he will be the Arbiter of all Europe, and will very quickly bring Lewis the great to a much humbler posture, and will acquire a much juster Right to the Title of great than the other has ever yet done.

As this glittering prospect floated before his eyes, Burnet chided himself. 'I must remember that I am a Historian and not a Prophet. Therefore I do now interrupt the thread of this History; whether I shall live ever to carry it on any more is only known to that God, to whom I must humbly resigne my life and all that is dear to me; thus I conclude at the Hague the 3rd of October.'[11]

A few weeks later, the winds changed and the Dutch fleet set sail. The ships of the Royal Navy – confined to their bases by the very winds which were wafting the Dutch up the Channel – were unable to intervene. On 4 November, Prince William celebrated his thirty-eighth birthday on board his flagship within sight of the Devon coast. The next day – the most auspicious in the Protestant calendar – he landed unopposed with his army at Brixham in Torbay.

For two weeks the nation watched and waited. Although the gentry of the south-west, both whig and tory, went over to Prince William, the planned uprisings in the north and midlands proved slow to materialize. At the same time, there was a singular lack of response to King James's call for the nation to rally against the foreign invader. The armies, not the people, would decide the issue. And they would, it seemed, decide it in battle. To Prince William's chagrin, there was only a handful of defections from the King's army based at Salisbury.

The rival armies were roughly equal in numbers, but the Prince's force was superior in all other respects, not least leadership.[12] In his youth, King James had been a brave and resourceful soldier. But when he reached Salisbury on 19 November, the fire had gone from his belly. Shocked to the core by the treachery of the Prince and Princess of Orange, unnerved by the apparent indifference of the populace to the Dutch invasion and convinced that his army was riddled with traitors, King James was in no mood to fight. Nor were his generals. At a Council of War on 23 November, the King accepted their advice to retreat. That night, King James's favourite, John Churchill, and his other son-in-law, Prince George of Denmark – both of whom were up to their necks in the Orangist conspiracy – slipped out of the camp and went over to the Prince. It was part of a growing trend. In the previous week Derby, Nottingham and York had all declared for the Prince and a free parliament.

As the King's army made its demoralized way back to London, whig exiles in Prince William's entourage pressed him to strike for the crown. The Prince would have none of it. Such a move would alienate the tories. It was also unnecessary. With a powerful army at his back, and the support of the political classes, the Prince's bargaining position was immensely strong. He could get what he wanted – control of England's foreign policy – without the embarrassment of having to topple his father-in-law.

When King James returned to London on the 26th, he received still more bad news. His younger daughter, Princess Anne, and her closest friend, Sarah Churchill, had followed their husbands' lead and gone over to the Prince of Orange. It was the final blow. In the depths of despair, the King sought the advice of the tory peers. At their urging, he called elections for a new parliament, and dispatched three commissoners to negotiate with the Prince at Hungerford.

The King, however, had no intention of reaching a settlement with his treacherous son-in-law. He was all too aware of the weakness of his hand, and he did not like it. The thought of being King in name only was unbearable. He was also mindful of his son's position. In his *Declaration*, Prince William had called for a parliamentary inquiry into the circumstances surrounding the child's birth. This filled King James with dread. At worst, it could pave the way for his son's dispossession. At best, it would result in the King losing control of the boy's education. And the possibility of his son succumbing to the 'northern heresy' was simply too horrible to contemplate. To make matters worse, he feared for his own safety and that of his family in a capital apparently on the verge of an anti-Catholic explosion. The bloody fate of deposed English monarchs – not least that of his father, Charles I – weighed heavily upon him. King James was determined not to go the same way. On 9 December he sent his wife and baby son to France. In the early hours of the 11th, after destroying the writs for the new parliament and ordering his soldiers not to resist the Dutch, King James followed suit. Later that day, as anti-Catholic mobs roamed the capital, a group of peers and bishops met at Guildhall and formed themselves into a provisional government.

While the peers sought to restore order in London, Prince William was hastily revising his plans. He had not come for the crown, it was true. But King James's flight had transformed the situation, creating a vacuum at the very heart of government. It was an opportunity too good to miss. For the first time, the Prince set his sights on the throne itself.[13]

Once again, however, events took an unexpected turn. The Prince was at Windsor on 16 December when he received the shock news that King James was back in London. His attempt to flee had ended in ignominy on the Kent coast where, mistaken for a Jesuit, he had been detained by local fishermen. Rescued by a unit of guards despatched by the Guildhall peers, the King had been brought back to London and reinstalled at Whitehall to the cheers of the crowds. It was a moment of revelation. For the first time King James realised that the Londoners loathed his religion, not his person.

The warmth of his reception appears to have given the King new heart. At all events, he was now ready to negotiate. On 17 December, in a meeting with the bishops, he promised to abide by the laws, maintain the Church's privileges, accept the Protestant monopoly of office, place the powers of war and peace in Prince William's hands and grant the Prince control of ecclesiastical and political patronage.[14] These were terms which delighted the bishops and would have more than satisfied the Prince had they been on the table a week earlier. But Prince William was no longer prepared to talk. King James had scorned one chance of a negotiated settlement. He would not be given another.

By 17 December, the Dutch army had advanced to the outskirts of London. Just before midnight, as the King was going to bed, the vanguard reached Whitehall. Its commander had orders to secure the palace and then 'escort' King James out of London. Finding the palace occupied by Dutch soldiers, the King offered no resistance. He left his capital under armed guard the next morning. Later that day, with his troops lining the streets, Prince William made a triumphant entry into London and set up court at St James's. There, on 23 December, he received the news he had been expecting. After being placed under the laxest of guards at Rochester, King James had at last made his way to France. The Prince's path to the throne was now clear.

Even before the King's second flight, Prince William's drive for the crown had been gathering pace. On 20 December he had summoned an assembly of peers in the hope that it would further his ambitions. When the peers proved hopelessly divided, the Prince called an unprecedented and highly selective assembly of commoners. On 23 December – the day of King James's flight from Rochester – he sent out invitations to selected members of the Corporation of London and all the surviving members of Charles II's parliaments then in town. But the Prince pointedly excluded those commoners who had sat only in the tory parliament of 1685. In that parliament, the Church party had first signalled its hostility to King James's policies. Like the London crowds, however, the MPs of 1685 remained inherently loyal to the King. For that very reason, they were ignored by a Prince intent upon securing an assembly sympathetic to his regal aspirations.[15]

The prospect of a whig-dominated assembly, coming hard on the heels of King James's flight, forced the peers' hands. At a meeting on Christmas Eve, they asked Prince William to summon a Convention of peers and commoners, and invited him to govern the realm until it met. Two days later, the assembly of commoners made a similar request. The Prince formally assumed the reins of government on the 28th. That same day, he issued circular letters for a Convention.

After elections early in the new year, the Convention opened at Westminster on 22 January. Six days later, in its first substantive debate, the Commons voted that King James had 'abdicated the government', and that the throne was 'thereby vacant'. But at this point, the Prince's serene progress to the throne hit an obstacle in the House of Lords.

Ever since King James's expulsion from Whitehall, the Church party had become increasingly uncomfortable with the course of events. It was one thing to support the Prince in restoring the nation's liberties: quite another to assist him in usurping the throne. As tories pointed out, Prince William's pre-invasion *Declaration* had made no mention of deposing King James.[16] Many of the peers and bishops still hoped for the King's restoration, and favoured the establishment of a regency in the interim. When that proposal was put to the vote in the Lords, it was defeated by only three votes. Nor was that the end of the story. Among the anti-regency majority were a number of tory peers who regarded the notion of a vacant throne as a constitutional nonsense. They readily accepted another Commons motion, 'that it hath been found, by experience, to be inconsistent with the

Figure 2   King William and Queen Mary, from Richard Cox's Hibernia Anglicana, *1689. The constitutional arrangement worked out in February 1689 was unique. William and Mary would reign as joint sovereigns, but William alone would hold the sovereign power. During the King's absences abroad, the Queen ruled as her husband's regent, assisted by a select group of ministers – the 'cabinet council'.*

safety and welfare of this Protestant Kingdom to be governed by a Popish Prince.' But if King James's reign was indeed over – and one discounted the popish and 'suppositious' Prince of Wales – it followed that Princess Mary had already succeeded to the throne. So in an attempt to secure the throne for Mary alone, and thereby preserve the principle of hereditary succession, they made common cause with the loyalists in voting down the 'vacancy'. This in turn encouraged tory commoners to stick their heads above the parapet. When the Commons debated the issue anew on 5 February, 151 die-hard tories – Maryites rather than Jacobites – voted to agree with the Lords. But the majority of the house still insisted that the throne was vacant.

With a stalemate between the two houses, the Prince might have been tempted to claim the throne by right of conquest. That was, after all, the reality of the situation. Yet it would not have sat easily with his professed objective of restoring the liberties of the English people. Nor would it foster good relations with parliament, a prerequisite for bringing King Louis to heel. So instead Prince William threatened to return to the Netherlands unless he was given the throne, leaving England to the mercy of King James and his protector, the King of France.

In the face of the Prince's ultimatum, the resistance of the Lords began to crumble. It collapsed entirely on 6 February after Princess Mary made it known that she would not dream of taking precedence over her husband. A unique constitutional arrangement was now agreed. William and Mary would reign as joint sovereigns, but with the King having sole responsibility for the administration of government. If Mary predeceased William, he would continue to rule as King. However, any children of a second marriage would follow Princess Anne and her offspring in the line of succession.

This ingenious compromise removed the final obstacle to Prince William's accession. In a ceremony at Whitehall on 13 February, William and Mary accepted the Convention's offer of the throne. At the same time, the Lords and Commons presented the new King and Queen with their Declaration of Rights, a largely anodyne statement of constitutional principles which has assumed a greater importance for historians than it ever possessed for contemporaries. True, it declared unlawful the Crown's power to suspend statutes, together with the dispensing power as it had been 'assumed and exercised of late'. It also broke new ground by declaring a peacetime standing army unlawful without parliamentary consent. But it left untouched the Crown's power to summon and dissolve parliaments at will, to veto legislation, to appoint and dismiss ministers, to declare war and make peace.[17]

In short, the Declaration of Rights – given legal effect as the Bill of Rights only in December 1689 – did not cause a radical shift in the balance of power between Crown and parliament. It simply made it illegal for the new

King to act as the old one had done – no great loss for King William since he had no intention of acting like King James. William the Dutchman, like William the Norman six centuries earlier, had won the crown by conquest. For the second William the Conqueror, however, winning the crown was not an end in itself. He had come to England to contest the power of France. To do that, he would need parliamentary supply. It was inevitable, therefore, that he would have to rule in partnership with parliament, just as he ruled in partnership with representative bodies in the Netherlands. Of course, he would not gladly surrender any of the Crown's prerogatives. But what really mattered was persuading parliament – the Convention having declared itself a parliament on 23 February – to commit England's resources to the struggle against Louis XIV. And over the next eight years, albeit often grudgingly, parliament would do just that. For all the tribulations he would suffer as King – and there would be many – William of Orange essentially got what he wanted. He was not only the architect of the revolution. He was also its principal beneficiary.

The revolution's great loser – other than King James – was the King of France. True to his word, King Louis had declared war on the Netherlands within days of Prince William's landing in England. He had, however, been unable to give King James any military assistance. As a result, the strategic balance in Europe had been tilted against the French King. It was only a matter of time before English ships and soldiers joined the fight against him. But King Louis had no intention of waiting for King William's declaration of war. Instead, he would strike first by making the British Isles a seat of war.

The obvious point of intervention was Ireland where the Catholic majority had gained control of the civil and military administrations during the rule of King James's viceroy, the Earl of Tyrconnell. At the French King's insistence, this intervention would be led in person by his guest, the deposed King of England.[18] King James arrived in Ireland on 12 March, accompanied by French military advisers. Seven more French convoys reached Ireland in the following months, bringing much-needed weaponry and supplies for the Irish army. Despite being reorganised by French officers in the Spring, this almost entirely Catholic force remained more notable for its size – some 35,000 men – than its quality.

King James intended to use Ireland as a platform for a landing in Scotland. Once established in his family's 'ancient kingdom', he would swoop down into England and drive the usurpers from the throne. His plans soon suffered a blow. The collapse of the King's rule in England had created a power vacuum in Scotland, a vacuum filled by his bitterest enemies, the fierce presbyterians of the south-western Lowlands. In mob violence starting on Christmas Day 1688, the Cameronians – the most extreme of the presbyterian groups – destroyed the episcopalian establishment in the south-west. They then seized the initiative at Edinburgh where a Convention of the Estates assembled on 14 March to consider Scotland's response to events in England.

The Convention met in an atmosphere not entirely conducive to free and reasoned debate. Edinburgh castle was held by a beleaguered Jacobite garrison, but the capital's streets were controlled by armed Cameronians, over a thousand of them, ready and willing to help the Convention reach the right decisions.[19] Not that the Convention needed much encouragement. Many of its members were committed revolutionaries, eager to deliver the *coup de grâce* to the old regime. Others did not take kindly to a threatening letter from King James, warning them of the frightful consequences of rebellion. Thus even before the disheartened Jacobites seceded from the assembly on 18 March, the outcome was certain. Forty years earlier, when the English had last deposed their king, the Scots reacted by proclaiming his son King of 'Great Britain'. The result was an English invasion and the forcible incorporation of Scotland within the Commonwealth. In 1689 the members of the Convention did not repeat the mistake. On 4 April they declared that the King – James VII to the Scots – had 'forfaulted' the Scottish throne. A week later, the Covention proclaimed William and Mary King and Queen of Scots.

Nevertheless, the deposed King still had his partisans in Scotland, notably John Graham of Claverhouse, Viscount Dundee. He was already attempting to raise the Highlands for his master, and was urgently in need of support from Ireland. King James promised to send him several regiments post-haste. In the event, no Irish troops were sent to Scotland until July, and then all that could be spared was a mere 400 raw recruits.[20] The rest of the King's soldiers wasted their energies investing Londonderry, held for King William by its Protestant citizens. After enduring a three month siege, the garrison was relieved by Williamite forces on 28 July.

It was the second disaster to befall King James's cause in two days. On 27 July Dundee's Highlanders fell upon a Williamite army at Killiecrankie, and literally cut it to pieces. But the clansmen's victory was rendered pyrrhic by the death of their commander, hit by a stray bullet at the moment of victory. For a few weeks, the leaderless Jacobites continued to menace the Lowlands. But after suffering a mauling from the Cameronians at Dunkeld on 21 August, and with no immediate prospect of reinforcement from Ireland, they retired to their Highland fastnesses. Eight months later, a planned foray into the north-eastern Lowlands came to grief at Cromdale, a defeat which destroyed the Jacobite army as a cohesive force. Yet it was not until January 1692 that a combination of bribes and threats finally induced the clan chiefs to submit to the new regime. Even then, King William felt the need to teach the clans a lesson, a decision resulting in the cold-blooded slaughter of the Jacobite Macdonalds of Glencoe.[21]

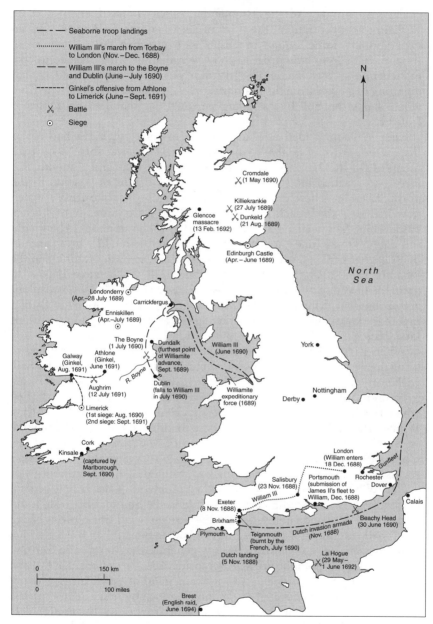

Map 1   The Glorious Revolution and the War in the Channel, 1688–94

The containment of the Highlanders after Dunkeld enabled King William to concentrate on the third of his kingdoms. In August 1689 an expeditionary force landed in Ulster to commence the reconquest of Ireland. It made so little progress, however, that the King decided to take matters into his own hands. The Irish war was becoming an acute irritant, diverting resources from the main theatre of conflict in Flanders. The King would lance the boil by assuming personal command of his forces in Ireland.

King William landed at Carrickfergus in June 1690. He had at his disposal an army of 37,000 men, whose backbone was formed by regiments of Dutch, Danish and Huguenot soldiers. By the end of month, this force had reached the River Boyne, a natural defensive position to the north of Dublin. There its path was blocked by the Jacobite army – which now included six French batallions – led by King James himself. The battle which had been avoided in England in 1688 was about to be fought in Ireland. On 30 June King William was hit in the shoulder by a cannonball ricochet while viewing the enemy positions, sparking rumours in the Jacobite camp that the usurper had been killed. He gave the lie to them the next day by leading a successful assault on the Jacobite positions across the river. King James fled the field, stopping only briefly in Dublin before slinking back to France. Never again would he set foot in any of his kingdoms.

When King William entered Dublin on 6 July, he was determined to bring the war to a swift end. This meant taking Limerick where the Franco-Irish army had taken refuge after the Boyne. The King arrived before the town on 9 August. However, his hopes of taking it by storm were dashed when the Jacobite cavalry destroyed most of his siege artillery. King William raised the siege at the end of the month and returned to England. In September John Churchill – now Earl of Marlborough – recaptured Cork and Kinsale in a brilliant three-week campaign. But the King's reverse at Limerick ensured that the war would drag on for another year.

The Williamite army, now under the command of the Dutch general Godard van Ginkel, resumed its offensive in the Summer of 1691. It did so against a depleted enemy. Seeing the way the wind was blowing, King Louis had withdrawn his troops from Ireland in September 1690. He had, however, sent out one of his most fiery generals, the Marquis de St Ruth, to command the Catholic army. After losing Athlone to Ginkel at the end of June 1691, St Ruth decided to make a stand at Aughrim in County Galway. The two armies met on 12 July. A much bloodier affair than the Boyne, the battle hung in the balance for much of the day. But as night fell, St Ruth and 7,000 of his men lay dead on the field. Catholic Ireland had suffered its most terrible defeat.

After destroying the Jacobite field army, Ginkel prosecuted the mopping-up operations with vigour. Galway capitulated a week after

Aughrim, leaving Limerick as the last major centre of resistance. After a five-week siege, the city surrendered on terms on 3 October, bringing to an end the revolutionary war in Ireland.

Such were the events which later generations called the 'Glorious Revolution'. Their consequences are the subject of this study.

2

King William and his Contemporaries

In this book, the reader will be introduced to a large cast of characters. Some will play starring parts, while others will enjoy only a fleeting moment in the limelight. The leading man, unquestionably, will be William Henry of Nassau, Prince of Orange, captain-general of the United Provinces, Stadholder of five of its seven provinces, and King of England, Scotland and Ireland. Yet King William may well emerge from the pages of this study as a rather shadowy eminence, an emblematic rather than a flesh and blood character. If that is so, then it is in part a reflection of the man himself. Unlike his two Stuart uncles, William of Orange was noted for his reserve, and was ill at ease in the public eye. However, the elusive role which the King will play in this book is also indicative of its aims. It seeks to describe and explain the perceptions, attitudes and debates engendered by King William's policies, and does not explore in any depth the processes by which those policies were made. Nevertheless, it can hardly be denied that King William was himself the greatest issue of the reign. The irregular manner in which he had come to the throne meant that England was afflicted with the worst evil that could befall a personal monarchy: a disputed succession. No matter what the Convention might say, King James did not consider himself to have abdicated the throne. Worse still, many of the late King's subjects refused to accept the overthrow of his regime. As we saw in the first chapter, Irish and Scottish Jacobites fought to preserve King James's rights in his Celtic domains between 1689 and 1691. In England, it is true, there were no risings against the new regime. But Jacobite conspiracy would remain a threat for much of the 1690s. On top of this, King James's deposition also plunged the Church of England into crisis. As we shall see in a later chapter, some 400 clergymen, led by Archbishop Sancroft of Canterbury, preferred to lose their livings rather than swear allegiance to the revolution monarchs. Some of these so-called nonjurors would become leading lights in the Jacobite press, keeping up an incessant literary barrage on the Dutch usurper. But it was not only avowed Jacobites who harried King William. The King's open preference for all things Dutch, and barely concealed disdain for his English subjects, were the objects of much adverse comment throughout the 1690s. In the last years of the reign, they helped to provoke (from the King's point of view) some thoroughly obnoxious parliamentary legislation. The personal affronts which King William suffered at the hands of MPs between 1699 and 1701 will be described in the final section of this chapter. It begins, though, with a review of the main themes of Williamite and Jacobite propaganda.

1. God's Warrior

At the end of each year, it was the custom of the nonconformist minister Oliver Heywood to pen a review of the 12 months which had passed. Since the purpose of this exercise was to trace the working of God's providence in the world, Heywood's review of the year 1688–9 had a very special significance: 'there have', he wrote,

> been the strangest Revolutions and preventions that ever England saw, a black day grew upon us, a bloody cloud hanged over us, of popery, massacre when all on a sudden a bright sun appeared out of the East, I mean the prince of Orange who landed near Exeter in the West Nov[ember] 5 [16]88 with 14000 and Nobility, gentry flock to him, souldiers fell to him this bright sun scattered the clouds, and our feares, K[ing] J[ames] fled into France papists fled, or were taken, a pa[r]l[iamen]t called, sate, chose W[illiam] P[rince] of O[range] King proclaimed him, day of thanksgiving celebrated through the kingdom, the whole face of things changed next to a miracle once in 3 months time, so the managem[en]t of all things is put into other hands and the scene of things so altered as if it were a new world, and great hopes of further mercy, and gracious dispensations both in state and church: from this time it shall be said what hath god! my dear Lord helpt my heart in the afternoon of that day to give him the glory of these prodigious acts of providence in these publick concernes: and my Lord made it a sweet day to my soul notwithstanding many avocations by several friends.[1]

Heywood's breathless account faithfully reflects the interpretation of the revolution favoured by ardent Williamites: a providential deliverance of the English people from the iniquities of popery. As the astrologer John Tanner wrote in 1689, King James's regime had seen

> . . . truth mangled, into Dungeons thrust,
> Goodness and good Men prest to lick the dust.
> Dark and most dismal clouds obscur'd the skie,
> We groap'd in darkness, no man knew his way;
> Heavens light besmeared by Rome's Sorcery.

From this sorry state of affairs, Englishmen had been rescued not by their own efforts but by the hand of God. 'Thus', Tanner continued,

> . . . in despaire all sinking to the ground,
> No hopes of help beneath Heaven to be found,
> Heaven heard us, and immediately decreed,
> In mercy to remove our sad distress:
> And that without our aid we should be freed
> From those that cruelly did us oppress:
> Inspir'd a Prince, and rais'd his mind so high,
> Above what mortal contemplations try.
> Who operates like the Celestial Sun,
> Whose warmth softeneth the Clouds and makes them fly,
> Then shews his Face, shines forth and all is done,
> All Fogs and Vapours banish'd from the Sky . . .[2]

And since the revolution was a divinely-inspired deliverance, it necessarily followed that King William was the chosen instrument of divine providence. Just as King David had been 'safely guarded, by a constant, signal, watchful Providence', declared a preacher in 1690, so 'our Illustrious Deliverer' had been 'conducted by a special Providence, which loudly proclaim'd all along, that it was God who had raised him up, to restore our Israel, to deliver our Bodies from the Tyranny of Men, and our Souls from the Doctrines of Devils'.[3] This view of King William is nicely illustrated by a print published to mark the first anniversary of the revolution. A manacled Albion is about to be despatched by the Pope. But flying to the rescue, like some seventeenth-century Superman, is the Prince of Orange. He parries the fatal blow, while an accompanying guardian angel prepares to plunge his sword into the Beast.[4] In the nick of time, God's champion saves the day.

There is no doubt that King William's supporters genuinely believed their hero to be a heaven-sent deliverer. But as Tony Claydon has rightly stressed, the rhetoric of providential deliverance was also an essential tool in legitimating a ruler who lacked the traditional sanction of hereditary succession.[5] In the 1650s Cromwellian propagandists, faced with a not dissimilar predicament, had taken to depicting the Lord Protector as an Old Testament hero, rescuing God's people from the clutches of those without the law.[6] Four decades later, the biblical analogies again flew thick and fast. To Tanner, King William was a Joshua, sent to 'lead us safely into the Promis'd Land'.[7] In a sermon delivered in April 1696, the Norfolk clergyman Henry Meriton reminded the congregation that King William was

> truly Religious, sent to redeem our Captivated Ark, out of the Philistins Hands; to spread himself like an Elijah upon the poor dying Shunamite; fainting and languishing Protestancy, and restore her to life again, as a Moses, with the lifting up of his Rod, and a puff of his Mouth, to blow away all the

Locusts of Rome, and swarms of Mass Priests that pestered this Nation, and threatened a Spiritual Famine to it; instead of the Calves of Dan and Bethel, to restore to us the worship of the true Jehovah, instead of a latine mummery, an intelligible Devotion.[8]

Figure 3 'In Memory of ye Deliverance from Popery & Slavery by King William III in MDCLXXXVIII', 1689. To Williamites, the revolution of 1688 was a providential deliverance from the evils of popery – a view vividly illustrated in this print. The heroic Prince of Orange, assisted by guardian angels, prevents the Pope from striking down a manacled Albion. In fact, Pope Innocent XI tacitly supported the revolution which he saw as a blow against his enemy, King Louis of France.

King William's supporters, like Cromwell's before them, were especially enamoured with the Moses analogy.[9] In 1699, when the King was beset with parliamentary crises, the writer Richard Blackmore attacked those who longed to return to Egyptian bondage and 'spoke of Stoning the Moses that rescu'd them'.[10] Ten years earlier, in a poem called *The Murmurers*, the story of the revolution was retold using the familar characters and imagery of the Book of Exodus. The people of Israel/England lie gasping before the feet of the tyrannical Pharaoh/James II. But their plight has not escaped the attention of Moses/the Prince of Orange:

> His injur'd Peoples woes too well he knew,
> Too well he saw, and seeing felt 'em too.
> He saw each Privilege and Grant was vain
> Confirm'd in any other Pharao's Reign,
> When the fair Compact with Israel was made,
> And in blest Goshen they might freely trade . . .
> New Task-masters thro Egypt sent he saw,
> And Pharao's Will was their unrighteous Law.
> Israel they ground, still made the Land more thin,
> And suck'd the last free drop of blood therein.
> He saw the brutish Idols they ador'd,
> Which all their Rivers, Fields, and Gardens stor'd . . .[11]

Seeing the misery of God's people, Moses resolves to act:

> These miseries he saw, and all the rest,
> And deep revolv'd in his sagacious breast.
> He saw those happy days approach, foretold
> So oft in holy Oracles of old,
> When happy Israel shou'd be Slaves no more,
> Nor Idol-Kings, nor Idol-Gods adore;
> No more their stupid Patience now be shown,
> Nor labor in those Kingdoms not their own.[12]

Before embarking on his mission of deliverance, Moses seeks divine guidance:

> . . . Sinai-Mount, and Horeb Hills he trod,
> And in the flaming Thicket talk'd with God.
> There he Instructions had, and Courage too
> For all the mighty things he was to do.
> He came to drive and purge the guilty Land,
> No Sword, no Spear, adorn'd or fenc'd his hand,
> He only wav'd about the wondrous Wand.
> He came, – th' Egyptian Gods before him fell,
> And knew, and fled the God of Israel.[13]

At this point, the Moses analogy breaks down. King William may have led the people of England out of a popish Egyptian bondage, but he had not done so merely by waving a wand. Instead he had come to England as a prince in arms. Not that this troubled Williamite writers. On the contrary, they gloried in the martial virtues of 'Our warlike David',[14] contrasting his military prowess with the ineffectiveness of his two immediate predecessors. In July 1690, following the French victory over the Anglo-Dutch fleet off Beachy Head, a Williamite newspaper suggested that 'Nothing but a William III can be able to rouze up the martial Genius of England, which the soft reign of a Charles II had laid asleep.'[15] And by 1695 the King had done just that, leading from the front in the great war against France. 'Remember,' urged a preacher, 'He is a Prince, who after many Years Effeminacy, Luxury, Ease and Softness, (wherein the English Valour so famed heretofore, lay withering and fading, unactive and rusting) hath renewed to us the Memory of those great Kings who headed English Armies abroad; and hath done more in his own Person, than all the Crowned Heads of this, or (for ought I know) any other age.'[16] Writing in 1699, Richard Blackmore similarly praised a King who, by 'his Courage', had 'rekindled the decaying Fire of this Warlike People, taught them by his Conduct, and provok'd them by his Example to equal the Atchievements of their Valiant Forefathers, and thereby restor'd to England the ancient Reputation of her Arms'.[17] Like 'the Noble Caesar', averred the military chaplain John Petter in 1694, King William 'was never heard to say, *Ite milites, sed venite*; not go, but follow me; as if he scorn'd in all his on-sets to be any thing else but still a Leader'.[18] He was 'A brave, bold Prince, not [like King James] a poor runing King'.[19]

Here then at last was the man to pluck the proud French cockerel. 'March and the King go out like a lion', wrote the Gloucestershire gentleman William Lawrence on King William's departure for Flanders in 1693:

> the arms of the House of Orange, the Belgick and the British arms are all lions: these he carries in his banners, but he bears a fiercer in his breast. Richard the First had not a greater heart. He succeeds a lazy race of Princes, a race unlike his own and so given up to ease and venery, that he seems not so much destined to possess the throne as to strengthen and reform it. He hath our old enemy the French to deal with, an enemy that hath been often and notably foiled in former ages; and why not now, since in his single person are revived the courage, activity, and martial genius of all our ancient Kings?[20]

Such qualities, alas, were not sufficient in themselves to secure victory on the battlefields of Flanders. In the Summer of 1692, as we shall see in a later chapter, King William was worsted by the French at Steenkirk. A year later, he suffered a still more serious reverse at Landen.[21] It was a classic case of virtue going unrewarded. 'Merit and success are seldom coupled together long', lamented Lawrence in October 1693. The King, he noted, 'hath this Summer suffered both in his allies and his own arms: valour was every where oppressed by number, and he that deserved a triumph, returns with the only honour of being admired for his personal courage and conduct'.[22] But the successful campaigns of the next two Summers, culminating in King William's capture of Namur in August/ September 1695, gave Williamites fresh cause to sing their hero's praises. 'Pray when had the Kingdom of England, / so valiant a Monarch before?' asked a balladeer on the King's triumphant return from the 1695 campaign:

> To Battle he goes, still facing his Foes,
>   where Cannons like thunder does roar,
> Whilst Lewis lies close at his ease,
>   who likes no such Battles as these . . .
> He sways both a Sword and a Scepter,
>   like great Alexander of old,
> Then through Christendom, for Ages to come,
>   his Deeds shall stand fairly enroll'd;
> For when was a Prince ever known,
>   so freely to go from his Throne,
> Through Fire and Water and Battles of Slaughter,
>   but valiant King William alone?[23]

Thomas Yalden lauded King William in similarly extravagant terms:

> Where'ere in Arms the great NASSAU appears,
> The Extream of Action's there:
> Himself the thickest Danger shares,
> Himself th'informing Soul that animates the War.
> Heroes of old in wondrous Armour fought,
> By some immortal Artist wrought:
> Achilles Arms, and Ajaxs seven-fold Shield,
> Were proof against the Dangers of the Field.
> But greater WILLIAM dares his Breast expose
> Unarm'd, unguarded to his Foes:
> A thousand Deaths and Ruins round him fled,
> But durst not violate his Sacred Head;
> For Angels guard the Prince's Life and Throne,
> Who for his Empire's Safety thus neglects his own.
> Had he in Ages past the Scepter sway'd,
> When Sacred Rites were unto Heroes paid:
> His Statue on ev'ry Altar stood,
> His Court a Temple been, his greater Self a God.[24]

As Yalden's poem suggests, Williamite writers viewed the King's many close encounters with death – notably the cannon ball which grazed his shoulder at the Boyne – as further evidence that King William was the chosen instrument of divine providence. 'He is Bold and Valiant', preached Henry Meriton in 1696, his enemies must acknowledge him the most intrepid, that ever faced a Danger; there seems not to be a jot of that Passion of fear in his Constitution; he converses with 1000 of Deaths every day, as familiarly as Job did, that calls Death Father, Mother and Sister; he was never daunted though Death made never so near approaches to himself, as at the Boin when it claspt him on the Shoulder, as if it had Arrested him; but blessed be God, it was not in the King of Heavens Name, and so he escaped.[25]

As John Petter preached to the army in Flanders, King William 'seems to be one that the supream God hath taken particular care of, by Death's coming often so very near him, yet passing him by, and shunning him when it hath swept away almost all about him. I need not tell you the many narrow Escapes he lately had, nor how often he hath been miraculously and particularly defended in the midst of the greatest Dangers.'[26] One such escape, during the Flanders campaign of 1691, was recalled by a balladeer that same year:

> A Canon Ball did fall,
>   Iust where the King had sate,
> Two Minutes, scarse was gone,
>   but comes the Bullet straite,
> Thus he by Heaven is guarded,
>   and blest in every thing:
> And we will with Consent,
>   All say God save the King![27]

The message of providence was plain: God had preserved King William's life for a special purpose. And that purpose was the smiting of popery, both at home and abroad. When Prince William arrived in London in December 1688, he had been acclaimed as the 'Protector of the Protestant Religion throughout the World' by the author of the following acrostic on the Prince's name:

> **W** elcom, Great Prince, the most August in Name,
> **I** mportant Time did ever bring to Fame.
> **L** ive ever Crown'd with Merit of Renown;
> **L** ong may You live, and see the World Your Own.
> **I** n After-Times may Crowns of Bliss attend You;
> **A** nd may the Lord of Life (the Lamb) Defend You;
> **M** ay Righteousness Espouse You, Glories End You.
>
> **H** appiest of Princes, all Good Mens Delight!
> **E** xcelling Virtues shine in You most bright;
> **N** oble in Blood, but Nobler far in Mind;
> **R** eligion groans to be by You refin'd:
> **Y** our Safe Protection She implores with Tears;

P ut her not off, till You redress Her Fears.
R escue Her from the Toyls of *Babel's* Whore;
I nsulting *Rome* bring prostrate on the Floor.
N ip *France's* Pride, Pull Hell's Great *Lewis* down;
C onfound his Glory, and Debase his Crown:
E nquire into the Time; for it is Now.

O ld Antichrist must to the Christian bow.
F ight then, Great SIR, Christ's Cause, His Faith defend;

O bserve His Laws, and on His Word depend:
R aise up His Standard, and proclaim His War;
A ccept the Guardian Sword of Eighty's Star.
N one shall Oppose and Prosper, but shall Fall.
G reatly confide in God, whose Armies shall
E xtirpate the False Prophet, Beast and All.

A ssume the Titles which await Your Brow;
N ot such as Potentates do covet Now.
D ispose Your Self Protector for to be,

N ot of *Baal's* Legions, but Protestancie.
A ccelerate Your *Gideonick* Force;
S teer to the Kingdom void of all Remorse:
S ecure under Heavn's Banner You shall Fight,
A nd Vanquish Them: yea, put them all to Flight,
W here they shall perish in Eternal Night.[28]

In December 1688 the destruction of Baal's legions was, in reality, far from the mind of a Prince whose anti-French strategy demanded close ties with Catholic Austria and Spain. He repeatedly assured the Emperor and the King of Spain – and through them the Pope – that his intervention in England was aimed against their common enemy, the King of France, not English Catholics. On the contrary, he promised his Catholic allies that he would succour their co-religionists in England.[29] He kept his word. The King was probably behind the bill to protect private Catholic worship, introduced in the Lords in December 1689. This measure proved abortive, and there were no further moves to establish a formal toleration for English papists. But there was no persecution either. The laws imposing fines for failing to attend the Established Church – the recusancy legislation – became a dead letter. And while Catholic landowners faced a fresh hardship after 1692 – double payment of the land tax – Roman priests ministered to their flocks unmolested.[30]

King William's liberal policy towards his Catholic subjects was not simply a product of diplomatic expediency: it was also a matter of personal conviction. As Bishop Burnet noted in 1691, the King 'does think that the

Conscience is Gods Province, and that therefore it ought to be left to him; and from his experience in Holland he does look upon Tolleration as one of the wisest measures of Government. He was not satisfyed with this Tolleration of Dissenters but also stopt some severe acts that were designed against Papists.' At the same time, King William made no secret of the wider policy considerations at work. According to Burnet, the King wanted his subjects to consider

> that France would make use of any severitys against these [English Catholicks], to alienate all the Papists of Europe from us, and would hope from thence to forme a new Catholick League, and to make the war a quarrell of Religion which might have very bad effects, nor could he have credit enough to protect the Protestants in Hungary, unlesse he might also protect the Papists in England: This was so well understood that all those hot motions were lett fall, so that the Papists have enjoyed the effects of the Tolleration tho they were not comprehended within the Law that was made for it.[31]

Not surprisingly, King William's official iconography shied away from anti-Catholic themes, portraying the King not as an explicitly Protestant figure but as the muscular mythological hero Hercules, protecting all Europe from the Hydra of French tyranny.[32] To his English supporters, however, King William remained, first and foremost, the great defender of Protestant liberty. 'We have', sang a balladeer in 1690,

> . . . a Prince, whose mighty hand,
> From Popish Ills protect our Land.
> The Scarlet Whore he has o'er come,
> And pluck'd down all the Pride of Rome . . .[33]

That same year, preaching before the Lord Mayor and Aldermen of London, Samuel Barton shuddered at the memory of King William's close shave at the Boyne. 'We may even tremble to think how near we were to ruine', he reminded the congregation, 'when the Breath of our Nostrils, the Anointed of the Lord, so narrowly escap'd that fatal Bullet, and how dismal the consequence must in all probability have bin not to us only but to all the Protestant Churches abroad had he fallen by it.'[34] Six years later, in the wake of the 'Assassination Plot' revelations, Barton averred that more than ever did the people of England regard King William

> as a particular gift from Heaven, sent us in the most needful time for our Deliverance! A Prince in whom all the Virtues of his Ancestors shine very bright, and who, like them too, but in a more high and eminent degree, has that peculiar Honour done him by the wise Providence of God, to be set as the Bulwark of True Religion, the Patron of Laws and Liberties, and the Grand Opposer of Tyranny and Oppression in all this part of the World.[35]

By delivering England from the popish tyranny of James II, and contesting the power of the persecuting King of France, William of Orange had, in the eyes of his partisans, become the greatest champion of Protestantism since the Reformation. As a pamphleteer wrote when war was again looming in 1701,

> King William is justly acknowledged the Atlas on whose Shoulders, the whole Protestant Interest hangs, and as such we ought to value him, since under that Character the Papists fear him, and give a charge like that of the King of Syria to his Chief Captains, I Kings 22. 31. Fight neither with small nor great, save only against the K[ing] of Israel. We have chose him for our Chieftain, who is the first English Prince that since the Reformation, opposed Popery with Sword in Hand. By our assisting him, we may not only secure our selves and Religion from forreign Usurpations, but may Replant the Protestant Faith, where it is now trod under foot, and make the Name of English Men famous in after Ages.[36]

2. The Dutch Usurper

Predictably enough, supporters of King James saw the revolution and its principal engineer in a rather different light. To Jacobites, the revolution was nothing less than a hellish rebellion against a rightful and virtuous king, which had resulted in the impoverishment and enslavement of England at the hands of a tyrannical foreign usurper. In John Sergeant's *Historical Romance*, published in 1694, King James appears in the guise of Eugenius, pacific ruler of Utopia, and King William as Nasonius, 'Hydra-holder' of the abominable Hydropick Republic. Eugenius is a noble king, devoted to the welfare of his subjects, promoting their prosperity by maintaining a strict neutrality in the ruinous war fought by his son-in-law Nasonius against the invincible giant Gallieno (Louis XIV). Eugenius, in fact, has only one fault: an excess of piety which blinds him to Nasonius's ambitions. Nasonius lusts after the wealth of Utopia, and is intent upon seizing his father-in-law's realm. Before embarking upon that devilish enterprise, he seeks the counsel of Lucifer himself. For his part, Lucifer bids Nasonius

> not to fear, for he was his Friend, and knew well his Design; which was to drive his pious Father out of his three Kingdoms, and get them for himself. Know then, continued he, that it was I that inspired thee with this Thought, and I will carry thee through: only thou must wed spiritually . . . my eldest Daughter Ambitiosa Superba; That is, thou must give thy whole Heart to her, hold to her constantly, and follow all her Motions and Inspirations, which done, she with her Maids of Honour will easily bring that design of thine to Perfection.

Nasonius's infernal bride then appears, accompanied by her equally fiendish handmaidens, Rebelliosa, Fictitiosa and Fatuitosa. Each of them promises to put their dark arts at Nasonius's disposal. Rebelliosa vows to 'fill the Hearts, Heads and Tongues of the Utopians with Murmurs and

Discontents against their kind and lawful King Eugenius', just as she had in the past 'inspir'd them to make War against his Father Eusebius [Charles I]'. Fictitiosa promises to 'spread thousands of horrid lyes against Eugenius, his Queen, and their Son all over Utopia, to disaffect his Subjects, and make them hate him'. The spirit of folly, Fatuitosa Credula, pledges to 'beset and infatuate the People of Utopia, that they shall give full Credit to Fictitiosa's Lyes, tho never so monstrous and incredible'. What was more, she would stir up the Utopians 'to make War against the Powerful and Politick Giant Gallieno, tho' to their vast Charge, and the utter destroying their Traffick and Commerce. I will inspire them with that refin'd Folly, that they shall voluntarily and contentedly beggar themselves to maintain the War of the Hydra [the Dutch], tho' they cannot but know that it laughs at them for it, as great fools; and in their Hearts hates them.' Diabolica, the Spirit of Ingratitude, also offers her services to Nasonius. She promises to make Eugenius's servants, particularly in the army, forget the debt of gratitude they owed to their master. Diabolica also has words of advice for Nasonius. Once he had won the Utopian throne, Nasonius should be sure not to show

> the least Gratitude to the Utopians, though they foolishly serve thee against their own Interest: But both disoblige those who have first and most assisted thee, and do all thou canst to requite the Kindnesses of that Sottish Nation with their utter ruin. Huff their Nobility as occasion presents, and imprison them Lawlessly; Pay not their Souldiers, nor any who are so foolish as to trust thee with their Goods, Stores, or other Commodities. Regard not the Seamen though most useful to thee, nor pay 'em their Wages: Only give the Fops good Words, and some little Pittance to keep up their Folly to trust and serve thee further. Give the Royal Assent to no National Bills, that may in any wise serve to support or secure their pretended Rights, Liberties, and Properties; nor to any others that do not strengthen thy Power, enable thee to crush their Persons, and obtain their Pockets.[37]

And so, alas, it had come to pass in England. Aided and abetted by the spirits of rebellion, deceit, folly and ingratitude, the ruthlessly ambitious Prince of Orange had seized his father-in-law's throne, and then bled England dry in his hopeless war against Louis XIV. The deluded people of England, lamented a Jacobite writer, had

> obliged [King William] infinitely, for we have abdicated our lawful prince, and accepted him, though a foreigner, for our king: To do this we have violated the most fundamental laws of England, by traversing the immediate succession. We have engaged ourselves in the costly, dangerous, and (in like-lihood) the lasting war of the confederates against France, which we were free from before: a blessing to England, which (amongst diverse such others) he brought over with him. We have exhausted ourselves, to give him vast sums of money, besides what we have kindly lent him out of our pockets; and, as things stand, upon very slight security.[38]

Too true. As we shall see in a later chapter, the war imposed unprecedented burdens on English taxpayers. It also crippled the nation's trade.

And as the war dragged on, so the impoverishment of the kingdom grew apace. 'If we tax and poll on for a year or two more,' quipped a Jacobite poetaster in 1695, 'The French I dare say will ne'er touch on our shore, / For fear of the charge of maintaining our poor.'[39] Nor had the cost in men's lives been any cheaper. 'He came to save your throats from Popish knives,' rhymed another Jacobite, 'Yet by his war, he has widowed half your wives.'[40] In *Advice to a Painter*, a poem written shortly after the end of the war in 1697, the author urges an artist to depict the horrors of King William's reign:

> Here, Painter, here employ thy utmost Skill;
> With War and Slavr'y the vast Canvas fill:
> And that the Lines be easier understood,
> Paint not with fading Colours, but with Blood;
> Blood of our bravest Youth in Battel slain,
> At Steenkirk and at Landen's fatal Plain . . .[41]

The contrast with King James's pacific reign could hardly have been greater. 'We cannot but remember,' wrote the polemicist Nathaniel Johnston in 1690,

> that in King James's time, and for a great part of King Charles II's, for almost fifteen years, there had neither been land-tax nor poll; the whole country enjoyed the unspeakable benefits of peace and plenty, at full liberty to improve, to the utmost advantage, the production of their labour and industry, without one penny of charges for all the ease and safety they enjoyed; the tenants and farmers grew rich; the landlords had their rents well paid, and their estates improved; nothing was wanting but a true sense of their happiness, and a desire to preserve it.[42]

But then, of course, King James was 'owned by his very enemies to have had a true English spirit and tender affection to all his subjects; a zeal and delight in advancing their peace and plenty at home, and honour abroad; to have been an excellent, good-natured, generous prince, the most constant friend, the best father and master in the world, and the most merciful to his enemies'.[43]

King James's reign, it was true, had not been free of blemishes. But these, claimed the author of one Jacobite piece, had been the responsibility not of the King, but of wicked counsellors, secretly working to bring about the revolution.[44] In any event, King James had been ready to redress all grievances before the Prince of Orange's invasion.[45] As a Jacobite versifier remembered, when King James had become aware of the Prince's intentions, he had desired

> . . . to know,
> What his Pretensions were,
> And how without his Leave, he durst

> Presume on Landing here.
> Declaring what was deem'd amiss,
> 　Should soon amended be,
> And whatsoe're should be desir'd,
> 　He would thereto agree.

But the King's offer had been scorned by the Prince of Orange, and that 'Surly Bruit' had

> . . . to our Cost repair.
> With several Thousand Belgick Boars,
> 　All chosen Rogues for spight,
> Join'd with some Rebels who from hence
> 　And Justice had ta'ne flight.
> Who arm'd with Malice & with Hopes,
> 　Soon threw themselves on Shoar;
> Crying, our Religion and our Laws
> 　They came for to restore.[46]

For that shameful deed, there could be no possible justification. The Jacobite writer Charlwood Lawton acknowledged that 'King James's ministers gave great provocations', and he 'could have joined with any but a foreigner to have rescued our liberties'. Yet he could not 'tell how any provocations that were given the people of England can justify the invasion of a nephew and a son-in-law.'[47] Another Jacobite writer conceded that King James might possibly have hearkened too much to popish priests and wicked counsellors. But that could not justify the deposition of a monarch who 'had the public virtues of a king, and the private ones of a gentleman', whose 'courage, constancy, justice, liberality, and frugality, in their due places, befitted him more properly for the government of England, than any king perhaps, who governed it before himself'. However much King James had been deceived, 'he generally aimed laboriously at the good and glory of the nation.'[48] He was, indeed, the very model of monarchical virtue,

> A King whose rights his foes could ne'er dispute.
> So mild, that mercy was his attribute.
> Affable, kind, and easy of access,
> Swift to relieve, unwilling to oppress,
> Rich without taxes, yet in payment just,
> So honest, that he hardly could distrust.
> His active soul did ne'er from labours cease,
> Valiant in war, and sedulous in peace,
> Studious with traffic to enrich the land,
> Strong to protect, and skilful to command,
> Liberal and splendid, not without excess,
> Loth to revenge, and willing to caress.
> In sum, how godlike must his nature be,
> Whose only fault was too much piety.[49]

In contrast, the wronged King's son-in-law was a monster, an aberration of nature whose repulsive looks – 'his Slavering Mouth, Lean-Chaps, Spindle-shanks, and Paramount Nose' – were the outward manifestation of an inner rottenness.[50] This showed itself not least in the usurper's base and unnatural sexual appetites – his alleged homosexuality. How could King William truly profess any religion, asked the Williamite-turned-Jacobite Robert Ferguson, when he 'doth indulge himself in the practice of such abominations as are repugnant to the light of nature and to the ethics of pagans, as well as to the doctrines and precepts of the Bible, and which are made capital by the laws of all nations'? Englishmen, added the scurrilous Scot for the benefit of readers who may have missed the point, were filled 'with contempt and hatred of themselves, for enduring a Catamite to rule over them'.[51] Nor was Ferguson unique in making such an allegation. 'For the case, Sir, is such,' wrote a Jacobite poet,

> The people think much,
> That your love is Italian, your Government Dutch
> Ah! who could have thought that a Low-Country stallion
> And a Protestant Prince should prove an Italian.[52]

The object of that 'Italian love' was said to be none other than King William's closest confidant, the Dutchman Willem Bentinck, Earl of Portland.[53] By 1697, however, Jacobites claimed that Portland had been superseded in the King's affections by his younger compatriot, Joost Keppel, Earl of Albemarle. 'Artist retire,' urged the author of *Advice to a Painter*,

> . . . 'twere Insolence too great
> T'expose the Secrets of the Cabinet;
> Or tell how they their looser Moments spend;
> That hellish Scene would all chast Ears offend.
> For should you pry into the close Alcove,
> And draw the Exercise of Royal Love,
> Keppell and He are Ganymede and Jove.[54]

King William's depravity further showed itself in his abnormal lust for power and glory. According to one writer, ambition was the 'master-ingredient' of the King's soul, so much so that he regarded 'no person living, longer than they serve his ambitious, proud, revengeful, or covetous ends; for whatever such gross sycophants, as his new chaplains of the first orb may say, these truly are his cardinal virtues'.[55] As Nathaniel Johnston jeered, King William had 'but one principle, that gain is great godliness'.[56] He had first put that maxim into effect in the United Provinces, where he had come to power in 1672 'by perjury and murder of two of the best patriots of the Dutch republic' – the republican De Witt brothers.[57] And it was the same maxim which 16 years later led the Prince into the ultimate act of filial impiety, the deposition of his father-in-law, King James. On more than one occasion, but notably in Arthur Mainwaring's poem, *Tarquin and Tullia*, King William was depicted in the guise of Tarquin, the proud Etruscan who slew his father-in-law, Servius Tullius, to gain the Roman throne. 'In times', wrote Mainwaring,

> . . . when Princes cancelled nature's law
> And declarations (which themselves did draw),
> When children used their parents to dethrone
> And gnawed their way like vipers to a crown,
> Tarquin, a savage, proud, ambitious prince,
> Prompt to expel yet thoughtless of defence,
> The envied scepter did from Tullius snatch,
> The Roman King, and father by the match.[58]

Yet it was not necessary to delve into ancient history to find a villain comparable to the Prince of Orange. Time after time, Jacobites coupled the Prince with a more recent usurper – Oliver Cromwell. The parallel between 'O[liver] P[rotector]', who murdered the father, and 'P[rince of] O[range]', who deposed the son, was simply too good to ignore. When in 1690 William Sherlock, hitherto a staunch nonjuror, belatedly decided that it was no sin to swear allegiance to a monarch chosen by providence, a Jacobite satirist summed up the turncoat's philosophy in the following ryhme:

> So let O.P. or P.O. be King,
> Or anyone else, it is the same thing,
> For only Heaven does that blessing bring.[59]

And just as William was following in Oliver's footsteps, so his supporters were treading the very path taken by their rebellious fathers four decades earlier. An obvious example was King William's Lord Keeper, Sir John Somers. According to the author of *Father's Nown Child*, a satire penned in 1694, Somers was a chip off the Cromwellian block. His father – a captain of horse in the New Model Army – had served the old usurper. Now Sir John was serving the new. 'And this', wrote the satirist,

> . . . is, in short, the true pedigree
> Of P.O's Lord Keeper, who's greater than he
> That did love and serve his Highness O.P.[60]

As for P.O, he had shown himself a more than worthy successor to O.P. Indeed, he had out-Cromwelled Cromwell. 'O.P.', wrote Ralph Grey in his mock *Coronation Ballad,*

> . . . did but smell at the crown in the Rump
> But though four were before, P.O., with a jump,
> Did venture his neck to saddle his bumb.[61]

Vaulting ambition was not the only sin which linked Orange to Oliver. The new usurper, like the old, was an implacable enemy of the episcopal

Church of England. While it was fair to say that King William was utterly devoid of any true religious feelings, his sympathies, such as they were, clearly lay with the presbyterians. As the Irish nonjuror Charles Leslie reminded his readers in 1694, 'the present king had the misfortune (to himself and to us) to be educated under the Geneva model, made Erastian [subordinate to the state] in Holland: And it cannot be imagined, that the alteration of his present circumstances have wrought as great a change in his principles'. On the contrary, he was 'as zealous for his religion as any other king at least'.[62] There was plenty of evidence to back up this charge. In Scotland, as we shall see in a later chapter, King William had presided over the destruction of episcopacy and the re-establishment of presbyterianism.[63] In England too, according to Nathaniel Johnston, the King was intent on introducing 'a Scotch reformation', but he had 'counted noses, and finds the Church of England the major part'. The usurper had therefore pursued a more subtle strategy south of the Tweed. Rather than launching a frontal attack on episcopal church government, he had sought to undermine it in three ways. First, he had settled 'an indulgence upon all dissenters' – the Toleration Act of 1689. Then he had deprived 'the chief and most zealous of our bishops, and others of the regular clergy' – the nonjurors led by Archbishop Sancroft of Canterbury. Finally, he had advanced 'upon all vacancies of sees and dignities ecclesiastical, men of notorious presbyterian, or, which is worse, of Erastian principles' – the likes of the Scot Gilbert Burnet (Bishop of Salisbury from 1689) and the one-time presbyterian John Tillotson (Archbishop of Canterbury from 1691). Such measures, concluded Johnston, were 'the insensible ways of undermining episcopacy'.[64]

In view of King James's much-vaunted support for liberty of conscience, it might be thought that Jacobite writers would have felt some diffidence in attacking the Toleration Act. Not a bit of it. Nonjurors such as Johnston and Leslie saw the Act as a key element in King William's plan to destroy the Church of England. Leslie also castigated the King for presiding over a general rise in irreligion. 'There is', he wrote, 'a spirit of atheism gone out into this land, especially among the gentry of first magnitude; and books are daily published, and greedily bought up, to render what they call priestcraft the object of all people's hate and contempt.'[65] This state of affairs, claimed the Catholic writer John Sergeant, could be directly attributed to King William's 'Dutch' policy of 'unlimited' toleration: 'let all Sects whatsoever, even Atheists, and Socinians [anti-trinitarians], which are next to them, hold and teach what they will, as does my Servant the Hydra', Sergeant has Lucifer advise Nasonius. 'For that's the only plausible way to make Mortals be of no religion at all.'[66]

The King's Dutchness was a theme to which Jacobite writers returned again and again. According to one writer, 'neither the air of England, the honour, benefit, and riches the Prince of Orange hath got by it, hath rendered him more English than ever he was, being wholly and entirely Dutch in soul and body.'[67] And like all Dutchmen, the Prince of Orange was determined to make his new realm a miserable fiefdom of the United Provinces – England's principal commercial rival and her enemy in three great naval wars fought between 1652 and 1674. In Sergeant's *Historical Romance*, Nasonius, before launching his invasion of Utopia, assures the Heads of the Hydra (the Dutch States General) that 'he could not but retain his chief Affection for the Hydra; and that he was willing to sacrifice the Men, Money, and Interest of Utopia to that of his own dear Country-men'. As a condition for obtaining the Hydra's support for his expedition, Nasonius promises that 'some of the greatest Personages of the Hydropick Commonwealth should go over with Nasonius, whom he is to advance to high Dignity, making some of them his Prime Ministers of State, and his most secret Council; and communicate to them all his Actions, and consult with them about all his Affairs'.[68]

Unfortunately for England, the Prince had kept his promise. 'Our eyes tell us, that no Englishmen is trusted in any thing,' wrote the author of *Observations upon the late Revolution in England,*

> no not those who for form-sake sit in places of trust, for as our English estates are often settled in trust, our English trust itself is in trust now; the fine titles worn by our ministers and privy-counsellors of England being nothing but gay liveries, to make them show the handsomer tools to finish up the work cut out by Dutchmen in the closet. And our reason will tell us we cannot complain, nor expect it ever should be otherwise. For no wise prince will trust a man whom he has cause to suspect will not be true to him; and our K[ing] W[illiam] cannot forget that he was not born in England, that he did not inherit the crown, that he cannot reign without wars and taxes.[69]

According to Nathaniel Johnston, King William's 'important and essential consults and resolutions are all managed by a few foreigners, in a secret cabal of Dutchmen'. And that cabal had resolved to impoverish and weaken England to such an extent that 'we should not be able to do any thing for one hundred years but in conjunction with the Dutch'.[70] King William's design, averred a Jacobite writing in the guise of a Dutchman, was to 'fleece that proud and pampered nation, and leave them neither men nor money, nor ammunition, nor ships, nor any thing to enable them to make war against us, or carry on a trade'.[71]

A particularly sinister aspect of the conspiracy was King William's policy of inundating England with Dutch and other foreign soldiers. While brave English troops were sacrificed on the battlefields of Flanders, the Dutch soldiery had 'spread like locusts over the whole kingdom'.[72] This was a potent charge. For obvious reasons, King William doubted the loyalty of the army which he had inherited from his father-in-law. Until the Spring of 1690, he garrisoned London and its environs with Dutch, German and

Huguenot soldiers.[73] This mercenary force, claimed Jacobites, would be used by the King to extort money from the capital once the nation's generosity had been exhausted. 'Talk not of law,' wrote a Jacobite pamphleteer,

> necessity, that knows none, will demand it; and a necessity too the most pressing and extreme that can be; for otherwise the war against King James cannot be upheld, and so the grandeur of the Tamer would be abased, the high elevation depressed, and the glorious character darkened and defaced. In such a desperate case, then, immense sums are absolutely needful; and when the lending hand draws back, for fear of none-solvency, necessity will be put to speak its own language, and cry, I must and will have it. And how must it be extorted? Not by our own countrymen; this cannot be expected; it can only be wrung from us by foreign hands, and by the help of those sober men above-mentioned [Dutch, Danish and German soldiers], whose prey, though they whet their courages first in Ireland, England is in all likelihood designed to be: For, if the great commander of them and us be . . . so over fond of glory, and hurried towards it with such an impetuous affection that he will hazard his own ruin rather than abate one tittle of the (in comparison) contemptible authority of the stadtholder of Holland, do we think he will stick to ruin us, rather than lose the majesty of a sovereign King of England, Scotland, France and Ireland, which he esteems to be infinitely above his former condition? And by what means can he do this, and wreak the revenge he so threatens to the diminishers of his glory, but by outlandish instruments?[74]

Nathaniel Johnston agreed. King William's 'janiseries', he wrote in 1690, were supposedly to be used in the reduction of Scotland and Ireland. But 'their last service and reward', Johnston maintained, 'will be the enslaving of England, as was experienced by us in the Cromwellian army, after the like success in those countries'. In the meantime, Englishmen were 'in a great degree enslaved already, by the numbers of foreign troops we have at present'. Indeed, it was 'because of the awe of those, as it was of Cromwell's army, that our parliaments deny no money, nor the making of any laws which are for the security of the government'.[75] Overawed and corrupted by King William, the parliament of England would soon 'signify no more than those of Paris, and be of no use but to register edicts of the sovereigns, and impose the taxes on the people'.[76]

In short, Englishmen had little reason to feel obliged to the Prince of Orange,

> unless we are to thank him for altering our constitution of government, destroying our laws, and hawling our men to the shambles, giving away our trade to the Dutch, perjuring the clergy and laity, squeezing those many millions of money from us, and transporting them to Dutch land, beggaring one part of the subject with taxes, and another [in Ireland] with his outrageous soldiers, who for want of pay and discipline, live upon rapine and free quarter, as if they were in an enemy's country.[77]

As Nathaniel Johnston grimly concluded, the revolution 'has brought along with it all the plagues we dreaded under others, and gives us nothing but the dismal prospect of all the misfortunes which can befall a nation, which hath greatly provoked God Almighty's anger'.[78] And from those plagues, the sinful people of England could be delivered only by King James's restoration. 'O England!' declaimed the author of *The Belgick Boar*,

> ... when to future Times
> Thy Story shall be known
> How will they blush to think what Crimes
> Their Ancestors have done.
> But after all, what have we got
> By this our dear-bought King?
> Why that our Scandal and Reproach
> Throughout the World does ring.
> That our Religion, Liberties,
> And Laws we held so dear,
> Are more invaded since this Change
> Than ever yet they were.
> Our Coffers droin'd, our Coin impair'd,
> That little that remains;
> Our Persons seiz'd, nay Thoughts arraign'd
> Our Freedom now is Chains.
> Our Traffick ruin'd; Shipping lost,
> Our Traders most undone;
> Our bravest Heroes sacrific'd,
> Our ancient Glory gone.
> A Fatal Costly War entail'd,
> On this unhappy Isle;
> Unless above what we deserves
> Kind Heaven at last does smile.
> And bring our injur'd Monarch Home,
> And place Him on his Throne;
> And to Confusion bring his Foes
> Which God grant may be soon.[79]

3. William and Mary

In their attempts to drive a wedge between King William and his subjects, Jacobite writers stressed the King's contempt for England and Englishmen: 'we are strangers to him, and he to us', asserted the disaffected Scottish whig, Sir James Montgomery; 'his affections, as well as his birth, are foreign, he distrusts and despiseth us, as treacherous to our former king; he may "love the treason, but hate the traitors".'[80]

Here the Jacobites were pushing at an open door. A man of immense reserve and few words, King William lacked the easy affability which wins men's hearts. 'He has a coldness in his way, that damps a modest man extreamly,' wrote Gilbert Burnet while in exile at the Stadholder's court before the revolution, 'for he hears things with a dry silence that shows too much of distrust of those to whom he speaks.' Burnet saw squalls ahead should William become King: 'if the Prince does not in many things

Figure 4 'William III', by Gottfried Schalcken, 1692. The artist has splendidly captured King William's reserved and taciturn nature – that 'coldness' which 'damps a modest man extreamly', and the 'dry silence that shows too much of distrust of those to whom he speaks' (Gilbert Burnet). These characteristics did not endear the King to his subjects.

change his way,' mused the shrewd Scot, 'he will hardly gain the hearts of the Nation: his Coldness will look like contempt, and that the English cannot bear, and they are too impatient to digest that slowness that is almost become natural to him, in the most considerable things; and his silent way will pass for superciliousness.'[81]

William, alas, did not change his ways. On the contrary, he infuriated his subjects by openly preferring Dutch counsellors and generals over their English counterparts. As early as March 1689, Goodwin Wharton, the son of a whig peer, recorded 'great discontents' in England, 'and complaints of all hands, of his [the King's] pride, and neglect of the English nobility in favour of Benten and his dutch favorites'.[82] The picture is confirmed by Burnet. 'The King', he later recalled,

> was thought to love the Dutch more than the English, to trust more to them, and to admit them to more freedom with him. He gave too much occasion to a general disgust, which was spread among the English [army] officers and the nobility: he took little pains to gain the affections of the nation; nor did he constrain himself enough to render his government more acceptable: he was shut up all the day long; and his silence, when he admitted any to an audience, distasted them as much as if they had been denied it . . . And the strain of all the nation almost was, that the English were overlooked, and the Dutch were the only persons favoured or trusted. This was national; and the English being too apt to despise other nations, and being of more lively tempers than the Dutch, grew to express a contempt and an aversion for them, that went almost to mutiny.[83]

Public opinion was particularly incensed by the exclusion of Englishmen from senior commands in Ireland and Flanders. King William's disdain for English generals was in large measure a matter of practicalities: the English senior officers, generally lacking experience of large-scale warfare, could not match their Dutch rivals for professional skill. But the King's lack of confidence in English generals was also a manifestation of his deep distrust of officers who had made their careers in King James's army.[84] Whatever King William's motives, there was widespread disgust at the favour he had shown to foreign generals. When in January 1692 the House of Commons was moved to vote thanks to the Dutch general Ginkel for his services in Ireland, some MPs were decidedly underwhelmed. 'I am not very fond of this way of this House giving thanks', Sir Christopher Musgrave told MPs. 'But if you do, I hope you will do the like for the English officers and soldiers who behaved themselves very bravely.'[85] Nor was the cause of Anglo-Dutch harmony helped overmuch by the widely-reported failure of another Dutch commander, Count Solms, to come to the aid of hard-pressed English troops at Steenkirk in August 1692. 'There is one thing, I confess, I do not like', Goodwin Wharton confided to the Commons in November, 'the putting foreigners over your men. You see the mischievous consequences of it the last year in Flanders where, for want of your men being seconded, you lost the prospect of a great victory.'[86] Wharton's fellow whig, Sir Peter Colleton, was of a like mind:

> I think it is not consistent with the interest of this kingdom for to have foreign officers over an English army when we have so many brave, courageous men amongst us. The Englishman can have no interest but the good of his own country; what foreigners may have I cannot tell. There are few persons but have heard of the action last summer at Steinkirk and how your men were served. I fear it may be of fatal consequence, and therefore I think it a head worthy of your advice that our English armies may be commanded by natives of our own.[87]

Yet still King William took little heed of the sensibilities of his subjects, making lavish grants of land to his foreign favourites. One such grant– to the Earl of Portland in 1695 – provoked the Welsh MP Robert Price into a general denunciation of Dutch influence. 'I must confess,' Price informed the Commons,

> I am strangely troubled with strange apprehensions of our deplorable state: We are in a confederacy in war, and some of those confederates are our enemies in trade, though planted among us; some in the king's council, some in the army, and the common traders have possessed themselves of the out-skirts of the city: we find some of them naturalized, others made denizens . . . We see most places of power and profit given to foreigners . . . How can we hope for happy days in England, when this great lord [Portland], and other foreigners (though naturalized) are in the English and Dutch councils? If the strangers (though confederates) should be of a different interest, as most plainly they are in point of trade; to which interest is it supposed these great foreign councils would adhere? So that I see, when we are reduced to extreme poverty, (as now we are very near it) we shall be supplanted by our neighbours, and become a colony to the Dutch.[88]

As King William's particular favourite, Portland was the chief butt of English criticism. In *A Dialogue between the Ghosts of Russell and Sidney*, a verse satire written in 1689, the spirits of two whig heroes 'martyred' by Charles II six years earlier express their dissatisfaction with the new regime. High on their list of grievances is King William's elevation of 'Dull Bentinck', the 'low-country footman' who now topped 'the English Lord'. Once, complains Sidney's ghost,

> His purse was as empty as now is his head;
> Now set off with titles, and ill-bestowed graces,
> He wafts over coin by selling of places.[89]

Although this piece may have been written by a Jacobite, there is no doubt that many whigs did indeed despise Portland at this time. In 1689–90, as we shall see in the next chapter, King William threw off his initial dependence on the whig party, and moved towards the tories. Whig true-believers, such as John Hampden, attributed this turn of events to Portland's baleful influence. 'Who would have thought that so unhallowed a Mother as a Republick could have produced children that are such Heros for Episcopacy & the divine Prerogatives of Monarchs?' asked a bitter Hampden in November 1690, 'or that my Lord Portland should become a bulwark of Monarchy, & Protector & eldest son of the Church of England?'[90]

By 1690 whig partisans were convinced that King William had sold the pass to the Church party. Yet the tories too had misgivings about the King, and these proved longer-lasting than whiggery's. For tories, King William was a double-headache. His accession flew in the face of their belief in the hereditary principle. Worse still, he was a Dutch Calvinist with no sympathy for the tory party's brand of Church of England exclusivism – a point rammed home as early as March 1689 when the King attempted to open up office to Protestant nonconformists. True, he subsequently sought to reassure the Church party through the agency of his ecclesiastical propagandists.[91] But precious little good it did him. As we shall see in later chapters, the King's establishment of presbyterianism in Scotland, his emancipation of dissent in England and his packing of the episcopal bench with 'latitudinarians' – the very men who were penning his propaganda – cast over him a veil of tory suspicion which proved impossible to lift.[92] In this sense, the 1690s provide an object lesson in the limitations of propaganda. King William's bishops could 'spin' to their hearts' content: the tories preferred the evidence of their own eyes.

In the early 1690s the revolution regime was made more palatable to the Church party by King William's reliance upon his tory Secretary of State, the Earl of Nottingham.[93] An equally reassuring figure, for moderate tories at least, was Queen Mary. Not only was the Queen English-born, she was also King James's legitimate heir (if one discounted the popish and 'suppositious' Prince of Wales). More importantly, Queen Mary was widely perceived to be 'a true tender Nursing Mother to the best of Churches' – the Church of England.[94] According to the royal chaplain, William Payne, the Queen was devoted to 'Building up and Repairing the whole Church of England, and making it like Mount Sion, the joy of the whole Earth'.[95] In future chapters, we shall see plentiful evidence to support that assertion. But we shall also see that Queen Mary was no bigoted Churchwoman.[96] In the words of Bishop Fowler of Gloucester, the Queen's 'love to this Church did not leven Her Mind, with any sour Prejudices against Other Protestant Churches, as That of Holland found by experience; nor lessened Her Charity towards Sober Dissenters among Our selves'.[97] Coupled to these broad Protestant sympathies was a personal piety which, though undoubtedly exploited for propagandist ends, was as deep as it was unaffected. 'She expresses so-deep a sense of Religion and so true a regard to it', recorded an enthusiastic Bishop Burnet in 1693. 'She has so right Principles and true Notions.' Nor was it a passive piety. As Burnet explained,

> the Queen was not satisfyed with an example to the Nation, that did shine in all the parts of it, but she was promoting all the methods that could be thought of for reforming it. She took the Ladys [of court] off from that Idleness, which not only wast their time but exposes them to many temptations, and engaged them to work; She wrought many hours a day her self, and had her Maids of honour and Ladys working about her: And whereas the female part of the Court had been in the former reignes subject to much just scandall, She has freed her Court so entirely from all suspitions, that there is not so much as colour for discourse.[98]

Add to this a charm and openness so singularly lacking in her husband, and it is easy to see why, according to the Lincolnshire clergyman Abraham de la Pryme, Queen Mary 'was universally well beloved of every one, and the most esteem'd of any [monarch] that ever was since the death of Q[ueen] Eliz[abeth]'.[99]

Figure 5 'The death of the Queen', by Romeyn de Hooghe, 1695. As her life ebbs away, Queen Mary receives spiritual instruction from Archbishop Tenison of Canterbury while her husband (centre) looks on helplessly. The Queen was widely mourned, but Jacobites saw her premature death as divine retribution for filial impiety.

De la Pryme's reflections were prompted by the Queen's death from smallpox in December 1694. Her passing, at the age of just 32, was deeply felt, not least by King William. The marriage between William and Mary had started life in 1677 as a typically cold-hearted dynastic match. Indeed, the prospect of spending life with her Dutch cousin – unprepossessing in looks, cold in demeanour and 12 years her senior – had initially filled the lively 15 year old princess with horror. But from those inauspicious beginnings, a powerful bond had developed between husband and wife. Its severing left the King distraught, much to the surprise of Gilbert Burnet. King William's 'affliction for her death', the bishop recorded,

> was far beyond what any body thought was in his nature, it was as great as his occasion was just, he went beyond all bounds in it. He was during her illness in an Agony that amazed us all, fainting often, and breaking-out into violent lamentations. When she dyed his Spirits sunk so entirely that there was great reason to apprehend that he was following her. For some weeks he was so little Master of himself that he was not capable of minding his affaires, nor of seeing any Company. He gave himself much to the meditations of Religion and Prayer.

Burnet was equally devastated:

> I never admired any Person so intirely as I did her. The more I knew her, I still saw the more reason to admire both her understanding, her Piety and her vertue, without discovering the least defect or fault in her. The purity and the sublimity of her mind was the perfectest thing I ever saw; I never felt my self sink so much under any thing that had happened to me as by her death; it is a daily load upon my thoughts, and gives me great apprehensions of very heavy judgments hanging over us: for I am afraid that in loosing her, we have lost both our strength and our glory.

'She was', Burnet insisted, 'the most universally lamented Princess, and deserved the most to be so, of any Person in our age, or in our History.'[100]

It was no great exaggeration. 'You inform me', wrote the Gloucestershire gentleman William Lawrence to a friend in London, 'how sad the City is without and within at the death of the Queen; the sorrow was begun but doth not dwell there; it spreads apace, and these remoter parts equally feel the loss and follow the example. The throne never was nor ever will be filled with so much virtue . . . She seemed not only born to rule but to reform a corrupted age; some murmured at her life, but all suffer on her death.'[101] 'Her death', wrote Thomas Brockbank from Oxford, 'is lamented by all true sons of [the] Church of England, since while alive she was such a Nursing Mother to it; and I think there is none [that] is not sorry for [the] loss of so good, so vertuous a Queen.'[102] Writing to one of her Harley cousins from Derby in March 1695, Abigail Pye asserted that the Queen's death 'has clad our nation in mourning & filled all good peoples hearts with greif'. Yet mourning was not quite universal. Jacobite sympathisers had no reason to shed any tears for King James's rebellious daughter, and they made no pretence of doing so. Pye's cousin, Abigail Harley, had told her that Herefordshire Jacobites were celebrating the Queen's death. And in Derby, too, there were some who 'expressed their joy tho they durst not soe publickly as Bells & bonfires.'[103]

In her lifetime, Jacobite writers had denounced the Queen for her complicity in King James's overthrow. She was a 'Tullia' fit to rank along-side William's 'Tarquin', a faithless daughter gleefully riding over the stricken body of her royal father. 'Oft have we heard of impious sons before, / Rebelled for crowns their royal parents wore', hissed a satirist in 1689,

> But of unnatural daughters rarely hear
> 'Till those of hapless James and old King Lear.
> But worse than cruel lustful Goneril, thou!
> She took but what her father did allow;
> But thou, more impious, robb'st thy father's brow.
> Him both of power and glory you disarm,
> Make him, by lies, the people's hate and scorn,
> Then turn him forth to perish in a storm.
> Sure after this, should his dead corpse become
> Exposed like Tarquin's in the streets of Rome,
> Naked and pierced with wounds on every side,
> Thou wouldst, like Tullia, with triumphant pride
> Thy chariot drive, winged with ambitions fires,
> O'er the dead body of thy mangled sire.[104]

In fact, despite appearances to the contrary, Queen Mary had taken no real pleasure in ascending the throne. 'The next day after I came [to England],' she had recalled in her journal,

we were proclaimed and the government put wholy in the princes hand. This pleased me extreamly, but many would not believe it, so that I was fain to force my self to more mirth than became me at that time, and was by many interpreted as ill nature, pride, and the great delight I had to be queen. But alas, they did litle know me, who thought me guilty of that; I had been only for a regency, and wisht for nothing else; I had ever dreaded being queen, liking my condition much better (and indeed I was not deceived); but the good of the public was to be preferd and I protest, God knows my heart, that what I say is true, that I have had more trouble to bring myself to bear this so envyed estate then I should have had to have been reduced to the lowest condition in the world. My heart is not made for a kingdom and my incli-nation leads me to a retired quiet life, so that I have need of all the resignation and self denial in the world, to bear with such a condition as I am now in. Indeed the princes being made king lessend the pain, but not the trouble of what I am like to endure.[105]

This was an age in which princesses kept their inner torments to themselves. But even if the Queen had made her true feelings public, she would have found it difficult to deflect the harsh words of her Jacobite critics. What possible value, they asked, could be attached to the outward piety of a lady who had shown such flagrant disregard for that most sacred commandment, 'Honour thy Father and thy Mother'? 'For God's sake, and the sake of your soul, and the sake of your queen's soul,' Charlwood Lawton had implored Archbishop Tillotson of Canterbury,

> study the fifth commandment; though the performance of it has the promise of length of days in this life, the breach of it (if any religion be true) will plunge her into miseries of longer duration: She has partaken with thieves and liars against her own father; she is a receiver of what has been by them from him wrongfully taken away, unless it can be proved that the crown of England is elective, the kings of it punishable and deposable.[106]

And when the Queen's days proved anything but long, Thomas Ken, the nonjuring Bishop of Bath and Wells, saw the hand of God at work. 'You take notice more than once, of the shortening the life of this Illustrious Princess, that she was taken away in the midst of her days . . . at thirty three years old . . . in the flower of her Age . . .', he wrote in a critique of Thomas Tenison's hagiographic funeral sermon,

> but you take no notice of that which most probably occasioned it, for the Fifth Commandment is not to be evaded, Honour thy Father and thy Mother, (which is the first commandment with Promise) that it may be well with Thee, and thou mayst live long on the Earth, and if any, even Princes, for the Command makes no exception, do visibly Dishonour Father and Mother, and their lives are cut short, the very Command of God assigns the cause of it, and I hope the surviving Princess will consider, and take warning, and repent, lest God be provoked, to cut her life as short as her Sisters.[107]

Ken's sentiments were echoed by a Jacobite versifier. 'Here', he mocked,

> . . . lies King James's disobedient Daughter
> who was addicted very much to laughter
> And liv'd as if there was no world hereafter
> She & her Ugly Nassaw both as One
> Depos'd the Father & usurpd the Throne
> But she from thence by death was rudely torn
> Gods fifth Comand is righteous just & true
> But she long since did bid it quite adieu
> For which her reign was short, her days but few
> With Heavens & Natures Lawes she was at strife
> Yet unconcernd she led a Merry life
> And childless died tho' sixteen years a Wife.[108]

While some Jacobites crowed that the Queen had received her just deserts, the normally abrasive Charles Leslie took a different tack. Well aware of the late Queen's immense popularity, Leslie declined to join the attack on her reputation. Instead, writing in the guise of a distressed juring clergyman, he portrayed her death as a calamity for the Church of England. The Church, he complained, was groaning under the rule of a presbyterian king who had already imposed his religion on Scotland, and was itching to do the same in England.[109] But now, Leslie lamented,

> to add to our misfortunes and dangers, already so many, we have received a fresh blow, by that irreparable loss of our most incomparable queen, who was our patroness, from a zeal she had for our religion, our true and orthodox church; in whose doctrines her judgement was entirely satisfied, and under whose strictest discipline she had her education, and whose truest and most genuine sons were always most in her favour, and had most interest and influence with her.

Who was there now to protect the Church of England? Certainly not King William. For he knew full well that Queen Mary's death had, in the eyes of orthodox clergymen, stripped his regime of its one fig-leaf of hereditary legitimacy. 'By her death', Leslie explained,

> we also lost all pretence to share in King William, and that because we have no pretence left of serving the present government upon our own principles: For though all the world should agree that King James abdicated his throne, and that the Prince of Wales was suppositious, yet King William's title being now become by her death merely elective, and all matrimonial right ceasing with her, we that are of the church of England, and have ever declared our constitution to be hereditary monarchy, can no longer have those salvoes for our compliance which heretofore gave some ease to our consciences.

'King William', Leslie concluded, 'can't but know this too; and therefore, whatever disguises he may think necessary to put on, he must be laying his foundation upon, and giving secret assurances to, those of the whiggish party.'[110] Queen Mary's death had thus left the Established Church exposed to the tender mercies of a king whose rule could only be grounded on a whiggish bottom.

At a time when, as we shall see in a later chapter, the 'whiggish party' was dominant in court and parliament, Leslie's arguments skilfully played on tory fears for the Church. But the most dangerous aspect of Leslie's piece was the way it used Queen Mary's death to delegitimise the King. This was a ploy to which King William's supporters were acutely sensititve. They responded by stressing the Queen's devotion to the King, and her wish that loyal subjects 'might all love him as she had done'.[111] 'While She lived,' observed a preacher at the Chapel Royal in the Tower,

> She loved, honoured and admired Him: She knew his worth beyond what we do; and besides His many other Accomplishments, which His very Enemies admire in Him, She knew, that in His greatest Undertaking, His chiefest Aim was the Interest and Good of Europe; and especially that part

of it which needed most his Help, and to which He was in all Respects most obliged to give it, Great Britain and Ireland.

For the Queen's sake, then, all good subjects should venerate the King. 'She best knew Him,' continued the preacher, 'and therefore justly valued Him: And surely if the Saints departed have any knowledg of what passes here below, we cannot perform a more grateful Service to her Memory, than to value Him, to love, honour and admire Him too.'[112] Indeed, now that Queen Mary was gone, it was necessary to 'place a double Value upon Him, whom God in his Mercy yet spares to us, our Gracious King. Let this heavy Stroke render his Life more dear to us: Let us pray more constantly, and more fervently, for his Health, his Happiness, his Safety, and his Success.'[113] So, far from dissolving the subject's loyalty to the revolution regime, Queen Mary's death would result in that allegiance being focused more sharply than ever on King William. 'The Learned affirm,' wrote another Williamite, 'that as in the loss of an Eye the kind concentring optick Nerves unite and convey their double force to the other remaining Light: so may we live to see the same verified in the Royal surviving Luminary of these Kingdoms. And let it be no less the Nation's particular Care and Duty to be tender of the greatest surviving Light, because 'tis our ALL.'[114]

Such appeals to public sentiment may have proved something of a two-edged sword. After all, they threw into relief all that had perished with the Queen. No longer would she be able to shield her husband from the xeno-phobia of his subjects or the suspicions of the Church party. Gone too was the cloak of hereditary legitimacy, flimsy though it was, which the Queen had flung across King William's shoulders. Small wonder, then, that Williamites once again fell back upon the language of providential deliv-erance in their efforts to shore up the regime. 'But as for our selves,' mused William Sherlock in a sermon at the Temple,

> though we must acknowledge that we have received a very great Loss, in the Death of an Excellent Queen, yet we have no reason to quarrel at Providence, while God preserves our King to go in and out before us. We had indeed perpetual Day; and no sooner was one Sun withdrawn, but another ascended our Horizon, with Equal Lustre and Brightness: This was a peculiar Happiness which we never had before, and which the Necessity of our Affairs, required now; but though God has cut us short in this, we have a King still, the Terror of France, and the Protector of Europe; a King whom Affection, as well as Blood, has Naturalized to us; who loves our Nation and our Church, which he has once delivered, and God grant he may live long to settle and protect both.[115]

In similar vein, Thomas Bowber, another London clergyman, urged his parishioners to prize King William 'as God's Vice-gerent, as the anointed of the Lord, as the breath of our Nostrils'. 'Let us', he urged, 'offer our most humble and devout Prayers to God for him, beseeching him to Crown His Arms with success both by Sea and Land, that he may be a terror to his, and our Enemies, to cover him with his Providence, as with an impenetrable Shield, preserve his Sacred Person from all the Plots and Attempts of his Enemies both at home and abroad.'[116] For, as Bishop Fowler observed, 'the loss of King William, would be the Greatest, that (Humanly speaking) can befal us: Since those are worse than Blind, who will not see, That the Safety of these Nations, and of at least all our Protestant Neighbours, doth wholly, under God almighty, depend upon His Precious Life; and must necessarily so do in the Eye of Reason, while our Circumstances continue as they are Abroad.'[117]

But no amount of eloquent preaching could protect King William from the malice of his enemies. Within a year, the King's 'Precious Life' would be under direct threat as English Jacobites plotted their most audacious attempt to reverse the revolution.

4.   The Triumph of Providence

Throughout the early 1690s, Jacobite conspiracy was endemic in both Scotland and England. In 1690 unsuccessful conspiracies were hatched in the northern kingdom by the disaffected whig, Sir James Montgomery, and in England by a motley group of plotters which included King James's Quaker friend, William Penn, the nonjuring Bishop of Ely, Francis Turner, and Queen Mary's ultra-tory uncle, the Earl of Clarendon.[118] Two years later, King James – adopting the plan patented by his son-in-law in 1688 – sought to foment risings in England in support of a planned French invasion. One of those drawn into the Jacobite intrigues was Admiral Edward Russell, a key player in the Orangist conspiracy of 1688. Although he had received high command from King William, Russell had been disgusted by the cavalier treatment meted out to his brother officers in the English armed forces. But while the Admiral was exasperated by the high-handedness of the new king, he would not contemplate the unconditional restoration of the old. Unfortunately, King James – confident that he would soon be restored by force of French arms – was disinclined to give many promises as regards his future behaviour. True, in April 1692 he published a Declaration designed to rally the people to his cause. But its tone was more menacing than reassuring, and the document gave the 'Compounders' – those ready to countenance the King's conditional restoration – few crumbs of comfort. Certainly not enough to satisfy Admiral Russell who went on to preside over the destruction of the French fleet – and with it King James's immediate hopes of restoration – off La Hogue in May.[119]

The defeat of the French fleet, coupled with strong pressure from King Louis, compelled King James to change his strategy. A second Declaration of May 1693 – in which the late King promised to honour post-revolution legislation, rule with parliament, abide by the Test Act and maintain the Church's privileges – was clearly an attempt to win over potential 'Compounders'.[120] Their ranks had been joined by such luminaries as the Earl of Sunderland – once King James's Secretary of State but now a confidant of the new King – and the Earl of Shrewsbury, King William's Secretary of State until 1690. An ardent Williamite during the revolution, Shrewsbury had been a natural choice as Secretary of State in 1689. But a year later he resigned, appalled – like his fellow whig, Russell – at the King's growing dependence upon the Church party. Since King William had betrayed the whigs, why should they not see what King James had to offer? And that is precisely what Shrewsbury did. As for Sunderland, he was convinced that King William was guaranteeing his own ruin by alienating his natural supporters and placing his trust in the unreliable tories. To insure himself against the prospect of another abrupt change of regime, Sunderland sought to make his peace with his old master.[121]

The 'Compounder' who sailed closest to the wind was John Churchill, Earl of Marlborough. In the Irish campaign of 1690 Marlborough had demonstrated the innate military genius which was to make him the greatest soldier of the age. But his earlier betrayal of King James – a prince who had showered him with honours – marked Marlborough down as a man not to be trusted, least of all by the beneficiary of that treachery. A satirist captured King William's sentiments perfectly when he wrote that

> William, with all his courage, must be afraid
> To trust the villain who has James betrayed.
> For sure, nothing can e'er redeem thy crime
> But the same brutal trick a second time.[122]

So, notwithstanding Marlborough's brilliant Irish service, King William pointedly overlooked the unscrupulous Earl when handing out commands for the campaigns of 1691. Marlborough took the snub badly. By the end of the year, he was seeking to organise an unprecedented 'general strike' – a mass protest by the English senior officer corps against the King's predilection for Dutch generals. It was probably this, rather than his lack of trust in Marlborough, which prompted King William to strip the soldier-courtier of all his posts in January 1692.[123] But in April Marlborough was among a number of suspected Jacobites required to take up quarters in the Tower of London.[124] As it happens, the Earl was almost certainly innocent of the charges which landed him in the Tower. There is no doubt, however, that he was up to his neck in Jacobite intrigues.[125] Released from the Tower in September 1692, Marlborough remained *persona non grata* with the King. And in May 1694 the earl committed an act of treachery breathtaking even by his standards: he disclosed to the French a planned English raid on Brest.[126]

Marlborough's motives for betraying the Brest operation remain obscure. Perhaps he was driven by desperation at his continued exclusion from military and political office. Alternatively, he may have been animated by jealousy of the raid's commander, Thomas Talmash, the only English officer to be entrusted with senior command by King William. If so, things could hardly have worked out better for Marlborough. The raid on Brest turned into a bloody shambles, with Talmash among the many fatal casualties.[127] Whatever the earl's motives, one thing is clear: in previous reigns, many men had lost their heads and innards for considerably less.

In betraying the raid on Brest, Marlborough displayed that readiness to take a risk which was so marked a feature of both his political and military careers. This was not a characteristic found widely among the 'Compounders'. By the Autumn of 1695, it had become painfully clear to the Jacobite court at St Germain that, while several prominent English politicians were prepared to consider King James's restoration, they would do precious little to bring it about. But just as King James's hopes began to fade again, King Louis of France reopened the more direct route home. Having suffered a series of setbacks in the campaigns of 1694 and 1695, the French King was becoming increasingly anxious to knock England out of the war. The one certain way of achieving that objective was the restoration of King James. And that in turn could be accomplished only by means of French military intervention. Accordingly, King Louis was now ready to deploy 12,000 French troops in an invasion of England planned for the Spring of 1696. However, he did not wish to be seen to be imposing King James upon an unwilling nation. So the French King insisted that his soldiers would land in England only *after* King James's supporters had risen against the usurper. The exiled King readily agreed.[128]

To pave the way for the planned risings, King James dispatched a number of agents to England. Among them was a former army officer, Sir George Barclay. It proved an exceedingly bad choice. Once in England, Barclay rightly concluded that it would be too risky to launch an uprising in advance of the French invasion. Instead, he grossly exceeded his authority by hatching a plan of his own. Although he had often been pressed to do so, King James had consistently refused to countenance any attempt to assassinate his son-in-law. This, however, was precisely the path on which Barclay and his fellow conspirators were now set. Together with his colleagues in the 'Select Number', the secret Jacobite organisation modelled on the Royalist 'Sealed Knot' of the 1650s, Barclay would strike down the usurper while he was riding in his carriage in Richmond Park.[129]

The blow was never struck. On 24 February 1696 King William informed both houses of parliament that he had discovered a plot against his life.[130] Barclay and the 'Select Number' had been betrayed by some of their own number. In the subsequent clamp-down, hundreds of suspected

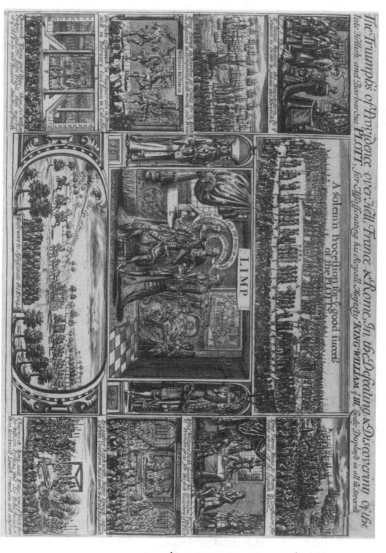

Figure 6 'The Triumphs of Providence', 1696. The story of the 'Assassination Plot', told in comic-strip form. In the bottom centre, the all-seeing 'Eye of Providence' protects King William from the conspirators who then receive their just deserts (bottom right). In the central panel King Louis of France, sickened by the failure of the plot, vomits up his conquests.

Jacobites were rounded up.[131] As for the planned French invasion, this was scuppered by the swift concentration of the English fleet in the Channel.[132]

The revelation of the 'Assassination Plot' led to an outburst of Williamite fervour not seen since the revolution. 'You cannot imagine', wrote a correspondent of Lord Hatton on 25 February, 'how this has renewd the affections of the generallite of the people to this King.'[133] Before long, gentlemen up and down the country were banding themselves into 'Associations' which swore vengeance upon any who dared touch the King.[134] But it soon became apparent that the danger had passed, and that the plotters had merely succeeded in adding another chapter to the Williamite saga of providential deliverance. To the London nonconformist Elias Pledger, it was plain that the 'Assassination Plot' had been uncovered 'by the wonderful providence of god'. ' Oh how many times', he mused in his diary, 'has this sinful nation been delivered. God seems to be loath to give us up, but Oh how many a Time have we provoked him, how easy a prey would our enemies make of us if god would but let them loos upon us. Blessed be god that that pit which they dug and designed for us, they are fallen into it themselves.'[135] The Gloucestershire JP, Sir Richard Cocks, was of like mind. Addressing his county's grand jury at the Easter Sessions of 1696, Cocks reminded the jurymen that 'there has been allmost as visibly the hand of god in our revolution as was in bringing the Children of Israell out of the Aegyptian thraldom'. The latest instance of divine intervention had been the discovery of the plot against King William's life. For that plot was 'so cunningly, so well laid that no human foresight could either dive into it or prevent it. Nothing but the immediate hand of providence could have delivered'.[136] Once again, the all-seeing eye of divine providence had come to the rescue of King William and the Protestant cause. 'And now', runs a Williamite verse,

> . . . the Assassins come to give the Blow,
> (Which had it took, had wrought all Europe's Woe)
> The very Day is fix'd, the Ambush laid,
> Which should the Life (so dear to all) invade:
> But then High Providence (whose Piercing Eye
> Did into their most secret Counsels pry)
> Bring their Dark Deeds to Light; that thereby all
> The Ills they meant, on their own Heads might fall.[137]

And fall they did with a vengeance. When the mood took it, King William's regime could be every bit as vicious as its predecessors. In 1693, for example, it had pursued William Anderton, a Jacobite printer, all the way to the gallows.[138] But hitherto, due to a combination of lenience and lack of will, the King had generally shied away from draconian measures against Jacobite conspirators.[139] This time there was to be no mercy. Eight Jacobites were convicted of treason, and suffered the grisly penalty which the law laid down for traitors – hanging, evisceration and quartering. A ninth, Sir John Fenwick, was attainted by parliament, and went to the block in January 1697.[140]

The unflinching ends made by the condemned men enabled Jacobite propagandists to salvage something from the shambles. Far from expressing remorse, the execution speeches of the conspirators, suitably embroidered for publication, rejoiced in the principles which had brought their authors to the scaffold. 'My religion', Fenwick was reported to have told the crowd at his execution, 'taught me loyalty, which I bless God is untainted; and I have endeavoured in the station wherein I have been placed, to the utmost of my power, to support the crown of England in the true and lineal course of descent, without interruption.' Another of the Jacobite martyrs, Sir William Parkyns, explained that it was his 'duty, both as a subject and an Englishman, to assist [King James] in the recovery of his throne'.[141] But brave words could not disguise the disaster which had befallen English Jacobitism. The 'Select Number' had been destroyed. Worse still, King James's cause had been thoroughly discredited. As John Evelyn observed, 'tho many did formerly pitty K[ing] James's Condition, this designe of Assassination, & bringing over a French Army, did much alienate of his friends'.[142]

Nor were the parliamentary consequences of the 'Assassination Plot' less far-reaching. As we shall see in the next chapter, the plot revelations, together with the subsequent reluctance of many tory parliamentarians to sign a document describing King William as the 'rightful and lawful' King, revived the old whig prejudice that the Church party was a nest of Jacobites. The upshot was a general closing of whig ranks in parliament, and the destruction of a nascent bi-partisan opposition to the 'Junto' whig administration. This in turn ensured that the King had few worries at Westminster as he negotiated an end to the war with France.[143] When the peace was finally signed at Ryswick in September 1697, it dealt another massive blow to the Jacobite cause. For in the treaty, King Louis promised to give no further succour to King William's enemies.[144]

By the Autumn of 1697, thanks to the Treaty of Ryswick, King William could at last wear the crowns of the three kingdoms with a modicum of ease. But peace would bring him a new and, in some ways, more trying set of problems. In a verse satire penned during the peace negotiations, King William's confidant, the Earl of Sunderland, warns his master of the difficulties to be expected after the war:

> Consider, Sir, your present situation
> And fickle temper of the nation:
> The senate now will sit and vote
> Your money, while they're worth a groat.
> But, if the danger once is o'er,
> Never expect one penny more.

> They then will saucily command
> That you your forces shall disband,
> Make strict enquiry what was lent in,
> And how paid out and what 'twas spent in;
> Nay, maybe what you gave to Bentin.[145]

It proved to be one of the more prophetic satires of King William's reign.

5. King William at Bay

In the next chapter we shall see how, in the eighteen months following the Peace of Ryswick, parliament's efforts to slash King William's army shattered the administration of the whig 'Junto'. Caught between Scylla (the King's insistence upon retaining a substantial peace-time army) and Charybdis (the thirst of MPs for swingeing cuts to the army), the whig ministry at first floundered and then sank with all hands. The climax came in the Commons' votes of January 1699. As Bishop Burnet later recalled, King William's

> ministers represented to him, that they could carry the keeping up a land force of ten or twelve thousand, but they could not carry it further: he said, so small a number was as good as none at all; therefore he would not authorize them to propose it: on the other hand, they should lose their credit with their best friends, if they ventured to speak of a greater number. So, when the house of commons took up the debate, the ministry was silent, and proposed no number; upon which those who were in the contrary interest named seven thousand men, and to this they added, that they should be all the king's natural born subjects.[146]

The principal victims of the Commons' vote were the blue-uniformed Dutch guards. This elite regiment was King William's favourite, and he regarded it as a personal affront when parliament refused his request to keep it on the English payroll.[147] But Burnet believed that King William was, once again, the author of his own misfortunes. 'Hitherto', wrote the bishop in his memoirs,

> the body of the nation retained a great measure of affection to him; this was beginning to diminish, by his going so constantly beyond sea, as soon as the session of parliament ended; though the war was now over. Upon this, it grew to be publicly said, that he loved no Englishman's face, nor his company: so his enemies reckoned it was fit for their ends, to let that prejudice go on, and increase in the minds of the people; till they might find a proper occasion to graft some bad designs upon it.[148]

One such 'bad design' was the so-called Act of Resumptions.

In the early 1690s MPs had hoped, and expected, that the cost of the Irish war would be met by the sale of the estates of unpardoned Jacobite rebels. The King, however, had other ideas. Instead of selling the forfeited estates for the public good, he parcelled them out among his favourite courtiers, including the Countess of Orkney, reputedly the King's mistress; the Earl of Portland and his heir, Lord Woodstock; and the King's young favourite, the Earl of Albemarle. While the whig 'Junto' ruled the parliamentary roost, King William's largesse escaped censure. But in the unmanageable 1698 parliament the grants were subjected to close scrutiny by MPs determined on retrenchment in the public finances. In April 1699 parliament established a commission to investigate the disposal of the Irish estates. To the fury of MPs, the commission's inquiries revealed that the lion's share of the forfeited lands had gone to seven foreign-born courtiers. The upshot was the most humiliating episode of the King's reign – the Act of April 1700 revoking all of his Irish grants.[149]

The fires of English xenophobia, reignited by King William's cavalier disregard for his subjects' sensibilities, were furiously fanned by the anti-Dutch polemicist, John Tutchin. In his scurrilous poem, *The Foreigners*, written shortly after the passage of the Resumptions Act, Tutchin heaped abuse upon the Earl of Portland. Using the imagery of the Old Testament, Tutchin portrayed Portland as a rapacious alien, grown fat at the expense of God's Chosen People. The Earl, he sneered, was

> Of mean Descent, yet insolently proud,
> Shun'd by the Great, and hated by the Crowd;
> Who neither Blood nor Parentage can boast,
> And what he got the Jewish Nation lost:
> By lavish Grants whole Provinces he gains,
> Made forfeit by the Jewish Peoples Pains;
> Till angry Sanhedrims such Grants resume,
> And from the Peacock take each borrow'd Plume.

But the attack on Portland served merely as a prelude to a general denunciation of the Dutch, that nation of 'Gibeonites'

> . . . void of Honesty and Grace,
> A Boorish, rude, and an inhumane Race;
> From Nature's Excrement their Life is drawn,
> Are born in Bogs, and nourish'd up from Spawn.

Why, asked Tutchin, should such loathsome creatures

> . . . our Land engross,
> And aggrandize their fortunes with our loss?
> Let them in foreign States proudly command,
> They have no Portion in the Promis'd Land,
> Which immemorially has been decreed
> To be the Birth-right of the Jewish Seed.[150]

Tutchin received a tart reply from the literary critic, John Dennis:

> If Judah's Sons are false, and Gibeon's just,
> Gibeon has right to share in Judah's Trust;
> And serve abroad whom she at home rever'd,
> By Gods approv'd of, and to Men endear'd.

And no 'son of Gibeon' was more worthy than Portland. Far from fleecing his adopted country, the Earl had

> . . . for thy Rights and Honours stood,
> And made an Israelite, sought Israel's good,
> Dispell'd the Tempests gathering from a far,
> and next Agrippa [King William] hush'd the Din of War.[151]

In his celebrated satire, *The True-Born Englishman*, Daniel Defoe also leapt to Portland's defence:

> Ten Years in English Service he appear'd,
> And gain'd his Master's and the World's Regard:
> But 'tis not England's Custom to Reward.
> The Wars are over, England needs him not;
> Now he's a Dutchman, and the Lord knows what.[152]

But such ingratitude was next to nothing beside the shameful treatment Englishmen had meted out to their Deliverer. 'Ye Heav'ns' regard!' beseeched an indignant Defoe,

> . . . Almighty Jove look down,
> And view thy Injur'd Monarch on the Throne.
> On their Ungrateful Heads due Vengeance take,
> Who sought his Aid, and then his part forsake.
> Witness, ye Powers! it was Our Call alone,
> Which now our Pride makes us asham'd to own.
> Britannia's Troubles fetch'd him from afar,
> To court the dreadful Casualties of War:
> But where Requital never be made,
> Acknowledgment's a Tribute seldom paid.[153]

Why, then, should King William be condemned for preferring loyal foreigners to faithless Englishmen? 'We blame the King', mused the poet,

> . . . that he relies too much
> On Strangers, Germans, Hugonots, and Dutch;
> And seldom does his great Affairs of State,
> To English Counsellors communicate.
> The Fact might very well be answer'd thus;
> He has so often been betray'd by us,
> He must have been a Madman to rely
> On English Gentlemens Fidelity.[154]

This battle of rhyming couplets was something of an internecine struggle: all of the combatants were strong whigs. As such, Tutchin was by no means a typical supporter of the Act of Resumptions. In contrast to the disbandment of the army, which had won broad parliamentary support, resumptions was essentially a tory policy.[155] In his poetical joust with Tutchin, Dennis had accused his opponent of taking a tilt at Portland in order to strike at the King:

> But Envy's not contented to Prophane
> Agrippa's Friend, but dares his Master's Reign;
> Under the Subject, it reviles the Prince . . .[156]

It may well be that whig backbenchers took a similarly jaundiced view of the motives of those urging the revocation of the King's grants. If so, they were pretty close to the mark. The Resumptions Act was, in large measure, a sign of growing tory animus towards Dutch William. This had been escalating steadily during the years of Junto whig dominance since 1693. But by the Spring of 1700 that dominance was a thing of the past. The whig leaders were on the rack, and the Act of Resumptions added to their agony. When the House of Lords threatened to block the legislation, its promoters in the Commons vented their spleen on the ministers who had aided and abetted the plundering foreigners. 'The whole nation', they complained,

> must be exposed to misery, and all for preserving the grants of those who would beggar the kingdom to enrich themselves; who were foreigners, and had not the bowels of Englishmen, but would be contented to see this country destroyed, when they are not to get their wills of it; they had been assisted by a servile corrupt ministry, who for a share of the plunder, had been the tools to foreigners, and served them in all their rapines.[157]

As can be imagined, such language did nothing to endear the Church party to King William. Not that this troubled the tories overmuch. Why should it? After all, they possessed the future in the plump form of the heir to the throne, Princess Anne. A more rigid Churchwoman than her elder sister, the Princess had long been the darling of true-blue tories. As early as 1689, Church party MPs had courted the King and Queen's displeasure by sponsoring an attempt to increase the Princess's annual revenue.[158] After that move was thwarted, Princess Anne had made common cause with the more extreme tories in mocking the godly tone of her sister's court. As Queen Mary lamented, her cold relations with the Princess had 'proved dangerous to the publick afairs of the nation in making a party; and that all the High Churchmen seemed to endeavour, and she herself affected to find fault with every thing was done, especially to laugh at afternoon Sermons, and doing in litle things contrary to what I did'.[159] Nor were sisterly relations improved by the Queen's refusal to allow her brother-in-law, Prince George of Denmark, to serve at sea with the fleet. But it was Princess Anne's intimate friendship with Sarah Churchill – wife of that notorious troublemaker, the Earl of Marlborough – which brought about

Figure 7   A print in honour of William, Duke of Gloucester, second in line to the throne, 1700. The 10-year old Duke plays at soldiers with his friends, watched over by his doting parents, Princess Anne and Prince George of Denmark. The boy's death in July 1700 ensured the extinction of the Protestant branch of the House of Stuart.

a complete rupture in the royal family. When King William stripped Marlborough of all his offices in January 1692, the Princess responded by establishing a rival court at Syon House.[160] These events left the Queen harbouring some gloomy thoughts about the consequences of filial impiety: 'in all this', mused that tortured soul,

> I see the hand of God, and look on our disagreeing as a punishment upon us for the irregularity by us committed upon the revolution. My husband did his duty and the nation did theirs and we were to suffer it, and rejoice that it pleased God to do what he did. But as to owr persons it is not as it ought to be, tho' it was unavoidable, and no doubt that is a just judgment of God, but I trust the Church and nation shall not suffer, but that we in our private concerns and persons may bear the punishment as in this we do.[161]

Not until December 1694 would the family feud be healed, and then only in the final hours of the Queen's life.

Queen Mary's death left the Princess but a heartbeat away from the throne. And as King William's hold on life became more tenuous in the late 1690s, so the Church party looked forward with growing expectation to the accession of an authentically 'cavalier' Queen. What was more, there was every chance of a prolonged sequence of tory monarchs. For after Anne would come her young son, the Duke of Gloucester. But on 30 July 1700 a thunderbolt struck. The MP Robert Harley, of whom we shall be hearing a great deal more later, recounted the tragic events in a letter to his father. 'The D[uke of] Gloucester danc'd on his [eleventh] birth day, was ill the next, fryday Dr Harnes orderd him to be let blood, & blister'd, he had some spots, had eat fruit; smal pox was suspected, he had a looseness al the time, dyed this morning at one a clock.' For once, the workings of divine providence seemed unfathomable. 'Gods ways', pondered Harley, 'are unsearchable – he reigns – thats the true comfort.'[162]

Divine providence, so often invoked in the past as the ally of the Protestant monarchy, had now placed a huge question mark against its long-term survival. Princess Anne's many fruitless pregnancies had broken her health, and there was no prospect of her producing another heir. As for the King, he would not countenance remarriage even for the sake of the Protestant succession. Thus the death of the young Duke ensured that the Protestant branch of the Stuart family would expire with his mother. Who, or what, would come after?

The whig leaders were determined to prevent a Jacobite succession at all costs. According to one report, they were even contemplating the establishment of a Commonwealth.[163] There was, however, a monarchical alternative to King James and his son: Sophia, dowager Electress of Hanover, 70 year-old Protestant granddaughter of King James I. In August 1689, when the Duke of Gloucester was a sickly newborn babe, parliament had considered expressly including the Hanoverian family in the line of succession.[164] Unlike Princess Anne's other children, however, Gloucester had survived infancy, and the Electress Sophia soon faded into the background. The young Duke's unexpected death brought her back into prominence as the nearest Protestant in the line of succession. But would Englishmen in general, and the Church party in particular, be able to stomach another foreign monarch? The auspices were not favourable. 'The House of Hanover is much spoken of', reported James Vernon on 15 August. 'The objection is, "What, must we have more foreigners?" which', added Vernon dryly, 'is not very obliging towards the King.'[165]

All this was music to Jacobite ears. The Duke of Gloucester's death had rekindled the flame of hope at St Germain. The evident queasiness of many Englishmen at the prospect of a Hanoverian Succession made that flame burn more brightly still. By early September it was reported that 'they are laying wagers at St Germains that they shall be called home, before Christmas by the parliament.'[166] Nor was this simply a case of wishful thinking. 'I reckon whenever the Prince of Wales comes hither,' opined Vernon at the end of August,

> it will be by so strong a hand from France as will subdue this nation for them-
> selves, and make him the pretence only for obtaining an easier conquest. I
> am sorry, therefore, to hear what the Archbishop [of Canterbury] told me
> yesterday, that by his advices out of the country, he feared there was an ill
> spirit working towards the Prince of Wales. I asked him if the clergy gave
> into it; he said, not those he corresponded with, but one may conclude they
> observed it in some others.[167]

Six weeks later Vernon wrote that he shared the Earl of Sunderland's view 'that if there be not a visible successor, the Prince of Wales will be put upon us very soon'.[168] But soon there would be a visible successor, and it was not the Prince of Wales.

In March 1701 a bill was introduced in the Commons settling the succession after Princess Anne on the Electress Sophia and the heirs of her body. Over the next next two months, it passed all its stages without a single division in either house.[169] This curious turn of events has never been satisfactorily explained. As good an analysis as any was provided by a Jacobite agent during the early stages of the bill's progress. The unwonted show of parliamentary unity, he believed, was a by-product of ministerial changes made before the beginning of the session. To pave the way for a new parliament, 'it was resolv'd to shift the Ministry of affaires from the Whigs to the Church Party . . . but to doe it in such a manner, as not to put the party remov'd in despair of being restor'd, so as to gain one party without loosing the other.' Thus 'the two Parties one to preserve the posses-sion, the other to regain it have been like Rivals at strife to promote the Court Projects, which has been one great occasion of the late Unanimity.'[170]

But the agent also saw another factor at work: the Church party's distaste for the Hanoverians had been outweighed by its fears of an intolerant popish successor. The Prince of Wales, wrote the agent, was believed to be under the influence of Lord Melfort, leader of the Catholic revanchist faction at St Germain. That belief had 'induc't severall well inclin'd persons', who had initially declared themselves against the Hanoverians, 'to change their minds, and to act as they have done contrary to what they have hitherto profest'. Faced with a choice between the popish Prince of Wales and a dynasty of foreign Protestants, the Church party had, for the time being at least, plumped for the latter as the lesser of two evils: 'tho they confess themselves uneasy in their present State, tho they have really endur'd more by what they call their deliverance, than they could have suffer'd by a Succession of twenty lawfull Tyrants, yet as long as any appearances last to nourish the imagination of greater difficulties they seem resolv'd to submit to what they feel, and this has been another cause of the late unanimity.'[171]

That there was no great enthusiasm for the Electress and her brood was apparent from the remaining provisions of the Act of Settlement. Tacked to the succession legislation was a series of measures which would come into force upon the Hanoverian Succession. In future, no monarch, 'not being a native of this kingdom of England', would be able to commit the nation to 'any war for the defence of any dominions or territories which do not belong to the crown of England, without the consent of parliament'. Nor would any monarch be allowed to set one foot outside the British Isles without parliamentary consent. As for foreign-born subjects, the Act prohibited them from sitting in the privy council or parliament, holding any office under the Crown, or receiving any grant of Crown lands, whether or not they were naturalized. Provisions such as these were designed to ensure that never again would the English ship of state be steered by a foreign rudder. It was less easy to legislate for the conscience of a future monarch born and bred, like King William, in the ways of a foreign church. But while the law could not make the Lutheran House of Hanover fall in love with the Church of England, it could at least oblige all monarchs of that line to 'join in communion with the church of England, as by law established'.[172]

Although these provisions were not to come into force until the advent of the Hanoverians, they were plainly a slap in the face for King William. At the beginning of his reign, as we shall see in a later chapter, the King had sought to repeal the sacramental qualification for office.[173] Twelve years on, parliament had effectively extended that selfsame test to the person of a future foreign monarch. In 1689 King William had led England into a war to curb the overweening ambitions of the King of France. By 1701, four years after the struggle had ended, many of his subjects still shuddered at the memory of a hideously expensive war from which only the Dutch had profited. In 1688 the Prince of Orange had vowed to rid England of the baleful influence of 'evil counsellors'. But as King, he had dismayed his subjects by showering favours and offices on a new breed of evil counsellors, that pestilential crew of Dutchmen and other equally ghastly foreigners. If there was no love lost for the Hanoverians, it was because Englishmen feared they would rule too much like King William.

For the devotees of toryism – a creed which despised the Dutchman and the dissenter almost as much as the Pope and the Pretender – this was an especially disturbing thought. True, fear of popery had forced the tories into the arms of the Lutheran Electress. But the embrace was a reluctant one, and would become progressively more so as the Hanoverian Succession moved from the realm of distant contingency to that of imminent reality. The upshot, in the succession crisis of 1713–16, was a chronically divided party, unable to commit itself wholeheartedly to either Hanover or St Germain. And the price of indecision would be the destruction of the tories as a party of government.

All that lay in the future. In 1701 the Church party could put the Hanoverian Succession to the back of its mind, and look forward instead to an altogether more appealing prospect: the accession of Anne, a princess with a true English heart and a Church of England soul. Of course, that happy event would come only on the death of King William. But the tories would be shedding few tears for the 'Great Deliverer'. The reasons for this will become clearer in the following chapters.

3

Parties and Politics

1. Whig and Tory

At some point in the early 1690s Thomas Papillon, puritan merchant and politician, penned a note on the state of English politics. He began his analysis with two bald assertions. 'The Kingdom of England is made up of Papists and Protestants. The Protestants are divided, and of late years distinguished by the name of Tories and Whigs.'[1] The second of Papillon's dichotomies, the partisan schism between tory and whig, was the cardinal fact of English political life in the 1690s, and would remain so for a further five decades.

The whigs and tories of the late seventeenth century were not the institutionalized political parties we know today. Referring to the political divisions of the early 1680s, when the historic party names were born, Jonathan Scott has written that there was 'a polarity, not of organization, but of belief'.[2] Much the same could be said of the post-revolution period. After 1689, it is true, political life acquired a more regular form. The demands of war finance transformed parliament from a rather erratic event – it had sat only once between 1681 and 1689 – into a permanent institution, and the timing of elections became more predictable thanks to the Triennial Act of 1694. These developments in turn stimulated a more systematic approach towards political organization both in parliament and the constituencies, resulting in the emergence, by Anne's reign, of an informal type of national party organization.[3] If, however, we wish to seek the origins of modern political parties, we should look to the middle of the nineteenth century, not the end of the seventeenth. For the parties of the 1690s could boast no centralised institutions. They had no single leader, no electoral organisation at national level, no mechanism to secure the attendance of 'their' members at Westminster, no means of disciplining erring MPs.

Nothing better illustrates the intangible quality of late-seventeenth-century party than the fog of uncertainty shrouding the results of the Williamite general elections. Since electoral organization was a local matter, it was extremely difficult to determine the party allegiance of many newly-elected MPs. Hence the partisan complexion of the House of Commons usually became clear only *after* the new parliament had sat. The returns for the second election of 1701, for example, left some observers estimating a whig victory by thirty seats, while others were equally confident that the tories had triumphed.[4]

Late-seventeenth century parties were more nebulous entities than their modern successors. They also had to contend with a phenomenon unknown in today's political system: a head of government with an agenda of his own. To King William, the squabbles of his subjects were a distraction from the real business of government, winning the war against Louis XIV. He was willing to employ anyone who would help him achieve that end, irrespective of their party allegiance. The result, in the early 1690s, was a hotchpotch administration in which men of violently-opposed principles rubbed shoulders uncomfortably with each other. True, the King gave his administration a distinctly more whiggish tinge after 1693. But the whigs never gained a monopoly of office. Even at the height of their dominance, in 1697, there were still some thirty tory placemen in the Commons.[5] And an administration which included men of both parties also contained men of none – King's servants like William Blathwayt, Secretary at War from 1690 to 1704, and William Lowndes, Secretary to the Treasury from 1695.

King William's administrations, then, were not the single-party affairs so familiar to us today. Nor were the parties of the 1690s centralized political organizations in the modern sense. Not surprisingly, therefore, we will make little sense of the political history of King William's reign, with its intra-party divisions and shifting political alliances, if we persist in viewing the parties of the period in anachronistic institutional terms. Instead, the labels whig and tory should be understood to denote two broad and mutually hostile political traditions, nothing more and nothing less.[6]

What were these rival traditions? A perceptive analysis was provided by an anonymous radical pamphleteer in 1692. The tories, he explained,

> have it for their End to see the Church establish'd in as high Power as ever; to see it freed from the Eye-sore of Dissenters and Fanaticks; to remove the ill precedent of [the establishment of presbyterianism in] Scotland; to set up Episcopacy in such strength as is requir'd by the Clergy-men themselves, to put them out of fear of every thing; and to have a King governing with as large a Prerogative as may be; but still by the means, and under the Tuition of such a Church.

In contrast,

The Whigs dread such a Power in the Church, and are so dissatisfy'd with what it has of that kind already, fearing what may come, that they expect a greater Security than is given them at present, that those who are Dissenters from, or under the Mark of the Church for being ill Friends to it, may never see it in a Condition to take its Revenge, or give them any Disturbance. These men exclaim generally against all Arbitrary Power, but more especially that which the Church would introduce, and that their Enemies would most profit by.[7]

To our writer, then, the ideological polarity between whig and tory was rooted, above all, in religious controversy.

While religion, as we shall see more fully later, did indeed form the fertile soil of party conflict, that soil was watered by the political struggles of the recent past. Needless to say, these were interpreted in very different ways by whigs and tories. Both parties could agree that under James II a popish plot had been afoot to undermine the liberties of Protestant England. But to the adherents of whiggery, King James's reign was merely the culmination of a conspiracy which had been hatched under Charles II. As the MP Jack Howe pithily asserted in 1689, 'The Door was opened in King Charles II's time, and the goods were stolen in James II's time.'[8] The evils that had befallen England in King Charles's days were later described by the anti-clerical writer, John Toland. To that 'profligate and Villainous Reign', he wrote in 1698,

we are to ascribe the loss of all the considerable Charters of England, the deaths of our best Patriots, the encouragement and almost establishment of Popery, the decay of Trade, the growth of Arbitrary Power, the ill effects of dishonourable Leagues [with France] . . . the progress of all sorts of Debauchery, the servile compliances at Court of a rampant [Church] Hierarchy in the kingdom, the insolent deportment of the inferior Clergy both in the Universities and elsewhere, their slavish doctrine of Passive Obedience and Nonresistance; in short, a general depravation of manners, and almost utter extirpation of Virtue and moral Honesty.[9]

Indeed, in the view of many whigs all that distinguished Charles II from his younger brother was greater discretion in prosecuting the popish cause.[10]

In their wicked contrivances against the nation's religious and political liberties, the Stuart brothers had been aided and abetted by those rogues, the tories. Writing in 1693, a whig pamphleteer acknowledged that knaves could be found in both parties. Yet there was still 'a Distinction to be made, betwixt our Party, who not only profess, but have maintain'd to the Death, the Religion, Rights and Liberties of their Country; and yours, who in King Charles's and beginning of King James's Reign gave up all these things.'[11] As for the subsequent opposition of the tories to James II, this, wrote another whig, was simply a case of thieves falling out – the behaviour of men who 'herd with, or connive at Robbers, till they come to divide the

Spoils, and then fall from them and make Discoveries, because they are not allowed that share which they merited'.[12]

Of the whole accursed Restoration period, the early 1680s were remembered by whigs as an especially dark age, redeemed only by the heroism of their 'martyred' brethren, notably Lord William Russell and Algernon Sidney who had both gone to the block in 1683.[13] To tories, on the other hand, the last four years of King Charles's reign constituted a golden age. Between 1681 and 1685 – the years of 'tory reaction' following the defeat of exclusion – they had enjoyed a monopoly of office and had enthusiastically assisted the King in crushing his whig enemies. For the tory party viewed the whigs as subversive incendiaries, intent on nothing less than the overthrow of the Crown and Church of England.[14]

As this suggests, the tory mental world was informed by a still longer historical perspective. When the tories looked into the faces of their whig opponents, they saw the roundheads and regicides of the 1640s. Thus in January 1696, when whigs held the reins of power, the high tory Edmund Bohun noted that it was 'almost fifty years since the blood of Charles the First was shed, in this very month, by this very party'. Although divine vengeance had not yet been wreaked upon that party for its heinous crime, Bohun looked forward with confidence to a time 'when that blood shall be required; and the sooner because they still go on in the ill principles that occasioned that murder, and persecute all those that will not joyne with them in those ill principles and worse practices'.[15] Six years earlier, the tory MP Thomas Clarges had invoked the memory of 'what they did in Charles I's time, and the consequences' when justifying the removal of whigs from the London Lieutenancy Commission, the body which controlled the capital's trained bands.[16]

Tory rhetoric was, in fact, steeped in the memories of the 1640s. In 1694, shortly after the whig party had gained pre-eminence in the King's administration, a tory parliamentarian warned the Commons of the danger that would arise 'if the civill power is taken out of their hands who are the friends, & the Supporters of the Church. I have read the History of the late times, & know that Puritans, men that could qualifie them Selves [for office], men that went to the Church first got power into their hands, got within these walls, & then under the notion of Reformation pull'd down the Episcopall Order, laid aside all our Ceremonies & covenanted against our very Liturgy.'[17] A still more explicit parallel between old roundheads and modern whigs was drawn by another tory parliamentarian. London whiggery, he correctly pointed out, was dominated by occasional conformists – dissenters who qualified for office by occasionally taking communion in the Established Church. While the whigs fulminated against 'Church-papists' – crypto-papists within the Church – it was these 'Church-fanaticks' who were the real danger. For were they not the same breed of men 'that destroyed our monarchy & our Church in the late times?'[18]

The cry that '41 is come again' was ever ready to trip from tory tongues. When in May 1701 the whiggish 'Kentish petition' implicitly attacked the tardy response of a tory parliament to renewed French aggression in Europe, Sir Edward Seymour, doyen of true-blue toryism, insisted 'that it was high time to looke in the commissions of the peace and to put a stop to such proceedings which would destroy our constitution and bring us to 41'.[19] A similar view of the motives of the Kentish petitioners was expressed by an outraged tory versifier:

> While Fearful of Invasions from a far,
> At home they meditate a Civil War,
> And hatch Rebellion underneath a Zeal,
> To save, and to promote the Common-Weal,
> As they for Mutinies most humbly sue,
> And would revive the Crimes of Forty Two.[20]

In tory eyes, then, the struggle with whig 'fanaticks' was merely a continuation of the old conflict with the roundheads. Nor was it difficult to find evidence to nourish this prejudice. Some whigs made no secret of their sympathy for the 'old cause'. In 1689, for example, Lord Wharton was indignant when the cause for which he had fought as a young man was branded a rebellion.[21] And in the late 1690s came that noisy group of commonwealthsmen responsible for publishing the memoirs of the regicide, Edmund Ludlow, and the works of the regicide's apologist, John Milton.[22]

The regicide itself was something of a taboo subject in whig circles. When Ludlow, the last of the regicides, returned to England from his long Swiss sojourn in September 1689, the parliamentary whigs kept their heads down. They made no attempt to shield Ludlow from the tory onslaught which soon forced him back into exile.[23] Nevertheless, many whiggish writers were willing to denounce the Church party's veneration of Charles I and his fellow 'martyr', Archbishop Laud. According to the French Protestant, Jean Gailhard, the High Church sanctification of the late King teetered on the brink of popish idolatry. King Charles's execution was undoubtedly 'an horrid murther, execrable, as black as words can make it'. Nevertheless, Charles I was no martyr, for 'his being a Christian was not the cause or pretence of his being put to death'. Rather 'the pretence was, (how true or false I dive not into it) his following evil council, encroaching upon the liberties, carrying on designs for arbitrariness, casting into prison men for refusing to lend him money, raising money without parliament, as in the case of ship-money, for designing to bring in popery and other such things . . . As to this last [charge],' he added pointedly,

> I must say in his time (whether or not of his own contrivance I cannot tell)
> a design was carrying on to reconcile us to the church of Rome, whose

interest here did much thrive through the queen's favour; the persecution of puritans, the prayer-book sent into Scotland, bringing in Arminianism, setting up crucifixes upon the communion-tables, by them called altars, as ministers were and are still by the name of priests, thus promiscuously bringing in names and things; those and many more, were evidences of the project then in hand.

None of this, Gailhard concluded, could justify the regicide. Nor, however, did King Charles's death 'prove him a martyr'.[24]

Other writers were equally forthright in their denunciations of Charles I's misrule. 'The first Fifteen Years of his Reign', wrote the polemical historian Roger Coke in 1694, 'were perfectly French, and such as never before were seen, or heard of in the English Nation; this brought on a miserable War in all the three Kingdom's of England Scotland and Ireland, and destruction upon the King, whenas it was not in the power of those which first raised the War against him, to save his life which they would have done.'[25] As for Archbishop Laud, he was a 'Fire-brand' who 'set all three Nations into the Flame of a Civil War'.[26] Writing in 1698, the violently whiggish John Trenchard claimed that Charles I had

> brought unheard of Innovations into the Church; preferred men of Arbitrary Principles, and inclinable to popery, especially those firebrands, Laud, Mountague, and Manwaring, one of whom had been complain'd of in parliament, another impeach'd for advancing Popery, and the third condemn'd in the House of Lords. He dispensed with the Laws against Papists, and both encourag'd and prefer'd them. He called no parliament for twelve years together, and in that time govern'd as arbitrarily as the Grand Seignior. He abetted the Irish massacre . . . It is endless to enumerate all the oppressions of his Reign. [27]

In 1690 another whig writer grudgingly accepted that Charles I had not favoured 'Down-right Popery'. But he had become enamoured of 'a Laudean Prelacy, or British Patriarchate, which was little better'.[28] While this accusation was more than enough to raise the hackles of the Church party, tories would have been rendered positively apoplectic by the musings of the whig astrologer, John Partridge. In his almanac for 1692, Partridge began with a chronology of events from 1625 to 1648. This helpfully reminded readers that it was fifty-one years since 'Shipmoney-Judges questioned; they were that kings dispensing Judges'; that forty-eight years had passed since 'Bishop Laud Beheaded for bringing in popery, and Treason against the Nation'; and, most startlingly of all, that the same length of time had elapsed since 'The Battle of Naseby, fatal to the then Tories and Pap[ists]'.[29]

Few whigs had either the inclination or the nerve to stigmatize the royalist cause of the 1640s by associating it with the latter-day tory party. But the notion that toryism went hand in hand with popery was a mainstay of whig rhetoric. The tories, wrote a whig pamphleteer in 1693, owed their rise 'to the horrid and execrable Designs of the two late Kings to set up Arbitrary Power and Popery amongst us'.[30] And to those abhorrent designs, the tory party was still devoted. For one thing, the tory creed, with its stress on the exclusive privileges of the Church of England, helped popery by sowing divisions among Protestants. The passage of the Toleration Act, it was true, seemed to preclude a renewal of the persecuting toryism of the early 1680s. Yet even after 1689 the tories persisted with their divisive religious policies, notably by opposing the abolition of the sacramental qualification for office. 'I am sure of this,' wrote an opponent of the test, 'that he that is at this day for weakning the Protestant Interest, is more than half a papist by his Acting, whatever his external profession may be; and I know nothing can weaken it more than keeping up this Sacramentary Test.'[31] Nor did the tories' hostility to the comprehension plans of 1689 – proposals to bring moderate dissenters back to the Church by broadening the terms of its communion – evince a deep yearning for Protestant union on their part. As one jaundiced versifier put it, 'Tories had rather see Protestants burn, / Than that their old Liturgy should not serve the turn.'[32]

In addition to pursuing religious policies injurious to the anti-popish cause, the tories were also deeply suspect on the crucial issue of the Protestant succession. It was, after all, the tories of the early 1680s who had made possible the popish tyranny of James II by crying 'up a Popish Successor as the only means to preserve the Church of England'.[33] Nor had the unhappy experience of King James's reign disabused the tory party of its pernicious notions. In the Convention, tory support for the succession of William and Mary had been deeply equivocal, and for the most part High Churchmen acknowledged them only as monarchs *de facto*, not *de jure*.[34] Small wonder, then, that the whig protagonist in *A Dialogue betwixt Whig and Tory* should tell his tory counterpart that 'your Education in Toryism, your Obligations to King James, and, which is more than both, your present Hopes from him, will make you so averse to this Government, that no Favour, no Courtship can engage you heartily in its Interests; and it is Nonsense to expect you should fight for a Title you have always declar'd to disapprove of.'[35] As another whig declared, 'who ever will not own King William to be King of Right, what do they, but playnely call him Usurper, An Usurper being nothing but a king in Possession without Right, And how ready they will bee to joyn with the King of France, Who call Him soe, or any body else, to out him is easy to judg.'[36] Here then was the kernel of the rival party traditions. While tories smelt in whiggery the whiff of Civil War 'fanaticism', the whigs were convinced that tory principles aided and abetted England's popish enemies.

The whig tendency to couple toryism with popery naturally infuriated the self-proclaimed Church party. 'I have heard formerly very much concerning Church-Papists,' complained a tory parliamentarian in 1694, 'but to this day wee have not discovered any great number of them.' Indeed, he was 'sure many of those who were soe nick-named have since appeared the boldest asserters of the Protestant religion, & the sincerest supporters of the Church of England, but, tho we have not found out many of these Church-papists, we know the Church-Fanaticks are a numerous brood.'[37] When tory gentlemen were greeted by 'the phanatic Rabble' with cries of 'Church-papist' at the Suffolk election of 1690, one Church party eye-witness was moved to an indignant response: 'would not any man be struck with wonder & amazement!' he asked,

> that these people who were so ready to comply with King James, calling him a most gracious prince, & caressing him with their fulsom & even blasphemous addresses [in thanks for the Declaration of Indulgence], encouraging him in his methods for destroying the Church, & approving his dispensing power by accepting places without qualifying themselvs according to law, whilest our pious & reverend Bishops were imprison'd & divers others cast out of their preferments for stoutly opposing of popery, that these men should have the impudence already to call us papists, who dare never open their mouths against popery all his Reign. [38]

It was a most powerful rejoinder. In 1686–8 the Church of England had indeed borne the brunt of the opposition to James II's policies. The dissenters, in contrast, had either kept their mouths shut or actively supported the King after he had granted them toleration and civil equality.[39] This the tories could neither forget nor forgive. 'Those who stood to the Protestant Religion were the Bishops', Charles Godolphin reminded the Commons in March 1689, 'those who were against it were those who managed Brent's regulation of Corporations' – a reference to Robert Brent, the Catholic lawyer who had co-ordinated King James's remodelling of parliamentary corporations.[40] In April 1690 Sir Edmund Jennings, another Church party MP, remembered that 'the Gazettes were stuffed with Addresses to King James, to stand by him in the Dispensing Power with Lives and Fortunes: Quakers, Anabaptists, Presbyterians, and other Sects; they either stood by King James, or assisted him.'[41]

At the moment of crisis in 1688, King James's attempt to woo the dissenters had availed him naught. True, a handful of his whiggish supporters – notably the Quaker leader William Penn and his friend Charlwood Lawton – remained devoted to King James's cause throughout the 1690s.[42] But the loyalty of most of the King's whigs ran considerably less deep, and evaporated entirely in the wake of the successful Dutch invasion. During the succession crisis of 1688–9, whigs of all shades of opinion had rallied to the cause of the Prince of Orange. Indeed, as Robert Beddard has shown, whig politicians played a crucial role in securing the crown for the Dutch prince.[43] Not surprisingly, they now expected to be handsomely rewarded by *their* new King.

2. Whiggery Discountenanced, 1689–91

By March 1689 the whigs seemed on the brink of entering the promised land of political preferment and influence. Not without reason, King William distrusted his new subjects, and throughout his reign the Dutch King was to show himself disinclined to repose his full confidence in English politicans. But in the earliest days of his reign, King William appeared to be in cahoots with one body of English politicians. Much to the disgust of the Church party, these were hot whigs – characters such as William Harbord, John Wildman, Richard Hampden and Lords Delamere and Mordaunt. As a tory letter-writer observed in mid-March, 'tis but to vissible he espouses their Interest'.[44] Nor did the King's initial ministerial appointments do much to smooth ruffled tory feathers. A disproportionate share of office, both greater and lesser, was conferred upon the whigs. The plum appointment of principal Secretary of State went to the Earl of Shrewsbury, the brightest young star in the whig firmament. Delamere, Hampden and Mordaunt were all appointed to the Treasury Commission, while Wildman took office as Postmaster-General. Along with many other whigs, William Harbord was given a niche on the Privy Council.[45] These appointments confronted tories with their worst nightmare: the prospect of a 'roundhead' administration. Thus on 12 April John Evelyn, a life-long constitutional royalist, ruefully noted that the new Privy Council had 'a Republican Spirit, & manifestly undermining all future Succession of the Crown, and prosperity of the Church of England: which yet, I hope, they will not be able to accomplish so soone as they hope: though they get into all places of Trust and profit'.[46] In fact, the apparently irresistible advance of whiggery was about to come to a grinding halt.

While the whigs looked upon King William as *their* King, the new monarch himself had no desire to be King of the whigs. He realized that the whig party had been instrumental in securing his ascent to the throne. But he also suspected that the whigs hoped to diminish his prerogative, an aspiration which he found utterly abhorrent. As for the tories, King William remained unconvinced of their loyalty to the new regime. At the same time, he had no wish to exclude the tory leaders from office, fearing that proscription would only serve to drive the Church party into King James's camp. Nor could he afford to alienate the tories when a war with France was imminent. Naturally, national unity would be at a premium in time of war. But the undeniable administrative experience of the old tory ministers would be no less of an asset in the struggle against Louis XIV.[47] Such was the thinking behind King William's decision to confer high office upon four politicans detested by whig partisans.

The second Secretaryship of State was given to the tory lawyer, Daniel Finch, Earl of Nottingham. A faithful servant of Charles II in the early 1680s, Nottingham had been the first of the old King's ministers to break with his brother. For he was, above all, a devoted Churchman who saw King James's policies as a direct attack upon his beloved Church. Yet, like so many other tories, he found it difficult to accept the constitutional propriety of King James's deposition, and in the Convention he spoke vehemently against the proposition that the throne was vacant. Once that battle was lost, however, Nottingham came to terms with the new regime. He could not, in all conscience, accept that William and Mary were the rightful and lawful monarchs. But he was prepared to swear allegiance to them as *de facto* King and Queen.[48] A leader deeply respected by rank and file tories, Nottingham's subsequent appointment to the secretaryship helped to persuade the Church party that King William would be no whig stooge. As Bishop Burnet wrote in 1691, 'Nottinghams being in the Ministry was lookt upon by them as no small part of their security: They knew that he would lay before the King the Right and Prerogatives of the Crown, and that he would represent to him, that the Church party were those he must trust, who would prove him his surest and firmest freinds.'[49]

Unlike Nottingham, George Savile, Marquis of Halifax, the new Lord Privy Seal, had precipitately thrown in his lot with the Prince of Orange when King James fled the country in December 1688. Yet while his apparent opportunism had disgusted tory loyalists, whigs could forgive neither the part he had played in the defeat of the second Exclusion Bill in 1680, nor his prominent role in the subsequent 'tory reaction'.[50] Although the trimming Marquis had emerged from the revolution crisis as King William's closest English confidant, 'no body thought that his Mercuriall witt would suite the kings phlegm long, So the Whiggs were inflamed to a mighty violence against him.'[51]

Equally obnoxious in whig eyes was the appointment of Sidney, Lord Godolphin, to the Treasury commission. An administrator of real ability, Godolphin had held high office without interruption since 1679, and had been loyal to King James to the bitter end. Indeed, in December 1688 the King had chosen Godolphin, along with Nottingham and Halifax, to negotiate on his behalf with the advancing Prince of Orange. This was more than enough to damn Godolphin in whig eyes, and he made the most incongruous of colleagues for the rabidly whiggish Treasury commissioners, Delamere and Mordaunt.[52]

In stark contrast to Godolphin, Thomas Osborne, Lord President of the Council and newly-created Marquis of Carmarthen, had been at the very heart of the Orangist conspiracy against King James. To whigs, however, Carmarthen was forever tainted by his association with the 'popish and arbitrary' policies pursued by Charles II in the mid–1670s when, as Earl of Danby, he had been that King's chief minister.[53] Not surprisingly, therefore, whig partisans viewed with dismay Carmarthen's prominence in King William's counsels. As a satirist glumly noted a little later,

> David, we thought, succeeded Saul,
> When William rose on James's fall;
> But now King Thomas governs at Whitehall.[54]

The favour shown by King William to the 'guilty men' of the two previous reigns had a disastrous effect on his relations with the whig party. Writing in 1691, Burnet remembered how Nottingham's appointment, in particular, had been 'very unacceptable to all that party that had shewed the greatest zeal for the King, and it gave a present and Sensible Change to the state of affaires, for the Whiggs grew sullen and became jealous upon it that the King would fall in with the Church party, and grow fond of prerogative Notions.'[55] This sense of alienation grew apace in the second half of 1689. In November the presbyterian diarist Roger Morrice was told by a disgusted whig MP that 'the Decicion seemed to be over, and that by not comeing over to his Friends it was plain he [the King] was gone over to his enemies, and from his own true Interest, and that the Regents or Hierarchy will have as great Dominion and Tyranny as ever over us.'[56] 'Look in to your Books,' John Hampden implored the Commons in December, 'and you will find those now employed, voted "Enemies to the King and Kingdom, and favourers of Popery".' Pouring his invective directly upon Halifax, Nottingham and Godolphin, the fiery whig expressed his outrage that 'these three men who came to Hungerford from King James, should be the greatest men in England'. 'If we must be ruined again', Hampden indignantly concluded, 'let it be by new men.'[57]

By Christmas 1689 the frustrations of the violently whiggish Comptroller of the Household, Thomas Wharton, boiled over into an outrageous letter to the King. It 'was thought a fatality upon your Majesty', wrote Wharton, 'that you should pick out the most obnoxious men of all England for your Ministers, when the Declaration you publish'd at your coming over was principally against Evil Ministers, & that you made Male-Administration the chief ground to Justify your taking Arms'. 'This', he continued,

> has been of unspeakable prejudice to you for it is visible to all men & the meanest People reason upon it, That we must expect the same Councills & the same Government from the same Men. If you did not come over to support our Religion & repair the breaches that were made in our Laws and Constitution, what can you urge but Force to justify what you have done, which would destroy the Glory of your Enterprise? We have made you King, as the greatest return we could make for so great a Blessing, taking this to be your Design; and if you intend to govern like an Honest Man, what occasion can you have for knaves to serve you? Can the same Men who contrived

and wrought our Ruin be fitt Instruments for our Salvation? Or with what Honour can you employ those against whom you Drew your sword?

While the evil counsellors of the late reigns were flourishing under King William, those who had risked all for him were coming to 'repent their too forward Zeal for a Man who despises his best & only true Friends, & mistakes the right way to advance both his own, & his people's Interest & Glory'.[58] Wharton's outburst reached its climax in a suitably insolent peroration:

> Your coldness and slowness in business hath made your Enemies think you are afraid of them, & your trimming between Parties is beneath both you & your cause; had you made use of those Men alone who always appeared true to the Interest of England, your Enemies would not have had the confidence to have opposed you in any thing; your business would have gone on smooth and undisturbed, and your Reign would have been glorious; but employing a medley of men, who can never act heartily together, your Friends could not serve you, and your Enemies were encouraged to intreagues against you.[59]

The King's 'trimming between Parties' was not the only aspect of royal policy which angered whig stalwarts. The whig party had confidently expected that the new regime would bring to justice all those implicated in the 'crimes' of the 'tory reaction'. Above all, whigs thirsted for vengeance against the 'murderers' of Russell and Sidney. Thus in March 1689 Sir Robert Howard, a strong whig, urged the Commons to 'free ourselves from the guilt of that blood spilt, to all Posterity, and not leave ill Ministers, by these Examples, to do the same again. 'Tis impossible we should live, and not have blood upon us, if we pass this by unpunished.'[60] 'Blood no mortal man can forgive', insisted John Hampden three months later.[61] It is clear, in fact, that the whigs hoped for at least some degree of restitution by blood. 'That which lies heaviest upon the Nation, is Blood,' the veteran puritan John Birch warned the House in May. 'I would have some Blood, though little, rather than be stained with what they have shed.'[62] Once again, however, whig aspirations were unfulfilled. In February the Commons established a Committee of Grievances to investigate the misdemeanours of the 'tory reaction', but it made little progress in bringing to justice either the greater or lesser 'criminals' of the early 1680s. Small wonder, then, that in June a group of whiggish Londoners complained to the Commons that they

> have not found their Grievances redressed, nor any of those persons brought to justice who were the instruments of introducing that tyranicall Government under which we groan[ed], but on the contrary your Petitioners observe that many of those persons who were the authors and advisers of our late miseries, some of which stand now Impeached in Parliament, boldly concerne themselves in the management of publick affaires, which makes

your petitioners to have just cause to apprehend that if these Grievances be not speedily redressed they shall fall into the same calamity.[63]

Whig opinion was particularly inflamed by the King's attitude to the question of indemnity. Determined to foster national unity in time of war, King William could see no point in raking over the alleged misdeeds of the tory party. Hence in March he urged parliament to pass a general indemnity bill, excepting only a few named individuals from the pardon.[64] Tories were naturally delighted by the King's resolve to cast a veil over the 'tory reaction'. To whigs, however, such a policy seemed a flat contradiction of the Prince of Orange's pre-invasion *Declaration* which had denounced King James's evil counsellors. 'There is scarce one word against King James in your Declarations', Tom Wharton justly reminded the King. 'The Evil Ministers are complain'd of, yet King James alone is punish'd, and the same Evil Ministers or worse are employ'd, when you might have found Honest Men to have served you in places.'[65] The whigs were being driven to distraction. They wanted to make the tories eat dirt – for the good of the nation, of course. But their deluded King would not let them.

Although whig parliamentarians were able to block the passage of the Indemnity Bill in the sessions of 1689–90, this could not compensate for the King's refusal to chastise tory 'criminals'.[66] Whiggery's thirst for blood was unslaked. 'The Government', claimed Roger Morrice in November 1689, 'cannot be served if one or two malefactors amongst us in England be not put to death, for a terrifying Example, for we can never answer it to the Justice of the Nation, nor to the World if we should finde no faults in any but King James.'[67] The blood of the whig martyrs, wrote a polemicist some months later, 'crieth against the Nation, for their neglect of avenging of it; for until this be done, God's wrath, which is kindled against us, will not be turned away, nor his Anger cease, nor his Judgments be diverted, but will be poured out more and more upon us, so long as these cursed Acan's remain in the Camp of our Israel'.[68] But by the time this jeremiad was penned, during the election campaign of March 1690, the whigs had been given still further cause for gnashing of teeth.

As the months passed, King William became steadily more exasperated with the antics of the parliamentary whigs. Not only were whig MPs blocking the King's policy of indemnity, they were also incessantly sniping at his tory ministers. Indeed, by December 1689 King William's whig ministers were badgering him to dispense with the services of their tory 'colleagues'.[69] Rather than promoting a united national war effort, the whigs, it seemed to the King, were more intent upon fighting their own party corner. In January 1690 King William's patience finally snapped. On the 10th he helped thwart a whig move to proscribe all those who had supported the forfeiture of corporation charters in the last four years of Charles II's reign. King Charles's systematic attack on the charters – the so-called *quo warranto* campaign – had been designed to break whig power in the corporations following the defeat of exclusion. For that very reason, it had won the enthusiastic backing of countless tories. Thus the abortive disabling legislation, sponsored by the whig MP William Sacheverell, would have driven a large segment of the Church party from public life. Sweet revenge, no doubt, for the 'tory reaction', but hardly conducive to national unity.[70]

Worse still, the whigs appeared determined to scupper the King's planned Irish expedition. When King William first made plain his intention to take personal command in Ireland, whigs were both perplexed and alarmed. 'It is thought a most unaccountable resolution,' wrote Roger Morrice in early January, 'and many fear it was suggested and cherished by his enemies.'[71] Convinced that the King's absence in Ireland would imperil the security of the regime in England, and that the planned expedition must therefore have been cooked up by tory 'evil counsellors', whig peers prepared a motion urging the King to abandon the foolhardy scheme. It was the final straw. Taking a leaf out of the book of his uncle, Charles II, King William prorogued parliament without warning on the morning of 27 January. Ten days later he dissolved the legislature, and called elections for a new parliament to meet on 20 March.[72]

The King's actions left the whig party dumbfounded. Although the Convention parliament had not lived up to whig expectations, especially on religious issues, it was still revered as the body which had effected the revolution. As was his wont, Roger Morrice smelt a tory rat. 'We are not sure what might be the speciall motives to this resolution,' he wrote upon the dissolution, 'but in generall the Toryes advised it in hope that they should have a parliament altogether for their turne, wherein they should be able to carrey what Votes and consequently what Lawes they pleased.'[73] In reality, the dissolution had rather more to do with King William's desire to clip the wings of whig extremists. This, he hoped, would have a moderating effect upon whiggery as a whole. So the King soon made it known that he looked for the return of 'moderate men of the Church party' to the new parliament.[74]

Apart from his well-publicised endorsement of moderate toryism, the King remained aloof from the election campaign. Much to the chagrin of the tory leaders, King William refused to deploy Crown resources on behalf of Church party candidates, and instead the election was allowed to run its natural course. It proved to be a hotly-disputed affair with contests in a record 106 constituencies.[75] As usual, the election results were determined by the complex interplay of magnate, gentry and corporate influence, not to mention numerous local issues.[76] To add to the complexity of the electoral mosaic, voters were also confronted with competing ideological appeals for their allegiance.

A novel feature of the general election of 1690, and one which helped to solidify party identities, was the blacklisting of opponents by the rival parties. Whig propagandists produced a list of the 151 tories who had refused to vote the throne 'vacant' in the Convention. This was to help the electorate choose 'none but such who are entirely in his Majesties and the Kingdoms Interest, which, as it is impossible to believe of them, who acknowledge him only a King in Fact, but not by Right, so it is not easie to conceive how they should be forward and zealous to support him in the Throne, who opposed his coming to it'.[77]

The tories responded by listing the 146 'commonwealthsmen' who had voted in favour of the disabling 'Sacheverell clause'. Reminding voters that the King had 'lately by Actions, as well as Promises, declar'd himself for the Interest of the Church of England', the author of the anti-whig black-list asked how any could be 'true to the Interest of that Church, who endeavour'd in the last Session to incapacitate some of the best members of it; and who were so far from granting that Amnesty which the King desir'd and propos'd, that they carried their Fury back to more than one preceeding Reign, and set aside all Acts of Indemnity, but that, which most of them need, in the Year 1660?'[78] Another Church party polemicist urged the voters of Cambridgeshire not to choose men of 'that restless Spirit of Malice, and Sedition, which will be satisfied with nothing less, than the ruin of the Government in Church and State'.[79]

The terms of the struggle could not have been clearer. While whigs insisted that a tory vote was a Jacobite vote, the tories retorted that a vote for whiggery was a vote for 'fanaticism'. Small wonder, then, that while Cambridgeshire dissenters were reportedly disseminating electoral propaganda on behalf of the local whigs, the episcopal clergy up and down the country were busily exerting their influence in favour of the Church party. In London, for example, the young whig Edward Harley bitterly complained that 'the parsons bestow more pains for votes than ever they did for soles.'[80] Going onto the counter-attack, an anonymous whig writer reminded voters of the crimes of the early 1680s, and branded their perpe-trators 'cursed Amalekites that hinder us from going to Canaan!' The polemicist continued his apocalyptic exhortation to the electorate:

> O cast out, cast out the Accursed thing from among us, for it is the setting up and preferring of these cursed Amalekites, that in all likely-hood did bring those unusual Storms which have cast away and destroyed so many of our Ships, both of War and Merchant-men, and drowned so many of our Seamen, and have and may yet do great damage on shore, may yet, without Reformation, bring the Plague. God may poyson the very Air we do breathe in, and send Fire, either from Heaven, or from Earth, and destroy us, or by Inundations of Water, or by Earth-quakes, or Famin, or Thunder and Lightning, or great Hail, or by the Sword, &c.[81]

Alas for the 'Camp of Israel', the election returns served only to strengthen the hands of the Amalekites. Although the results, like those of all the elections of the 1690s, are difficult to quantify precisely, contemporaries were convinced that the trend favoured the Church party.[82] The election returns certainly seemed worth celebrating to one tory balladeer. 'The true Church of England', he crowed,

> . . . may lift up her Head,
> Since in her own Bosom this Senate was bred;
> Whose worthy brave Members are taught to maintain
> The Rights of their Mother, 'gainst Schismaticks vain:
> No Commonwealth-broachers shall longer prevail,
> Away with the Rump and her Factious Tail.[83]

The biggest reverse for the 'Commonwealth-broachers' came in London where the votes of the City liverymen unseated the whig incumbents and swept four tories into the Palace of Westminster.[84]

After the election the political tide continued to run against the whig party. The London Lieutenancy Commission, hitherto a hotbed of unadulterated whiggery, was remodelled in favour of the tories. Ministerial changes, though not all that the leaders of the Church party desired, further tilted the political balance in favour of toryism.[85] All this proved too much for King William's favourite whig, Secretary of State Shrewsbury. At the end of April, much to the King's consternation, Shrewsbury returned his seals of office.[86]

As the resignation of the mild-mannered Shrewsbury indicates, whigs of all temperaments and opinions were dismayed by King William's swing to the Church party. But it had a particularly shattering effect on the devotees of that pure brand of whiggery notable for its strong identification with the Civil War parliamentary cause, a commitment to reining-in the royal prerogative, and an implacable animus towards 'prelacy'.[87] Of these, none was more disillusioned than John Hampden, grandson of the puritan hero of the same name, and self-conscious champion of true whig principles. By November 1690 it was painfully clear to Hampden that the fruits of the revolution were to be left unpicked. 'You say you do not understand the present Scheme', he wrote to his bewildered kinsman, old Sir Edward Harley. 'I don't know who does & that which is most melancholy & discouraging is that there seems to be no Scheme at all. The only maxime that I see followed is this, Secure the Church; No Bishop no King.'[88]

The final straw for Hampden came in March 1691 when his friend, the ex-Leveller leader John Wildman, was dismissed from his office of Postmaster.[89] With over forty years of radical politics emblazoned on his escutcheon, Wildman was the very embodiment of the true whig faith and its heroic traditions.[90] His dismissal confirmed what Hampden had long suspected: King William had turned his back on the revolution whigs. 'We thought being for the Bill of Exclusion, venturing our lives to bring this king in & setting him upon the throne, in despite of those who had murdered our friends & betrayed our Libertys, had been things of great merit', a dispirited Hampden wrote to Harley on their friend's dismissal, 'but we were deceived, for they were the greatest of crimes & certain marks of Republicans.'[91]

This turn of events may not, in fact, have come as a complete shock to Hampden. In the early 1680s he had been an intimate of Algernon Sidney, and that most unyielding of commonwealthsmen had repeatedly warned of the despotic ambitions of the House of Orange. In his unpublished *Court Maxims*, for example, Sidney had explained how in the Netherlands, as well as in England, the ruling house wove a web of deceit in order to win unlimited power.[92]

In the early 1690s a Sidneyesque voice of republican scepticism is heard once again, notably in *The State of Parties*, a remarkable pamphlet published in 1692. According to its anonymous author, King William was playing a nefarious game with the whigs and tories. 'Neither of these two Parties', he explained,

> towards the Satisfaction they desire, go now about the making of any new laws, or attempt any Alteration in the present Settlement: But their labour is, the gaining of the King, and the gettting those of their Fraternity (whatever otherwise they be) into the Government. This is the only Means by which they, at this time, think to serve their Interest. This is the only Pledg they now ask for the Success of their respective Parties: Each promising to themselves that within a little time, or whenever his Majesty has made an end of his Enemies, He will declare for them, and for the future employ only the Men of their Stamp.

However, the parties were deluding themselves. If King William won the war, there were two possibilities: 'either he will be immediately absolute, and have it in his Power to act as he fancies, or he will be as he now is, under the Restraint of Laws, and Parliaments to be struggl'd with.' If the latter prognosis proved to be more accurate, then what more could satisfy the Crown 'than the present Construction of Whig and Tory in Parliament? Is there any thing that the Court cannot carry? Whereas, if one Party were declar'd for, it would not be so. As to the Whigs,' he continued,

> the thing is the same. This Balance that the Court has got is too useful, and shall never be departed from (so as that the Whigs shall be a jot more advanc'd) whilst the Court must use a Parliament: and if that time once come to be over, tho it is not to be thought that the Court will ever act for the zealous Church-men according to their Expectations . . . yet on the other side, to think that then any thing will be done more for the Whigs, for the Advancement of their Persons, or in favour of their Principles, is what the least of all can be imagin'd, and is the most absurd.[93]

While there is something to be said for this analysis, it is not wholly persuasive. For one thing, as we shall see later, the King's attempt to play off one party against the other eventually caused him more problems than it solved. Nor had the parliamentary whigs entirely abandoned their commitment to reform. Indeed, whigs of all shapes and sizes – Court placemen, backbench MPs and independent peers – gave at least some degree of support to the bill for triennial elections which passed both Houses in February 1693.[94] When King William vetoed the Triennial Bill as an intolerable encroachment upon his prerogative, whig disenchantment with the King reached its apex. 'I must confess to you', says a character in a whiggish dialogue,

> nothing prevail'd with me to concur with our King in his Pretensions to restore our Parliaments, and the Laws to their due Authority, than my own knowledg, that the late Civil Wars in this Kingdom, and the Subversion of our Religion, Laws and Liberties, were principally occasion'd by the Powers usurp'd in several late Reigns, to refuse the calling of successive Parliaments, and to continue the same Parliament for many Years, to form them into a compliance with their Designs of Despotick Power.

But in the wake of King William's veto of the Triennial Bill, it was readily apparent that 'we are no more secur'd against the Slavery we fear'd by subverting our Constitution, than we were before the Convention of the People for a Settlement, when King James had just abdicated the kingdom.'[95] As another whig commentator put it, the revolution had apparently effected 'a Change, without an Alteration'.[96] The same writer sternly warned King William not to walk in the footsteps of his Stuart predecessors. Their vices, he claimed, 'will appear with a worse grace in You, who have declar'd and made war against these [arbitrary] Practices, than in your Predecessors: For as St Paul says, Thou who hast said, Ye shall not commit Adultery, dost thou commit Adultery? Thou who hast said, Ye shall not steal, dost thou steal?'[97]

The most stinging rebuke of all came from one of the King's former ministers, the violently whiggish Henry Booth, Earl of Warrington. 'To be deliver'd out of the Hands of an oppressing King is a great Mercy', he mused to the Chester Grand Jury in April 1693, 'yet when such a Prince is put into the Hands of any People, it is seldom improv'd as that Mercy ought to be; for Tacitus makes this Observation upon the Fall of Nero, that the first day after the Reign of a Tyrant is always the best. This', the Earl pointedly added, 'is a great Truth, and a Rule that yet hath no exception.' Warrington continued with a loaded gloss upon the Roman historian's dictum. One explanation for Tacitus's observation, he surmised,

> may be this, Because he that is the chief Instrument of their Deliverance, altho he appear'd very zealous on their behalf, yet he aim'd at nothing but getting the Crown; as it was when the Dauphin of France came over to assist

the Barons against King John: His Declaration was full of nothing else but the English Liberties, and yet it afterwards appear'd, that his Design in assisting them was only to get into the Throne, and not ease that Nation's Oppressions. So that in such Cases a Revolution does the People no good; for he that hath got the Crown, thinks that whatsoever is done for the Good and Security of the People, is so much Loss to him of what he hop'd to get by coming over.[98]

All this from the man who, as Lord Delamere, had been one of the first Englishmen to take up arms for the Prince of Orange in November 1688.[99]

In January 1689, during the debates on the settlement of the crown, Delamere had told the Lords that 'it was long since he thought himself absolved from his allegiance to King James; that he owed him none, and never would pay him any; and if King James came again, he was resolved to fight against him, and would die single, with his sword in his hand, rather than pay him any obedience.'[100] Despite Delamere's subsequent alienation from the Williamite regime, there is no reason to believe that this champion of the 'Old Cause' ever came to revise his attitude towards King James. The same, however, could not be said of all the revolutionaries. For one consequence of King William's discountenancing of whiggery was the emergence of that paradoxical phenomenon, revolutionary Jacobitism. Earliest and most startling convert to the Jacobite cause was the Scot, Robert Ferguson. A leading player in both the Rye House Plot against King Charles in 1683 and Monmouth's rebellion against King James in 1685, Ferguson was one of the few to emerge unscathed from those shambolic episodes. In 1688, having been an exile in Holland since Monmouth's defeat, the Scotsman at last backed a winning horse. But barely a year after accompanying the Prince of Orange on his triumphant expedition, Ferguson's addiction to plotting had swept him into the arms of King James. Implicated in a conspiracy organised by Sir James Montgomery, another disaffected Scottish whig, Ferguson went on to become perhaps the most scabrous of all the Jacobite propagandists.[101]

The rapid conversions to Jacobitism of Ferguson and Montgomery owed not a little to personal pique: the two Scots felt they had been ill-rewarded for their parts in the revolution.[102] But the murky Jacobite dabblings of the Earl of Shrewsbury and Admiral Edward Russell, both of whom had received favour from King William, betokened a deep disgust at the King's rapprochement with the 'Jacobite' tory party, and a conviction that such a misguided policy made King James's restoration a more than likely prospect. Two yet more violent whigs, the Earl of Monmouth (formerly Lord Mordaunt) and his crony John Wildman, similarly began intrigues with St Germain once it became clear that King William would not countenance the extermination of toryism.[103]

Unlike his old friend Wildman, John Hampden did not tread the crooked path which led from revolution whiggery to Jacobitism. Instead, having lost his seat at the 1690 general election, he sank deeper and deeper into the mire of despair. Towards the end of 1696, a vacancy in a Buckinghamshire county seat temporarily revived his hopes of a return to the fray at Westminster. But the local whig establishment wanted nothing to do with the spent firebrand which Hampden had become. Already tormented by the memory of lost opportunities and unfulfilled promise, this latest rebuff was too much for Hampden to bear. In December he put a blade to his own throat.[104] So perished the man who had once been the torch-bearer of the pure whig faith.

3.   Court and Parliament, 1691–93

King William's swing to the tories after the general election of 1690 did not signal a complete break with the whigs. While many devotees of whiggery found the King's actions unforgivable, some 85 whig MPs could still be classified as Court supporters in April 1691.[105] Prominent among these were the Chancellor of the Exchequer, Richard Hampden (John's father), and the Solicitor-General, John Somers, both of whom were personally devoted to King William. But the Court whig group also included the Comptroller of the Household, Thomas Wharton, who most emphatically was not. As we have seen, 'Honest Tom' shared many of the prejudices of the hottest anti-Court whigs. He was, however, distinguished from them by a readiness to accept – albeit grudgingly – that politics are the art of the possible. Purity of the faith was all very well. But it was coming to be seen by Wharton and other whig placemen as an indulgence incompatible with their aspirations for personal advancement, not to mention detrimental to the best interests of whiggery in general. It is this note of pragmatism which is the key to understanding the emergence of 'Court' whiggery. Like their 'Country' brethren, Court whigs were appalled by the favour King William had shown the tories. However, they sought to convince him of the error of his ways not by obstructing his business but by doing all in their power to promote it. Thus the Court whigs would show King William that whiggery produced more efficient and reliable royal servants than toryism.

The pragmatic strategy of the Court whigs inevitably led to some fudging of traditional whig policies. In November 1692 parliament was considering a bill to reform the procedure in treason trials in favour of the accused. Designed to prevent a repetition of the rough justice meted out to Russell and Sidney in 1683, the Treason Trials Bill had obvious appeal to whig parliamentarians. Not so to King William. He had no wish to make it easier for accused Jacobites to escape the rigour of the law. This placed the Court whigs in an invidious position. If they opposed the bill, they might be accused of apostacy by outraged backbenchers. If they supported it, they would find themselves in King William's bad books. They decided to stick by the King. When the measure was debated in the Commons on 18 November, it was opposed by Court whigs such as Sir John Somers, now Attorney-General, and Sir Thomas Littleton. Although they were able to marshal some sound whiggish reasons for opposing the bill (above all, that a reform of the treason law would make it harder to convict Jacobite conspirators), the apparent volte face of the Court whigs drew a caustic response from the young whig MP, Robert Harley:

> I cannot but take notice though some gentlemen are now against this bill, yet they complained much of the misconstruction that was made in the last reign in cases of trials in treason. It is what you took notice of when you presented the crown to Their Majesties and made it one of the heads of grievances against the late King. But now some of those gentlemen that were so zealous then are against it now and say it is not timely.[106]

The Court whigs, it seemed, were too ready to sacrifice their principles on the altar of political expediency.

As well as seeking to curry favour with the King through loyal and efficient service, the Court whigs were also determined to discredit their tory ministerial 'colleagues'. For much of the early 1690s, in fact, the so-called 'Court party' was at war with itself. When it suited their purposes, whig courtiers would happily support parliamentary attacks on government maladministration. Of these, there were many. For the spiralling costs of the war, not to mention the general lack of success with which it was being prosecuted, led to growing disgruntlement with the administration's performance among backbenchers of all persuasions. This inchoate sense of discontent was given form and direction by the House of Commons Commission of Accounts. Established early in 1691, the Commission was initially riven by partisan feuding. But under the leadership of Sir Thomas Clarges, a distinguished tory MP, the Commission's members soon sunk their ideological differences in a united attack upon all aspects of government mismanagement.[107]

While the Commission's activities were genuinely impartial, its attacks upon maladministration could easily be twisted to partisan ends. A good example is provided by an incident in November 1691. During a debate on the management of the war at sea, Clarges and his whig colleague Paul Foley proposed a scheme for parliamentary supervision of naval officers. The whig placemen, however, turned the debate into an attack upon the conduct of the principal tory ministers, Nottingham and Carmarthen.[108] It was episodes such as this which doubtless lay behind the wry comment of one observer in December 1691: 'whig & Tory endeavoured to unite or mix at the beginning of the session, yet so soon as the mouse appeared, the lady turn'd cat again, I mean both partyes flew for their interests, & hopes of prey.'[109]

In November 1692 a debate on the mismanagement of a 'descent' on

France provided the whigs with another stick with which to beat the tory courtiers. 'At first all matters went on very successfully,' insisted Sir Walter Yonge, 'but since some men have come into employ all things have gone backwards, matters have been very dilatory, and your intelligence has done little service. Therefore I am for an address that the King will be pleased to employ only such men as are for his interest against that of the late King and such as think this government to be *de jure* as well as *de facto.*'[110] In similar vein, Tom Wharton observed that

> Your chief men that manage matters are such as submit to this King upon wrong principles – because he has the governing power – but will be ready to join another when he prevails. They are such as came not into your government till it was late, and I think it no policy to take men into a government because they were violent against it. I will not at present name these persons, but I would address to His Majesty against them in general (for he knows them best) and that he would be pleased to receive such men only under him who are of known integrity and will come up both to the principles and His Majesty's right to this government.[111]

Although they had not named him during the debate on the 'descent', everyone knew that the whigs were gunning particularly for the Earl of Nottingham. Not only was the Secretary of State deeply implicated in the miscarriage of the 'descent', he was also perhaps the most influential advocate of the *de facto* theory of allegiance.[112] And in early December Nottingham's whig ministerial 'colleagues' resumed their anti-tory offensive by attempting to outlaw the Secretary of State's *de facto* beliefs. A bill introduced by Sir John Somers provided for the imposition of severe penalties on all who asserted or implied that the King and Queen were merely *de facto* monarchs. What was more, all office-holders would be required to swear a new oath against King James. It was a blatant bid to force Nottingham and like-minded tories from office. So it was fortunate for the Church party that the bill failed in the Commons.[113] Nevertheless, the embers of the controversy were still burning on 20 December when Comptroller Wharton told the Commons that it was 'not fit for the safety of this government that all things should depend on one man who is not of an opinion for the title of the King and Queen'. 'For my part', concluded 'Honest Tom', 'I cannot act, nor I think any honest man, as long as he is at the helm, and therefore I move you for an address to his Majesty to remove this Lord from his presence and councils.' The Comptroller of the Household's open attack on Secretary Nottingham provoked a forthright response from the tory placeman, Peregrine Bertie: 'Since it is plain there are men in employ in direct opposition to one another, I am for advising His Majesty to consult only with men of one principle and interest.'[114] Over the next eighteen months King William did indeed shift his administration decisively towards 'men of one principle and interest'. But it was not in the direction that Bertie wanted.

4. Whiggery at the Helm, 1693–97

At the beginning of 1693 parliament was on the brink of full-scale mutiny against the Court. In January a bill to bar all placemen from the Commons was defeated by only two votes in the Lords.[115] Worse was to follow. Legislation providing for annual parliamentary sessions and triennial elections passed both Houses after winning the support of many whig placemen, and was thwarted in March only by use of the Royal veto.[116] King William's administration seemed more beleaguered with every passing day.

The root cause of the administration's troubles was readily apparent to the tory Licenser of the Press, Edmund Bohun. 'The whig party, tory, and Jacobite', he confided to his diary on 12 February, 'all joyned against the king, as one man, to force him to take a party; so that no man, but his servants, stuck to him.'[117] In fact, as the voting on the Place and Triennial Bills revealed, even the King's servants were not entirely reliable. Nevertheless, the essence of Bohun's analysis holds good: by attempting to please all sides, King William had pleased none. Such had long been the conclusion of King William's latest confidant, the Earl of Sunderland.

Robert Spencer, second Earl of Sunderland, was the most reviled politician of the age.[118] He had first come to prominence by supporting exclusion in 1680. Yet five years later this arch-opportunist was serving King James as Secretary of State. Indeed, no man was more closely associated with the King's policies. Not only was he the principal architect of King James's rapprochement with the dissenters, he even embraced Catholicism in order to ingratiate himself with his master. Here, then, was the very epitome of an 'evil counsellor', and when 'Jack' fell down and broke his crown, 'Jill' came tumbling after. But an event which might have spelt permanent ruination for a less slippery customer proved a mere interlude in Sunderland's career. Exiled in Holland after the revolution, he was soon attempting to work his passage home. All through King James's reign, the Earl announced to an incredulous world, he had been a secret servant of the Protestant cause, working tirelessly to bring about the downfall of his popish master. If Sunderland's imaginative account of his role in the revolution raised eyebrows at King William's court, it caused fury at King James's. So it was that Sunderland eventually achieved the unique feat of being excluded both from King William's 1690 Act of Grace and King James's general pardon of 1692. Yet while King James could never bring himself to forgive his ex-minister's latest apostasy, King William bore no malice towards the oily Earl. As early as May 1690 Sunderland had wormed his way home, and before long his counsel was being sought by a King whose administration was rapidly disintegrating.

Sunderland's advice to the King, enunciated with increasing vehemence

from the Spring of 1692, was straightforward. He should stop shilly-shal-
lying with the parties – a policy which was merely serving to undermine
his government – and instead commit his favour to the talented new generation of whig leaders. This was not at all the sort of advice which King
William wanted to hear. He had not forgotten the insolent behaviour of
the whig party in the Convention parliament. Nor had the continuing
factiousness of the whig ministers done much to recommend them to the
King's favour. On the contrary, it served to convince him that the whigs
were little better than republicans. At the same time, he had come to see
the tories as the natural allies of the Crown. This view brought forth a
characteristically barbed rejoinder from Sunderland: 'it was very true that
the tories were better friends to monarchy than the whigs were, but then
his majesty was to consider that he was not their monarch.'[119]

Although the Court's parliamentary difficulties escalated markedly in
the course of the 1692–3 session, King William remained disinclined to
act upon Sunderland's counsel. In the Spring of 1693, it is true, the King
had demonstrated his growing confidence in Attorney-General Somers by
elevating him to the post of Lord Keeper. More startlingly, he had
conferred the vacant second Secretaryship of State upon Sir John
Trenchard, one-time ally of the Duke of Monmouth.[120] Yet far from propitiating the whigs, King William's gestures merely fuelled their demands for
a wholesale purge of tory office-holders. Once again the cry went up to
cast the ungodly tories out of the camp of Israel. 'Throw out, Sir, these
Achans to be ston'd by the People,' a whig polemicist implored the King,
'who will otherwise (I fear) prevent God's Favour to You; who blast Your
Success Abroad, and rob You of the Affections of Your Subjects at Home,
with their Accursed Thing, I mean that Tinsel Power with which these
Miscreants dazzle the Eyes of Princes, and lead them out of the right
way.'[121] As ever, the chief target of whig abuse was Secretary of State
Nottingham, a man

> whose Father [Charles II's Lord Chancellor, Heneage Finch, first Earl of
> Nottingham] and Family was rais'd by K[ing] C[harles] and K[ing] J[ames]
> for prostituting the Law (and his nauseous Rhetorick) to the Designs of those
> two Brothers, who himself was a Privy-Counsellor with Father Peters [James
> II's Jesuit confidant], and chosen by K[ing] J[ames] at the time of the
> Revolution to treat with your Majesty at Hungerford, in order to delay your
> Progress to London; and lastly, who so violently oppos'd your Majesty's
> being crown'd King, as to lay an eternal Obligation on K[ing] J[ames] by it.[122]

The renewed assault upon Nottingham was played out against a background of military and naval disaster which left the administration in still
more disarray. In July 1693 King William was defeated at Landen in
Flanders. That same month, a richly-laden merchant fleet fell into French
hands while en route to the Turkish port of Smyrna. 'Our want of

Intelligence of all the motions of our Enemys while they seeme to know every thing that we are doing, cast a great Reproach on our whole ministry,' noted Bishop Burnet after the loss of the Smyrna fleet, 'which is now so broke in pieces that there is no union nor conduct among them, and every one justifys himself and throws the blame upon others.'[123] 'God knows what will become of Us,' lamented a correspondent of Sir William Trumbull in October 1693, 'but it is certain Our affairs are in a very bad Condition, and people say here publickly that if the King dont change both his Ministers and his Measures, We are ruined beyond recovery.'[124] By early November, King William had come to a similar conclusion. On the 6th he asked for Nottingham's resignation as Secretary of State. The next day, Nottingham's whig bête noire, Admiral Edward Russell, was given command of the fleet.[125] With deep misgivings, King William had at last decided to throw in his lot with the whigs. As the King told an equally disconsolate Queen, he thought 'his case so bad that he was forced to part with Lord Nottingham, to please a party who he cannot trust.'[126]

In the months following Nottingham's dismissal, the whigs tightened their grip on the levers of power and influence. Having apparently won an assurance that the King would approve a new Triennial Bill, Shrewsbury resumed office as Secretary of State in March 1694.[127] During the Summer, the Customs and Excise commissions were refashioned in favour of the whigs.[128] The remodelling of the revenue commissions was not based solely on political considerations. Some of the commissioners, including one or two whigs, were removed on grounds of corruption or inefficiency. Nevertheless, most of the victims of the purge were tories, and nearly all the beneficiaries were whigs.[129]

The remodelling of the Excise commission was of particular political significance. As Sir John Somers informed the King in June,

> Those commissioners have yearly the disposition of 100,000 l. in salaries to inferior officers, and these officers they appoint without any control, and if this great sum be distributed to the worst men which can be picked out, and it be considered how great an influence these inferior officers have upon great numbers of your subjects, and how they are spread in every part of the kingdom, it will be plain that nothing can tend more to the poisoning of the people.[130]

In order to protect the country from that Jacobite poison, the new Excise commission – headed by whig stalwarts Edward Clarke and Foot Onslow – launched a vigorous purge of its minions. By January 1695 some 121 excise officers – almost ten percent of the Excise Office's personnel – had been removed from their posts.[131]

Nor were the Commissions of the Peace beyond the reach of the vindictive whigs. Although King William would not sanction a general purge of tory JPs, at least twenty-five county benches suffered some degree of partisan remodelling.[132] Little wonder that in September 1694 Edmund Bohun, himself a victim of an especially severe purge of the Suffolk bench, should complain that the 'loyal party' was 'every day more oppressed than before'.[133]

As is vividly illustrated by a collection of parliamentary speeches preserved in the British Library Stowe MSS, the advance of whiggery filled the Church party with dread.[134] 'The Church of England, the Orthodox Church of England is now plainly in danger', declared one irate High Churchman.[135] Another tory parliamentarian inveighed against the regulation of the Commissions of the Peace recently carried out by Lord Keeper Somers. 'Wee all know how he has already changed the Commissions, & wee must have satisfaction in that matter, or petition for his removall, or, lastly be contented to see the whole Orthodox Church-Party insulted by Whiggs & Fanaticks, & at long run, nay perhaps in a short time, our discipline & our Forms of Worship changed.'[136] A third speaker warned that tories were being removed from all offices of profit in the country. 'Wee could be, we were content that some Whiggs should have preferment but we see that Tories, true Church men, must be turned out of all.' Particularly ominous was the investigation by the JPs of disaffection among the Excise officers. 'Considering who made these Justices, & what sort of men they are, & who it was that set this whole matter on foot in the Excise Office, wee may easily imagin for what end this scrutiny is designed, & that few men will be left even in the inferior offices of that part of the Revenue who have any tolerable love for the true Orthodox Church of England.' Such a purge would have far-reaching political consequences. For 'the Excise Office influences Corporations, & as soon as it is well setled by the Generall Excise being given, may return a Whigg & Church-Fanatick parliament.'[137]

In fact, the Church party saw itself faced by a return of the nightmare of 1687–8: a King in cahoots with the 'fanaticks' at the behest of that knave, the Earl of Sunderland. 'It was falling in with this Fanatick Faction that begot the generall disgust [with King James]', an indignant tory MP recollected. 'The prince of Oranges's [sic] Declaration seemed levell'd against that measure, was all over Church of England, & evidently pointed at the man who misguided King James, & now misleads his majesty into an exorbitant favouring of those that Dissent from our Church. And can it be thought', the MP bluntly continued, 'that those that love the Church will think it secure when soe much trust is put into their hands who can meerely quallifie themselves for their posts [by occasionally conforming to the Church]? Can his Majesty be secure if he disobliges the Church?'[138]

Another parliamentarian saw in the exaltation of whiggery an alarming parallel with the conduct of affairs north of the border. 'I have observed for these many yeares last past that our Princes have begun in Scotland to set on foot those things which they designed to bring about in England, &

that the deluges that have overflowed our State & Church have proceeded from the Innundation that were in that Northern kingdom. Wee know how Episcopacy has been been treated there, that presbytry is there settled by a law.' Particularly sinister was the King's reliance upon Scots presbyterians such as James Johnston, the Scottish Secretary of State, and William Carstares, King William's chaplain and confidant:

> we know how inward Secretary Johnston is wth his Master upon the affaires of this, as well as his own Nation, & wee know too that the famous Carsteers is Mr Johnston's Deputy when the King resides in Flanders, & since his Majesty was bred a presbyterian, has been perswaded to the setling presbytry in Scotland, has such a Secretary for Scotland eternally at his ear when at home, & admitts such an importunate Solicitor for that Faction to be alwaies about him when abroad, & since the late Regulations of the Commissions for the Lieutenancy, & the Peace have put soe great authority into hands that are enclined to it [presbyterianism], wee must have the least foresight, or the least love for it, of any men that ever professed to be of the Church of England, if wee can forbear venting our honest & Religious Resentments, & beseeching his majesty to give us further Securities for the Church of England.[139]

The King's abandonment of the politics of balance left the Church party fuming, but it succeeded, for the most part, in winning over whig MPs to the support of the Court. In the sessions of 1693–4 and 1694–5, whig placemen and backbenchers formed the core of a more solid Court party in the Commons.[140] This should not surprise us. After all, King William was at last beginning to act the part of King of the whigs. True, there were still a number of tories in office, most of them cronies of Carmarthen, now Duke of Leeds.[141] But Leeds himself had been marginalised into insignificance, and Nottingham sent packing. On top of this, King William made one crucial concession to whig ideological sensibilities. In January 1694 the King had disgruntled backbenchers of both parties by refusing his assent to another Place Bill.[142] In December, however, he more than made up for this – in whig eyes at least – by approving a fresh bill for triennial elections.[143]

The first general election held under the Triennial Act took place in late October and early November 1695. Compared to its predecessor of 1690, the general election of 1695 was a sedate affair. Only seventy-nine constituencies were contested, and there was a general dearth of the partisan electoral propaganda which had been such a notable feature of the 1690 poll. Having had plenty of time to prepare for the election, the Court was broadly satisfied with the returns. In contrast, the tories, who had been unable to create a new 'Church in danger' agitation, were extremely gloomy about the prospects for the new parliament. Nevertheless, the unusually high number of new members returned at the election meant that all predictions about the forthcoming session were fraught with uncertainty.[144] Nor could the Court be confident of the backing of the whig MPs from the Welsh Marches. They looked for leadership not to the whig ministers but to the member for Hereford, Paul Foley, and his nephew by marriage, Robert Harley.

The whig credentials of Robert Harley were impeccable. His grandfather, Sir Robert Harley of Brampton Bryan, had been the leader of the puritan cause in Herefordshire in the 1640s. Sir Robert's son, Edward, proved to be a fitting heir to the old puritan. A passionate champion of Protestant union and godly reformation, Sir Edward turned Brampton into a haven for dissenting ministers after the Restoration. He was also a remorseless opponent of popery, supporting exclusion in the parliaments of 1679–81 and rallying to the Prince of Orange in November 1688. Elected as one of the members for Herefordshire in January 1689, he was eventually joined in parliament by his eldest son, Robert, returned for Tregony at a by-election later that year.[145]

Although the younger Harley was already drifting away from his father's brand of 'Church presbyterianism', he had imbibed something of Sir Edward's godly sensibilities. Yet this did not prevent him from enjoying some of the less godly delights of London life, notably its ale houses. The divergent pull of nature and nurture produced a young politician who cherished his family's tradition of disinterested public service, but was also determined to cut a figure in the Commons. The two strands of Harley's political personality were to lead him down some crooked paths in later life, but in the early 1690s they consorted harmoniously enough. As a member of the Commission of Accounts, he soon made a name for himself through his attacks upon government maladministration. What really distinguished Harley from his contemporaries, however, was a genuine aversion to partisan politics. In the Convention parliament, it is true, Robert behaved like an orthodox whig. Like his father, he supported the 'Sacheverell Clause', and for his pains was 'blacklisted' by the tories during the 1690 elections. But Sir Edward's defeat at the polls in 1690 freed Robert – by now the member for New Radnor – from his father's tutelage, and as early as March 1691 he was finding 'fault on both sides'.[146] The following year, Harley – together with Paul Foley – scandalized fellow whigs by opposing a bill to outlaw the *de facto* theory of allegiance.[147] For his part, Harley was disgusted by the factiousness of the whig ministers in the 1692–3 session, and he reacted coolly to the fraternal gestures made to him by the party leadership after Nottingham's fall. While his father, who had been re-elected to the Commons in 1693, happily dined with the triumphant whig leaders, Robert kept the party chiefs, especially Wharton, at arm's length.[148] So by 1694 his politics could already be described as more 'Harleyite' than whiggish.[149]

Harley's uncle, Paul Foley, had been a still more distinguished member of the Commission of Accounts in the early 1690s. Together with his tory colleague Sir Thomas Clarges, he had become the voice of backbench disquiet with the conduct of the war.[150] When the Court whigs sought to woo their 'Country' brethren after Nottingham's fall, Foley was naturally one of the principal recipients of their blandishments. Though it cut little ice with his nephew, the administration's charm offensive was not entirely fruitless. For in the first half of the 1694–5 session there was something of a rapprochement between Foley and the Court.[151] The honeymoon, however, did not last long. A man with a strong sense of his own importance, Foley soon took umbrage at the increasingly high-handed behaviour of Tom Wharton and Charles Montagu, the principal Court spokesmen in the Commons. Nor was he best pleased by the administration's plan to impose an excise on leather, a move which would have damaged the economic interests of Foley's stamping ground in the Welsh March.[152]

The breach between Foley and the whig leaders widened still further in March 1695. Having engineered the expulsion from the House of Speaker Sir John Trevor, a creature of the Earl of Sunderland, the Court whigs had attempted to bounce MPs into selecting one of their own number as his replacement. This backfired badly. While they were happy enough to see the back of the corrupt Trevor, whig backbenchers did not take kindly to the Court's hamfisted attempt to influence the election of his successor. As a result, a number of normally reliable Court supporters joined the tories and the Welsh March whigs to block the election of the Court's candidate. The Chair went instead to Paul Foley who, in any case, was thought by many members to be the more experienced candidate.[153]

Although efforts were made to patch up relations between the whig factions in the run-up to the 1695 general election, Foley and Harley were coming to see themselves as an alternative whig leadership in the Commons to Montagu and Wharton.[154] And in the first months of the new parliament, the hold of the Court whigs over the lower House seemed increasingly tenuous. The first serious blow against the whig managers was struck in January 1696 when the Court was defeated by one vote in a crucial division over the proposed Council of Trade. What made this defeat especially ominous was the composition of the 'Country' majority. The Court could expect to be opposed by the Church party and the phalanx of Welsh March MPs led by Foley and Harley. But it was a shock to see the long-standing malcontents joined by an array of newly-elected whig members, upon whose loyalty the Court had counted.[155] Some of these new MPs – for example, Lord Ashley, heir to the Earl of Shaftesbury – were imbued with a genuine suspicion of the Court and its ways. The motives of others were rather less disinterested. Feverishly ambitious young men, such as Sunderland's heir, Lord Spencer, hoped to secure speedy offers of place by making a thorough nuisance of themselves on the backbenches.[156] Whatever their motives, many of the new whig members again trooped into the 'Country' lobby during the elections for the

Commission of Accounts, guaranteeing a heavy defeat for the Court's candidates.[157] For the first time in over two years, there were clear signs that the King's administration was losing its grip on the Commons.

The situation was saved in late February by the revelation of a Jacobite plot to assassinate the King in advance of a planned French invasion.[158] Presented with a golden opportunity to revive the Court's fortunes, the whig ministers lost no time in driving a wedge between the whig malcontents and the Church party. When an 'Association', threatening 'revenge' upon King William's 'enemies', was drawn up in the lower House, whig MPs rushed to sign it. In contrast, as many as eighty-nine tories baulked from putting their signatures to a document which referred to the King as 'rightful and lawful'. In the Lords the terms of the 'Association' were somewhat less offensive from a tory viewpoint. But some nineteen tory peers, led by the Earl of Nottingham, still refused to sign the 'Association'.[159]

The 'Assassination Plot' proved a serious blow to Foley and Harley. Since the election of 1695 at the latest, their strategy for harassing the Court had been centred upon the construction of a bi-partisan 'Country' alliance. And by February 1696 that plan was apparently beginning to work. It was, however, a strategy built upon rickety foundations. Whig backbenchers might be out of sorts with the Court, but they were not eager to fall into bed with a party of crypto-Jacobites. Sure enough, the Assassination Plot, and the subsequent refusal of so many tories to sign the 'Association', shattered the embryonic 'Country' alliance. The tyros on the whig backbenches rallied to the Court, and the opposition to King William's administration was emasculated. Foley and Harley, supported by their kinsmen and friends from the Welsh March, kept up the attack on the Court. Indeed, Foley's antipathy towards the whig ministers turned to hatred after the collapse of his cherished Land Bank scheme in the Summer of 1696, a debacle which he blamed on the machinations of Charles Montagu.[160] But the loyalty to the Court of backbench whigs, so dubious in the first half of the 1695–6 session, was unshaken even by the terrible financial crisis of 1696. With the war entering its dangerous final phase, backbench whigs were simply too scared of the French and the Jacobites to risk rocking the administration's boat. This state of affairs made the Court's position virtually unassailable. As Shrewsbury's Undersecretary, James Vernon, cheerfully noted in October 1696, 'the opposition is weak at present, and while this union [among the whigs] last, whatever is pre-resolved is sure to be carried.'[161]

The continuing pre-eminence of whiggery in the body politic left a true-blue tory like Edmund Bohun utterly despondent. When King William turned to the whigs in 1693–4, Bohun had considered his move to be a purely temporary expedient. If the King 'can finish the war to his contentment', he wrote in August 1694, 'he will then, most certainly, pull down these men faster than he now settes them up; without which he will lose all his royal authority and be reduced into a state of servitude; which in his temper he abhorreth, no man more.'[162] Yet by January 1696, this once devoted Williamite had come to see whig political hegemony as a sad but inevitable consequence of the revolution – whiggery's pay-off for bringing about King William's accession and supporting his war. 'The king that now reignes came in by this party', mused Bohun,

> and not only obtained the first possession but the continuance of the crown for his life from them. His right was founded upon the queen's, as he set forth in his Declaration against king James, and, being matrimonial, was to end with her life. Here this party plaid their first prize. The throne was to be declared 'vacant', that they might pretend to elect him for his life with, but before, the queen, and to reigne after her if she should happen to die before him, as by the divine disposal it happened . . . And now who can blame a prince that came in by these men, that reignes by their arts, that is to spend so much of their blood and treasures, and to see so much more ravished from us by the French, if, after all, he makes one oblation of all the loyal party in the nation to them? Assuredly we are not to complaine or wonder he doth that by us king James would have done if he had prevailed and, if we had not flattered ourselves too, too far, what we ought to have expected from the first. All kingdoms are preserved by the same means they were gotten. King William the third is as wise as William the first, though not so open now, because never well settled.[163]

In the event, Bohun's earlier analysis was to prove rather closer to the truth. The administration had been built to fight the war. The coming of peace in September 1697 would not only place unbearable strains on the King's ministry. It would also shatter the unity of the whig party.

5. The Fragmentation of Whiggery, 1697–1700

Within three months of signing the Treaty of Ryswick, King William lost three of the key ingredients in his wartime ministerial cocktail. Sir William Trumbull, junior Secretary of State since 1695, resigned on 1 December 1697. A lukewarm tory, Trumbull had owed his appointment to the King's desire to retain some semblance of balance in the upper reaches of his administration, and he had always felt out of place in a ministry dominated by whigs. Excluded from the fruits of influence and power by the whig ministers, Trumbull's resignation evinced his exasperation at being treated 'more like a footman than a Secretary'. Trumbull was followed out of the administration a few weeks later by his patron, the Earl of Sunderland. Despised by parliamentarians of all shades of opinion, Sunderland lived in constant fear of impeachment. For that reason, he had been reluctant to assume ministerial responsibility, preferring to exercise influence behind doors, and it was not until April 1697 that he accepted the largely honorific post of Lord Chamberlain. By December, however, Sunderland was convinced that he was about to face a concerted parliamentary attack. He pre-empted it by resigning.[164]

Sunderland's anxiety had been compounded by his distrust of the Junto, as the principal whig ministers had come to be known. The Earl was well aware that the Junto whigs did not regard him as 'one of us', and he was convinced that they would happily feed him to the parliamentary dogs at the first suitable opportunity. He was not far short of the mark. Certainly Thomas Wharton, who had succeeded to his father's barony in 1695, made no secret of his loathing for the Lord Chamberlain.[165]

Although the whig leaders had never trusted Sunderland and were not sorry to see the back of him, the slippery Earl had performed a vital service for them by acting as an intermediary with the King. Among the whig leaders, only Somers – now Lord Chancellor – and Shrewsbury enjoyed the King's personal confidence. Of those two, Shrewsbury – elevated to a dukedom in 1694 – was at most a semi-detached member of the administration by the end of 1697. A political dilettante, he had never concealed his reluctance to shoulder the burdens of high office. After months of imploring the King to release him from business, Shrewsbury retired to his country estate in early December, although he remained nominally the Secretary of State.[166] Deprived of the courtly services of both Sunderland and Shrewsbury, the whig ministers would stand almost naked to the King's wrath should the tide of parliamentary affairs turn against them.[167] And that tide was already beginning to turn.

The issue which proved fatal to the Junto was the army controversy of 1697–9. During the course of the war, the King's army had expanded massively.[168] With the coming of peace, MPs on all sides were determined to obtain a 'peace dividend' for English taxpayers. This meant, above all, swingeing cuts to the bloated army. For his part, the King, while appreciating the inevitabilty of some reduction, was anxious to maintain a substantial force, preferably in the region of 35,000 men.[169] But he made life hard for his ministers by refusing to name a figure which they could present to the House of Commons. Hamstrung by the King's reticence, and knowing only too well that whig backbenchers were looking for massive cuts to the army, the ministers put up a half-hearted performance in the Commons debates on the army in the session of 1697–8. The upshot was a series of votes on supply designed to reduce the army to a mere 10,000 men. Among the 'Country' majorities were many normally loyal Court supporters.[170]

The parliamentary attack on the army was accompanied by a flurry of publications from a group of dissident whigs – centred upon Lord Ashley and the Anglo-Irishman, Robert Molesworth – who saw in the ancient Roman Republic the paradigm of civic and religious virtue.[171] The army's parliamentary critics had aired old charges that a standing army posed a threat to English liberties. In this, they were probably influenced by the principal luminary of the 'Roman whigs', John Trenchard. 'What if they [the army] should come into the Field and say, You must choose these Men your Representatives; Where is your Choice?' he asked in an influential pamphlet written at the beginning of the 1697–8 session. 'What if they should say, Parliaments are seditious and factious assemblies, and therefore ought to be abolished; What is become of your Freedom? Or, if they should encompass the Parliament-House, and threaten if they do not surrender up their Government, they will put them to the Sword; What is to become of the old English Constitution.'[172] While Trenchard led the way, the most spectacular contribution to the literary campaign of the 'Roman whigs' was the publication of Edmund Ludlow's *Memoirs*. Heavily edited (and in some places virtually rewritten) by John Toland, another of Lord Ashley's friends, the *Memoirs* provided a telling reminder of the iniquities of military tyranny. As Toland wrote in the preface to the third volume of the *Memoirs*, 'Men may learn from the issue of the Cromwellian tyranny that liberty and a standing mercenary army are incompatible.'[173]

Ominously for the whig ministers, the literary campaign against the army broadened into a general denunciation of the drift of whiggery under the Junto. Whereas the radical pamphleteers of 1691–3 had concentrated their fire upon the King's tory evil counsellors, the 'Roman whigs' of the late 1690s, deprived of suitable tory targets by the Junto's political successes, levelled their guns upon the edifice of Court whiggery. This they damned as an apostate creed which had perverted the principles of the true whig faith. 'Who can enough lament the wretched Degeneracy of the Age we live in?' asked Toland in 1698:

> To see persons who were formerly noted for the most vigorous Assertors of their Country's Liberty, who from their Infancy had imbib'd no other Notions than what conduc'd to the public Safety, whose Principles were further improv'd and confirm'd by the advantages of a sutable Conversation, and who were so far possest with this spirit of Liberty, that it sometimes transported them beyond the bounds of Moderation, even to unwarrantable Excesses: to see these Men, I say, so infamously fall in with the arbitrary measures of the Court, and appear the most active Instruments for enslaving their Country, and that without any formal steps or degrees, but all in an instant, is so violent and surprizing a transition from one Extreme to another without passing the Mean, as would have confounded the imaginations of EUCLID and PYRRHO.[174]

Trenchard too accused the ministerial whigs of 'infamous Apostacy', reminding readers of the whig party's consistent opposition to standing armies before the revolution.[175]

The effusions of the 'Roman whigs' did not go unanswered. One pro-Court writer stigmatised the radicals as 'a sort of republicans of the old stamp, that are for subverting monarchy itself, to set up an idol, they know not what, in the room on't; and care not what becomes of king and parliament, and kingdom too, so they can gratify their own pride and peevishness, and advance the Dagon of a commonwealth'. For such men were 'so averse to all kings, that if God should send them one from heaven, they'd never like him two days together; nay, if they were in heaven themselves, 'tis to be feared they'd be turned out again, for attempting against the monarchical power of God Almighty'. Turning the apostacy charge on its head, the same writer accused the commonwealthsmen of aiding and abetting those inveterate enemies of liberty – the tories, Jacobites and papists. Though they were 'as opposite to the Jacobites in their principles, as they are to peace and loyalty, yet they both agree in opinion and practice against King William and his government, and take the same methods of lying and slandering and raising fears and jealousies to weaken and destroy it'.[176] Writing in response to Trenchard, another pro-Court pamphleteer argued that, far from being a threat to English liberties, the army was the bulwark of the nation's freedom. As long as the power of Louis XIV remained undiminished, it would be essential to maintain a standing force to defend the nation.[177] Nor did this writer permit Trenchard's yearning for the good old days of whiggery to go unchallenged: 'perhaps our Author is of the Opinion of a Gentleman, who told me, He was for Whigs as Whigs were 15 years ago; But tho . . . I am – a – Whig, and I fancy as hearty a Whig as the Author, yet I must own I am not for being a Whig as Whigs were 15 years ago, that is, I am not for being Imprison'd, Fin'd, Whip'd, Pillory'd, and Hang'd, as Whigs were then, and as we maybe again, if we come into our Author's Scheme.' Instead, all true whigs would place their faith in the King's army to defend the revolution from its enemies.[178]

While the 'paper war' between establishment and 'Roman' whigs escalated, the Junto's credit with the King was steadily diminishing. Although Lord Somers had produced perhaps the most skilful defence of the army in the press, King William's appreciation of his Lord Chancellor's literary efforts were outweighed by the Junto's feeble performance in the parliamentary debates of December 1697.[179] That the King's confidence in the Junto was waning seemed to be indicated by his behaviour in the general election of July 1698. As Somers subsequently noted, King William had conspicuously failed to endorse the Junto upon the dissolution of the old parliament.[180]

From a partisan perspective, the election of 1698 was by no means a disaster for the whig leaders. There does not appear to have been a marked upturn in the fortunes of the Church party.[181] Nevertheless, Somers had been deeply disturbed by the tone of the election campaign, and was not optimistic about the Court's prospects in the forthcoming session. 'The elections were made on an ill foot; uneasiness at taxes and the most dangerous division of a Court and Country party; so that there is reason to doubt the behaviour of many of your best friends.'[182] Needless to say, this state of affairs boded ill for the King's hopes of salvaging the army.

When the new parliament met in December, matters went from bad to worse for the Court on the army issue. Far from sanctioning an army in excess of 10,000 men, as the King had hoped, the Commons was intent on cutting it still further. On 16 December MPs voted to reduce the army to a paltry 7,000 men.[183] Once again, the King bears a large measure of responsibility for the debacle. Despite the votes of 1697–8, he had kept on foot nearly 15,000 soldiers in England and had attempted to 'hide' others on the separate Irish military establishment. These clumsy attempts to circumvent the will of parliament helped to provoke the move to cut the army still further.[184] And even when he was faced with the prospect of a 7,000 man army, the King would still not authorize his supporters to defend a force of 10,000 men. On 17 December James Vernon, now Secretary of State, complained to Shrewsbury that the 'Committee [which voted to reduce the army to 7,000] yesterday would in all probability have come up to 10,000 men for England, if any had authority to propose it, and that the managers had come warmly into it; but it now was as the last year, that his Majesty would not declare himself on that point, thinking less than the present number insufficient'.[185]

For their part, the whig leaders found themselves caught between the devil and the deep blue sea. 'At present we are under a great perplexity', Vernon wrote on 31 December:

> Those that are convinced in their judgments that a greater force is necessary, are apprehensive of the ill consequences if such a question be carried upon a division, which fixes people in a party, so that no good is to be expected during the rest of the sessions. If it be not attempted, the King will be disobliged, and may be told if there were not more troops, it was because nobody pressed it. This dilemma is a little staggering.[186]

In the event, the ministerial whigs at last rallied to the defence of the King's army. When the Disbanding Bill received its third reading in the Commons on 18 January 1699, the Court's 'opposition to it was made with more vigour at first than has appeared hitherto in any of these debates, and beyond what was expected'. Moreover, 'many [whig] country gentlemen' came 'in voluntarily, and without any concert, to declare their dislike to so small a number'.[187] But the Court's rally could not save the day. With some thirty to forty whigs voting with the tories and the Foley-Harley group, the Court went down by 221 votes to 154.[188]

Although the division of 18 January had seen some whig backbenchers return to the Court fold, the army controversy had been an unmitigated disaster for the Junto. Afraid that a strong campaign in favour of the army would antagonise many whig MPs, the King's managers had, for the most part, put up a woeful performance in the key debates. The result was a severe loss of credit in both Court and parliament. While the diffidence of the Court whigs over the army issue had greatly diminished their standing with the King, even a lukewarm defence of the army was sufficient to sully them in the eyes of many backbench whigs. This much became clear on 4 February when the placemen were told to stay away from a meeting of whig MPs at the Rose Tavern, a favourite whig haunt.[189]

Under the twin pressure of backbench rebellion and apparent royal disfavour, the Junto began to disintegrate. First to jump the sinking ship was the nautical Earl of Orford (the former Admiral Edward Russell). Attacked in the Commons, and, so he believed, slighted by the King, the temperamental Orford resigned as First Lord of the Admiralty in May 1699.[190] His colleague Charles Montagu, First Lord of the Treasury and the Court's chief manager in the Commons, took an alternative route to the political wilderness. Finding the task of managing an increasingly irascible House both irksome and futile, Montagu decided to keep his head down and all but abandoned his parliamentary responsibilities. In November he was happy to exchange the principal office at the Treasury for a sinecure.[191]

As the Junto's star waned, Robert Harley's began to wax strong. Paul Foley's death in November 1699 left Harley both the head of the dissident Welsh March whigs and the most influential voice in the Commons. With nobody willing to step into Montagu's shoes as Court business manager in the Commons during the session of 1699–1700, Harley filled the vacuum himself. He began, in effect, to manage the King's business from the back-benches. 'Mr Harley now manages the whole business of supply', wrote an MP in January 1700, 'and the House hath hitherto entirely approved of his scheme.'[192]

Harley's influence in the Commons, based on his reputation as an honest and disinterested country gentleman, ensured that his name would loom large in any major ministerial reconstruction. But that reconstruction was a long time coming. Although the whig leaders had been declining in the King's estimation since 1697, and began to slip out of high office during the course of 1699, King William had no reason to feel favourably disposed towards the leaders of the Church party in either Lords or Commons. As Somers informed Shrewsbury in March 1699, the King believed that the tories were bent on humiliating him.[193] Furthermore, the Junto's parliamentary position was by no means hopeless. A clear partisan issue, such as an election dispute, could still produce a closing of whig ranks and an impressive Court majority. 'One may observe what a strength there is like to be in the Whig party, if they do not moulder again by being put upon unpopular things', mused James Vernon after one such success in December 1699. 'If they cannot do everything that the King may think a gratification to him,' he went on, yet I believe he may depend upon it they will keep the government upon its present basis, which is no small consideration; but then they must be at liberty not to meddle with things they see reason to despair of; and, as circumstances now stand, no prudent man will act but with a good deal of caution, and have some regard to his own safety, since the compensations are like to be so small, for any hazards he shall run.[194]

King William, however, was not inclined to take a sympathetic view of the predicament of the whig leaders. He was particularly galled by his ministers' inability to prevent the passage in April 1700 of the Act of Resumptions, a measure revoking the King's grants of forfeited lands in Ireland. Although, as David Hayton has shown, this was a largely tory-inspired measure, it was the leader of the Junto, Lord Chancellor Somers, who bore the brunt of the King's displeasure. Believing that Somers had shown insufficient vigour in opposing the popular Resumptions Act, the King dismissed him from office on 27 April 1700.[195]

The dismissal of Somers meant that all the whig leaders were now out of high office. As yet, however, no successors had emerged to assume their leading role in the King's administration. Reluctant to give office to the tory leaders, King William had shored up the ministry in 1699 and early 1700 with a series of stop-gap appointments, political second-raters who could never hope to form a viable administration.[196] Not until the Summer of 1700 did the King come to accept an unpalatable truth: with the good ship whiggery rudderless and listing, the Court's parliamentary business would be unmanageable without the support of the Church party. So in July 1700 King William began to court tory heavyweights like Lord Godolphin and the Earl of Rochester. But the key figure in the negotiations was Robert Harley. He was already recognised as a peerless parliamentary operator, and the King and the tory lords were eager to enlist his services on behalf of the new administration. For his part, Harley was reluctant to take office lest it jeopardise his reputation for political independence. Instead, he made it clear that he would assist the Court if he were elected Speaker in the new parliament. For as part of the deal with the tory leaders, the King had agreed to dissolve parliament and call fresh elections. In December the agreement was implemented. Godolphin was appointed First Lord of the Treasury, and Rochester was given the Lord Lieutenancy of Ireland. That same month, the King dissolved parliament, and in the ensuing weeks the nation again went to the polls.[197] A new political experiment was about to begin.

6. The Reunification of Whiggery, 1700–1701

When the new parliament met in early February 1701, King William was keen to complete his political jigsaw by securing the election of Harley as

Speaker of the Commons. A number of whig members, however, were determined to resist this because of Harley's alliance with the High Church zealot, Rochester. Thus at the beginning of the session some 125 or so whig MPs met at the Rose Tavern to co-ordinate opposition to Harley's election.[198] Their efforts met with ignominious failure. On 10 February Harley won the Chair by 249 votes to 125.[199]

The scale of Harley's triumph is only partly attributable to tory successes at the general election of January 1701. As the Dutch ambassador observed, it was clear that 'a great party of Whigs' had also supported Harley's bid for the Chair.[200] In fact, Harley's success was testimony to the unique position he had acquired in the House of Commons. Although he was now closely associated with Rochester and other High Tories, Harley still retained the goodwill of many whig parliamentarians. Even the hot Gloucestershire whig Sir Richard Cocks, who had been at the heart of the moves to resist Harley's election, could not 'beleive Mr Harley in the main to be in any interest but that of the country tho I confes I do not approve of many of his words and actions'.[201]

Eleven months later the face of affairs had changed. When Harley again stood for Speaker after the general election of November 1701, whig MPs rallied to the rival Junto candidate, and Harley scraped home by a handful of votes.[202] What had happened in the intervening months to restore whig solidarity and the pre-eminent role of the Junto in the party's affairs?

The answer is clear: the events of the 1701 parliament had given a fresh lease of life to a range of issues central to the rival party traditions. In the first place, an abortive tory attempt to penalize 'occasional conformists' showed whig MPs that the religious principles of their old enemies were as narrow as ever.[203] Once again, tories were prepared to sow dissension among Protestants in order to maintain the supremacy of the Church of England in the state. This episode proved deeply embarrassing for Harley, since it pitted his new allies in the Church party against his old presbyterian friends. Even a politician of Harley's legendary dexterity could not emerge unscathed from such a confrontation. At the end of March, Harley received a plaintive letter from Daniel Williams, the celebrated presbyterian minister. On more than one occasion, Williams explained, 'my assurance of your upright ends obliged me to vindicate you . . . against the suspicions your [tory] company exposed you to'. But he was now 'amazd to see the clauses that party hath inserted against dissenters, in a bill now in your hous'. Could Harley have forgotten the nonconformists who stood for English liberties when they were 'under the axe'? Did he not remember

> that the dissenters were persecuted because they struggled for civil libertys, and not because dissenters? can you equally confide in late converts, whom a short memory must conclude *miraculously* changd, or now pleading against prerogative for liberty from some fixd design? will an establishment of civil

rights be reputable, strong and lasting, which incapacitates the most sober and usefull dissenter from being in any civil office, and yet leave him punishable by his townsmen for not serving in the office to which they shall call him [the practice of fining citizens who refused to accept certain irksome local offices]? this very thing will soon be equivalent to a persecution.

Even if Harley himself did not support this pernicious measure, he was, at the very least, guilty by association: 'tho I cannot believe you do concur in this attempt against us, yet I bewayl it as an unhappiness that it happens when you fill the chair, and in the effort of those with whom you are reputed to concert affairs'.[204] The Speaker's many admirers on the whig backbenches were doubtless equally distraught.

While the occasional conformity issue had caused Harley acute embarrassment, his parliamentary skills were seen to advantage during the debates on the bill settling the succession to the throne upon the eventual demise of Princess Anne, the last surviving Protestant in the Stuart line. The Speaker took the lead in piloting the measure through the Commons, and with surprisingly little dispute both houses agreed to settle the succession upon the Hanoverian branch of the Royal Family.[205] But the easy passage of the Act of Settlement did not succeed in burying the old whig prejudice that the Church party was popery's best friend. On the contrary, that prejudice was exacerbated by the tardy response of tory politicians to the deepening crisis in Europe.

In November 1700 Charles II, last of the Spanish Habsburgs, bequeathed his domains to Philip of Anjou, a grandson of Louis XIV. Three months later, the Spanish government invited King Louis to send his army into Flanders, sweeping away the fortified zone which shielded the Netherlands from France. The Dutch, scared out of their wits, asked parliament for assistance, only to find that the tory majority in the Commons preferred words to action. True, in the Summer English troops were at last despatched to Holland.[206] But the earlier diffidence of tory ministers and MPs had given new life to a central tenet of whiggery: the Church party could not be trusted to defend the Protestant cause.

The dramatic impact of these events on whig opinion – explored more fully in the next chapter – is well illustrated by the views of the Earl of Shaftesbury. As Lord Ashley, he had been one of the leading anti-Junto whigs. And in November 1700, Shaftesbury still looked upon Court whiggery with distaste. 'The Whiggs, you know,' he wrote to a friend in the Netherlands, 'have for severall years & in these last Parlemants especially, been shamefull in their over great Condescencions to the Court, & by this have lost their Interest much in the Countryes.' At the same time, though he was less than enamoured with the Church party's imminent return to power, he believed that political insecurity would encourage the tories to 'carry on the Face of tollerable Patriots'.[207] Yet by early March 1701

Shaftesbury was writing that the French and tory interests were 'one & the same'.[208]

If a whig was someone who believed that tories were soft on popery, his convictions would have been amply confirmed in the first half of 1701. He would also have had another article of faith reinforced – that the Church party was the handmaiden of arbitrary power. In May the whig-inspired petition of the Kent Grand Jury urged the Commons to vote supply so that the King 'may be enabled powerfully to assist his Allies before it is too late'. In response, the tory majority in the Commons voted the petition 'scandalous, insolent, and seditious', and ordered the imprisonment of the five gentlemen who had brought it up to Westminster.[209] This action, argued the young firebrand Daniel Defoe, was 'illegal; a notorious breach of the liberty of the people, setting up a dispensing power in the House of Commons, which your fathers never pretended to, bidding defiance to the habeas corpus act, which is the bulwark of personal liberty, destructive to the laws, and betraying the trust reposed in you'.[210] Englishmen, complained Defoe, had rid themselves of an arbitrary monarch in 1688 only to be enslaved by an equally arbitrary House of Commons thirteen years later:

> Posterity will be ashamed to own,
> The actions we their ancestors have done,
> When they for ancient precedents enquire,
> And to the journals of this age retire,
> To see one tyrant banished from his home,
> To set five hundred traitors in his room.
> They'll blush to find the head beneath the tail,
> And representing treachery prevail:
> They'll be amazed to see there was but five,
> Whose courage could their liberty service,
> While we that durst illegal power dethrone,
> Should basely be enslaved by tyrants of our own.[211]

With the tory party displaying all its old 'popish' and 'arbitrary' tendencies, whig parliamentarians put aside their misgivings about the Junto. This became clear in April 1701 when the tories attempted to impeach Somers, Orford and Charles Montagu (now Lord Halifax). A symptom as much as a cause of the growing tension between the parties, the impeachments were a blatant attempt by the tories to decapitate whiggery. As James Vernon commented when the impeachments were first mooted, 'it is visible these heats don't arise upon the subject matter [the alleged role of the whig peers in negotiating the Partition Treaty of 1700], but are resolutions formed to take any occasion for excluding those they have so great an aversion to from ever coming into power again.'[212] Faced with this attack on their old leaders, whig MPs knew where their loyalties lay. Although the surviving whig placemen in the Commons generally kept their heads low, the rest of the party rushed to the defence of their 'Brother-Whiggs'.[213]

The attempted impeachments of the Junto lords came to grief in June in the House of Lords.[214] And though the tories continued to hold sway in the Commons, the whigs were also giving as good as they got in the press. The author of *Jura Populi Anglicani* – possibly Lord Somers himself – launched a particularly vicious attack on the Church party. 'The Case in short is this', he wrote,

> To this loyal Tory-Party (as they would be esteem'd) we find all those attach'd, whose Principles imbib'd in the late Reigns, makes them firmly adhere to the interest of K[ing] James: Here we find all those in a manner who were against the Abdication [of King James], Recognition [of William and Mary], who would not allow his present Majesty to be rightful King, and refus'd to enter into the Association to preserve him and his Government: In this Party are all those likewise whome either the Love of Mony, or of the St Germain Family, or Popery has reconcil'd to the French Interest. 'Tis most certain that there is not a Man in the House ingag'd in any of these Interests, who is not one of this Party; and as certain it is that all the Papists, Friends of King James, and the French King, without doors, applaud their proceedings, and own they are fairly represented by them.[215]

The pamphleteer did not content himself with name-calling. He also sought to undermine the legitimacy of the tory-dominated Commons by broaching that most radical of doctrines, the sovereignty of the people: 'we are told', he observed, 'that by the Constitution of our Parliament, the Members are left to the Freedom of their own Debates, and are to act without Controul; they therefore who take upon them to intermeddle in their Business, invade that Freedom, and consequently our Constitution.' This, he averred, was the most pernicious of doctrines:

> They who tell us that the Representatives of the Freemen of England have such a Freedom as this, and are to act without controul, cannot sure mean that they have delegated their whole Power to them, so that 'tis free for them to do whatever they please, without any regard to the Inclinations or Interest of those who employ them. 'Tis not to be supposed that he who takes what Servant he pleases, is oblig'd to suffer him to do what he pleases. The Knights, Citizens, and Burgesses, sent by the People of England to serve in Parliament, have a Trust reposed in them, which if they should manifestly betray, the People, in whom the Power is more perfectly and fully than in their Delegates, must have a right to help and preserve themselves.[216]

It was a theme taken up by Defoe in *Legion's Memorial*: 'though there are no stated proceedings to bring you to your duty,' he warned the lower House, 'yet the great law of reason says, and all nations allow, that whatever power is above law, it's burdensome and tyrannical, and maybe reduced by extrajudicial methods: You are not above the people's resentments; they that made you members may reduce you to the same rank from whence they chose you; and may give you a taste of their abused kindness, in terms you may not be pleased with.'[217] Defoe's rhetoric became still more menacing: 'if the House of Commons, in breach of the laws and liberties of the people, do betray the trust reposed in them, and act negligently or arbitrarily and illegally, it is the undoubted right of the people of England to call them to an account for the same, and by convention, assembly, or force, may proceed against them as traitors and betrayers of their country.'[218] In the event, the tory House of Commons was overthrown by more conventional means, another change in the King's policy.

By the beginning of September it was clear that a renewal of war with France was inevitable. This prospect led King William to reconsider his political options, and he again turned for counsel to the Earl of Sunderland. As the King explained, he was reluctant to break with the tories. Although he had been less than pleased with the conduct of tory parliamentarians in the 1701 session, he was concerned that 'if he should quit those he now employs, and that the others should not be able to serve him, then he shall have no resource'. For that reason he was inclined 'to try again what the present ministry and their party will do; with a resolution to change upon the first occasion they shall give'.[219] The King's strategy received short shrift from an exasperated Sunderland. The tories, he contended, were at best unreliable and at worst downright disloyal. Thus King William had no option but to repose his trust once more in the whigs. To this end, continued Sunderland, the King should arrange immediate consultations with Lord Somers.[220] For once, King William acted promptly upon the Earl's advice. In October he made overtures to the leader of the Junto, and when the two men met in early November Somers urged the King to call fresh elections. Within days, King William dissolved his fifth parliament.[221]

The second general election of 1701 was an indecisive affair, and the King did not live to complete his planned ministerial changes.[222] Nevertheless, the heats of 1701 had brought a renewed sharpness of definition to the issues which divided King William's subjects. As England prepared for the renewal of the great struggle with France, the parties within the state girded themselves for an escalation of the domestic conflict. Few would have guessed that the war against Louis XIV would be fought and won before the battle between whig and tory was at last decided.

4

King William's War

1. The Meaning of War

On 16 April 1689 Sir Edward Harley informed his son Robert that the 'House of Commons this day Voted to Suport the King in a War with France when he please with his Allies to declare it. This', he added, 'is a great Vote, the Lord may in mercy give his blessing.'[1]

For King William, the vote came not a day too soon. Five months earlier, in response to the Dutch invasion of England, Louix XIV had declared war on the United Provinces. Since then, the Dutch had been waiting impatiently for their Stadholder to bring England into the lists, and he in turn had been urging parliament to come to the aid of his countrymen.[2] Now his efforts had met with success. The upshot was the most revolutionary aspect of the revolution: a radical reorientation in England's foreign policy.

Under King James, England had not been at the hub of European affairs. Unlike his brother Charles II, who in 1672 had joined Louis XIV in attacking the Dutch, King James had no intention of entering into an offensive alliance with France. Nor, however, was he to be drawn into the emerging anti-French confederacy in Europe. Instead, he had remained aloof from Continental entanglements, concentrating instead on the implementation of his controversial domestic policies.[3]

The King's neutrality was to prove his undoing. With war between France and the Netherlands imminent, his son-in-law the Prince of Orange was determined to bring England into the struggle against Louis XIV. This imperative, above all, prompted Prince William's invasion of England, an invasion supported to the hilt by the Dutch government.[4] As the Marquis of Halifax later commented, William 'hath such a mind to France, that it would incline one to think, hee tooke England onely in his way'.[5] So well-known was Prince William's animosity to the French King that as early as December 1688 a balladeer was portraying him as the nemesis of France:

> The Fury of your Sword, Let the French feel,
> That Kingdom is Designed by you to reel;
> Pull down their Gaudy Pride which long hath stood,
> And their own Fields Manure with their own Blood.[6]

In the event, it was King Louis who opened Anglo-French hostilities by sending aid to the Irish Jacobites in March 1689. Thus in his reply to a Commons address of 25 April calling for war, King William was able to claim that it was 'already declared in effect by France against England', and that it was 'not so properly an act of choice as an inevitable necessity in our own defence'.[7] Twelve days later, on 7 May, the King of England formally declared war on his cousin, the King of France.[8] So began the great war against Louis XIV, a war which would be fought in alliance with the United Provinces, Austria and Spain.

Since the 1960s, King William's war has become something of a growth-area in the world of historical research. The role of the war as a motor for administrative, financial and constitutional development has been well-chronicled.[9] But with the exceptions of court-sponsored propaganda and the controversy over war strategy, there has been little investigation of the ideological context of the war.[10] This is a mountainous subject, and the following pages are no more than an exploratory tour of the foothills.

Our central question is straightfoward: what did contemporaries think the war was about? The answer for many was religion. The chief end of the war, wrote John Hampden in 1692, was 'the preservation of the Protestant Religion against Popery and Idolatry'.[11] Preaching at Whitehall in 1694, Dean Comber of Durham averred that King William's 'chief End, in all his Councils, and principal Aim in exposing his Life, is to establish the True Religion, and preserve a happy Peace for all that profess it'.[12] According to *The Loyal States-Man*, a ballad dating from late 1695 or early 1696, King William, the 'English Caesar',

> . . . espouses our quarrel;
> Predestin'd to stand
> Against Lewes le Grand,
> And wear his now flourishing lawrel:
> The cause that is best
> Now comes to the test,
> For Heav'n will no longer stand newter,
> But pronounce the great doom,
> For old Luther or Rome,
> And prevent all our doubts for the future.[13]

As another balladeer had sung in 1690, 'The True Religion is the Stake, / Which Tyrant Rome now void wou'd make.'[14]

At first sight, such views seem trite. Since Louis XIV was intent upon restoring King James to the throne, it was self-evident to Williamites that the war was one of self-defence against popish tyranny. But the religious dimension of the war tended to be set in a much broader context: the defence of the 'reformed interest' in Europe from French aggression. As Dean Comber reminded his listeners at Whitehall, the sword which the French King was now brandishing against the Church of England was 'yet reeking with the Gore of a Sister Reformed Church' – the French Protestant church, destroyed by King Louis in 1685.[15] In a sermon delivered in 1690, the conformist clergyman Samuel Barton claimed that the revolution had benefited all European Protestants. But for the revolution, he declared, 'not we only but even all the Christians of the Reformation had in a little time, in all probability, bin reduc'd to as deplorable a Condition, as those of France or Savoy have bin.' Thankfully, however, 'the whole Protestant interest which was in a manner expiring, is now thro' Gods wonderful Providence beginning to revive again' – a matter of indifference only to 'narrow souls' who criticized the revolution and 'Bigots' who 'would cut themselves off from the Body of the Reformation'.[16] So rather more was at stake in the clash with Louis XIV than the fate of England alone. 'I looke upon the cause wherein King William and Q[uee]n Mary and the Parliament of England are now ingaged', wrote the whiggish judge Thomas Rokeby in May 1689, 'to be the cause of God and Christ against Satan and Antichrist.'[17]

Like Mr Justice Rokeby, Archbishop Tillotson of Canterbury saw the French war in an apocalyptic light. Preaching before the King and Queen at Whitehall in October 1692, Tillotson drew a comparison between Louis XIV and the biblical King of Babylon. Just as that wicked monarch had sworn destruction upon ancient Zion, so now the French King said, 'I will destroy the Reformation, I will extirpate the Northern Heresie.' But the rout of the French fleet at Barfleur in May had shown that God was about to humble the haughty King of France. Indeed, the French naval defeat was nothing less than the fulfilment of scriptural prophecy. 'I have sometimes heretofore wondred,' he confided to the congregation, 'Why at the destruction of Modern and Mystical Babylon the Scripture should make mention of great wailing and lamentation for the loss of Her Ships and Seamen [Rev. 18v17]: Little imagining, thirty years ago, that any of the Kingdoms who had given their power to the Beast would ever have arrived to that mighty Naval Force: But the Scripture', Tillotson reassuringly concluded, 'saith nothing in vain.'[18]

The war, then, presaged the downfall of popish tyranny. As a ballad of 1690 warned,

> . . . Pope and Monsieur, have a care,
> 'Twill prove to both a fatal War,
> Whilst England shall successful be,
> In plucking down of Popery . . .
> The haughty Monsieur we'll pluck down,

> And make him bow to England's Crown:
> Our Papist Foes our Pow'r shall know,
> We'll bring their Cross and Miter low,
> Old England's Glory to Advance,
> We'll scare the Pope and King of France.[19]

For who could doubt that the forces of true godliness would eventually overcome those of popish flummery. 'Our Enemies no doubt have sought their Holy Fathers Benediction, applyed to the Saints and the Blessed Virgin', sneered Dean Comber,

> But we call only upon the Name of JESUS CHRIST; and I hope it will prove, as it did of Old, in the great Battle of Poictiers, when the French, who had got the Pope's Blessing, were beat by the English, who trusted in CHRIST their Saviour; Men said . . . Behold the Pope was on the French and JESUS on the English Side; so that we have seen this Day, which of these can do most for his Friends.[20]

Although the idea of a war of religion was not the preserve of any one party, it was particularly widespread among the whigs, party of pan-Protestantism. The notion of a war of the 'reformed interest' dovetailed neatly with their domestic political agenda, for whigs maintained that Protestant unity abroad must be matched by Protestant unity at home. This meant, above all, scrapping the sacramental qualification for office. When the House of Lords voted to retain the sacramental test in March 1689, six whig peers protested. As they explained, the setting of

> Marks of distinction and Limitation on any Sort of men who have not rendred themselves justly suspected to the Government, as it is all times to be avoided by the makers of just and equall Lawes, so may it be of particularly ill effect to the Reformed Interest at home and abrode in the present Conjuncture, which stands in neede of the united hands and hearts of all Protestants against the open attempt and seacret endeavours of a restless party, and Potent Neighbour, who is more zealous than Rome itselfe to plant Popery in these Kingdomes and labours with his utmost force to settle his Tirany upon the ruin of the Reformation all through Europe.[21]

Seven years later, the ultra-whiggish cleric William Stephens similarly lamented that due to the sacramental test 'the Nation cannot act vigorously in its own defence, being debarr'd the Use of one Moiety of it self.'[22]

It was a central tenet of whiggery that toryism, with its insistence on the exclusive privileges of the Church of England, impaired the English war effort by sowing division among Protestants. Whigs also contended that the narrow religious principles of their tory rivals precluded the close alliance with foreign Protestants that the French threat demanded. Whereas the whigs, asserted the veteran puritan Thomas Papillon, 'do own the foreign Protestant Churches as Churches of Christ, and hold communion with them', the tories 'comprehended all those that cry up the

Church of England in opposition to the Churches of Christ in foreign parts'.[23] Writing in June 1689, the presbyterian diarist Roger Morrice complained that

> the enemies of King William are very many amongst all ranks of men, many are professed enemies to him that yet openly aver they will never receive King James back again, yet King William they would remove rather than Coalesce with the Reformed Interest abrode, which King William can alone be supported by, for that they say will destroy the Tory interest in England, so that they cannot divid the Spoil of Church and State amongst themselves, and Tyranize over their neighbours as they have done for many yeares last past.[24]

This whiggish perception of high church bigotry found theatrical expression in the figure of Sir Humphrey Maggot, the debauched Jacobite alderman in Thomas Shadwell's comedy, *The Scowrers*. Upon hearing that French forces have crushed the Protestants of Savoy, the Vaudois, Maggot is beside himself with joy. 'Heaven be praised,' he enthuses, 'they are damn'd Presbyterian Fellows, and hate the Church, for my part, had I my will, I would put all the Phanaticks in Christendom in pitch'd shirts, light them, and let them blaze like City Funerals.'[25]

As might be expected, the whigs were not over-subtle in their interpretation of tory attitudes towards European Protestants. Only the most extreme highflyers, such as the nonjuror Henry Dodwell, believed that Continental Protestants were beyond the pale of the true church.[26] And against the likes of Dodwell should be set Bishop Compton of London, the tory prelate who was the Huguenots' best friend on the episcopal bench.[27] Nevertheless, the whigs did have a point. As we shall see in a later chapter, the first year of King William's reign witnessed various abortive proposals for comprehension – the broadening of the Church's terms of communion in order to bring moderate dissenters back into the Establishment. These schemes – fiercely opposed by most tories – were seen by the whigs in a European, rather than a purely domestic, context. Comprehension, they argued, was necessary not only to unite Protestants at home, but also to show that the Church of England believed itself part of the European Protestant community. Thus in March 1689 Sir Henry Capel warned the Commons that 'If we do not comprehend, and make our entrance broad, at this time, you may create jealousies at home and abroad.'[28] Three months later, the nonconformist leader John Howe reportedly told the King that the proposed comprehension should 'allow for the time past such Ordinations as is allowed in Holland and other Reformed Churches for we [dissenters] can never concur to any clause that condemnes their Ordination'.[29] Failure to recognise the validity of presbyterian orders, wrote another dissenter, 'destroys the Church State, not only of Dissenters, but of all other Protestants in the World, except of those in the Church of England, nulling their Ministry, Sacraments, and Discipline'.[30] In similar vein, Roger Morrice complained that the rejection of comprehension would inevitably 'keepe up the schism betweene the Church of England and all other Reformed Churches, and by dividing and separating from the Protestant Churches abrode, they actualy reduce themselves to that same narrow bottom they had been upon these late yeares, and so consequently in a little time will be overcome by, and make way for Popery to enter'.[31] From Morrice's perspective, then, it was simply inconceivable that the Church party could have its heart in the war against France. For by their hatred of comprehension, the tories had shown that they did not feel themselves part of the brotherhood of European Protestantism.

The King himself may have had some sympathy with this view. Before the revolution, according to Gilbert Burnet, he believed that the Church of England should be 'softned a little, both with relation to the Non-conformists at home and to the forrigne Churches beyond Sea'.[32] After the revolution, as we shall see in a later chapter, he pressed unsuccessfully for the repeal of the sacramental test and the introduction of some form of comprehension.[33] Unlike the whigs, however, King William was reluctant to describe the war in religious terms. Since the corner-stone of his anti-French strategy was an alliance with Catholic Austria and Spain, this is not altogether surprising. As we saw in an earlier chapter, the King was always wary of offending the religious sensibilities of his Habsburg allies, and this was an important factor in his relatively tolerant policy towards British Catholics.[34] Hence the Jacobite writer Thomas Wagstaffe could claim with some justice that Englishmen were 'encouraged to give supplies to maintain the inquisition in Spain, and in the empire, persecution of protestants, and toleration and liberty to papists in England, Scotland and Ireland'. Indeed, Jacobites heaped ridicule upon the Protestant credentials of King William's war. As Wagstaffe scornfully remarked,

> the emperor, who hath severely persecuted his protestant subjects in Hungary, and the King of Spain, under whom the bloody inquisition reigns, are like to be admirable defenders of the protestant religion; and yet these are the persons you must court, and you are invited to maintain an expensive and devouring alliance with the most bigotted papists in the world; and no doubt in defence of the protestant religion. The sheep may as well confederate with the wolves, and they will be as helpful guardians for their lambs as the inquisition is for the protestant religion.[35]

It was a nonsense, averred another Jacobite writer, 'To be roaring at Popery with Popish Confederates', 'To think the French Popery so much worse than the Spanish; and the House of Bourbon more an Enemy to Protestants, than the Bloody House of Austria'.[36]

It was not only Jacobites who found it impossible to accept the good faith of King William's popish allies. There 'is a most deepe conspiracy a carrying on among the Popish princes under the covert of this war for the destruction of the Hollanders and of us', warned an anonymous informant in October 1691. In the next year's campaign in Flanders 'our King William will bee shot or stabbed by the Spaniards and in an instant afterwards they and all other Popish forces then in conjunction with ours will joyne with the French and make as horrid a massacre as ever they can on all the Protestants they can finde, and while wee are in that confusion in these parts the Popish forces on the Rhine will doe the same.' The informant acknowledged, with a modicum of understatement, that this would seem 'strangely incredible upon the account that it is the interest of the Popish princes to see France brought within modester bounds, and that wee can hardly imagine that they should kill so many of one another, if they were not engaged in a state of reall hostility'. But that was a measure of the depth of the plot, designed 'to blind the eyes of the Protestants and to catch them the more secure asleep then the Prince of Orange did the justly discarded K[ing] James'.[37] If the English troops in Flanders were ever in mortal danger, wrote a whig pamphleteer in 1692, they would find the local population 'such bigotted Papists, as would rather cut the Throats of our English in such cases of distress, than afford them the least Succour'.[38]

For the most part, though, King William's subjects had little difficulty in reconciling themselves to the Habsburg alliance. True, Spain and Austria still had unsavoury reputations as persecutors of Protestants. But just as Stalin became the acceptable face of totalitarianism in a war against Hitler, so the Habsburgs were the acceptable face of popery in a war against Louis XIV. Certainly, in English minds King Louis had long since supplanted his Habsburg enemies as the very epitome of popish evil. With good reason. In 1682 the King of France's soldiers rampaged through the Protestant principality of Orange, Prince William's tiny patrimonial territory in southern France. Far worse came in 1685. After years of harrying his Protestant subjects, King Louis formally revoked the Edict of Nantes, the royal decree of 1598 which had supposedly guaranteed the religious liberties of French Protestants. The Huguenots fled in their thousands, most of them finding refuge in England and the Netherlands. Four years later, the French King's image as a popish tyrant was reinforced when his troops laid waste to the Palatinate, a largely Protestant territory in the Rhineland.[39]

The sufferings of the Huguenots and the Palatines, suitably embellished in the telling, were etched into the public consciousness. 'While good Princes are tender and mild,' observed a balladeer in 1689, King Louis 'rips up the Mother and stabs the Child.' And all in the name of his warped religion. 'Firing Cities', the balladeer continued,

> ... (Oh! that True Wit is)
>   It carries on the good Catholick Cause,
> To burn the Corn in the Field,
> Which to Babes Food should yield,
>   are not these lovely mild Roman Laws?[40]

Another ballad portrayed the French King, sunk deep in a drunken stupor, disturbed by the sight of

> ... an Army of Martyrs,
>   which he hath Murder'd by Fire and Sword;
> Men and Wives with both Sons & Daughters;
>   The Sight of which did much horrour afford:
> These Martyrs bore a Banner before,
>   now with this Inscription in a Protestant Gore,
> Lewis shall flye from France: for why?
>   the innocent Bloud do's for fearful Vengeance cry.

The ballad concludes with King Louis nervously awakening, and

> Saying, I fear my Ruine draws near,
>   For to me a Vision this night did appear,
> The Protestants they will advance,
>   And make their King William the Monarch of great France.[41]

Since King Louis was the champion of persecuting popery, his defeat would constitute a great triumph for the Protestants of Europe. It was readily acknowledged, however, that the humbling of the overmighty King of France would be a blessing to Christendom as a whole. For Louis XIV's boundless ambition had made him a threat to all the peoples of Europe, Protestant and Catholic alike. King William 'has not declared it a War of Religion,' wrote George Story, a veteran of the Irish campaign, 'but is linked in a Confederacy with a great many Princes of the Romish Church, that have all the same reason to dread the growing-Power of France, who neither spares Protestant when he has an opportunity, nor a Papist when he can gain by it.'[42] The Gloucestershire JP, Sir Richard Cocks, similarly stressed Louis XIV's universal menace: 'this war', he informed his county's Grand Jury in 1695, 'is for the defence and protection of the laws libertys customs and religion as well papist as protestant from the barbarous and avaricious tiranny and invasion of the French King.'[43] To another Gloucestershire gentleman, William Lawrence, the King of France was 'the hostis humani generis [the enemy of the human race]; who like the hawk is always in arms, and without distinction preys upon every thing that is weaker than he.'[44] Lawrence's views were echoed by John Hampden. 'The Enemy with whom we have to deal', he wrote in 1692,

> is the French King, who is not only our Enemy, but, in some sort, may be said to be the Enemy of Mankind. If there be any thing dear and valuable to Mankind, he has given the Example of tearing and ravishing it from them,

without the least pretence or colour of Justice; if there be any thing sacred and binding, if Contracts and Engagements have any Force or obliging Virtue, 'tis he that has grounded his whole Politicks upon infringing and trampling upon those sacred Ties, both with his own Subjects and Strangers. It has been the Design of his whole Life to establish in Europe what they call an Universal Monarchy; which may more properly be call'd, the enslaving of all Europe.[45]

Louis XIV's quest for the 'Universal Monarchy' of Christendom is a recurrent theme in the anti-French sentiment of the period, as it had been since the 1660s.[46] For one thing, it provided a convincing justification for the Habsburg alliance. Preaching to the army at Ghent in 1694, John Petter, a regimental chaplain, argued that the Protestant and Catholic powers had a mutual interest 'to adventure their distinct Power and Interest in one common bottom, and to hinder the obstinate pursuit of his [Louis XIV's] project of Universal Monarchy'.[47] King Louis' design 'was universal', averred the Irish cleric William King, 'and aimed at the destruction and enslaving all the Kingdoms and States of Europe: No distinction of Protestant or Papist, Enemy or Ally. All were equally devoted to destruction in it'. For the French King's grand aim was to advance to 'the universal Monarchy of the West', and to make himself 'as great and as pernicious to the Western Princes and States, as the Turk has been to the Eastern'.[48]

William King was not alone in comparing Louis XIV to the Turk. For centuries, the Kings of France had borne the honorific of 'Most Christian King'. But King Louis, quipped a balladeer in 1689, was now called 'Most Christian Turk', a more fitting title for 'A Tyrant great, as e'er was born'.[49] According to John Petter, the French King's actions showed

that he makes the Maxims of the common Enemy of Christendom the Rule and Measure of all his Actions, and that absolute Power at home, with the universal Empire abroad is his aim as well as the Turk's; and seeing that by these principles (which 'tis plain he hath taken up) all the duties of Christianity are laid in the dirt, it were difficult to determine, should absolute Conquest (which God forbid) attend his Arms, whether under French or Turk Christendom would obtain the fairest quarter.[50]

King Louis, averred George Story, 'has no other Prospect nor regard to Men and Things, but his own Greatness and Ambition; not sparing even those of his own Perswasion, when they stand in his way. Every one sees, that his Brother of Constantinople and he, agree much better than his Holy Father at Rome and he ever did, or are like to do; because the former is more favourable to his Designs than the other.'[51]

True enough. Louis XIV, the hammer of the Huguenots, might see himself as a loyal son of the true Church. But during the 1680s he had been at loggerheads with Rome more often than not, clashing with Pope Innocent XI over control of the French Church, the rights of the French

THE USURPERS HABIT

He begins to wrigg

How proudly Lewis sitts upon his Throne
Embroider'd o're with Towns were not his own
As Æsops Iay did from the feather'd Race
Snatch Plumes to look with more Majestick grace
But all the Birds affronted at the Thief
Ofs borrow'd feathers did him soon bereave

So that proud Monarch must his fate Deplore
And all his Thefts and conquests soon restore
Mons, Strasbourg, Nice, & Other Towns Hee Stole
Will follow Athlone, Limerick, Carmagnole
This mighty Work for William is Design'd
The Scourge of France, and Darling of Mankind

1. Strasbourg.	5. Suze.	9. Bauillon.	13. Maubeuge.	17. Dinant.	21. Ville Franche.
2. Carmagnole.	6. Cambray.	10. Lemerick.	14. Nice.	18. Galloway.	22. Philisbourg.
3. Athlone.	7. Slego.	11. Treuer.	15. Fribourg.	19. Orango.	23. Valenciennes.
4. Charlemont.	8. Landau.	12. Luxembourg.	16. Ipre.	20. Mons.	24. Philipville.
					25. The Crown.

Sold by I. Savage at ý Golden head, in ý Old Baily.

embassy in Rome and the election of the Archbishop-Elector of Cologne. By the Autumn of 1688, relations had sunk so low that King Louis was seriously contemplating an invasion of the Papal States. As a result, the French fleet spent that fateful Autumn in the Mediterranean when it might have been better used confronting the Dutch in the Channel. The wrangles between Rome and Versailles thus played a part in the demise of England's last Catholic monarch.[52] Not that Pope Innocent shed many tears for King James. On the contrary, the Pope tacitly supported the revolution which he saw, quite rightly, as a blow against the King of France.[53]

In contrast to his fraught relations with Rome, King Louis was on excellent terms with the Ottoman court, making common cause with Sultan Suleiman II against the Emperor Leopold. Indeed, the Sultan owed the French King a real debt of gratitude. After their defeat outside Vienna in 1683, the Turks had been driven from Hungary and the Serb lands by the Emperor. But in the Autumn of 1688, French aggression in Germany compelled Leopold to abandon his great offensive in the Balkans. The Sultan now took the initiative against depleted Imperial forces, driving them back towards the Hungarian frontier.[54] Thus the affinity between the two great enemies of Christendom went far beyond a common world-view. 'With Mahomet, I am Brother sworn, / 'Gainst Christendom and Popery', declares King Louis in a ballad of 1689.[55] To James Smalwood, chaplain of Ormonde's regiment, Louis XIV's greatest crime was 'his entring into a League Offensive and Defensive with the Turk, at a time too when that Empire was in its Declination'.[56] In 1690 a pamphleteer claimed that the Confederate powers were, in part, fighting to punish the French King's 'Impiety, in calling into Europe the much-more-Christian Turk'.[57] So it was entirely appropriate that in Nicholas Rowe's play *Tamerlane*, written towards the end of King William's reign, Louis XIV should appear in the guise of the fourteenth-century Ottoman Sultan Bayazit, a man

> . . . Proud, impatient,
> Of Ought Superior, ev'n of Heav'n, that made him.
> Fond of false Glory, of the Savage Pow'r
> Of ruling without Reason, of confounding
> Just, and Unjust, by an Unbounded Will;
> By whom Religion, Honour, all the Bands,
> That ought to hold the jarring World in Peace,
> Were held the Tricks of State, Snares of wise Princes,
> To draw their Easy Neighbour to destruction.[58]

Figure 8 'The Usurpers Habit', a satire on Louis XIV, 1691. To Englishmen, the French King was both the epitome of popish evil and 'the Enemy of Mankind', a ruthless tyrant thirsting for the 'Universal Monarchy' of Christendom. In this print, King Louis wears a suit of clothes representing the towns seized by him since the 1660s. He removes his hat – the Irish town of Limerick, recaptured by Williamite forces in 1691 – prompting the gleeful observation, 'He begins to unrigg.'

While the war was often portrayed as a struggle to free all Europe from the clutches of a devouring tyrant, it could also be seen in a more parochial light, an opportunity to renew England's ancient enmity with France. In December 1688 a poetaster, anticipating the outbreak of hostilities, recalled the glories of the Hundred Years War:

> The terrour still of our Third Edward's Name,
> Rebukes their Pride, and damps their swelling Fame,
> Nor can the Tide of many rowling years,
> Wash the stain'd Fields of Cressy and Poictiers,
> A Conscious terrour strikes their Bosoms still,
> When they behold that famous fatal Hill,
> Where Edward with his Host Spectator stood,
> And left the PRINCE to make the Conquest good.
> Nor has the black Remembrance left their Brest,
> How our Fifth Harry to their Paris prest,
> While France wept Blood for their hot Dauphin's Jest.[59]

Five years later, at a low point in the war, a balladeer invoked the spirit of the past to spur his countrymen on to greater efforts in the present:

> 'Tis Edward the Black Prince, and Henry doth call,
> Brave Talbot and Clifford, stout Nevill and all,
> 'Tis Cressy and Poitiers, nay, Ag-in-court too,
> That know if you may all them outdo,
> Why will you be then thus in sluggishness lost,
> When bravely attempting you may gain the post?

The songster concluded with a patriotic exhortation:

> Now if you have more than the heart of a hen,
> What your ancestors have done you may do agen:
> Then play the man briskly, let it not be said,
> That Lewis or James e'er can make you afraid,
> Let them mumble and grumble, you may tread such a dance,
> As bravely shall lead to the conquest of France.[60]

Such florid triumphalism brought forth a scornful response from the author of *An Honest Commoner's Speech*, a pamphlet written late in 1691. 'Conquering of France, which some hot heads dream of, is not our business, if it were in our power, and therefore must be the passions of fools and the hopes of women.' As the pamphleteer explained, Edward III and Henry V had 'rather showed France and the world what they could do, than what they could keep; and made the experiment at the expense of that blood and treasure that we were the worse for our glory, even while we could maintain it: But that failed us also at length, and we ever lost all back again, with more dishonour than we got it with reputation'. What was more, the France of Louis XIV was incomparably stronger than the enfeebled state which England's warrior kings had fought centuries earlier.

Instead of pursuing the chimerical conquest of France, the national war effort should be confined to the sea. 'Our part is little more than defensive, scour the coast and you secure the island and the trade, which is the life of it.'[61]

The *Honest Commoner's* call for a 'blue-water' strategy was echoed by other writers, although they usually visualized it in rather more aggressive terms. Thus one pamphleteer argued in 1692 that England should seek to ruin Louis XIV 'in his West-Indian Trade, and cut him off his Sea-Men; To shut up his Commerce Northwards, thro[ugh] our own Seas; To spoil him (as might be) some of his chief Harbours and Sea-Port Towns; destroy the rest of his Ships of force, and ruin his Trading, even in the Mediterranean'.[62] Such a campaign, wrote the author of another 1692 tract, *An Impartial Inquiry*,

> had been a perpetual Spring to supply our Expences; the Monys had return'd as it were in a Circle, unto the Gentlemen, Tradesmen, and Mariners, because the Beef, the Pork, the Bread, the Pease, the very Clothing of the Seamen had been of our Growth and Manufacture; and the more Ships had been equipp'd for Sea, the more had Trade and the Price of our Commodities been advanced, and our Force had been increas'd by using it, in regard more of our laborious Youth would have apply'd themselves to the Sea-Affairs upon such Encouragement; and increase of their Numbers would naturally and necessarily have promoted Trade and Power, and made all the Nations court our Friendship.

But, alas, the King had instead embarked upon a ruinous campaign in Flanders which 'must exhaust his own Kingdom's Mony to maintain his Troops abroad'.[63] The result of the Flanders strategy, lamented another writer, was 'the exhausting of the Wealth, the Stock of the Nation, in the vast Sums drawn out from thence, for the Use of Foreign Countries, and the numerous Troops paid in those Countries: And at the same time that our Sustinence goes out, it is hindred [by the French] from coming in to us'.[64] Nor was it easy to see what England could possibly gain from the Flanders campaign. 'I have often ask'd the most knowing Men I meet with,' wrote the author of *An Impartial Inquiry*,

> what benefit our king or kingdom could expect from this mighty War in Flanders, if it should succeed beyond most Mens hopes? And the Answer I could ever get, hath been no more, than that we should weaken the Power of France. But I was bold to pursue my question, and ask, Whether we thought to beat him in Flanders, that he should give up his Fleet and Naval Store to pacify us; or whether we hope this Summer or the next, to gain his Frontier Cities and Garrisons, which it hath cost him near thirty years to compleat, and many Millions to fortify? Or was it design'd to gain part of his Country from him, for the English to inhabit; or to over-run his whole Kingdom and possess the Crown of France, and to plant the Protestant Religion there by the Hermaphrodite Swords of Papists and Protestants?[65]

Running through these attacks upon the land war is a vein of violent whiggery. The *Honest Commoner* was fearful of the large army that a Continental campaign required. 'I cannot forget that I have read Caesar's story, what he did with his victorious army when he returned home, and have seen something to the same purpose in our own Country [under Cromwell].' The writer further revealed his republican sympathies by lauding the cheap and efficient war management of the Rump Parliament.[66] So pernicious was the Flanders strategy, believed the author of the *Impartial Inquiry*, that it could only be a contrivance of the King's evil counsellors – tories, of course. By dissipating the nation's strength in futile land war, these secret traitors hoped to pave the way for King James's restoration.[67] But hostility to a heavy land commitment was by no means the preserve of undiluted whiggery. As we shall see later, many tory politicians were also thoroughly alarmed by England's growing entanglement on the Continent.[68]

Compounding concerns over war strategy was the conviction that England was bearing a disproportionate share of the Confederacy's war effort. 'The army the king asks is for the continent, and not an island, and what have we to do there?' asked the *Honest Commoner*. 'Is not our quota enough? Are any but the Dutch concerned in the charge at sea? And of that do we not bear a double share? Besides, have any of the confederacy assisted us in the reducing of Ireland? Let us', he concluded, 'observe proportion.'[69] In 1692 John Hampden indignantly asserted that 'we suffer our Allies, and all the World, to carry on a lucrative Trade with France, while we our selves are forc'd to bear almost the whole Burden of the War, and are thus shamefully made the Cullies of the Confederacy.'[70] Such views were also aired in the Commons, notably by the chief spokesmen of the Commission of Accounts, the tory Sir Thomas Clarges and the whig Paul Foley. 'England bears almost the charge of the war and others reap the benefit of it', Foley told MPs on 26 November 1692.[71] On 6 December Foley joined Clarges in condemning the subsidies granted to foreign princes.[72] Three days later, Clarges renewed the attack upon the subsidies. He also took a swipe at the Dutch. 'I cannot but take notice that though we were drawn into this war by the Dutch – they being the principals – yet we must bear a greater share of the burden.' This sorry state of affairs he attributed to excessive Dutch influence in the conduct of the war.[73] In December 1693, when the Court sought supply for over 90,000 soldiers, Sir Christopher Musgrave similarly smelt a Dutch rat. 'One would think that this was Dutch Counsel', he commented, 'else we should never be put to contribute at this rate, to ruin England to preserve Flanders.'[74]

The anti-Dutch gripes of Clarges and Musgrave may well have been rooted in their toryism. Although whigs resented the King's predilection for Dutch counsellors and generals just as much as tories, the Church party's prejudice against the United Provinces – a state bereft of bishops as well as kings – generally ran deeper. As the Marquis of Halifax had observed in 1689, the Church party 'hated the Dutch'.[75] This was no great exaggeration. Sir Edward Seymour's reported comment in December 1689 – 'that all our trade and riches were carried to Amsterdam, and that in exchange we were likely to bring from thence nothing but their religion' – was a typically bilious expression of tory disdain for the Dutch.[76] And as the war dragged on interminably to England's cost, tory resentment of the Dutch grew apace. When a correspondent of the Derbyshire tory, Thomas Coke, wrote in July 1696 that 'I am sure you Cannot have a Worse Opinion of the Devills Children then I & all English men Ought to have', he was referring to the Dutch, not the French.[77]

All this would have been music to Jacobite ears. It had long been a stock theme of Jacobite propaganda that 'this war, and all the charges we have been at, was purely for the Dutch.'[78] The pretences of the revolution were, in fact, but 'a flat Cheat of the Dutch, and other Confederates, to gull silly England, at the expence of their Blood and Treasure to maintain *their* War'.[79] This bare conspiracy theory was embroidered by the disaffected Scottish whig, Sir James Montgomery. The Confederate powers, he claimed in 1692, had 'wanted our money and our troops to carry on their several pretences'. To this end, they had helped to engineer the overthrow of King James, whom they knew to be 'a good husband of his treasure, and they were afraid would never be induced to part with any of it to them, but for equivalent returns of glory and profit to the nation'. The Prince of Orange, in contrast, 'had a weak side, which might be better wrought upon'. As Montgomery explained, Prince William's 'towering ambition, and vast unlimited desires after command and a noisy fame, exposed him continually to the bait they designed him, which was to pay him in airy titles, empty compliments, and feigned pretences of service and obsequiousness, for our good English gold and brave English troops. The plot hath succeeded,' Montgomery sadly concluded, 'and we paid them very handsomely for the trick they put upon us.'[80] The octogenarian nonjuror Sir John Bramston subscribed to a similar, if rather less vitriolic, interpretation of the revolution. 'It is evident now,' he wrote in 1690, 'and hath longe been so in my thoughts, that the whole confederate Princes made it theire business to disjoyne England from France, which could not be effected whilst Charles II or James II were on the throne, unless James could be brought to it by force, and the Prince [of Orange] had a good colour to use force to prevent his wife's disinherison and his owne.'[81]

As conspiracy theories go, the Jacobite interpretation of the revolution has more to recommend it than most. The Dutch invasion was indeed designed to remove England from the French orbit, and bring its resources to bear against Louis XIV. Not for nothing, then, did Jacobites castigate the Dutch as the chief orchestrators of the foreign conspiracy against England. But Jacobite writers embellished their tale by positing a further contrivance on the part of the Dutch: a fiendish plot to deprive England of her commerce. According to this theory, the Dutch, a godless and avaricious people, had feared that King James's policies would enable England to challenge their mercantile hegemony. 'Tis certain', acknowledges the 'Dutch ambassador' in a Jacobite piece of 1690, that

> England had robbed us of our trade in the two last kings' reigns, who by an unlucky neutrality had made the stream of traffick run that way. 'Tis certain also that the late King James was taking most mischievous measures to continue and augment their trade, and ruin ours; for if the liberty of conscience, which he was going to establish, had not been prevented, the most considerable of our merchants (who live amongst us because they are not molested in the free exercise of their religion) would have removed, and drawn their effects to England, where the ports being more secure, they would, without hazarding their religion, have run less danger of their goods. 'Tis manifest also, and foreseen by our wise men, that (whilst it was impossible for us to stave off a war with France) K[ing] James, whose industry and application to the advancement of trade made him embrace all occasions to encourage it, would have preserved a neutrality to our utter ruin. These, and many other considerations, (as I affirm,) made us willing to pluck the thorn out of our own foot and put it into another's; and therefore, after much consultation, nothing was found so expedient as to heighten the divisons in England, and join with the mal-contents.[82]

Another Jacobite tract attributed King James's sufferings to 'the sensibleness the Dutch had, that the king, by his granting liberty of conscience, and providing such naval and military stores, had a design to promote the traffick of his subjects, and oblige the Dutch to a juster and more equitable regulation of trade, than any of our kings could hitherto obtain. This gauled them in the sensible part,' the writer concluded, 'and they well knew they must either embarrass him at home, or they must forgo their cursed treacherous art in circumventing our trade.'[83]

This theme was taken up with gusto by the Catholic controversialist, John Sergeant. In his *Historical Romance of the Wars, Between the Mighty Giant Gallieno, and the Great Knight Nasonius*, the Dutch Republic is portrayed as a cunning and rapacious sea-Hydra, while King William appears in the guise of the 'Hydra-holder', Nasonius. The ruthlessly ambitious Nasonius covets the throne of his father-in-law, the pacific King Eugenius of Utopia. To further his ambitions, he seeks the assistance of the Hydra, reminding the monster 'how averse my father Eugenius is to joyn with the associates [in their war against Gallieno/Louis XIV], being resolv'd by preserving a Neutrality, and keeping his Country in Peace to advance the Trade and Riches of his Kingdoms, which with his giving Freedom from Persecution to tender Consciences, will bring the Traffick to them, and half ruin us'.[84]

Taking fright at this prospect, the Hydra promises to support Nasonius in his attempt on the Utopian throne. They negotiate a treaty, one clause of which provides

> That in regard Utopia is the only Competitor in Trade with the Noble Hydra, he [Nasonius] should do his utmost to advance the Hydropick Interest, and depress the Utopian, by denying them Convoys, though of their own Ships, as also to take Care that no Utopian should trade privately with Luyslandia [France]: But yet that he should connive at the Hydr[o]picks doing the same, which would impoverish Utopia, and enrich the Hydra: Than which nothing can be more grateful to their powerful patroness, the Goddess Mammoneta.[85]

The 'Hydra-holder' had kept his side of the bargain. Not only had King William made his new subjects pay for the privilege of being invaded – in 1689 parliament voted the Dutch £600,000 to reimburse them for the expenses of their expedition – he had also succeeded in running England's foreign trade into the ground, gaining for his countrymen through chicanery all they had failed to achieve by force in the three Anglo-Dutch naval wars of 1652–74. Thus in a tract of 1690, a Jacobite hack has the 'Dutch ambassador' laud King William for having procured for the Netherlands

> a long wished for liberty at sea, freed his Native country from the greatest obstacles to their trade, suppressed those who have always been the objects of our envy, rendered them for ever uncapable of standing in competition with us, diverted the channel of traffick to our own merchants, and all this in one year's time, without any charge to us; nay, on the contrary, with a considerable reward from our adversaries for their own destruction.[86]

Three years later, the execution speech of a Jacobite 'martyr' asserted that 'Under the Notion and necessity of a War They [the Dutch] deliver us from our Money, and from our Foreign Traffick and Commerce by which so great a part of the Nation is sustained.'[87] So the upshot of King William's war was the visible impoverishment of the English people: 'what a dismal sight it is', lamented Nathaniel Johnston in 1690,

> to behold the perishing state of such an infinite number of men, women, and children, in almost all counties of England, such as spinners, carders, weavers, &c., employed about the woollen manufactures; such as miners, and other labourers, in the lead, tin, alome, and iron works, who are now turned off, or so abated in their wages, that they are forced to beg, steal, or rob, for the subsistence of themselves and their families, to the continual terror of their neighbours who have any thing to lose, and to the cramming of jails with the carcasses of so many wretched criminals, who were before useful and necessary for the prosperity of the nation.[88]

Here the Jacobites were ploughing fertile soil. For it did not require great powers of perception to discern that the very real hardships of the 1690s

were a direct consequence of the war. 'Alas,' went the plaintive lines of a
balladeer in 1692,

> ... too well, we understand
>   what causes all our grief and care,
> It is the Wars by Sea and Land,
>   Alas, Alas, who can forbear,
> In these hard times, to sigh and weep,
>   There's nought but poor mens labour cheap.[89]

2. The Fortunes of War, 1689–95

By May 1689 William of Orange had achieved his ambition of drawing
England's human and material resources into the great struggle against
Louis XIV. These he hoped to concentrate on a direct confrontation with
the French in Flanders, the buffer territory between France and the United
Provinces held by King William's ally, the King of Spain. But in the early
years of the war, much to the King's chagrin, the side-show campaign in
Ireland forced a dispersal of the war effort. The campaign of 1689 having
ended in stalemate, King William took personal command of the forces in
Ireland the following year. On 14 June 1690, at the head of 15,000 reinforcements, the King landed in Ulster. Determined to bring the war in
Ireland to a swift conclusion, he promptly marched his troops south to seek
out King James and his army.[90]

The mid-Summer of 1690 produced the first real crisis of the war in more
ways than one. On 21 June/1 July the French general Luxembourg
defeated the allied forces at Fleurus in Flanders.[91] A few days later, the allies
suffered a still more serious reverse in the Channel. Hampered by
conflicting intelligence reports, and saddled with inflexible orders, the Earl
of Torrington, commanding the Anglo-Dutch fleet, fell in with a superior
French fleet off Beachy Head on 30 June. After several hours of unequal
fighting, Torrington prudently withdrew his fleet to the mouth of the
Thames. It was a move which saved the fleet from destruction, but at the
cost of surrendering the Channel to the French.[92]

The news of Torrington's defeat was greeted with consternation in
England. The French, it was assumed, would take advantage of their
victory by staging a major landing on the south coast. Alternatively, the
Gallic fleet might sweep into the Irish Sea, cutting off King William's line
of retreat. In the event, the French were unable to exploit their success.
King William's victory at the Boyne on 1 July led to the abandonment of
French plans to attack the line of communications between Ireland and
England. Nor was King Louis ready to launch an invasion of England.
Although the French fleet cruised up and down the Channel for some

weeks, its only aggressive action was a raid on the small Devon port of Teignmouth.[93] Nearly two years were to pass before the French King seriously turned his thoughts to the invasion of England.

In the Spring of 1692 a major invasion force was prepared in the French Channel ports. But this time it was Louis XIV's battle fleet which found itself outnumbered and outmatched. In a series of hard-fought engagements off Barfleur and La Hogue in May, the rejuvenated Anglo-Dutch fleet, now commanded by Admiral Edward Russell, inflicted a heavy defeat on its French counterpart.[94] With the French fleet defeated, the English government hoped to turn the tables on King Louis completely by launching a 'descent' upon the French coast. Although the plans for the operation had been drawn up before Barfleur, the 'descent' proved a good deal easier in theory than practice. After months of delay, logistical problems, compounded by Admiral Russell's reluctance to risk his ships on a treacherous coast, caused the 'descent' to be abandoned amid a welter of acrimony.[95] As Queen Mary lamented, 'all the expence was thrown away,

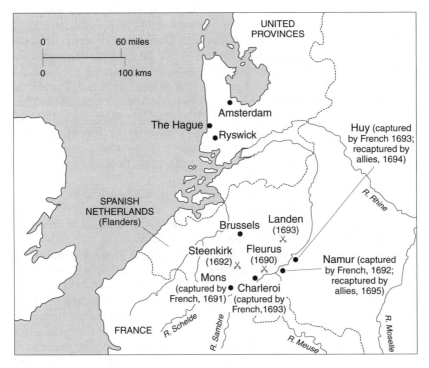

Map 2   The Low Countries during King William's War (1689–97)

the troops came back as they went, having made us ridicoulous to all the world by our great preparations to no purpose.'[96]

Like his consort, King William was exasperated by the incompetence which plagued the 'descent' of 1692.[97] Nevertheless, he did not greatly mourn its abandonment. For the most part, King William viewed the 'descent' concept as a strategic irrelevance, a mere sop to the prejudices of his English subjects.[98] It was the King's unwavering conviction that the crucible of war lay in Flanders. There the campaign of 1691 had gone badly. In April, as the allies discussed war plans at The Hague, the French captured Mons, the greatest fortress in the Spanish Netherlands.[99] The next year, following the successful completion of the Irish campaign, King William was at last able to concentrate England's resources in the Flemish theatre of operations. By 1692 there were over 40,000 troops in English pay in Flanders.[100] Yet this new concentration of effort failed to turn the tide. At the end of June, the French captured the frontier fortress of Namur. Stung by this fresh setback, King William decided to risk a general engagement with Luxembourg. On 23 July/3 August, he launched an attack on the French encampment at Steenkirk. It was bloodily repulsed, with the English and Scots troops bearing the brunt of the losses.[101]

During the course of the 1692 campaign, deep misgivings about the King's strategy emerged within the highest reaches of his administration. In July Secretary of State Nottingham urged that the 'descent' be given priority over the campaign in Flanders. While Nottingham accepted the need to defend Flanders, he saw little prospect of gaining a conclusive victory in that heavily-fortified province. A major landing in France, on the other hand, promised to strike a decisive blow against Louis XIV. This, Nottingham deemed to be imperative. If the Flanders stalemate continued, he warned the Earl of Portland, 'I may venture to foretell that the Parliament will not be induced to maintain an army abroad, nor with so vast an arrear and the necessary expence of a great fleet will they be able to find money if they would.'[102]

After Steenkirk, the Secretary of State's pessimism appears to have infected the rest of the Cabinet, the group of ministers appointed to assist Queen Mary during the King's absence. At the end of August, Nottingham informed William Blathwayt, the Secretary at War, of his colleagues' conviction that 'Parliament will find it very difficult, if not impossible, to raise upon any fonds so great a summe as was this year apply'd to the war, tho' they should be willing and desirous so to doe.' At most, MPs might be persuaded to vote £2,700,000, a sum that would be of little avail to King William. For it was the Cabinet's view 'that if the Parliament should be induced to give this summe, as it would not be sufficient to maintaine the fleet and so great an army as is now in pay, so they will not be perswaded to apply the money to the payment of an army in Flanders because the exportation of so great summes would drain the kingdom of the current coyn, of which there is already great want'.[103] Scarcely more comforting to King William was an analysis of parliamentary feeling proffered by another leading minister, Lord President Carmarthen. Most MPs, he wrote to the King in September, would come to see the necessity of maintaining the army at its present strength. But, like his colleagues, Carmarthen believed that parliament would question the army's continued deployment in Flanders. An attack on France recommended itself to country gentlemen, since the army could either live off the land or be provisioned directly from England. In contrast, supplies for the troops in Flanders were purchased from the local population, necessitating the export of vast sums of money from England. Thus the Flanders campaign was draining the nation of its specie, a phenomenon which MPs liked even less than high taxes.[104]

Sure enough, the Flanders strategy came under heavy fire when parliament met in November. 'We ought to have applied ourselves by sea and attacked them there,' declared Sir Thomas Clarges during the debate on the King's speech, 'to have burned his ships if possible so to have weakened him there, whereby we should have done ourselves the best service, and not to have gone into Flanders to attack him where he is strongest.'[105] On 3 December, when the Commons debated the army estimates, Clarges returned to the attack. 'The security of this nation with our interest', he insisted, 'lies in having a good fleet at sea and, if we can, to destroy that of our enemies, and not to send armies abroad which will drain the nation both of our people and our money, too.' Clarges coupled this assertion with his customary swipe at England's allies. 'I know it is a received opinion with the Dutch and the Germans that England is an inexhaustible fountain, but if you go on at the rate you have I am afraid you will quickly be drawn dry.'[106]

Sir Thomas Clarges had long been in the van of those critical of the Confederacy's contribution to the war effort. In contrast, the government placeman Sir John Lowther was anxious not to offend England's allies. Yet, like Clarges, he could see little good coming from the Flanders campaign. 'As to the war in Flanders', he confided to the House on 3 December, 'I do think we can do nothing in it; it is running our heads against a wall.'[107] A fortnight earlier, in the debate on the King's speech, Colonel Thomas Sackville had similarly denounced the futility of the 'pernicious' war in Flanders. 'The French have so many strong garrisons, there are so many rivers and passes, that [it] is almost impossible to do anything with the French there to our advantage. And though we could perhaps gain a town or two there, what benefit is it to us? It will put us to a greater expense and not compensate the charge of our men.'[108]

Not all MPs were quite so dismissive of the Flanders strategy. On 3 December Goodwin Wharton urged the Commons to 'Consider with yourself; if he [Louis XIV] swallows Flanders Holland must follow, and if

France be once master of Holland pray think what will become of you. Will your fleet alone be able to deal with that of France and Holland, too, for that will be the consequence.'[109] In the same debate, Sir Richard Temple put the case for the Flanders campaign rather more pithily. 'I am for the whole number [of troops requested]', he told MPs, 'because I had rather we should fight for Flanders than for England.'[110] Temple seems to have spoken for the majority of the House, for the Commons confounded expectations by approving supply for an army of 54,000 men. In all, more than £4,000,000 were voted by MPs for the supply of the Crown.[111]

The votes of supply in December 1692 showed that most MPs were ready to give King William the benefit of the doubt. Assured that one more big effort would settle all scores with the French King, parliamentarians once again loosened the nation's purse-strings. But far from securing a victorious conclusion to the war, the campaigns of 1693 marked the nadir of England's fortunes. In July Marshal Luxembourg inflicted another sharp defeat upon King William at Landen in Flanders. The French followed up their success by capturing Charleroi, another of the great frontier fortresses, at the beginning of October.[112] Nor was the war at sea progressing any better. In April an attack upon the French Caribbean island of Martinique ended in fiasco.[113] Two months later, the wealthy Smyrna merchant convoy fell foul of the main French battle fleet off the coast of Portugal. Despite the presence of an escorting Royal Navy squadron, the French succeeded in capturing or destroying the greater part of the merchant fleet.[114]

The loss of the Smyrna fleet was the worst of a series of disasters which overwhelmed England's international trade in the early years of the war. The transfer of human and material resources from the merchant marine to the Royal Navy; the loss of many ships to the elements because of unseasonable sailings; and, not least, the depredations of French privateers, all contributed to the collapse of England's overseas trade. The figures, for once, eloquently tell the story. By 1693–4 English exports to the Iberian Peninsula, the Canaries and the Mediterranean region had fallen by 25 per cent of their 1686 levels. The figures for the re-export of extra-European goods were worse still. After five years of war, re-exports to north-west Europe were 60 per cent lower than the figure recorded in 1686.[115] Colonial merchants were hit particularly hard. In 1694–5, for example, the Jamaica merchants lost cargoes worth over £68,000; the New England merchants suffered losses to the tune of £114,000; the Leeward Islands traders lost £138,000 worth of cargoes; and the Barbados merchants lost cargoes worth a shattering £387,000. The losses in shipping suffered by Bristol, chief home port of the colonial trade, make similarly grim reading. By 1695 Bristol had lost some 200 ships to the French.[116]

The misfortunes which befell the merchant fleet provoked indignation in England. As early as November 1689, the Commons resolved that 'the want of a Guard, or Convoys, for the Merchants, for the last Year, hath been an obstruction of Trade, and an occasion of great losses to the Nation.'[117] But, alas, trade could not be protected by parliamentary resolutions. After the Spring of 1692, when the French concentrated their naval effort on commerce-raiding, the losses of English merchantmen reached a new high. As Bishop Burnet noted in 1692, 'our Merchant-men suffered extreamly this Summer, for the French not being able to make head against us [in battle], suffered their Seamen to go into Privateers, with which the seas were covered.'[118] That same year, John Hampden lamented the collapse of England's overseas trade. 'Our Merchants', he wrote, 'are ruin'd by the loss of their Ships and Goods, and their best Opportunities of Trade are lost for want of Convoys. Our Seas and Coasts are not defended, and our Natives are forc'd to have recourse to Foreigners to guard and convoy their Ships, who carry away the Mony that should be earn'd and kept in England by our English Seamen.'[119] Hampden's fellow whig, the MP John Smith, similarly deprecated the Navy's failure to protect English commerce: 'for the taking so many merchant ships', he told the Commons in November 1692, 'the reason thereof is for want of cruisers at the mouth of your Channel to guard your merchants.'[120]

In truth, the manifold demands of war were stretching the Royal Navy's resources to breaking-point. As the Admiralty itself recognized, there were simply 'not ships enough, both to furnish-out a great [battle] fleet, and at the same time to send Convoys for securing the Trade'.[121] Nor did parliamentary legislation do much to ease the situation. Although an Act of 1693 required 43 men of war to be set aside for trade-protection, this figure was never achieved.[122] Not surprisingly, then, the French continued to take a heavy toll of the hapless English merchant marine. In the late Summer of 1695, for example, five richly-laden East Indiamen were captured by the French in the Western Approaches. The loss to the East India Company of just two of these vessels was put at a colossal £1.5m.[123]

The continuing depredations of French commerce-raiders caused more gnashing of teeth in England. 'The losses of this sort to the Nation has been immense', complained John Evelyn after the capture of the East Indiamen, '& all thro[ugh] the negligence & little care of the Government, to secure the same neere our own Coasts, of infinite more concernment to the publique than spending their time in bombing & ruining two or three paltry Towns [on the French coast].'[124] James Whiston, a writer on mercantile affairs, was rendered positively apoplectic by the insolence of the French privateers. 'Can we pretend to have English Blood in our Veins,' he wrote in 1696,

> and suffer the Insulting Monsieur to Ravish our Darling Mistress under our very Noses! To Commit a Rape upon our Trade in our own Channel, and on our own Coast? Have our Fore-Fathers with Expence of their blood and

almost insupportable Toyl past through an Ocean of hazards to Establish our Title, and Assert the English right to the Seas, to extend our Trade and Commerce beyond our Plantations, and join'd the most distant parts of the World in a Correspondence with us? Have they done thus much for us, and shall we disparage their Labours, and Reproach our selves by a Stupid and Supine Negligence?[125]

Although the Royal Navy had swept the French fleet from the seas, observed the Bristolian John Cary in 1695, '[we] do now suffer more loss in our Navigation than formerly we did'. For the French 'are come to a new way of fighting, they set out no Fleet, but their Privateers swarm and cover the Sea like Locusts, they hang on our Trade like Horse-Leeches, and draw from it more Blood than it is well able to spare, whilst we still go on as we did, without new Methods to countermine them.'[126]

This sorry state of affairs Cary attributed to the mishandling of matters mercantile by amateurs. 'I confess for my own part', wrote Cary,

> I value nothing that cannot be reduced to a certainty in its practice, things seem difficult to those who do not understand them, if we are to Besiege a Town we make use of Soldiers, if to storm a Castle, Engineers, if to build a Ship, Carpenters, and so in lesser things, and yet Gentlemen are thought fit to sit at the Helm, and steer the Ship wherein is Embarqu'd the Treasure of our Trade, who are altogether unskilled therein, on whose good Conduct the Nation's Weale or Woe depends; Thus things do fall into Confusion, whilst Men undertake what they do not understand, and set the Nation in a flame, whilst they injudiciously guide the Chariot of the Sun.

But if 'Heads well verst in Trade were set at work, Methods might be thought on to secure all with little Charge to the Government, and hereby the Kingdom might flourish'.[127] Thus Cary called for the establishment of a 'standing Committee of Trade' which would supervise all matters relating to commerce.[128] James Whiston advocated a similar panacea for England's mercantile ills. The management of the nation's trade should be placed wholly in the hands of a committee, established by statute and answerable to the legislature, but whose members were to be elected by the principal London trading interests.[129] With the management of the nation's trade in the hands of experts, England would have little difficulty in sustaining its war effort. For

> besides the Impoverishing and consequently weakning of France, by Their care of Securing our Navigation from the French Rapine, &c. They will likewise be able so far to Improve our present Trade, That our Additional Advantages thereby Gain'd to the Nation, shall more than pay for the War to the Easing of the greatest part of our Burthen, and thereby the Chearing our Cause, and Edging our Swords.[130]

Indeed, thanks to the skilful management of the Committee of Trade the 'General Inconveniencies' of the war 'would hardly be felt, and that which to others is an Impoverishment and Calamity, would to us be an Augmentation of Riches and Security'.[131]

In the winter of 1695–6 the agitation for the establishment of a council of trade reached the Palace of Westminster. A bill to establish such a council – its membership to be nominated by parliament – was introduced in the Commons. Sensing a challenge to his prerogative, King William drew up a warrant for his own trade committee. MPs were unimpressed. The King's committee, they feared, would be a mere talking shop, and so the Commons pressed on with their own measure. A clash seemed inevitable until the revelation of the Assassination Plot caused a general closing of Williamite ranks. The Commons bill was gently laid to rest, and in May the King established his own Board of Trade.[132] King William's Board was not quite the executive body that some writers and MPs had in mind, but it did go some way towards propitiating the anger caused by the collapse of England's trade.[133]

Although King William had made a gesture towards the commercial sensibilities of his subjects, the protection of trade still took a poor second place to the Flanders campaign in his strategic priorities. Needless to say, however, the King's defeat at Landen in July 1693 had done nothing to win over opponents of his strategy. In October 1693, a few weeks before the opening of the new parliamentary session, the tory ministers once more warned King William that the Commons was unlikely to vote further supply for the war. Since the King was determined to carry on the war at all costs, this gloomy prognosis forced him to reshuffle his ministerial pack. In early November King William dismissed his Secretary of State, the tory Earl of Nottingham. It was a move which signalled the King's intention to throw in his lot with the whigs.[134]

King William's swing to the whigs brought him immediate dividends. Far from refusing further supply, the Commons voted the unprecedented sum of £5,000,000 in the session of 1693–4. What was more, despite the murmurings of some MPs, the House agreed to augment the army by 20,000 men.[135] In the following year, the Court had little difficulty in obtaining another lavish vote of supply for the army in Flanders.[136]

The facility with which whig ministers gained supply for the army in 1693–5 should not lead us to think that their party whole-heartedly supported the King's Flanders strategy. Both within and without parliament, disquiet with the Flanders campaign had been fuelled by four factors: antipathy towards the large army which a heavy Continental commitment required; anxiety that the Flanders campaign was draining the nation of its specie; the belief that a war in Flanders was unwinnable; and the conviction that England's human and material resources were being sacrificed upon the altar of Dutch self-interest. Dyspeptic attacks upon the Netherlands – though not resentment of the King's Dutch favourites and military commanders – are chiefly to be associated with

High Church toryism.[137] It would be misleading, however, to identify any of the other anxieties with one party or the other.[138] What really distinguished whig parliamentarians from their tory counterparts was not zeal for the Flanders campaign, but rather a strong desire to maintain whig pre-eminence at home, and, we may surmise, a more general and deeper commitment to the defence of the Protestant cause abroad. If both were dependent upon supporting the King's strategy, then whig politicians would continue to support the campaign in Flanders, albeit with no great enthusiasm.

In the session of 1694–5, parliament's generosity towards the King was also lubricated by some long overdue military success. In March 1694 John Evelyn could justly complain of 'Unreasonable Taxes & Impositions layed on us by the Parliament to maintaine an hithertoo successles War with France, managed hitherto with so little discretion'.[139] But apart from a disastrous English raid on Brest in June, the year 1694 bore witness to a marked upturn in allied fortunes. In particular, the capture of the Flemish town of Huy went some way towards reversing the gains made by the French in the 1693 campaign.[140] The following year, fortified by plentiful supplies of ready cash thanks to the foundation of the Bank of England, King William resumed his offensive against weakened French forces. His reward was the recapture of Namur after a two-month siege on 26 August/ 5 September 1695.[141]

These years of allied success in Flanders also saw the Royal Navy take the offensive in the Mediterranean. In the summer of 1694, Admiral Russell was despatched to the south with the English main fleet and a Dutch squadron. The arrival of Russell's force in July compelled the French fleet to lift its blockade of Barcelona, and sent it scuttling back to its base at Toulon.[142] Having taken the unprecedented step of wintering at Cadiz, Russell's fleet re-entered the Mediterranean unchallenged in May 1695.[143] The western end of the Mediterranean had become, albeit temporarily, an English sea.

By 1695, with the French on the defensive on all fronts, some of the tension had gone out of the war. 'These warrs', observed the Lincolnshire clergyman Abraham de la Pryme in August 1695,

> went very hard the two or three first years after that the king came in, and there were general complaints about the heaviness of taxes, and everybody was anctious about the affairs of state, and full of cares, and doubts, and fears. But now the nation haveing become used to the taxes there is none that either now complains or that troubles them about the state affairs; the whole country being now in as much peace as if there were neither any taxes nor any warrs.[144]

Yet things were not as rosy as they seemed. As we shall see later, the next year was to prove the most difficult and dangerous of the whole war.

Figure 9   The siege
of Namur, 1695.
The recapture of the
fortress in August/
September 1695 was
King William's
greatest success of the
war. This Dutch
print illustrates two
factors which made
it difficult for either
side to land a knock-
out blow in
Flanders: sophisti-
cated fortifications
and numerous
waterways.

3. The Sinews of War, 1689–95

King William's war, as so many Englishmen grumbled, did not come cheaply. Whereas average annual expenditure under King James had been under £2m, government spending in 1689–97 averaged some £5.5m per annum.[145] In all, Crown expenditure during the war years amounted to £49.3m, of which £36.2m (74 per cent) were expended for military purposes.[146]

This vast increase in Crown expenditure was funded by lavish votes of parliamentary supply. Over the whole course of the war, the government's average tax revenues amounted to £3.64m per annum, a figure which was roughly double the Crown's annual tax income before the revolution.[147] This tax revenue derived from four principal sources: polls, the land tax, customs duties and excises levied upon various items of domestic consumption. Vigorously administered by Crown officials, the excise was a favourite tax at the Treasury. Throughout the war, in fact, Treasury officials hoped to expand the range of items on which the excise was levied. But their plans consistently fell foul of the House of Commons which feared that a 'general excise' would generate a vast fiscal bureaucracy beyond parliament's control.[148] Nevertheless, some £13.6m were raised by excise duties over the whole course of William's reign.[149]

The Treasury's biggest money-spinner was the land tax, a charge administered by local gentlemen rather than government officials. In 1696 the land tax accounted for no less than 52 per cent of the government's tax revenue, and it provided as much as 42 per cent of all tax receipts between 1689 and 1697.[150] Originally levied by a monthly assessment on all counties and boroughs, the land tax was raised by means of a uniform pound rate from 1693.[151] Other direct taxes included numerous polls and the notorious charge on windows introduced in 1696.[152]

Massive levels of taxation were not sufficient in themselves to meet the demands of war finance. As a result, the Crown was forced to borrow money on a hitherto unimaginable scale. By the time peace was signed in September 1697, the Crown's deficit stood at a staggering £16.5m.[153] Total borrowing was considerably higher than that. While no more than £7m were raised through long-term loans over the whole of King William's reign, a mammoth £32m accrued to the Crown through short-term borrowing between 1689 and 1697.[154] During the early years of the war, all government borrowing had been short-term, since it was considered undesirable by both executive and legislature to load the Crown with a standing financial burden.[155] But by 1693 the scale of short-term borrowing was jeopardizing confidence in government credit. Since tax receipts were falling well short of anticipated yields, a mound of uncancelled tallies (the government's official 'IOUs') was building up. With little prospect of repayment, desperate government creditors began to sell their tallies in the money market at massive discounts.[156] Not surprisingly, it became increasingly difficult for the Crown to obtain credit. By 1694, for example, the Navy Board was finding it virtually impossible to find contractors for the naval stores.[157]

The parlous financial situation forced the government to resort to long-term borrowing. The tentative first moves were the Million Loan of 1693 and the Million Lottery of 1694.[158] But by far the most important development was the foundation of the Bank of England in the Summer of 1694.

A scheme for a joint-stock bank, lending money to the Crown on an indefinite basis in return for a fixed-interest 'rent', had first emerged in 1692 from the fertile mind of the London Scots merchant, William Paterson. His ideas were subsequently taken up by a group of predominantly whiggish London merchants, led by Michael Godfrey, who hoped that such a venture would expand the stock market, and so diminish the overweening influence of the East India Company. When the merchants presented their plan to the administration, it immediately appealed to the hard-pressed Treasury Commissioner, Charles Montagu. And it was Montagu, working with Michael Godfrey, who was apparently responsible for the legislation presented to parliament in April 1694. This provided for the establishment of a chartered Bank of England which was to raise a stock subscription of £1.2m. That sum would in turn be lent by the Bank to the Crown for an indefinite period in return for an annual 'rent' amounting to 8 per cent interest.[159]

Having speedily won parliamentary approval, the Bank's subscription books were opened in June 1694. The flotation proved an outstanding success, thanks in large measure to the grim trade conditions of the early 1690s. Much of the capital of the London mercantile elite was lying idle, since merchants had become reluctant to invest in the increasingly risky business of war-time international trade. The Bank of England, on the other hand, promised an investment safe from the vagaries of the weather and the depredations of French privateers. So the merchants drew upon their surplus capital to buy up the bank's stock.[160] Within two weeks, all of the Bank's stock had been taken up. The money which accrued was promptly lent to the government.[161]

The Bank of England shored up tottering government finances in 1694–5. This was due more to the nature of the new institution than the size of its loan, welcome though that was. Since the Bank paid over much of the original loan in bank bills rather than cash, and because it was soon taking deposits from clients, the Bank had considerable cash reserves at its disposal. These it used to buy up tallies, so easing the pressure on the government to repay short-term loans. As for the Bank bills, they were used by the Crown to pay its contractors. For their part, the contractors were happy to accept the bills as payment for their services, since they could either cash them at the Bank or pass them on to their own creditors.[162] The upshot was that most wondrous of alchemical phenomena, the restoration of confidence in government credit. This in turn laid the basis of a marked upturn in the nation's military fortunes after the Spring of 1694. In short, then, the Bank of England, an institution established to provide long-term credit to the Crown, had helped to boost the war effort by salvaging confidence in government short-term credit.

As we have seen, the Bank of England scheme had been designed in part to increase the size of a stock market dominated by the magic circle which controlled the East India Company. In this, it succeeded beyond all expectations. But even before the foundation of the Bank, there had been something of a stock market boom as import merchants sought a secure and liquid outlet for surplus war-time capital.[163] And with the growth of the stock market in the early 1690s had come the emergence of the parasitic practice of 'stock-jobbing'. As early as January 1692, Sir Christopher Musgrave complained to the Commons that 'The trade of stock-jobbing is now become the sole business of many persons, which has ruined great numbers of tradesmen and others.'[164]

But what was 'stock-jobbing'? As P.G.M. Dickson has noted, it was a rather vague, though undeniably pejorative, term which was 'used to denote every kind of activity in the market'.[165] It implied, above all, the sacrifice of the public good to private profit. Thus in 1695 the Bristol merchant John Cary denounced 'Stock jobbing' which

> hath been the Bane of many good Manufactures, which began well, and might have been carry'd on to Advantage if the Promoters had not fallen off to selling Parts, and slighted the first Design, winding themselves out at Advantage, and leaving the Management to those they decoyed in, who understood nothing of the thing, whereby all fell to the Ground.[166]

In addition to his antipathy towards 'stock-jobbing', Cary was also alarmed that post-revolution financial developments were drawing the wealth of the provinces to London. The growth of taxes and government borrowing meant that 'all the Cash of England will center there in a short time, to the Ruining of the other Trading Cities, and disabling of the Country to pay future Taxes.'[167]

Cary's anxiety was shared by John Locke. In February 1695 Locke complained that the 'money in the Bank [of England] is, and I conclude always will be, managed by London merchants, whereby it will come to pass that they . . . and their friends will be sooner and easier supplied for their occasions than others, whereby I am apt to think the greatest part of our trade will in a little while by secret combinations be got into a few hands, even by this monopoly of money.' It more became the wisdom of parliament, Locke continued,

> to consider how money might be better distributed into the country, and other ports, and trading parts of England, than to set up a corporation, and by

law countenance its drawing all to London. For if you examine it I believe you will find trade in all our ports mightily decayed: one cause whereof I looked on to be the banking trade (formerly) in London, which is now authorised by a law, and such an establishment of it as I fear will cost dear to England. And whatever good effects are boasted of now in the infancy of the corporation will not last long when they are a little grown up and know their own strength.[168]

In similar vein, the Anglo-Irishman Francis Brewster asserted that the Bank of England 'will Ingross the Money, and consequently the Trade of the Nation, into one City; and will draw from all Parts of the kingdom those little Sums that do now in great measure support the Manufactoryes of the Nation'.[169]

Like Brewster and Locke, John Cary was no friend of the Bank of England. Writing in January 1697, when the Bank was facing severe financial problems, Cary insisted that banks 'ought chiefly to be Calculated for the Use of Trade, and modeled as may best content the Traders'.[170] On that score, the Bank of England was a sorry failure. As a private institution, it was vulnerable to the pernicious practice of 'stock-jobbing', and it was 'so shaken in its Reputation, as hath rendred it uncapable to be made the Foundation of a National Credit'.[171] Cary advocated instead the establishment of a state-owned national bank, based in London but with branches all over the country.[172] Such an institution would provide a secure investment for lenders, and, by forcing down interest rates, provide credit on easy terms for gentlemen, traders and the Crown.[173] Since it would provide the Crown with ready money at low interest, the state bank would also enable the government to abandon taxes detrimental to trade.[174]

Two years before Cary drew up his scheme, another alternative to the Bank of England had been proposed by John Briscoe. In his *Discourse on the late Funds*, Briscoe launched a frontal assault upon the Bank and the other long-term funds established in 1693–4. In the first place, the new funds were discouraging investment in trade by acting as a magnet for mercantile capital. Too many merchants, he lamented, had

> turn'd their Genius from Trade, quite another way; for whereas formerly a great Part of their Time was taken up in contriving how to improve their Money to the best Advantage in the way of their Trade, and to provide for their Families, by an honest Industry; now almost their whole Discourse is of Lottery-Tickets, Annuities, Bank-Bills, &c. and in contriving how they may draw their Money out of Trade, to put in upon some of the late Funds, upon the Prospect of the great Advantages they are capable of receiving thereby, beyond what they can expect to gain by their Trade, and that also free from Taxes.[175]

Worse still, the new funds were undermining the competitiveness of the few remaining overseas traders by raising the price of borrowing. Whereas Dutch merchants paid only 3–4 per cent for their credit, their English rivals were forced to pay a burdensome 8–10 per cent. Inevitably, the profits of the merchants would be eaten up in interest payments, and 'this in process of Time, will dishearten our Merchants, discourage Navigation, ruin our Trade, and will leave it in the Hand of those who can trade with less Disadvantages than we can, and who having once got the Trade in their Hand, will not easily part with it.'[176] Nor would landowners be unscathed by the new funds: 'for as the Taxes (necessarily laid on Lands) make Land less esteemed, and consequently less valuable than formerly; so this Encouragement given to the Contributors to the late Funds (which is in effect a creating a new sort of Purchases much more advantageous than Land) make Land less esteemed, and consequently less valuable than formerly.'[177] In short, the long-term funds were 'a Canker, which will eat up the Gentlemens estates in land, and beggar the Trading Part of the Nation, and bring all the Subjects in England to be the monied Mens Vassals'.[178]

To replace the ruinous long-term funds, Briscoe advocated the establishment of a land bank which would be administered by Commissioners appointed by King and parliament. Derived broadly from the ideas of the celebrated obstetrician and financial projector, Hugh Chamberlen, this was a bank whose subscription stock would consist of land rather than money, and would lend at a mere 3 per cent.[179] Such an institution, Briscoe confidently asserted, would shower blessings upon the country. It would provide easy and cheap credit for the Crown, while the low rates of interest would enable English merchants to undercut their foreign rivals. What was more, the land bank would also prove the salvation of the landed interest. Those gentlemen who 'lent' their land to the bank would enjoy tax exemptions and see their land rise in value. At the same time, the bank would provide cheaper mortgages for other landed men.[180] Thus Briscoe's land bank would cure all of England's financial and economic ills at a stroke.

Briscoe put his ideas into practice in June 1695.[181] That summer, a rather different sort of land bank was founded by John Asgill and Nicholas Barbon. This bore a closer resemblance to a modern building society than to Briscoe's scheme. The bank's stock consisted of liquid capital rather than land, while its assets were to fund cheap mortgages.[182]

In late 1695 the pressing requirements of government finance encouraged the rival land bankers to join forces in a new project. Briscoe, Asgill and Barbon proposed to raise £2m for the government through a cash subscription, and a further £140,000 in landed stock. In return, parliament would settle an annuity of £140,000 upon the new bank. Thus the land bank would help to finance the war, as well as continuing to provide cheap mortgages for penurious land owners.[183]

Alas, it was all too good to be true. Despite the misgivings of the head of the Treasury, Charles Montagu, a modified version of the scheme received the approval of parliament in the Spring of 1696.[184] But when the bank's books were opened in May, the subscription proved a disastrous failure.[185] The land bank had fallen victim to a liquidity crisis which would hasten the end of the war.

4. The Recoinage Crisis and the Coming of Peace, 1696–7

Throughout the early 1690s, the English coinage was systematically debased by coin clippers – rogues who sheared the edges off rimless pre-Restoration coins and then sold the silver clippings to equally unscrupulous goldsmiths. Although it had been a well-organized and thriving industry since at least the 1670s, coin-clipping was given an enormous boost by King William's war. The purchase of supplies for the army in Flanders necessitated massive exports of English bullion to the Continent. The consequent rise in demand for silver bullion led in turn to an acceleration in the pace of clipping. Indeed, it now seems clear that the rapid debasement of the coinage in the early 1690s was all that sustained the requisite bullion exports as the nation's trade collapsed. Thus England's war effort had come to depend in large measure upon organized crime.[186]

In the early years of the war, the debasement of the coinage provided a silver lining to England's financial woes, but at the cost of mortgaging the future. As coin-clipping increased, so public confidence in the coin would eventually be stretched to breaking-point. By 1695, when some of the silver coin had lost as much as 40–50 per cent of its metal content, the inevitable was at last coming to pass. Public confidence in the currency began to collapse, and before long a recoinage was deemed essential. In January 1696, after almost a year's deliberation, parliament passed the requisite legislation. This provided for the progressive demonetization of the clipped coin, and its melting down and coining anew by the Mint.[187]

On 4 May 1696 the clipped coin was accepted in payment of tax for the last time. This triggered the most severe socio-economic crisis of the 1690s. For in the interval between the demonetization of the clipped coin and the minting of the new, the circulation of money virtually ceased.[188] Much of the unclipped old coin was hoarded in mistaken anticipation of a sterling devaluation, while in many parts of the country the clipped coin was no longer accepted as a means of exchange. In mid-June the JP Charles Price found to his dismay that even coin which was not visibly clipped was being refused in south-east Wales. 'I was on Fryday last at Abergainy about the window tax', he informed Secretary of State Trumbull, '& it being Markett day, & the towne being great & Populous the People were in A great Consternation About the Money, not being able to Have any Commoditys for it, tho much of it to my apprehension being good money'. In order 'to satisfy the people & to prevent an uprore', Price acted immediately.

'I ordered the Beadle to Proclaime at the Markett Crosse that whosoever refused any sixpenny not clypped within the Innermost Ring, or any other punchable money, I would bind them over or Commit them'. This, he reported, 'did some good for the present, but how long I Cannot tell, new money we have none, & some will not take the old on any account, & the Poor cannot reach to gold'. Price concluded on a suitably glum note. 'I have declared that I will trust any honest poore till the new money doth Circulate, I suppose some other gentlemen will doe the like, but All will not doe it.'[189]

In other areas, the old coin was passing only on weight. In Suffolk the local magistrates tried to stamp out this practice, but their efforts proved sadly counterproductive. 'Our Justices of the Peace in Our last sessions threatened to prosecute all that Weighed the Silver money [before accepting it] and many were presented', reported Edmund Bohun from Ipswich at the end of July. But 'upon this the small money stopped and nobody would take it at any rate.' In consequence, the wheels of the local economy had ground to a halt. 'No trade is Managed but by trust', Bohun lamented. 'Our tenants can pay no rent, Our Corne factors can pay nothing for what they have had and will trade no more so that all is at a stand; and the People are discontented to the utmost. Many self Murders happen in sevrall families for want and all things look very black and should the least accident put the Mobb in motion no man can tell where it would end.'[190]

In the north of England, where the shortage of passable cash was even more acute than in the south, disturbances did indeed break out in the Summer of 1696. 'The cuntry is in so great distresse for want of current money,' wrote Roger Kenyon from Manchester on 13 June, 'that without some speedy supply, all traffick will cease. Our markets cannot be continued. The poor have been, in severall markets, tumultuously

Figure 10   The English silver coinage before and after the great recoinage of 1696: a Charles I shilling as minted (left), a clipped example of the same coin (centre), and a William III shilling of 1698. The recoinage caused hardship throughout the country and hastened the end of the war.

murmuring; and we are, I think, in great danger of greater unquietnes.'[191] A few days earlier, at Kendal in Cumberland,

> a great many of the rabble being ale house keepers, halfe drunk, went to the mayor and demanded of him how they were to get bread if their money could not pass. He gave them good words and said that he and I had resolved to accept all money not clipped within the innermost ring, in our dealings, and hoped that others would do the like. There [sic] were not satisfied but rambled about the town making a great noise. As they were far too strong for the civil power, we gave them some drink and they promised not to molest the town tonight but will have a frolic in the country. We can do nothing but give them good words or there will be bloodshed.[192]

Writing from York on 10 June, Hugh Todd reported that Lord Lonsdale, one of the leading magnates in the north-west, 'is in some danger from the Rabble, he having offer'd to weigh their old Money, & give other in proportion to the weight; and . . . he keeps a Gaurd upon his House, till the fury be over'. Disturbances had also occurred in the north Midlands and the north-east. 'In Darbyshire', Todd claimed, 'about 700 rose & went to the Sheriff; & their Representatives who were in some danger from them; & I fear the Tumult is not yet appeased.' At Newcastle, where the 'Coal trade is quite ceased because they have no money at London', a crowd of 'about 500 Colliers got together; & were very insolent'. Although the colliers were temporarily appeased by gifts of gold coin from the local MPs, Todd had subsequently heard that 'they are up again, & hinder people from bringing Victualls to the Town or seise it for themselves.' 'If something be not done,' he plaintively concluded, 'we shall have Intestine Confusions, in a very short time; & those that are forc'd to it by Want will plunder All that have any thing to loose.'[193]

Three months earlier, the revelation of the Assassination Plot had led to an outburst of Williamite fervour. The recoinage crisis did nothing to diminish King William's new-found popularity. Instead, the crowds vented their spleen on the politicians. As Hugh Todd noted in his account of the Newcastle disturbances, the 'Rabble . . . spoke dutifully of his Majesty, but were very seditious in their Expressions toward the Ministers of State & their Representatives'.[194] A similar dichotomy was observed by the Lincolnshire cleric, Abraham de la Pryme. 'Most people seems mightily dissatisfyed, tho' they love K[ing] W[illiam] very well', he confided to his diary on 8 June. 'Yet they curse this parliament, not for their design of coining all new, but for their ill mannagement of it in setting so little time, in taking no care to coin fast and send new monney out.' Indeed, times were so hard that 'Poor people are forced to let their clip'd shillings go for 6d., 8d., and some at 10d. a piece, and some at shops are forced to give as much more for anything they by as is ask'd for it . . . These are very hard things,' he concluded, 'and but that the nation is so mightily in love with the king they would all be soon up in arms.'[195] On the other side of the country, at Whitehaven in Cumbria, the colliery manager John Gale came to a similar conclusion later in the year. 'There is nothing in the world,' he wrote to his master, Sir John Lowther, in early November,

> that to me is a greater indication of the affections of the people to the government than the peacible temper under the present distraction about mony; for my owne part I am sattisfyed that if halfe the like disturbance had happened in the preceading raigne it would have putt the kingdome into a flame and I pray God there may yett no evill consequences attend it, for wee are not yett come to a crisis. I fear the markitts will stopp for want of a currency. When they doe, the poorer sort that live upon dayly wages, will be reddy to muttiny for want of dayly bread.[196]

Gale's fear of bread riots proved to be unfounded. In contrast to many other parts of the country, the Whitehaven area appears to have remained calm throughout the recoinage crisis. Yet even in those parts of England which did witness serious disturbances, social unrest failed to spill over into disaffection towards the revolution regime. The diary of Abraham de la Pryme provides an illuminating account of an incident in Lincolnshire in early June:

> This day [7 June 1696] I heard of one that is come from Lincoln, that the country people has been up at Stamford, and marchd in a great company, very lively, to the house of S[i]r John Brownley. They brought their officers, constables, and churchwardens amongst them, and as they went along they cryd, "God bless King William, God bless K[ing] W[illiam]" etc. When they were come to S[i]r John's, he sent his man down to see what their will was, who all answered – "God bless K[ing] W[illiam], God bless the Church of England, God bless the Parliament, and the Lords Justices and S[i]r John Brownley! We are King William's true servants, God forbid that we should rebel against him, or that anything that we now do should be construed ill. We come only to his worship to besieech him to be mercifull to the poor; we and our familys being all fit to starve, not having one penny ith' the world that will go," etc. S[i]r Jo[hn] hearing all this (as soon as his man) at a window where he was viewing them, sent them a bagg with fifteen pound in it of old mill'd [unclipped] money, which they received exceeding thankfully, but sayd the sum was so little, and number and necessitys so great, that they feared it would not last long, therefore must be forced out of meer necessity to come to see him again, to keep themselves and their familys from starving. Then they desired a drink, and S[i]r Jo[hn] caused his doors to be set open and let them go to the cellar, where they drunk God bless King William, the Church of England, and all the loyal healths they could think on, and so went their ways.[197]

The Jacobite crowd was widely feared in 1696, but it took the whig reaction of 1714–16 to bring it into being.

Although the Jacobites were unable to turn the recoinage crisis to their advantage, the scarcity of money nevertheless gravely imperilled the security of the Williamite regime. For in the Summer of 1696 the war effort all but ground to a halt. At the end of February, the fleet had put to sea at short notice in a successful bid to deter a planned French invasion.[198] But by early Summer, the navy's victualling service, starved of cash since March, had broken down. Poorly-provisioned ships were forced to return early to their bases, only to find dockyard stocks almost exhausted. To make matters worse, the food that was available was barely edible, for no fresh provisions had been purchased since the Winter.[199]

The army in Flanders was in an even sorrier state. Since supplies for the army were obtained locally, large-scale remittances had to be sent to the Continent in the early 1690s.[200] From the Autumn of 1694, the Bank of England began to take over the management of Continental remittances, and it assumed complete responsibility for the remittance business in the following Spring.[201] But in the second half of 1695 the collapse of the sterling exchange rate – itself a sign of the erosion of confidence in the English silver currency – had caused the Bank heavy losses.[202] After May 1696 the Bank's troubles escalated rapidly. On 6 May, two days after the final demonetization of the clipped coin, a run on the Bank by cash-hungry depositors jeopardized its liquidity. Nor was the Treasury able to help the Bank in its hour of need, for the state's cash reserves remained locked up in the demonetised clipped coinage. Faced with the prospect of imminent financial collapse, the Bank swallowed a bitter pill. In early July it reneged upon its commitments to Continental creditors. At a stroke, confidence in English credit evaporated, leaving the army paymaster in Flanders penniless. Not until October was the Bank able to resume remittances to the army, and then only thanks to a substantial loan from a worried Dutch government.[203]

At home, the economic malaise caused by the recoinage lingered into the Autumn in some parts. 'Money is every day worse and worse', wrote Timothy Banks from Westmoreland in early September. 'There is not a farthing to be had. About three weeks ago sixpences with the ring on, and shillings with some letters on, would have gone, but if ever shears have been on either they will not. Men cannot sell their beasts for ready money.'[204] In October, it is true, Abraham de la Pryme cheerfully reported from Lincolnshire that 'New Money beginns to grow plentyfull, there is no one almost but has some little quantity.'[205] But to John Gale of Whitehaven the gloom seemed unrelieved in the second half of November. 'For my owne part', he wrote to Sir John Lowther,

I propose noe comfort to myselfe till the warr be over, and the matter of the coynes regulated, that there be a settled currency of money without scruple, that every man may buy and sell in peace and safety. Noe man now knows what he hath, or what mony to take. Today he may be sent to prison for refusing the king's (unclipped) coyne, tomorrow a greater sufferer by takeing it.

These uncertaintyes make all things whatsoever dearer by a 3d. than formerly – and hence I conclude arise all discouragements of the poorer sorte, especially your poor [colliery] workmen and leaders and gives me nothing but melancholly and dispair of amendment till peace and more plenty come.[206]

Like John Gale, Francis Hopegood, an associate of the Derbyshire tory Thomas Coke, saw peace as the only panacea for the nation's ills. 'God send us a good and sudden peace,' he wailed to Coke in September 1696, 'or else it will be impossible for us to subsist much longer without money, which is harder every Day to come by.'[207] Three months earlier, in another letter to Thomas Coke, Hopegood had expressed his yearning for peace in terms which starkly reveal his tory prejudices. 'Wee have most Reason to Curse our selves for trusting our greatest Enemys to our own ruine. Butt what shall I say: from a D[utch] Alliance, a Greedy C[our]t, & mercinary P[arliamen]t, Good Lord Deliver us. Nothing butt a peace Can Retreive us.'[208]

Needless to say, King William and his whig ministers did not see things in quite the same light. The financial crisis of 1696 had nevertheless convinced them that the war must be brought to an end. Fortunately, King Louis of France, deeply embroiled in financial problems of his own, was just as anxious to reach a peace agreement. Overtures to the French King were made early in the new year, and the formal negotiations began at the Dutch town of Ryswick in May 1697.[209]

The peace talks were played out against a background of worsening financial crisis in England. To compound the problems caused by the recoinage, confidence in government short-term credit once more reached breaking-point in 1696–7. An over-extension of short-term borrowing, coupled with recurring deficiencies on the funds charged to debt repayment, again brought into question the Crown's capacity to repay tallies.[210] The so-called engraftment scheme, by which the Bank of England bought up as stock about 14 per cent of the floating tallies, helped to ease the pressure on government short-term credit in the course of 1697.[211] But there was still a severe shortage of ready cash. The provisioning of the fleet in the Channel, for example, remained problematic throughout the Summer of 1697: 'all I can hope for is to make up the provisions of the Fleete to a Month, and verie little Oatmeale and pease', lamented Admiral Rooke in mid-June, 'which makes me Apprehend we shall come in againe if not beaten, verie sickly, and att our Witts end for a Supply of provissions.'[212] The Admiral's claims, reported the Undersecretary of State, James Vernon, were disputed by the victualling commissioners. 'And yet', Vernon noted pointedly, 'what [provisioning] there was more they could not tell, but this they declared that without more money they could not make a further supply.'[213] By early August the fleet was in a dreadful state at anchor in Torbay. 'We are still in a most miserable condition for want of provissions', wrote Admiral Rooke from his flagship, 'some tymes comes a supply of eight or ten days breade, then we are choaking for beare; and upon the arrivall of tenn or twelve days beare, we are starving for breade; of which Specie we are now to our shame be it spoaken, at halfe allowance in our owne portes when the Dutch seamen never were fed in greater plentie.'[214] Not surprisingly, it took more Dutch loans to keep the English government's head (barely) above water in the last weeks of the war and the first of the peace.[215]

The French war was at last brought to a close by a treaty signed at Ryswick in September 1697. This accurately reflected the inconclusive character of the war by requiring all parties to surrender territorial conquests made since 1688. From the English point of view, the most important aspect of the treaty was the clause by which King Louis promised to give no further assistance to the enemies of King William. In effect, the French King had recognised the Protestant revolution of 1688.[216]

Since it left the power of Louis XIV pretty much untramelled, some observers felt that the peace of Ryswick left much to be desired: 'here is a peace', wrote one, 'obtained I doubt more in show than substance for us.' At a time of his own choosing, the French King would make himself master of the Rhineland and overawe the Dutch, 'unless that Monarch be grown more pious than formerly, or that he forbear troubling the World out of his affection to King William when he has fair occasion'.[217] Such scepticism, however, was submerged in a tide of joyous relief upon the end of the most expensive war in the nation's history. The news of the peace, reported a correspondent of Robert Harley, was greeted 'everywhere with wonderfull rejoycing, as it deserves'.[218] To a hard-pressed civil servant like James Vernon, the coming of peace was little short of a saving grace. 'When we consider all our circumstances,' he wrote to his patron, the Duke of Shrewsbury, 'never came a peace so seasonably to any people.'[219]

In spite of his obvious relief at the return of peace, Vernon was disturbed by the public rejoicing which accompanied it. 'We are the only people that have let joy break out upon the first news of the peace', the Undersecretary noted, 'there has been no such demonstrations of it either in France or Holland.'[220] Perhaps Vernon was aware of one rather unpalatable truth: no amount of rejoicing could altogether obscure the fact that a massive expenditure of blood and treasure had produced precious little wool for England. In this respect, the official peace celebrations, held in early December, provided a fitting epilogue to King William's war. 'Ther was in St James's Square a sort of triumphall arch built,' reported a jaundiced eyewitness,

> but very ill design'd, on ye topp of w[hi]ch were 4 figures made of wood and painted, one at each corner, and, had ther not been ye names of w[ha]t they were design'd for, noe person cou'd have guess'd what they were meant for.

Peace out of a cornucopeia flung out rockets of wild fire. Conduct had a
death's head in one of her hands. Concord held in a dish a flaming heart;
and Valour had by it a ravenous lyon. The whole was an emblem. Ther was
a great unnecessary expense of treasure; severall killed; a vast number of
crackers; and all ended in smoake and stinke.[221]

5. King William's Peace, 1697–1701

The peace signed at Ryswick in September 1697 rested upon the shakiest
of foundations, for it failed to address the key question in European diplo-
macy: who was to succeed to the Spanish throne and its vast imperial
territories upon the apparently imminent demise of the last of the Spanish
Habsburgs, Charles II? If the throne were to go to one of King Charles's
Austrian cousins, a renewal of hostilities in Europe seemed inevitable.
Faced with the old nightmare of encirclement, King Louis of France would
surely feel compelled to launch a pre-emptive strike upon the Habsburg
domains, including the Spanish Netherlands. That Flanders would again
be a prime target for the French was rendered all the more certain by the
evident lack of fight in a war-weary England. As Lord Somers told the King
in August 1698, 'there is a deadness and want of spirit in the nation universally, so as not at all to be disposed to the thought of entering into a new
war'.[222] If Englishmen were indeed content to watch a new European
struggle from the sidelines, it seemed only too likely that the French would
overrun Flanders and capture the Dutch 'barrier' fortresses in the province.
In short, then, a renewal of hostilities threatened to bring the French army
to the borders of the United Provinces.

Thus within a few months of the peace of Ryswick, King William found
himself once again contemplating a potentially mortal peril to his home-
land. Unable to risk another war, the King decided to negotiate with
Louis XIV a mutually acceptable settlement of the Spanish question.[223]
These talks bore fruit in a treaty signed in October 1698. The first Partition
Treaty, which named the young Electoral Prince of Bavaria as heir to King
Charles of Spain, was rendered obsolescent almost before the ink was dry
by the untimely death of the Bavarian princeling.[224] The second Partition
Treaty, agreed by England, the United Provinces and France in March
1700, named the Archduke Charles, younger son of the Emperor, as the
new heir to the Spanish throne. But this concession from Louis XIV was
won at the expense of surrendering most of Spain's Italian possessions to
the Dauphin of France.[225]

There was but one flaw to this neat arrangement: the partition of the
Spanish Empire was totally unacceptable to the courts of both Austria and
Spain. On the Austrian side, the Emperor Leopold was determined to

secure for his younger son the whole of the Spanish succession. As for the ailing King Charles of Spain, he shared his Habsburg cousin's wish to maintain the integrity of the Spanish Empire, but had no intention of preserving it for the benefit of the Austrian Habsburgs whom he heartily loathed. So when the Spanish King at last shuffled off his mortal coil in October 1700, he stunned Europe by leaving the entire Spanish Empire to Philip of Anjou, younger son of the French Dauphin. The lure of Bourbon dynastic aggrandizement now wrestled in the French King's mind with his treaty obligations to King William and the Dutch. It was an unequal contest. After a few days deliberation, King Louis accepted the will on behalf of his grandson, thereby consigning the Partition Treaty to the dustbin of history.[226]

King William was understandably mortified by this unexpected turn of events. His English subjects, on the other hand, seemed undismayed by the prospect of a Bourbon succession to the Spanish throne. 'I do not find that the death of the King of Spain makes any alteration in Trade', wrote a complacent Thomas Johnson from London in November 1700, 'oyles, by little and little, are advanced; most are of opinion all will be well, and pleased with the Duke of Anjou.'[227] There certainly seemed little reason why England should risk its precious Spanish trade for the sake of a dynastic squabble between the Bourbons and Habsburgs. Writing from Cadiz in early January 1701, the merchant Sir William Hodges simply could not believe 'wee or the Dutch shall bee drawn into a warre upon the Emperor's account'.[228] Two weeks later, his views were unchanged. 'I dont apprehend England will be brought into a warr upon the account of this Succession', he wrote to Samuel Pepys's nephew, John Jackson.[229]

As a prominent member of the English mercantile community at Cadiz, Sir William Hodges had much to lose from a rupture with France and Spain over the will. But his dislike of the Partition Treaty was shared by many of his compatriots. Pepys himself, though not overjoyed by the Duke of Anjou's succession, was at one with Sir William 'in preferring the Will to the Partition in most respects'.[230] Quite simply, it was widely believed that the Partition Treaty had conceded too much to the French in the Mediterranean. As one English observer had commented in July 1700, the treaty had 'given France not only the best and richest part [of the Spanish territories in Europe], but that which will enable him to be master of the rest whenever he pleaseth, and puts him into immediate possession, if he hath a mind to it, of all the Mediterranean trade'.[231] This prospect now seemed averted. The Spanish possessions in the Mediterranean would not go to the Dauphin. As for his younger son, the new King of Spain, he would not in the normal course of events inherit the French throne. On the contrary, it was hoped that he might one day emerge as an enemy of France. The 'newe Spanish King', noted a correspondent of the Norfolk whig, Robert Walpole, 'will be under a Regency for three yeares, in which the Spanish Regents will so discipline him as to make him a Spaniard so that upon a good occasion the new King will dispute his interest in opposition to his Father or Grandfather.'[232]

It soon became clear, however, that this was so much wishful thinking. In February 1701 King William's worst nightmare came true when French troops, acting on an 'invitation' from the Spanish government, entered Flanders and seized the Dutch garrisons.[233] The Cadiz merchants were dumbstruck. 'If I should acquaint you that all the English and Dutch in this place are more than half scared out of their sences, feareing a suddaine rupture, I should still keep within measure of what passeth', wrote Christopher Haynes to John Jackson on 23 February/6 March 1701. 'All the last weeke', he continued, 'many pack prosessions went about these streetts, so if you had been here you would have seen something resembleing a dispatch of the Galeonez.'[234] Not that Haynes's partner, Sir William Hodges, had given up all hopes of peace. 'I can't yet be perswaided it will bee for the interest of England to breake with France and consequently Spaine,' he wrote to Jackson that same day, 'neither do I believe France or Spaine will pretend to quarrell with us; the King of the first being aged and will gladly dye in peace, and the latter will have enough to do for some time in settling his new howse.'[235] In contrast, the Derbyshire gentleman Sir Edward Coke thought war was inevitable. 'I believe that the war is already determined', he wrote in the first week of February:

France acting in it with as absolute a power in the Spanish dominions as in her own is the necessary consequence of the Duke of Anjou being King of Spain. The advantages that France may propose to herself from this favourable juncture of affairs will probably make her dispute this war at a greater expense of blood and treasure than any she was ever engaged in, for I fear that it will lay the foundation of the Western Monarchy. I doubt the first step will be the parting with Flanders to France, and giving her the pre-eminence above all other nations. How far the consequence will affect England and Holland is so obvious I need not explain it: and if once these two Powers truckle to France farewell the liberty of Europe and the Protestant Religion.[236]

At Westminster, many MPs preferred Hodges' analysis to Coke's. True, the whig party had long been in belligerent mood. As early as 10 December 1700, a hostile observer reported that the 'Whigs at present are all for "To your tents, O Israel" and are very full of a war.'[237] But later that month, while elections for a fresh parliament were in progress, King William's new chief ministers, Godolphin and Rochester, warned him that they 'did not think the parliament of England would bee brought into a war against Spaine or if the dismembring any part of that monarchy were made the ground of it'.[238] They were right to be cautious. The House of Commons which assembled in February 1701 was dominated by tories, and they had no desire to rush into another war. When a motion was proposed to 'stand by [the] king and support the government for the safety of England the preservation of the protestant religion and for [the] peace of Europe', it was approved by only 181 votes to 163. For in the view of the minority, such a motion 'would insensibly bring us in and ingage us in a war'.[239] And what could England possibly achieve by engaging in such a war? Nothing but the loss of its valuable trade with Spain.

Over the next few months, the growing realization that Spanish foreign policy was being directed from Versailles led to a shift in opinion among tory MPs. Thus on 2 April the Commons voted *nem con* to assist the Dutch in accordance with existing treaties, a move followed on 9 May by a resolution promising to support the King and his allies 'in maintaining the liberties of Europe'. As a result, a small English army was sent to the Netherlands under the command of the Earl of Marlborough, now fully rehabilitated after spending most of the 1690s in the political wilderness.[240] Then on 12 June the Commons 'unanimously' resolved to support King William in moves to re-establish the wartime alliance with the United Provinces and Austria, 'for the preservation of the liberties of Europe, the prosperity and peace of England, and for reducing the exorbitant power of France'.[241]

Although the tories had come to accept the need to support the Dutch, the tardy and grudging nature of that acceptance played into the hands of their whig enemies. Riven by internal divisions since 1697, the whigs now seized the opportunity to re-establish their credentials as the party of Protestant patriotism. To this end, whig propagandists sedulously peddled the line that the tories were playing fast and loose with the safety of the nation and Protestantism in general: 'deserting the Dutch when the French are at their doors, till it be almost too late to help them,' insisted Daniel Defoe, 'is unjust to our treaties, and unkind to our confederates, dishonourable to the English nation, and shew you [the tory House of Commons] very negligent of the safety of England, and of our protestant neighbours'.[242] All those who were reluctant to assist the Dutch were branded friends of popery and France: 'under luscious terms of Peace', wrote another whig polemicist, the anti-war camp 'would introduce the Design of enslaving our Bodies under a French Yoke, or Tyranizing over our Consciences under a Spanish Inquisition'.[243]

The pro-war campaign escalated through the Spring of 1701, and reached its climax in early May. On the 8th, the petition of 'the Gentlemen, Justices of the peace, Grand-Jury, and other Freeholders' of Kent was brought up to Westminster by five of the petitioners. This implored the Commons 'to have regard to the voice of the people, that our Religion and Safety may be effectually provided for, that your Loyal Addresses may be turned into Bills of Supply, and that his most sacred majesty . . . may be enabled powerfully to assist his Allies before it is too late'.[244] The House's subsequent denunciation of the petition as 'scandalous, insolent, and seditious', and its decision to imprison the five principal petitioners, merely reinforced the impression that the tories were disinclined to take a strong line with France. Defoe once again wagged his finger at the lower House:

> Your actions all the World disgust,
>   The French are only glad;
> Your Friends your honesty distrust,
> And while you think you're wise and Just,
>   The Nation thinks you mad.[245]

The 'Kentish Petition' was by no means an impartial expression of county opinion: the five 'martyred' petitioners were all prominent figures in Kent whiggery. But there is no doubt that the anxieties articulated by whig propagandists were real enough. 'The House of Commons,' complained John Evelyn on 18 May, 'neglect the Affairs abroad most unseasonably, whilst the French secure themselves of Flanders &c., irreparable negligence.'[246] Like Evelyn, the Lincolnshire cleric Abraham de la Pryme was no natural whig. Scion of a presbyterian family, de la Pryme showed all the wonted zeal of a convert in his love of the Church and hatred of dissent. Yet this fierce High Churchman denounced the tory parliament of 1701 as 'seditious and mutinous'. 'The Dutch', he recalled at the end of the year, 'writ memorials and letters to the king and them [the Commons] of what great danger not onely they but this nation and the protestant religion was in, yet, for all they heeded none of them, but went on in their villainys, till the whole nation was enraged against them.'[247]

In the Spring and Summer of 1701 whiggery once again waxed strong by clothing itself in its old anti-French and anti-popish rhetoric. In response, tory writers produced a series of brilliant anti-whig polemics. Star of the tory effort was Robert Harley's friend, Charles Davenant. A shrewd and skilful polemicist, Davenant turned the tables on the resurgent whigs not by belittling the French threat, but by demolishing instead whiggery's pretension to be the sole custodian of the Protestant and anti-French cause. In his *Esssays upon . . . The Ballance of Power*, Davenant freely acknowledged the scale of the menace posed by the Bourbon succession to the Spanish throne. 'What English man can bear to see Flanders in French Hands?' he asked his readers. 'And what mischiefs to our Trade may not be expected from [the French] being in a manner Masters of the Ports of Italy and Spain?'[248] He was also happy to admit that some Englishmen 'seem at present willing to embrace peaceful Councils, and to decline entring upon immediate Action'. But this, he hastened to add, was not out of fear of, or sympathy towards, France. Rather, such men were fearful that a new war would revive the influence of that brood of vipers, the old whig ministers. As Davenant explained,

They [the anti-war tories] are jealous that War, as it first introduc'd upon the Stage of Business, so it will again bring into Play the very set of men whose Ruinous Conduct for Eight Years, was a greater Weight upon this Kingdom, than all our other Burthens: They are afraid the same Vipers will once more have an opportunity to rend and gnaw the Entrails of the Commonwealth: They are under Apprehensions of seeing a War carried on upon the same Foot as formerly, that is, by a numerous Land-Army and with a small Fleet: They are fearful that Forty Millions more will be handled by the same Men, and with the same profusion: They expect to see the same Set of Men raise yet larger Fortunes out of the Nations Treasure.[249]

Far from being selfless models of Protestant patriotism, the Junto whigs had impoverished England for their own gain during King William's war, and were now clamouring for a new war to provide themselves with fresh opportunities to beggar the nation: 'too many now call out for War (not to oppose France, or to preserve the ballance [of power], nor upon any motive of honour) but out of hopes it may afford new matter for their Avarice and Ambition to work upon.'[250]

Davenant returned to the theme of whig rapacity and war-lust in his famous dialogue, *The True Picture of a Modern Whig*. Speaking in the guise of 'Tom Double', a knavish Junto underling, Davenant averred that the whigs 'can reap no Advantage but by a long, bloody and expensive War, began and carry'd on against all Right and Reason'. For that party, as 'Double' explains, 'want such a War as no Body in the Nation but our selves will be willing to support, and then we shall have the fingring of all the Mony that must be given to maintain it, which is what we should be at.'[251] Small wonder, then, that support for the war-mongering whigs came only from that most rascally element of society, the sharp financial operators who had grown rich thanks to the Junto's conduct of the last war. 'Who is it sticks to 'em', asks 'Double' rhetorically, 'but those who are concern'd in Tallies and the new Stocks?' In contrast,

> The plain Country Gentleman, who has nothing to trust to but his estate, is for having 'em call'd to an Accompt for robbing the Nation; but we, who through their Means, have so many Years got fifteen or twenty per cent for our Mony, and who by their Help have had so many other ways of raising our Selves, Cry up their Innocence, and long to see 'em again at the Helm, that under their Countenance and Protection we may once more fleece the kingdom.[252]

It was a powerful and effective message. Concocted by Davenant as an antidote to the whig rhetoric of Protestant patriotism, the image of the self-serving whig, in cahoots with parasitic 'monied men', would be the mainstay of a rival tory patriotic discourse for years to come. As it was, the black legend of Junto rapacity was already taking hold in tory minds. In April 1701 the Welsh tory Thomas Mansell informed the East India Company's Thomas Pitt of political developments in England since the latter's departure for India. 'Our Ministry', wrote a cheerful Mansell, 'is chang'd much from what you left it & I am in hopes to see more of my friends daily come in to play'. But, he concluded, 'it had bin better for England those you left in employment had never bin in, for they came in beggars & have done all they cou'd to make all of us so while they have gott both Titles & Estates.'[253] Six weeks later, Lord De la Warr wrote to Pitt 'that all mankind which are for the Monarchy & the Church of England & the trade are resolved to exert theire utmost interest to support it [the tory ministry] & to prevent those Presbiterian Ratts from infesting the government, & plundering it any more'.[254] To that end, Church party MPs brought the impeachments of the Junto lords in the Spring of 1701.

While the partisan struggle in England was reaching new heights of intensity, the drift towards a more bloody confrontation between the great powers continued apace. In August negotiations for a peaceful resolution of the European crisis collapsed, and hostilities broke out between the French and Austrians in Italy. On 27 August/7 September the wartime alliance between England, the United Provinces and the Emperor was formally re-restablished at The Hague. Nine days later, on 5/16 September, King James died at St Germain. That same day, in a clear breach of the spirit of the Treaty of Ryswick, Louis XIV recognized the old King's 13 year-old son as James III of England and VIII of Scotland.[255] This caused uproar in England. Throughout the Autumn, King William was inundated with loyal addresses denouncing King Louis and demanding satisfaction for the insult he had dealt the King of England.[256] In a nation which had been edging gradually but most uncertainly towards war, Louis XIV's provocation had had a shock effect similar to that generated in the United States 240 years later by the attack on Pearl Harbour. As a correspondent of the tory MP Thomas Coke noted in early October, the French King's recognition of the Pretender 'has so opened the eyes of everybody, that no one dares hardly speak out against a war'.[257] By appearing to throw down a fresh challenge to the Protestant succession, King Louis had made another war between England and France virtually inevitable.

It was a prospect which filled the tory merchant Henry Whistler with dread. Mindful of the catastrophe which had befallen English trade in the last war, Whistler praised the caution of the 1701 parliament. 'The temper of the last parliament', he wrote to Thomas Pitt after its dissolution, 'saved us last year from a war and we have gott home great riches by it that we must have lost in a war.' But Louis XIV's recognition of the Pretender, he sadly conceded,

> gives us cause to fear that he should force him upon us. This you will see has caused so many addresses and makes us the more angry with the King of France, and for this indignity done to our King they say we must have a war

to make him eat his words. And as all things now stand I know not how we shall keep out of a war and at the same time I very much fear we shall not gett nor save by a war but may loose our trade & never get it again.[258]

Henry Whistler was a fully paid-up subscriber to the nostrum that the whigs wanted a war for their own selfish ends: 'under pretence to carry on their party', he wrote to Pitt, 'they cry up a warr with Spaine & France'.[259] But with all now set for the resumption of the great struggle against Louis XIV, the man who had done so much to foster the image of the war-mongering whig, Charles Davenant, began work on a book altogether different from his previous efforts. 'The Work I am at present upon & which shall be publishd at the Opening of the Parliament, will consist of two Parts', he told the Earl of Marlborough:

> In the First I shall show the Mischief of Divisions in a kingdom, & use all the strongest Arguments I am Master of, to reconcile the two Parties, & to incline our Friends [on the tory benches] to lay aside, for this time at least, their Resentments, in order to unite with more Vigor against France the Common Enimy. In the Second Part I show the dangers which threaten England from the immediate growth of the French Empire, & their strict Conjunction with Spain. With all the Force I can I recommend to the House of Commons Espousing the Interests of the House of Austria, & by speedy & effectual supplies to enable the king to make good the Alliances he has or shall form Abroad, not to dread the expences they shall enter into for the Preservation of themselves & of all Europe & rather fully to engage in a war than listen to unsound & dishonourable Proposals of Peace, & so to arm themselvs with Resolution as not to sheath their Swords til the Greatnesse of France shall be reduced. I shall show by several Reasons & Arguments how unable The French are to stand their Ground, if in this juncture they are pushd home. In short My Lord I intend to be the Dove of Peace here, & the Trumpet of War Abroad.[260]

Over the next decade, England was to show herself more than capable of curbing the ambitions of the King of France. The quest for domestic harmony was to prove an altogether more difficult task.

5

The Church of England

1. The Nonjuring Schism

The reign of James II was a traumatic experience for most clergymen, but for none more so than the Archbishop of Canterbury, William Sancroft. From his sequestration by the parliamentarians in the 1640s, through a period as a royal chaplain in the 1660s and 1670s, to his elevation to the primacy in 1677, Sancroft's life had been one long testimony of devotion to the House of Stuart. But his career had also supplied plentiful evidence of another unshakable loyalty, owed by Sancroft to the episcopal Church of England. Thus it was nothing short of a personal tragedy for the Archbishop when the King's policies put the Crown on a collision course with the Church. How Sancroft resolved his conflict of loyalties is well known. In the Spring of 1688 William Sancroft, life-long servant of the Stuart Monarchy, emerged as the leader of the opposition to King James.[1]

In the tense months which followed, the Archbishop was unflinching in his defence of the Church, even when it landed him in the Tower. Yet defiant as he was, Sancroft never allowed his aversion to King James's policies to descend into disloyalty to the King's person. It is true that Sancroft, together with the other bishops, refused to condemn the Prince of Orange's pre-invasion *Declaration* in October 1688.[2] The Archbishop was even prepared to confer some degree of legitimacy upon Prince William's enterprise by attaching his signature to the Guildhall Declaration of 11 December, the manifesto of the 'provisional government' which referred to the Prince's efforts to rescue the nation 'from the imminent dangers of Popery and slavery'.[3] But Sancroft would give no further sanction to the revolution. Conspicuously absent from the Convention, the primate adamantly refused to accept its resolution that King James had abdicated the throne. Nor would he swear the oath of allegiance to the new monarchs, which was to be imposed upon all beneficed clergymen upon pain of suspension and, ultimately, deprivation.[4] Swearing the oath, he believed, would be perjury, a forswearing of his oath of allegiance to King James. The consequences were inevitable. Suspended from office in August 1689, Sancroft was deprived six months later. His fate was shared by five of his fellow bishops and some 400 of the lower clergy.[5]

The nonjuring clergy represented but a fragment of the Church. Rather

Figure 11 '*William Sancroft, Archbishop of Canterbury*', *by Edward Luttrell, 1688. Sancroft led the Church of England's opposition to King James in 1688, but subsequently refused to swear allegiance to King William and Queen Mary. Nonjurors contrasted his unbending devotion to the Church's principles with the allegedly lukewarm churchmanship of his successor, John Tillotson.*

than troop down the road to deprivation, the overwhelming majority of England's 10,000 or so beneficed clerics leapt at the advice proffered by the Archdeacon of Carlisle, William Nicolson. 'We have now', he told his clergy in May 1689, 'a Prince and Princess seated on the English throne, in whom we are ready enough to acknowledge all accomplishments that we can wish for in our governors, provided their title to the present possession of the Crown was unquestionable; and therefore, methinks, we should rather greedily catch at any appearance of proof that may justify their pretensions, than dwell upon such arguments as seemingly overturn them.'[6] Yet many clergymen took the oath with tortured consciences. William Wake, for example, confessed in November 1689 that there 'was once a Time when the value I had for some persons of our church, made me almost suspect my own Conscience; and I was afraid I had done like a knave in taking the Oaths; tho at the same Time I could not but think myselfe very evidently convinced of the Lawfulnesse of it'.[7]

In the crisis of conscience which beset the Church in 1689, many clerics took refuge in the so-called *de facto* theory of allegiance. This was the notion, promulgated by many writers throughout the early 1690s, that allegiance was owed to William and Mary as *de facto* monarchs only, and that King James remained King *de jure*.[8] Precisely in order to accommodate that theory, parliament had omitted the usual 'rightful and lawful' formula from the oath to the new monarchs.[9] This in turn made it possible to argue that swearing allegiance to William and Mary was no act of perjury, since the new oath did not impinge upon King James's right to the throne. Hence the alarm of Archdeacon Prideaux of Norwich in December 1693 at reports that parliament planned to impose a new oath, abjuring King James's right to the throne. As Prideaux explained to his kinsman John Ellis, he had no objection to acknowledging the new monarchs as lawful King and Queen, for they 'beeing invested by those who had ye lawfull power to doe soe, are certainly lawfull King and Queen. But', continued the Archdeacon,

> ye word rightfull is that I cannot goe over; for that is to swear to King Williams title. Not [that] I have anything to say against his title, but that it may be good as far as I know; but before he can have a right and title, King James must have lost his, and of this we must be well assured before we can swear to ye right of ye other. Soe that it draws in this whole question, whither King James was rightfully deposed; w[hi]ch dependeing upon ye knowledge of soe many circumstances, matter of fact and matters of law, w[hi]ch private men can never have a clear inspect into, it is impossible one of us, who are strangers to ye whole action and know nothing of it but by news letters and news talk, can be so well assured of it as to swear it.[10]

The sophistry, nice distinctions and downright squirming of the swearing clergy earned them the scorn of their nonjuring brethren. 'I have

Read all the Books Written for taking the Oaths', declared the dying Bishop Thomas of Worcester in June 1689, 'in which I find the Authors more Jesuits than the Jesuits themselves.'[11] The previous March, Queen Mary's nonjuring uncle, the Earl of Clarendon, had bluntly informed his old friend William Lloyd, the juring Bishop of St Asaph,

> that I was fully satisfied, that I could not be absolved from the oaths I had taken; to which these new ones were contradictory; that, having already taken the former oaths, my allegiance was due to King James, and not in my power to dispose of; that I had taken the oaths according to the plain and common sense therein expressed, and would not admit of any explanations to be put upon them; which would look, in my opinion, but as equivocations against the letter of the oath, and which we condemn so justly in the Jesuits.[12]

On a Winter's evening ten months later, Clarendon dined with Bishop Lloyd and three other clerical friends, Bishop Turner of Ely and Dean Hickes of Worcester – both nonjurors – and Thomas Tenison, the juring rector of St James Westminster. After dinner the conversation turned, predictably enough, to the oaths controversy. Tenison freely acknowledged that 'there had been irregularities in our settlement; that it was to be wished things had been otherwise; but we were now to make the best of it, and to join in the support of this government, as it was for fear of worse.' Clarendon, naturally, did not agree. 'Strange doctrine!' he was moved to exclaim to his diary. But it was Bishop Lloyd's stance which truly raised his lordship's hackles. 'The Bishop of St Asaph', the earl recorded, 'said, that it was known, while things were in debate, he had voted against abdication and for a regency; but now, things being as they are, and that the Prince of Orange was crowned King, he looked upon acquisition to beget a right: upon which I interrupted him in great heat, and said, if he preached such doctrine, he should not preach to me.' At this point Bishop Turner intervened to soothe Clarendon's temper, leaving the earl to confide to his diary that he had indeed been 'too passionate; for which I am very sorry: but really to hear clergymen in these days so vary in their practice from what themselves have formerly taught, as if we were to change our principles as often as they change their humours, would give provocations'.[13]

More biting still in his condemnation of the swearing clergy was the Irish nonjuror, Charles Leslie. The jurors, he wrote in 1692, had taken the oath of allegiance 'with new coyn'd Distinctions and Declarations, point blank contrary to the declared Sense of the Imposers', and every swearing clergyman had 'had a particular Salvo for his own Conscience'. It was, scoffed Leslie, 'a severe Jest that the Common People have got up against the Clergy, That there was but one thing formerly which the Parliament could not do, that is, to make a Man a Woman: But now there is another, that is, to make an Oath which the Clergy will not take'.[14]

Deprived of their livings and abandoned by their brethren, the clerical nonjurors gained solace and fortitude from the notion that they alone were vindicating the ancient principles of the Church. As Thomas Wagstaffe exulted, the nonjurors had

> preserved themselves from contagion, and gave the same great proof of their invincible fidelity and constancy, whereby they not only secured the uprightness of their own consciences, but have withal maintained and upheld the honour and reputation of the church of England, which hath so terribly been impaired by the scandalous apostacy of so many others. And this is of such mighty consequence, that it must be confessed that posterity hath nothing left to vindicate the church and her avowed principles, but their heroick and memorable examples; and when after-ages shall come to dispute the principles of our church, they will have the piety and practices of these excellent men to counterbalance the general defection which hath overspread this unhappy nation.[15]

In their lonely stand against the revolution, the nonjurors perceived themselves to be following in the footsteps of the sequestered clergy of the 1640s. William Thomas, the nonjuring Bishop of Worcester, had in his youth been proud to number himself among the sequestered clergy. Brought to his deathbed in June 1689, the old bishop blessed God 'that I have Twice Suffered in the same Righteous Cause'.[16] Archbishop Sancroft was another who had suffered twice for upholding the principles of the episcopal Church of England. During the Commonwealth, remembered his biographer Thomas Wagstaffe, the young Sancroft 'became an actual sufferer for the very same principles, and chose to relinquish his interest in his native country, and submit to a voluntary exile, rather than advance himself by the rewards of ungodliness, and own the authority of an unjust, though prevailing usurpation. This therefore,' Wagstaffe continued,

> is not the first time he gave the world proof of his admirable constancy; he was a confessor near fifty years before, upon the very same account; and the very same reasons and arguments (that in those days were urged for rebellion and usurpation) which would not work upon him then, much less could they do it now, (though they had new names put to them) when his judgment and virtue were improved, and the truth of those principles confirmed by his most mature thoughts, and by long experience.[17]

The older Sancroft was revered as the very model of nonjuring self-sacrifice and resolution, splendidly free of the self-serving sophistry which had so tainted the post-revolution Church. 'He had no skill', mused Wagstaffe,

> to dive into the mystery of a people being conquered by themselves, and thereby deriving a title of conquest to a third person; he could not expound the riddle of conquering by vote, or that giving and taking were discriminating marks of conquest; nor could he submit his conscience to the maddest hypothesis that was ever broached by men. He had not the nice subtilty to distinguish between allegiance de facto, and allegiance de jure; for, as he knew that all duties whatsoever were founded in right, and flowed from it,

and there is no such thing in the world as a duty to wrong, so he knew likewise, that neither our own laws, nor any in the whole world, had been so contradictious and inconsistent, as to provide for a double allegiance in opposition to one another. These were fig-leaves, which some had sewed together to cover their nakedness; but the covering was so very thin and slight, that a far less discerning judgment than his would easily look through them; it needed no skill nor art, but plain honesty was sufficient to uncloath them, and to perceive that they served only to blind or shuffle with the conscience, by no means to direct or satisfy it. He knew an oath was too sacred and serious to be taken upon phantoms and shadows; upon such wild and ridiculous suggestions as have not the least being in nature, reason, religion, or the law. And he knew withal, that to take two contradictory oaths must necessarily involve a man in the guilt of perjury: In such a case, there is no medium betwixt swearing and forswearing. Upon this basis he stood, and he stood like a rock, firm and unshaken, and all the billows that beat upon him could not make the least impression. His high post and great revenues were mighty temptations, but when they came to be put into the balance with his conscience, he soon determined his choice, and gave a convincing demonstration that his virtue was superior to the world, and independent of it; that truth is better and far more eligible than riches and honour, when, for the sake of one poor persecuted truth, a man can, without the least hesitation, forsake all that is great and honourable in the world.[18]

Through such selfless loyalty, the nonjurors believed that they alone had upheld the ancient principles of the Church. Indeed, they held themselves to be the sole remnant of the true Church of England. For the established Church, averred the nonjurors, had unchurched itself by lapsing into the sins of heresy and schism. The key event here was not the perjury of the swearing clergy, heinous though that was, but the filling of the sees made vacant by the deprivation of the nonjuring bishops. In a manuscript tract probably written near the end of 1689, Henry Dodwell, the most brilliant of nonjuring theologians, had analysed the implications of such a move. An extreme clericalist, Dodwell contended that only a church council could deprive a bishop of his spiritual authority. Parliamentary deprivation of the nonjuring bishops was therefore totally invalid. That being so, it necessarily followed that appointments to the vacant bishoprics would be uncanonical, and all those who remained in communion with the 'antibishops' would be in a state of schism from the true church.[19]

The deprivation of the nonjuring bishops in February 1690 did not immediately cause the schism predicted by Dodwell. The King still hoped that a compromise might be reached with Sancroft and his followers, and to that end he kept vacant the dioceses of the deprived bishops. But when in late 1690 Bishop Turner was implicated in a Jacobite plot, King William ran out of patience. In April 1691 he nominated the Dean of St Paul's, John Tillotson, to the primacy. Assisted by the Archbishop-elect, the King and Queen now set about filling the other vacant bishoprics. This was no easy task. Painfully aware that filling the vacancies would forever shut the door on an accommodation with the nonjurors, King William's nominees proved none too eager to accept preferment. William Wake, perhaps the most gifted of the younger generation of clergymen, declined both the diocese of Norwich, made vacant by the deprivation of Bishop Lloyd, and that of Bath and Wells, previously held by the revered Thomas Ken. When William Beveridge subsequently accepted Bath and Wells, he found himself the victim of a merciless broadside from an old nonjuring friend: 'you make your abominable hypocrisy in Preaching up restitution to the wronged, and that upon pain of Damnation,' fulminated the indignant nonjuror, 'And yett you your self can receive and enter upon the right and possession of an other, An Innocent conscientious Bishop of our Church (yet in being and uncanonically turned out to beg his bread).'[20] Hit below the waterline, the hapless Beveridge reversed his initial acceptance of Bath and Wells. Ken's diocese was then passed on to Richard Kidder who, under massive pressure from Tillotson, reluctantly accepted.[21]

The new Archbishop was himself on the receiving end of a harangue from an outraged (and outrageous) Henry Dodwell. As Dean of Canterbury before the revolution, Tillotson 'must have promised Canonical Obedience to your then Archbishop . . . And that part of your Canonical Obedience will still oblige you, at least neither to make nor countenance any Schism against him within his own Jurisdiction. Nor can you own the Lay-pretended-law as sufficient to discharge you in Conscience from your promised Canonical Obedience. If you do,' Dodwell warned, 'you make it impossible for the Catholic Church to subsist as distinct & Independent on the State, which will fundamentally overthrow the very Being of a Church as a Society & be consequently more Heretical than many other propositions which are of worse repute with inconsidering Persons'. The finger-wagging went on remorselessly:

> We have born with all Scandals on our part rather than break from your Communion. If you will cut your selves off from us by Acts of your own, we cannot help it. Only we must appeal to our own comon Master, & your own Consciences, that you erect Altars against those Altars which you have owned your selves, & can pretend no justifyable cause for your not continuing to own them. You that have such Candor for Adversaries [ie the Dissenters], who can give no security of continuing yours upon any Concessions, whatsoever, for Gods sake have some for your own Brethren, who have principles obliging them in Conscience to continue yours, if you cutt not off your selves from their Communion.[22]

Alas, Dodwell's inspired penmanship proved to no avail. All the vacant bishoprics were eventually filled, and so Dodwell's nightmare became reality: the Established Church had separated itself from the communion of the 'true' episcopal Church of England, embodied in the nonjurors.

To protect himself from the contagion of schism, Dodwell took refuge at Shottesbrooke in Berkshire. There he became the leading light of a small nonjuring colony succoured by the local squire, Francis Cherry. The presence of the Dodwellian colony in the midst of his parish made life uncomfortable for the local minister, White Kennett. 'I am just return'd from Berkshire,' he wrote to a friend in January 1698, 'but am allwaies uneasie in that Place by the continued oppositions of Mr D[odwe]ll who I doubt will never be convinced of the singularity of his waies by any Occasional Paper, nor indeed by any Miracle if Providence would grant it . . . the Church forsooth has made a Schism from his House, and he will neither join Himself nor suffer Any, upon whom his judgment can have any influence.'[23] Yet Dodwell's views were by no means as singular as Kennett would have them. True, not all the nonjurors broke communion with the Established Church. But the conciliatory examples set by Bishops Frampton and Ken were outweighed by the well-publicized separatism of John Kettlewell, Samuel Grascombe, Thomas Wagstaffe, George Hickes and Bishop Lloyd of Norwich.[24] Needless to say, Archbishop Sancroft's views carried particular weight, and they were unequivocal. 'Throughout the whole course of his retirement, and more particularly during the time of his sickness,' remembered Wagstaffe, 'he never communicated with the swearing clergy, nor would permit them to officiate.'[25] Sancroft, indeed, eventually out-Dodwelled Dodwell. While Dodwell held that the schism should not be perpetuated beyond the lives of the deprived bishops, the old Archbishop came to believe that only the consecration of new nonjuring bishops could preserve unsullied the apostolic succession in the Church of England. To this end, in 1693 Sancroft obtained King James's approval for the elevation of Hickes and Wagstaffe to the nonjuring episcopate.[26] Thus for the first and only time in its history, the Church of England found itself condemned to a protracted contest for legitimacy between two rival hierarchies.

The nonjuring schism was to sear itself into the psyche of the post-revolution Church. Though they were relatively few in number, the nonjurors could lay claim to many of the most distinguished figures in the Restoration Church. Of the Seven Bishops of 1688, for example, no fewer than five (Sancroft, Turner, Ken, White of Peterborough and Lake of Chichester) refused the oath of allegiance to William and Mary. This was not lost on contemporaries: 'how strange a thing it will appear to the present Age and to Posterity', mused a juring clergyman in 1689,

> that those Prelates who had escaped the fury of Papists, and had made so glorious a Confession for Protestant Religion and English Liberties, should in so little a compass of time come to be disgrac'd, and depos'd and ruin'd under a Protestant Government, without any high Crime laid to their Charge, but only because they cannot prevail with their Consciences to take the Oaths; which tho' I think be just and necessary, yet cannot

but acknowledge to have some Circumstances that are unusual and extra-ordinary.[27]

Of the many paradoxes of the revolution, the fate of the episcopal heroes of 1688 was indeed the strangest. As a Jacobite writer wryly observed in 1693, it had been made 'a Capital Offence in King James, that he imprisoned the Bishops for refusing to read his Proclamation'. And yet it was now thought 'Just to deprive the very same Bishops, both ex Officio and Beneficio, to live upon Alms; because they scruple to own a new King out of the Line, and King James alive'.[28]

The deprivation of the nonjuring bishops had shorn the Church of some of her finest ornaments. But in the eyes of nonjurors, and not a few of the swearing clergy, the Church's loss was made infinitely worse by the allegedly lukewarm churchmanship of the new bishops. The deprivation of Archbishop Sancroft and his brethren, complained a Jacobite writer in 1693, had made room for the advancement of a 'latitudinarian gang' who would 'readily concur with [King William] to set up what religion he pleases, provided it will suit their turn, as well as his'.[29] 'We see among the new-made bishops those who were formerly fanatical preachers', wrote the scabrous Charles Leslie in 1694, 'and those who, of all our number, are least zealous for the church, and most latitudinarian, for a comprehension of dissenters, and a dispensation with our liturgy and discipline.'[30] Archbishop Sancroft's biographer, Thomas Wagstaffe, held the new order up to opprobrium by contrasting the old archbishop with his successor, the one-time presbyterian, John Tillotson. Unlike Tillotson, who was only too eager to dilute the Church in order to accommodate dissenters, Archbishop Sancroft had never been 'at the bottom of any project to give up the liturgy, the rights and ceremonies of the church'. Nor would he have shown any favour to the sort of men who now sullied the episcopal bench, prelates who were 'equally principled for Geneva as for England, or for any constitution besides; who were never true nor honest to the church in their inferior charges, and who are far better qualified to betray than to support her'.[31]

It was a powerful and effective message. For in their denunciation of the new bishops, the nonjurors came to articulate the sentiments of much of the swearing clergy. In 1689 a Williamite poet had depicted Archbishop Sancroft as an Aaron who, having 'dar'd fierce Pharo meet, and tell / The Grievances of groaning Israel', had subsequently abased himself before the Golden Calf of nonjuring.[32] But the parish priests, who found themselves at the sharp end of 'King William's Toleration', would never accept that the old archbishop and his fellow nonjurors had succumbed to the lure of a false god. Instead, they came to despise the new episcopate for presiding over the piecemeal destruction of that latter-day Israel, the episcopal Church of England.

2. The Revolution Religious Settlement

'It is now known, and believed by Men of good intelligence,' asserted the controversialist Edward Stephens in 1689, 'that not only the then D[uke] of York, but K[ing] Charles 2 also, were intangled in Popery before their Return into England. And it is therefore not to be question'd, but their Counsels, and the Parliament it self, being at first under a transport, and after corrupted by Pensions and Expectations, were through their Means influenced by the crafty and busy Romish Agents.' Those agents, Stephens explained, 'did really desire to have the king absolute: for a single person, they knew, was more easy to be dealt with, than a number of Men in Parliament'. But they had also sought the imposition of 'very strict Terms of Conformity and Severity against Protestant Dissenters'. For 'this they foresaw would the more effectually divide the Church and Nation, and so much the more weaken each part, and give them advantage against either, as they had occasion'. In this nefarious contrivance, the papists succeeded all too well. The Cavalier Parliament re-established the Church of England on a narrow basis, and then enacted a stream of anti-nonconformist legislation.[33]

Whatever the merits of Stephens's conspiracy theory, there is no doubt that the Restoration had been a disaster for the cause of Protestant union. Writing in early December 1688, the presbyterian diarist Roger Morrice painfully remembered that, instead of rewarding the presbyterians for bringing about the Restoration, the rigid episcopalians, or 'Hierarchists' as he termed them, had 'set themselves most treacherously to ruin them by all kind of vile Lawes they could call to mind'. Yet Morrice believed that King James's policies, particularly his attempt to forge a papist-nonconformist alliance against the Established Church, had at last made the 'Hierarchists' see the error of their ways. It was now blindingly obvious that if Protestantism was to stand against popery, the Church would be obliged to seek reconciliation with the nonconformists. According to Morrice, 'the principall men among them say, they will be content to reduce Church matters here to the State they are in in Reformed Churches beyond Seas, and herein they now speake with a morall Sincerity, and would do it while those feares are upon them for they say they cannot stand without such a Temperament.' At the Restoration, it was true, similar good intentions had soon given way to a narrow religious settlement and persecution. But it was clear that the Prince of Orange would not tolerate a return to the bad old days. It was 'morally certain', Morrice concluded, 'that while the King of France continues so formidable', Prince William 'must continue the visible publick head of the Protestant Interest in the World, and therefore will be under a necessity of using moderation and temper, and his civill interest will not admit him to be induced by any to depart therefrom'.[34] Morrice returned to this theme two months later. 'There is', he wrote in late January 1689, 'no doubt to be made but that the Prince will preserve Episcopacy and the Doctrine of the Church of England but he will not preserve the Tyranny, the Persecution, nor the Debaucheries of the Church of England.'[35]

Morrice's analysis was sound enough. If the coming war with France were to be waged successfully, then domestic harmony would be essential. And this in turn required a settlement of the old quarrels between Church and dissent. To this end, in March 1689 King William's Secretary of State, the tory Earl of Nottingham, introduced two bills in the House of Lords. The first, the so-called Comprehension Bill, sought to modify the terms of the Church's communion in order to facilitate the re-incorporation of moderate dissenters into the Established Church. As for those separatists who would be unable to conform to the new establishment, they would be granted a statutory Indulgence – an exemption from the penalties for nonconformity – by the second of Nottingham's bills.[36]

Nottingham's Comprehension Bill was something of a disappointment to Roger Morrice. True, the bill rendered optional certain obnoxious ceremonies, such as kneeling at the communion. But its terms, Morrice complained, were far less generous than those contained in an abortive measure of 1680. That bill, unlike its successor, had afforded some degree of recognition to presbyterian orders, and had not required a declaration approving the doctrine, worship and government of the Church of England.[37] Yet while Morrice moaned that the Comprehension Bill did not go far enough, there were many who believed that the proposed legislation went too far. As John Locke observed, the 'episcopal clergy' were showing themselves 'not very favourably inclined' to either the Comprehension or the Indulgence Bills.[38]

The general hostility of the Restoration Church towards the toleration of Protestant nonconformity is well known. But its aversion to comprehension was perhaps even more deeply rooted. As John Spurr has reminded us, many clerics feared that an accommodation with dissent, through a broadening of the Church's terms of communion, would simply import the nonconformist schism into the bowels of the Church of England.[39] Such views remained widespread in 1689: 'a Church that grows numerous by taking in Dissenters,' wrote an anti-comprehension pamphleteer, 'may be no stronger, than an Army that fills up its Company with Mutineers'.[40] Indeed, comprehension was felt by some to threaten the very fabric of the Established Church. 'I would have tender consciences come in at the door', Charles Godolphin told his fellow MPs in March 1689, 'and not pull down the rafters of the house to come in at the roof.'[41]

These anxieties were intensified by the favour King William showed to the whigs in the first weeks of his reign: 'whereas our former feares were of popery and Arbitrary Government,' wrote the tory Rupert Browne in mid-March, 'now it is of a commonwealth and the pressure of the Church

Figure 12 'A Trimmer Practicall', 1689. High Churchmen vehemently opposed comprehension – plans for bringing moderate dissenters back to the Establishment by modifying the Church's terms of communion. They claimed that comprehension would not end the nonconformist schism, but merely import it into the bowels of the Church – a proposition illustrated in this print. The central figure – a monstrous half-priest, half-presbyter – may represent Gilbert Burnet, the Scots-born Bishop of Salisbury.

by the Dissenters.' As Browne explained, thanks to a series of restrictive amendments Nottingham's Comprehension Bill no longer posed much of a threat to the Church. Yet 'some of the leading men that is feared councells the King' continued to give 'great jealousie and discontent to the Church of England Men.'⁴² Two weeks earlier, the Earl of Danby, one of the leaders of the Church party, had reportedly complained to the King that 'he did all things to encourage Presbutery and to dishearten the Church of England, and that he would absolutely prejudice himselfe and government by it.'⁴³

Already suspicious of King William's intentions towards the Church, tory parliamentarians were thrown into panic by the King's address to the two houses on 16 March. 'And as I doubt not but you will sufficiently provide against Papists', the King had told parliament, 'so, I hope, you will leave room for the Admission of all Protestants that are willing and able to serve.'⁴⁴ This statement, drafted by the leading whig Richard Hampden, was correctly interpreted as a call for the repeal of the sacramental test for office as it affected dissenters.⁴⁵ The Church party was outraged: 'great distaste', wrote the whiggish Edward Harley to his brother Robert, 'is taken at the King's last speech by the sons of the Church who resolve to unite in her defens to keep of[f] any thing that may eclips her dominion and Grandeur.'⁴⁶ In fact, some 150 tory MPs had already met at the Devil's Tavern to co-ordinate opposition to King William's religious policies.⁴⁷

The strength of feeling in the Commons against the principle of comprehension became clear in the debate on the new Coronation Oath on 25 March. When comprehensionist whig MPs attempted to insert in the Oath a promise to defend the Church 'as *shall be* established by law', they were defeated by 188 votes to 149. The Commons voted instead that the new monarchs swear to uphold the Church 'established by law'.⁴⁸ The implications of this rebuff,which reportedly left the whigs 'wonderfully down in the mouth', were not lost on Roger Morrice. The vote, he complained, plainly signified the Church party's 'purposes to bind the King from consenting to alter any thing in Ceremony Government or Worship that was Established by Law'.⁴⁹ By mid-April, indeed, it was clear to the Marquis of Halifax that the tories 'had rather turn papists then take in the Presbuterians amongst them'.⁵⁰

With Nottingham's Comprehension Bill becoming steadily more narrow in scope, and tory MPs openly set against the very notion of comprehension, the issue of Protestant union was brought to a head by Richard Hampden's still more whiggish son, John. On 8 April the younger Hampden introduced into the Commons a truly radical comprehension measure which would have opened the doors of the Establishment to ministers ordained by any Protestant church.⁵¹ In short, Hampden's bill sought to smash down the prelatical embankments constricting the natural flow of the English Church, leaving it free to surge back into the mainstream of European Protestantism. To put it another way, the bill would have made 'the Church of Englandmen Dissenters & not the Dissenters Church of Englandmen'.[52] Predictably, the measure caused a furore in the serried ranks of the Church party. When a day was moved for the bill's second reading, an irate tory bellowed that it was 'so destructive to ye Ch[urch] of E[ngland] he desired it ly on ye table till Doomsday'.[53]

He need not have worried. On ecclesiastical issues, the 150 or so tory die-hards could count upon the support of several more MPs who, though not committed tories, shared their anxiety for the security of the Church. As Roger Morrice glumly noted, 'the house of Commons was stronger by 80 or 100 Voices to Reform things amiss in the State than in the Church.' This left Morrice – who was coming to view Nottingham's Indulgence and Comprehension Bills as a devious sham – deeply pessimistic about the prospects for Protestant union: 'in such a juncture as this', he wrote in mid-April, 'none but malitious enemies and weake Friends to Dissenters would bring in any Bill for the uniting, or giving impunity to Dissenters, because all wise men knew they would be prostituted and made ineffectual to their end, and were intended so to be by those cunning men that brought them in, or influenced others so to doe, so that all true friends to the Reformation or to the uniting of Protestants would feigne have them laid aside at least till a better opportunity.'[54]

King William and his advisors appear to have reached a similar conclusion, for they were now prepared to sacrifice Nottingham's lacklustre Comprehension Bill in order to salvage the Indulgence. By mid-April, a deal was on the table. If the Church party agreed not to obstruct the passage of the Indulgence Bill, the King would abandon both the Comprehension Bill and the planned repeal of the sacramental test. In addition, King William promised to leave the issue of comprehension to a convocation of the clergy.[55] Since they regarded comprehension as a far more loathsome prospect than an apparently limited toleration, the tories jumped at the King's proposal. As a result, the Indulgence Bill passed smoothly through its remaining parliamentary stages, and on 24 May King William gave his assent to 'An Act for exempting their Majesties protestant subjects, dissenting from the Church of England, from the penalties of certain laws.'[56]

The Toleration Act, as the statute soon became known, removed the penalties imposed upon trinitarian dissenters for non-attendance of the Established Church, and also permitted them free public worship in licensed meeting houses.[57] Its passage both delighted and surprised nonconformists. Roger Morrice, for example, believed that the dissenters 'have great reason to be thankfull for it, for it answers its end, and gives them a due liberty with entire Security'. And yet, having only the vaguest inkling of the bargain between King William and the Church party, the usually well-informed Morrice was baffled by 'the Mystery of it, nor the true reason why the Lords Spirituall, and those Lords and Commons of their Sentiments did pass the Bill'. 'Certain it is', he noted, 'the [tory] Devil Tavern Club did call for it and did promote the passing of it.'[58] The veteran Lancashire congregationalist minister, Thomas Jolly, was similarly taken aback by the Toleration Act. 'The tydings of our publique liberty established by law', he wrote, 'must needs affect mee more than ordinary, having almost given up our hopes thereof, the majority of the Parliament being of such a [tory] complexion'.[59] Almost four years after its passage, the Toleration Act remained a source of wonder to the Yorkshire presbyterian, Oliver Heywood. 'No lesse [providential than the peace of the nation]', he mused in February 1693,

> is the wonder of publick liberty of the gospel, and spirituall priviledges main-
> tained and increased this year to great admiration: the vast numbers of new
> meeting-places erected all over the kingdom, the multitudes of hopefull
> young men sent out of private schooles yearly to supply them, the vast
> summes of money distributed through the kingdom from the fund at London
> for maintenance besides many private well-meaning gentlemen building
> meeting-places, and giving comfortable incouragement to ministers and all
> this by Act of Parliament, King, Lords and commons, in the open face of our
> Enemys, who gnash their teeth at it, but cannot hinder it, the laws being in
> force, but penalty taken off, prelacy in power, and many great ones bearing
> us no good will, and the rabble so much ag[ains]t us.[60]

By the time Heywood penned his paean to 'King William's Toleration', hopes for comprehension had long since sunk without trace. As part of the deal struck with the tories in April 1689, the King had agreed to refer consideration of comprehension to a convocation of the episcopal clergy. That body would not be able to meet for some months. In the meantime, King William set out to demonstrate his 'Princely Care for the good Order Edification and Unity of the Church of England committed to Our Charge and for the reconciling as much as possible of all differences among Our good Subjects and to take away all occasions of the like for the future'. He did so by establishing an ecclesiastical commission charged with the task of reviewing the Church's liturgy and canons, and overhauling the operation of the ecclesiastical courts.[61]

Tony Claydon has suggested that the ecclesiastical commission's warrant, with its stress on the King's care for the Church of England, was intended to counter 'the tories' perception of William as hostile to their church'.[62] If this is correct, then the plan failed miserably. When the commission met for its first, largely ceremonial, session on 17 September 1689, a number of its members, including the Archbishop of York and the Bishops of Carlisle and Exeter, were conspicuous by their absence.[63] These prelates were still nowhere to be seen when the commission got down to business in earnest on 16 October. But one who did attend, Thomas Sprat, Bishop of Rochester, was less than effusive about the commission's work.

After questioning the commission's legality, Sprat tore into its terms of reference. As John Williams, the commission's secretary recorded, the bishop 'urg'd further, that He could not see how We could enter upon such matters [changes to the liturgy and canons], having given our assent and Consent unto them, That it was to accuse the Church and condemn it, as if it needed [reform], That this was to prevent the Convocation, and that it could not be taken well by them to be call'd together to confirm that, which they had no hand in: That this would provoke the Parliament.'[64] It was the last the commission was to see of the Bishop of Rochester. Two days later, the Oxford dons William Jane and Henry Aldrich followed Sprat's lead. When their colleagues began to discuss the Church's ceremonies, the Oxford men stormed out of the meeting 'and came no more'.[65]

Designed to sabotage the work of the commission, the High Churchmen's boycott merely left the field free for the comprehensionists led by John Tillotson. By mid-November, this liberal rump – subsequently denounced by Jane as a group of men ready 'to part with any thing but their Church-preferments' – had prepared dozens of revisions to The Book of Common Prayer and drawn up new comprehension proposals. Among other things, the commission's scheme removed the obligation to make the sign of the cross in baptism; allowed the sacrament to be administered in the pews to those who objected to kneeling; empowered bishops to appoint, on the request of parishioners, alternative readers of the holy service in parishes where ministers refused to wear the surplice; and provided a compromise solution to the thorny issue of episcopal re-ordination.[66] But would the commission's proposals be acceptable to the forthcoming convocation? The prognosis was not hopeful, for events north of the border were casting a fresh shadow over the prospects of Protestant reconciliation in England.

In June 1689 King William had reluctantly assented to the abolition of episcopacy in Scotland. That event, together with the well-reported tribulations of the Scottish episcopal clergy at the hands of the triumphant presbyterians, stiffened clerical opposition to an accommodation with dissent in England. Writing from York in October, Thomas Comber averred that the 'successe of that party in Scotland ag[ains]t Episcopacy, and the opinion of their numbers and interest here hath lately advanced their pretences to liberty of Conscience into hopes of legall establishment and Dominion over all others, to which I know the great pillars of our Church will be cautious how they contribute'. Indeed, Comber was deeply sceptical about the whole concept of comprehension, fearing that 'our condescensions will only help them with arguments to upbraid us, not incline them to part with one opinion in order to a coalition'. There were, it was true, some moderate presbyterians who could be re-incorporated into the Church on reasonable terms. 'But the greater part of Dissenters here', Comber continued, 'are independents, who seem incapable of any thing but toleration, and cannot be taken in but by such concessions as will shake the foundation of our Church: and possibly by attempting to gain such as after all will be false friends, we may drive out many true ones both of considerable Clergy and Laity also.'[67]

Comber's disquiet was a portent of things to come. When convocation at last met in late November 1689, it soon became apparent that its lower house was set against any compromise with dissent. A contest for the pro-locutorship (chair) of the lower house resulted in a decisive victory for William Jane over John Tillotson.[68] In the ensuing weeks, convocation did not even condescend to debate the commission's proposals. But their fate was sealed by the furore surrounding convocation's address to the King. As Bishop Burnet of Salisbury explained a little later, the lower clergy

> rejected the Mention that was made in the draught of the Address which the Bishops sent them of the Protestant Religion in generall, as well as the Church of England in particular, for even that looked like an expression favourable to the Churches that had not Bishops, & tho the avoiding to name the Protestant Religion seemed to be a very invidious thing at ye time, yet they refused to do it rather than give the least advantage to any healing propositions. There were then but a few Bishopps in the upper House of Convocation, so they had not authority enough to governe the lower, and found it necessary to begg the Kings leave to put off their sessions which was done, and they have never met since.[69]

Burnet was dismayed by the blow which convocation had dealt to the cause of Protestant union. 'It raised a great out-cry against the Church', he recalled in 1691, 'when it appeared that after all the promises of modera-tion that had been made in King James's time the Convocation was not in a temper to bear the proposing of any thing which tended that way.' For their part, the bishop reported, the lower clergy 'said to justify them-selves that it was very visible from all the proceedings in Scotland that the King was no freind to the Church, and that therefore it was necessary for them to stand their ground and to stick firme to one another'.[70] Nor was the baleful impact of events in Scotland lost upon Burnet's colleague, Bishop Stillingfleet of Worcester. According to Robert Kirk, a visiting Scottish episcopalian, Stillingfleet was convinced that 'many of the Convocation, from whom he does not disassociate himself', were put 'upon not yielding a jot' by the disaster which had befallen the episcopalian cause in Scotland.[71] Intransigent the 'hierarchists' may have been. But who could blame them?

It would certainly be wrong to attribute continued Protestant divisions solely to High Church obduracy.[72] True, hardline Churchmen, in both parliament and convocation, had proved the nemesis of the 1689 compre-hension plans. But it is by no means clear that the terms on offer in 1689 would, in any event, have been acceptable to most dissenters. Roger Morrice, so often the voice of moderate nonconformity, contrasted Nottingham's Comprehension Bill unfavourably with its predecessors in the exclusion parliaments. 'In the three Parliaments in Anno 1678 1679 1680', he wrote in March 1689,

> The Hierarchists offered some generous and large concessions in a Bill they put into the House of Commons, which with a few additions would have made a rationall Comprehension Act That would have taken all the Dissenters in the Kingdome into the Nationall Church that were Comprehensible, and this no doubt were the true Nationall interest, But now they offer for a Bill of Comprehension no such generous Concessions nor none that will comprehend any Dissenters I thinke at all, and so force them all to run in with the Tollerated or those only which have impunity.[73]

Morrice's fellow presbyterian, Matthew Henry, was similarly un-enamoured with Nottingham's pallid bill. 'It pleases me well that the Comprehension Bill is for the present laid aside,' he wrote to his father in May 1689, 'for better none than uncomprehending.'[74] So Bishop Burnet was spot-on when he informed a foreign Protestant in July 1689 that, while the 'stricter Conformists' were convinced that the proposed terms were too generous, the dissenters were 'hoping for more'.[75] A great deal more in the case of the most senior nonconformist leaders, Richard Baxter, William Bates and John Howe. In January 1689, at the height of revolutionary excitement, those three worthies had even contemplated reviving 'many particulars' of the 1645 Uxbridge Treaty, an abortive Civil War settlement which had contained proposals for reforming the episcopal office along presbyterian lines.[76] To those who looked back to the puritan heyday of the 1640s, Nottingham's comprehension bill must have seemed very small beer indeed.

As we have seen, the bill's death did not spell the end of efforts to bring moderate dissenters back to the bosom of the Church. And in November 1689, when a new comprehension scheme was being drawn up by the ecclesiastical commission, Roger Morrice remained adamant that 'the Non-Conformists would for the interest of Religions sake be very forward to come into the Church in that there was a necessity of preserving the Nationall Church of England, because those that most neede instruction, will go to the publick Church if Turcisme, Judaisme, or Popery were intro-duced into it.'[77] Yet would the commission's scheme really have satisfied the presbyterians? William Wake, one of the younger generation of comprehensionist clergymen, thought not. In November 1689 he told Arthur Charlett, Master of University College, Oxford, that he expected 'little good' from the forthcoming convocation 'unless Gods providence do's wonderfully over-rule our passions'. Rightly believing comprehension to be doomed, Wake paradoxically welcomed the abuse being heaped upon 'men of latitude' like himself by the anti-comprehensionists. For it would show the world 'that it is not our fault that we do not take away all just grounds of dissent, from those, who when all is done will I fear never be persuaded to unite with us'.[78]

There was indeed one virtually insuperable barrier in the path of comprehension: the Church's long-standing insistence on the episcopal re-ordination of ministers who had received only presbyterian ordination. In the eyes of dissenters, that insistence amounted to a refusal on the part of the Church to recognise the validity of presbyterian orders. And as a nonconformist writer complained in 1689, such a refusal 'destroys the Church State, not only of Dissenters, but of all other Protestants in the World, except of those in the Church of England, nulling their Ministry, Sacraments, and Discipline'. Accordingly, any comprehension scheme which required episcopal re-ordination was 'none at all'. Rather it was a mere 'offer to Unite with Dissenters on their doing what is to them Impossible; They cannot renounce their Ordination, nor Consent to the Destroying their own, nor the Church State of Reformed Protestants Abroad'.[79] If, on the other hand, the comprehensionists agreed to drop the requirement of episcopal re-ordination, they risked opening a schism in the Church greater by far than the one they hoped to heal. In the Autumn of 1689 the ecclesiastical commission had sought to square the circle by means of a compromise. The orders of foreign presbyterians were to be recognized as valid but imperfect, and those seeking preferment in the English Church would be obliged to have their orders 'perfected' through the episcopal laying-on of hands. As for English presbyterians, those who aspired to minister in the Established Church would not be compelled to renounce their orders. But they would be required to undergo an ambiguous ceremony in which the officiating bishop was to recite the following formula: 'If thou art not already ordained, I ordain thee.'[80] This palpable fudge satisfied nobody, and it died a generally unlamented death when the good ship comprehension was torpedoed by convocation in December 1689.

The miscarriage of the ecclesiastical commission's plan did not destroy the cause of Protestant union. As we shall see in a later chapter, co-operation between the godly of all persuasions was the cornerstone of the societies for reformation of manners established after 1691.[81] The events of 1689 had, however, killed stone dead any prospect of a formal rapprochement between the Church and moderate dissent. John Tillotson's elevation to the primacy in 1691 promised for a time to breathe new life into the corpse. But after the mauling he had received in the 1689 convocation, the leader of the comprehensionist clergy was in no mood to take risks. 'I must needs acknowledge this which I know to be true,' wrote the well-informed Roger Morrice after Tillotson's death in 1694, 'that about the time when Dr Tillotson was Nominated Archbishop of

Canterbury, he would not consent for Peace Sake to Relax Reordination, Not because he could not have done so as to his own particular Judgement, but because many of their followers would have deserted, and separated from them if they should have so done, and they must not loose known old freinds for doubtfull new ones.'[82] From his own words, we know that Tillotson had indefinitely shelved plans for comprehension by February 1691. 'One thing in my opinion is to be deeply regretted', he wrote to a Dutch theologian, 'that there are many on both sides, of our church, as well as among the Dissenters, who know not the means nor way of peace. I cannot therefore foresee what will at last be the issue of these pacific counsels. As affairs now stand in England, I think nothing of this kind should be attempted for the present; but that we ought to wait till the times grow more disposed to a peace.'[83]

Like Archbishop Tillotson, John Hampden, author of the most radical plan for Protestant union in 1689, eventually turned his back on comprehension, although for rather different reasons. Hampden was suspicious of the motives of some of the comprehensionists, and feared that comprehension would be a pretext for curtailing toleration. 'I should be much for actuall Union among all Protestants in England, if I thought it could be obtain'd', he confided to a dissenting minister in 1693,

> but I have really laid aside all thoughts of Comprehension, ever since I saw plainly that the design of some who drove it was only to destroy obliquely, & by a sidewind, what had been gain'd, at a favourable time, in the Act of Toleration, which they durst not directly attempt to overthrow. 'Tis better to have half a loafe than no bread, & much more adviseable to stick at Liberty of Conscience, where we are, than with Esop's dog, to lose the Shoulder of mutton of which we are in possession, by chopping at the Shadows of another, which will deceive us.[84]

Yet, as we shall now see, even half a loaf and a single shoulder of mutton would prove too much for many Churchmen.

3.   Toleration, the Test and Occasional Conformity

During the last four years of Charles II's reign, church and state had worked hand in hand to crush political and religious dissent. From their pulpits, clergymen preached damnation against those who dared to resist the Lord's anointed. At the same time, the heavy hand of the law was brought down hard and often across the necks of Protestant nonconformists. This symbiotic relationship between the secular and the spiritual arms did not long outlive King Charles. Severely shaken by James II's Declarations of Indulgence, it was utterly broken by the Toleration Act of 1689. Many clergymen found this difficult to accept. 'Till the Tolleration is broke, and a persecution of Dissenters is set on foot', lamented Bishop Burnet in September 1693, the 'high sort of Church-men' in his diocese of Salisbury 'will still conclude that the Church of England is persecuted, or at least neglected, And they cannot with any patience bear a man that has declared himself so openly against those things as I have done'.[85] Six months later, the whiggish judge Thomas Rokeby was appalled when the preacher at the Dorchester assizes 'reflected upon ye indulgence by Act of Parl[iament] to Protestant dissenters, and s[ai]d ye wisdom of ye nation had giv[e]n every man liberty to spit in ye face of ye Church, & had taken away all ye means of correcting strife & envyings in ye Church'.[86]

Such clerics would doubtless have been enthusiastic readers of a critique of the Toleration Act, penned by the nonjuror Charles Leslie. Writing in 1694, Leslie contended that the statutory Indulgence had undermined the Church in both theory and practice. If the Church 'be jure divino', he reasoned, 'then it is out of the parliament's power to abolish it, or even to dispense with, or tolerate, any other form of government in the church'. Thus acceptance of the Toleration Act meant that 'we must give up our jure divino right, which we have endeavoured to hold out so long against the dissenters; and profess to hold hereafter by no other tenure than that of an act of parliament, which now grants equal liberty to the dissenters as to ourselves.' What was more, the Indulgence had

> rendered our church a perfect cypher; and if any, or all, of our flocks should desert us to-morrow, and go over openly to the dissenters, we have no power left us, by this act, to restrain any of them by ecclesiastical censures or any other way; and the whole nation have liberty to believe any of their communions to be as safe a way to heaven as our own. And they have made full use of that liberty; for how many do we meet with who do not believe it, and think it a thing indifferent which of our churches they go to, as they term the dissenters and ours? They think them all to be churches; and the law giving equal liberty to all, who dare quarrel with any for taking that liberty to go to any or all of these churches?

In short, Leslie concluded, the Toleration Act 'has divested us of all our authority over the people'.[87]

Leslie's claims were by no means without substance. In November 1693 William Lloyd, now bishop of Lichfield and Coventry, reported the grievances of his clergy to Bishop Stillingfleet of Worcester. Dissenting ministers had taken it upon themselves 'to baptize the children of all such as will send for them to their houses to do that office, as commonly their Parishioners will, if their Minister holds them to observe the laws of our own church in bringing their children to public Baptisme, & in many the like cases'. Deeply concerned by this state of affairs, Bishop Lloyd sought his colleague's advice 'on the best way of dealing with those dissenting Ministers: For to punish those Parishioners', he glumly concluded, 'would be to drive them from the Church & so to fill their congregations.'[88]

While Bishop Lloyd feared a drift away from the Church to the meeting house, other clergymen complained that the Toleration Act was being treated as a licence to attend no place of worship at all: 'they that continually stay at home, & never go to Church or meeting, do plead the Tolleration in their defence', reported a Bedfordshire clergyman in December 1692, '& many have no other notion of the Indulgence, but that it is a libertie to do what they please, & go where they please, & stay at home when they please.'[89] The previous June, Archdeacon Prideaux of Norwich had similarly bemoaned the consequences of the Toleration Act, which 'hath almost undon us, not in increasing ye number of dissenters but of wicked and profane persons; for it is now difficult almost to get any to church, all pleading ye licence, although they make use of it only for ye alehouse'.[90] Prideaux returned to this theme in mid-July: 'as to ye Toleration Act,' he wrote to his kinsman John Ellis, 'unlesse there be some regulation made on it, in a short time it will turne halfe the nation into downe right athiesme. I do not find it in my archdeaconry (and I believe it is the same in other places) that conventicles have gained anything at all thereby, but reather that they have lost. But', the archdeacon continued,

> the mischief is, a liberty being now granted, more lay hold of it to separate from all manner of worship to perfect irreligion then goe to them; and although the Act allows no such liberty, the people will understand it soe, and, say what ye judges can at ye assizes, or ye justice of peace at their sessions, or we at our visitations, noe churchwarden or counstable will present any for not goeing to church, though they goe noe where else but to the alehouse, for this liberty they will have.[91]

Nor did the diffidence of churchwardens lessen appreciably as the years passed. On the contrary, the problem seemed so great by 1700 that the recently-established Society for Promoting Christian Knowledge urged its correspondents to present to the JPs those wardens who had themselves failed to present parishioners for non-attendance.[92]

The advent of religious pluralism in the 1690s presented the post-revolution cleric with challenges largely unknown to his Restoration predecessor. No longer could clergymen rely upon the legal sanctions at the disposal of the secular arm to suppress nonconformity and enforce attendance at their churches. Nevertheless, given energy and the support of influential lay people, the lot of the parochial clergyman was far from hopeless in the new world created by the Toleration Act. When the Reverend Edward Bowerman came to the Bedfordshire parish of Caddington in 1691, he found his church poorly attended and the religious life of the parish in a most disorderly state. Among other things, the altar rails, torn down during the Civil War, had still to be re-erected; the communion table was given over to profane uses; and the behaviour of parishioners in church 'was the most indecent & irreverent that I ever beheld'. When 'I began to pray in the Pulpit', Bowerman recalled, 'some of them got upon their legs, & yawn'd & stretched themselves; & after I had named my Text many of them put on their hatts, tho it was in the most scorching time of July'. Yet, if Bowerman is to be believed, his tireless badgering of adult parishioners and catechising of the young, coupled with the pious example set by a newly-arrived gentry family, soon effected a remarkable transformation in the formal religious life of the parish. In 1691 only twenty-four of Bowerman's parishioners had attended the Christmas Day communion. But at Easter 1692 the cleric 'administered the sacrament to an hundred; and at Whitsontide twelve more were added to the number'. Bowerman's congregation had 'begun now to put on a new face, & much decency & order was seen in the Church; their irreverence & drouziness was changed into devotion & serious attention; & those that could read bore their parts in the service, & many now joynd in the responses & singing, which before were confined to the Clerk alone & all stood up when the Psalms were sung'. Not all, however, was rosy in Bowerman's garden. On more than one occasion, devotees of the old lax regime had alleged that his efforts to promote a more regular and seemly devotion were nothing but popery. Nor did Bowerman make much of an impression upon Caddington's Quaker and Baptist sectaries. The 'poor deluded People of those Opinions are so pouffed up with pride, & possessed with an assurance of their holiness & Election,' he reported to Bishop Tenison of Lincoln in December 1692, 'that they are deaf to the clearest Testimonies of reason & scripture, & deride the fairest means of conviction'. There was, in fact, 'not one of a thousand among them that knows what schism means, or beleive they are guilty of the crime, since they are freed by the Laws from the penalty of it'.[93]

As the years passed, clergymen found it no easier to come to terms with the emancipation of dissent. Particularly galling was the growth of unlicensed dissenting education. Although the Toleration Act had given no sanction to the establishment of nonconformist schools, dissenters interpreted the statute as doing just that. In this respect, the experiences of Bishop Lloyd of Lichfield and Coventry are once again revealing. In November 1693 Lloyd informed Bishop Stillingfleet of an encounter with one Woodhouse, an unlicensed nonconformist schoolmaster, during a recent visitation of his diocese. Summoned to show Bishop Lloyd his nonexistent licence, Woodhouse had coolly retorted that he was 'enabled to do what he did by the Act of Toleration'. When the bishop pressed 'him to shew me this in the Act', Woodhouse simply 'shewed me that clause where it is said that Dissenters, so qualified as the act requires shall not be troubled for non-conformity in Religion'.[94] Having been given an inch by the Toleration Act, the dissenters, it seemed, were intent upon stealing two or three miles. What was more, the secular authorities appeared disinclined to rein in the encroachments of dissenters like Woodhouse. Writing again to Bishop Stillingfleet in January 1694, Bishop Lloyd lamented that 'the Nursery of Schism, which to my great grief is within 7 miles of this place, to my greater grief you tell me of no way I have to suppress it but by the Justices of Peace who if they had any mind to do any thing of that kind might & would have done it before my coming into the Country'.[95]

Nonconformist attempts to broaden 'the toleration' reinforced the prejudices of those Churchmen who believed that the dissenters were bent upon the destruction of the Church of England. In December 1693 Anthony Wood, the Oxford antiquary, wrote scathingly of the 'effect of toleration – instead of enjoying their religion in peace without disturbance, they endeavour to pull downe the Church by their writings and preachings'.[96] Speaking in 1694, after King William's swing to the whigs, a tory parliamentarian averred that the presbyterians would never be satisfied with a mere toleration. Both the history of the 1640s and more recent events in Scotland showed conclusively that men of that ilk sought domination, not toleration.[97] In the mind of Abraham de la Pryme, High Church son of a presbyterian father, the nonconformist challenge assumed nothing less than apocalyptic proportions. 'Having been a little melancholy this day,' he confided to his diary on 10 October 1696,

> I was very pensive and sedate, and, while I remained so, there came several strange thoughts in my heart, which I could not get shutt of. Methought I foresaw a Religious War in the nation, in which our most apostolick and blessed church should fall prey to the wicked, sacriligeous, non-conformists, who should almost utterly extinguish the same, and set up in the place thereof their own enthusiastick follys, which God prevent! however, I foresee the downfall of those famous patriots the Bishops, and that those that shall be the authors thereof shall have far less religion and goodness in them than them, and that, whatever their pretence is, the chief thing that they shall pluck down this holy order for will be to get their lands and estates. Then will England be fill'd with all manner of confusion and horror, and shall stand like a drunken man, many years, untill that God have pour'd out all the wraith of his cup upon it.[98]

By the mid–1690s the 'high sort' of Churchman was fast coming to look upon the heyday of the 'Church state' in the early 1680s as a lost golden age, and the reign of King William as a living nightmare. Yet the revolution had, in fact, left untouched the central bulwark of the Caroline 'Church state', the sacramental qualification for local and central office required respectively by the Corporation Act of 1661 and the Test Act of 1673. At the revolution, dissenters had looked forward eagerly to the repeal of the sacramental test, viewing it as the surest way of demolishing the Restoration church settlement: 'once let these men [the dissenters] into the State,' wrote Roger Morrice at the end of December 1688, 'and they will let the Outed Ministers into the Church.'[99] For that very reason, tories insisted that the sacramental test should stay. And it was their views which had prevailed in the Convention parliament, to the bitter disappointment of dissenting ministers like Philip Henry. 'When you write to any of our law-makers', he had instructed his son upon the passage of the Toleration Act, 'acknowl[edge] their kindness & paines in procuring it with all thankfulness, but till the Sacramental Test bee taken off, our Business is not done.'[100]

Parliament's failure to repeal the sacramental test appalled the dissenters and their friends in the whig party. For one thing, the retention of the test deprived King William of the services of many loyal Protestants at a time of mortal peril to the nation. 'It is for the King's Interest that the Sacramental-Test should be taken away', asserted a pamphleteer in 1689. 'For by means thereof many worthy Persons and good Protestants, who are every way Qualified for Publick Employments, are made uncapable of serving His Majesty, the English Nation, or the Protestant Interest.' Thus 'nothing can be thought of, which at this Juncture will more Effectually promote the Interest of the Papists, than to continue a Test which does so unhappily divide Protestants one from another, making them unable to afford their Joynt-assistance against the Common Enemy . . . Shall we for a Ceremony which may lawfully be removed,' the pamphleteer asked, 'hazard the Ruin of the Nation! and the whole Protestant Interest in the World also?'[101] Similarly, in March 1689 six whig peers protested that the retention of the sacramental test was not only unjust but also incompatible with the national interest: 'it gives great part of the Protestant Freemen of England reason to complain of inequality and hard usage when they are excluded from publick Employment by a Law, and also because it deprives the King and Kingdome of divers men fit and capable to serve the publick stations, and that from a meer scruple of Conscience which can by no means render them suspected, much less disaffected to the Government.'[102] Thus the exclusion of nonconformists from office was an absurdity, making as much sense as a man ripping off 'the Limbs of his Body for a Spot upon the Skin'.[103]

As well as condemning the test for senselessly dividing the Protestant interest, its opponents also complained that the sacramental qualification for office was a shameful prostitution of the sacrament. As a pamphleteer wrote in 1689, the 'Holy Sacrament was not appointed by the Lord Jesus Christ, to be used as a qualification for Civil Offices, but for other Sacred Ends and Purposes'. Thus 'to use it as a Test for Civil Employments, is to Pervert and Corrupt an Holy Ordinance of God, and consequently to Transgress the Divine Law.'[104] This was a point taken up with some gusto by the French Protestant, Jean Gailhard. A 'great evil there is amongst us,' he wrote in 1694,

> that the posture of receiving the holy sacrament, an ordinance of God to seal the pardon of our sins, and strengthen our faith, is made use of for a trial of those who are qualified for worldly employments; to turn it to temporal ends, is an unaccountable profaneness of that holy institution: And though without such a bye-consideration I could receive it kneeling, I declare if I should receive it in that manner, upon the account of such a trial, I could not avoid believing I had eaten and drank my damnation.[105]

But not all dissenters were quite so scrupulous as Gailhard. On the contrary, many nonconformists were ready to qualify themselves for office by taking the sacrament in the Established Church at least once a year. In the City of London, for example, so-called occasional conformists formed the backbone of whig representation on the aldermanic bench and in common council.[106]

It would be wrong to view the widespread practice of occasional conformity as a mere device on the part of dissenters to circumvent the Corporation and Test Acts. There was still something of a grey area between conformity and moderate dissent. Presbyterians, in particular, were keen to keep one foot within the Church of England. But in the post-revolution context of open nonconformity and – after 1693 – whig political dominance, occasional conformity took on a thoroughly sinister appearance in tory eyes. 'Men of the Presbyterian principle can't be content with Toleration', argued a tory parliamentarian in 1694. In 'the late times it was by degrees that they had wormed out the Church. Wee must take care that they advance not too far now. The men that favour them will have all or nothing, & wee have experienced that we are not the safer because they can qualifie themselves by taking our Sacrament to disguise their purposes.'[107] 'And have not we seen', asked another devotee of the Church party, 'within these few yeares men qualify themselves by taking the Sacrament in our Church that they might be Sheriffs & Lord Mayors of London, who, before & since they were magistrates, went to Conventicles? . . . We are in danger,' he grimly concluded, 'of these Church-Fanaticks, these Sacrament-taking hyppocrites.'[108]

The prominence of 'Church-Fanaticks' in the civic life of the metropolis was vividly demonstrated in November 1697 by the actions of the Lord Mayor, Sir Humphrey Edwin. Having attended morning service at St Paul's, Edwin proceeded in full mayoral regalia to a presbyterian meeting house for afternoon sermons.[109] High Churchmen were scandalised. Writing in the wake of the Edwin episode, William Baron, a nonjuror, claimed that 'the Holy Sacrament goes down as glib with them [the dissenters] as the Covenant of old; there is no Scruple, when the Cause is concern'd.'[110] And that cause was the destruction of the episcopal

Church of England. For though, like the tribes of Israel, the dissenters were divided among themselves, 'yet the Judah of the Church of England, is the united Object of all their Spites, and what they study most implacably to supplant and destroy'.[111] By the end of King William's reign such fears had helped to make occasional conformity the principal bugbear of the Church party, and in the tory parliament of 1701 legislation was proposed to penalise the practice. This first attempt to legislate against occasional conformity proved abortive.[112] But it foreshadowed the controversy which was to dominate the early years of Queen Anne's reign.

4. Anti-Clericalism and Heterodoxy

After the revolution, the Church of England clergy discovered, to their cost, that two extremes can be brought together by a shared contempt for the middle ground. Denounced by nonjurors for clinging on to their livings at the expense of their principles, the swearing clergy also found themselves accused of time-serving hypocrisy by anti-clericals. For by abandoning their old shibboleth of non-resistance, and swearing allegiance to the revolution monarchs, clergymen had shown that expediency was their governing doctrine. 'When all the Argument is out', mused William Stephens in 1696, 'Tis Interest still resolves the doubt.' On that score, Stephens, who was himself a priest in the Established Church, could find nothing to choose between the Church of England and the Church of Rome: 'there is now no need of going over the Water to discover that the name Church signifieth only a Self-interested Party, and that the Clergy have no Godliness but Gain.'[113]

Once again like the nonjurors, although for very different reasons, anti-clericals denounced the *de facto* theory of allegiance in which so many clerics had taken refuge. Whereas nonjurors dismissed *de facto* theory as a blind to obscure the Church's abandonment of its old principles, anti-clericals took it to show that the clergy's allegiance to the new regime was no more than skin-deep. Most clergymen, it was true, had taken the oaths to William and Mary. But they had done so in a fashion so hedged about with qualifications that it was still possible for the Church to worm its way back into favour with its once and, perhaps, future king.[114] All this went to show that the Church of England was 'nothing but a Party', concerned only with preserving its privileged status.[115]

Nothing better illustrated the essential factiousness of the Established Church than its hostility towards Protestant dissenters. In his *Account of the Growth of Deism in England*, published in 1696, William Stephens denounced his own Church by purportedly reporting the views of an anti-clerical layman – a 'Deist' who rejects the Church of England's pretensions to religious authority. 'I have heard it said of late by another of the same Constitution', wrote Stephens,

> that as the Church of Rome was a modelled Faction against all other Christians, so was the Church of England, by Law Established, against all other Protestants, who were by Law excluded from every Office of Profit and Trust; who were made subject to the Piques and Malice of every Church-man, and become a constant Revenue to Apparitors and Spiritual Catch-poles [the informers who had taken a share of the fines imposed on conventiclers before the revolution]. And though at present there be a Toleration by Law granted, yet 'tis still opposed by the Spirit of the Church, as appears by Sermons Preached at Visitations, and the constant ordinary Discourses of the Clergy, in which the Church of England is always represented, as at this time, in greater danger than ever it was; though I shall think the danger had been as great in King James's Time: And notwithstanding the Toleration (said he) no Man can enjoy a place of Profit or Trust, though he be ever so dutiful a Subject, and ever so able or honest a Man, unless he hath a Conscience by Law Established: By which Church-device Men are deprived of the Privileges of their Country to which they are born, and for the discharge whereof they never did in any respect incapacitate themselves; and hereby it comes to pass, that the Nation cannot act vigorously in its own defence, being debarr'd the Use of one Moiety of it self; and notwithstanding this, they have the Confidence to tell us Lay-men, that we ought to love our Neighbours as our selves. Now if this be the way of Christians (concluded he) let my soul be with the Philosophers.[116]

Later in the same piece, Stephens rammed home his attack upon the temporal power and influence of the Established Church. 'I shall be cautious how I enter into Church-membership,' states his spurious interlocutor, 'since I plainly see that every Party of Christians embodied, organized, clegy'd and modelled into a National Church, casteth an awe upon the Sovereign Power, and suffereth it not to provide equally for the Common Good of the subject, but will appropriate the salus publica, and influence the Government to serve its own particular, its own private ends.'[117] And those private ends were invariably at odds with the civil and religious liberties of the subject. For if, claims the 'Deist',

> you will be a Son of the Church of England you must hold Kings and Bishops to be jure divino, the Apostolical Doctrine of Passive Obedience; you must not be indifferent to their Ceremonies, though declar'd but indifferent things; and the Reason is, because you must have a profound Respect for the Powers of the Bishops, by which these Ceremonies were ordain'd: And besides this, you must shew a perfect Abhorrence of all who do not submit to the Spiritual Royalties of their Diocesan Bishops; for your Churchmanship will not appear by any Mark so well, as by the Hatred you bear to all Dissenters, in Conjunction with a deep aversion to all the ancient Rights and just Liberties of your Native Country.[118]

The Church of England was not unique in concocting spurious doctrines to serve its own interests. Ever since the beginning of organised religion, averred Sir Robert Howard in his *History of Religion*, priests had laboured to manufacture mysterious doctrines so they might lord it over a bamboozled laity. As Howard explained,

> the more various and intricate they contrived the Methods and Rules of Devotion and Worship, so much the more there would be need of their Interpretations and Directions, and also of their Numbers. Things most ridiculous and improbable, nay impossible, were sometimes most proper for them to pronounce and teach: for what is rational carries its own Weight; and they could derive no Authority to themselves by such a Method of Religion. But things that are sublime, above the reach of servile Reason, things that Reason cannot understand or justify, if believed, must be an entire Submission to the sacred Authority of these Divinely inspired Persons, that are the Teachers of others: to this purpose they ever taught, that no Belief can or ought to be hard to an Active Faith; the Difficulty not being in the things we are taught to believe, but in the Perverseness or Imbecility of the Persons who want Faith to believe.[119]

It was indeed the chief contention of anti-clerical writers that true religion had been corrupted from its pure state by the obfuscations of a self-serving clerical caste. The clergy, they argued, had buried the simple truths of religion under an insupportable mound of superstitious mysteries and obscure doctrines. Thus had unvarnished natural religion, serving the good of society as a whole, been supplanted by the mumbo-jumbo of 'priestcraft', designed to keep the laity in thrall to the clergy. 'It hath been observed to me,' wrote the priestly enemy of priestcraft William Stephens,

> that where the Notion of a Church hath been carried on with the Highest Tide, there ever natural Religion is at the lowest Ebb; as in Italy of old, and lately in France, where gross Immoralities and Atheism are at the greatest height. And though in our Reformation we discarded some Idolatrous and Superstitious Doctrines and Practices, which were grown scandalous among the People, yet still Christ was made to serve that turn, which his Holy Vicar can no longer do, viz. Support an Holy Order of Men in as haughty Insolences, in as proud, ambitious and malicious Designs, as those which King Henry (though a Son of the Church) and his times could not bear.[120]

And it was self-serving priestcraft, rather than anti-clerical rationalism, which was once again threatening to bring religion into disrepute with the people. In Nicholas Rowe's play, *Tamerlane*, a Muslim cleric presses the eponymous hero – a King William-like champion of civil and religious liberty – to break faith with his Christian friends, and launch a holy war in alliance with the wicked Ottoman Sultan, Bayazit. For such a war, asserts the cleric, was an ordinance of the Prophet himself. His plea is given short shrift by Tamerlane:

No – thou do'st bely him,
Thou Maker of new Faiths! that dar'st to build
Thy fond Inventions on Religion's Name.
Religion's Lustre is by native Innocence
Divinely pure, and simple from all Arts;
You daub and dress her like a common Mistress,
The Harlot of your Fancies; and by adding
False Beauties, which she wants not, makes the World
Suspect, her Angel's Face is foul beneath,
And wo'not bear all Lights.[121]

In the view of many anti-clericals, the clearest example of the corruption of natural religion by priestcraft was the absurd doctrine of the Trinity. All churches 'agree the Belief of your Trinity is absolutely necessary to Salvation,' observes the sceptical layman in Stephens's *Account of the Growth of Deism*, 'and yet widely differ in what we must believe concerning it; whether three Minds or Modes, or Properties, or external Denominations; or else no more than a Holy Three, or Three Somewhats; or otherwise only one of these Three to be God in the highest Sense, and each of the other two to be a God without Self-subsistence and Independence.' That being so, it was plain that the Trinity could be no part of true religion. 'I am confident,' concludes the layman, 'if I should be perswaded that an Explanation of the Trinity were necessary to save my Soul, and see the learned so widely differing and hotly disputing what it is I must believe concerning it, I should certainly run mad through despair of finding out the Truth.'[122] Indeed, the doctrine of the Trinity was held by many anti-clericals, including Stephen Nye in his *Brief History of the Unitarians*, to be the source of all corruption in the Christian religion.[123]

Nye's *Brief History of the Unitarians*, first published before the revolution, was reprinted in 1691, probably under the auspices of Thomas Firmin. A London merchant, Firmin was perhaps the most celebrated philanthropist of the day. But he also gained much notoriety in the 1690s for sponsoring the publication and dissemination of Socinian (anti-trinitarian) tracts.[124] The brazenness of Firmin and the writers he sponsored, which increased still further after the end of press licensing in 1695, induced apoplexy in the champions of orthodoxy. 'What open Defiance hath of late been given to all the Sacred Mysteries of the Gospel, what barefaced Opposition hath been made to the Christian Faith, is well known, and is sadly Lamented by every serious and considerate Man', wrote James Lardner, a clergyman of the Established Church, in 1700. 'The labouring Press', he continued,

doth, almost every day, produce some sly Pamphlet or other; the design of which, is to Undermine our most Holy Religion, and Ridicule and Scoff at all the Professors of it: Nor do these things steal secretly into our Hands, or by their Privacy betray an inward Shame in the Author, but every Page doth publickly declare, that the Publisher of it is a profess'd Enemy to the Faith of Christ. The Opposition is made with so much Courage and Boldness, that a neer Stranger would hardly believe Christianity to be the Religion of our Country, or that the Gospel had the Protection of the Law to guard it.[125]

Thomas Bray, the rector of the Warwickshire parish of Sheldon, was similarly aghast at the rising tide of heterodoxy. Since the revolution, he lamented in 1696, the avowed enemies of Christianity had 'enter'd through our Breaches into the very heart of our City (as St Austin calls the Church of God)'.[126] That same year, to the boundless distress of its defenders, a good deal more of the City of God was overrun by John Toland's *Christianity not Mysterious*, the most notorious of all the heterodox tracts. By the late 1690s, then, the onslaught of the forces of anti-clericalism and heterodoxy was assuming ever more menacing proportions in the eyes of clergymen. How that onslaught might be contained and repelled was a question which preoccupied many ecclesiastics, not least the rector of Sheldon.

5.   The New Episcopate and the Reinvigoration of the Church

Between 1689 and 1691 the deprivation of the nonjuring bishops and the deaths of several other incumbents created no fewer than 18 vacancies on the episcopal bench.[127] This provided King William and Queen Mary with a unique opportunity to refashion the episcopate in their own image. They did not waste it. Onto the bench came clerics sympathetic to the broad Protestant ideals of the new regime. They included Prince William's chaplain during the invasion of England, Gilbert Burnet (Bishop of Salisbury from 1689), and a group of prominent London clergymen whom Burnet had recommended to the Prince in December 1688: John Tillotson (the Queen's favourite clergyman and Archbishop of Canterbury from 1691), John Sharp (Archbishop of York from 1691), Simon Patrick (Bishop of Chichester in 1689 and Ely from 1691), Edward Stillingfleet (Bishop of Worcester from 1689), Edward Fowler (Bishop of Gloucester from 1691) and Thomas Tenison (Bishop of Lincoln in 1691 and Tillotson's successor as primate in 1694).[128]

The new bishops, with the possible exception of Edward Fowler, were not whigs in any meaningful sense of the term. Many of them were close associates of the Earl of Nottingham, champion of moderate toryism, and may have shared his conviction that the whigs wanted to dismantle the Establishment.[129] Thomas Tenison, for one, reportedly urged his parishioners to reject the whig candidates during the Westminster election of 1690.[130] Yet for all this, the post-revolution bishops were a rather different breed of men from their 'hierarchist' predecessors. The distinction was most marked in their approach to the nonconformist issue. Whereas

Archbishop Sancroft had viewed the prospect of reconciliation with dissent in 1688 as, at best, a necessary evil, the new prelates – many of whom had been active members of King William's ecclesiastical commission – tended to look upon Protestant union as a wholly desirable political and spiritual objective. For that reason, they had been prepared to make real concessions to dissenters in 1689. [131]

As we have seen, the ecclesiastical commission's concessions may well have proved insufficient to entice significant numbers of dissenters back to the Church. But they were more than enough to expose the new bishops to the charge – vehemently pressed by nonjuring critics such as Charles Leslie and Thomas Wagstaffe – that they were at best lukewarm Churchmen, and at worst downright enemies of the episcopal Church of England.[132] Archbishop Tillotson was especially vulnerable to such accusations. In the first place, the cool rationality of the primate's sermons – which won the praise of that noted anti-clerical, Sir Robert Howard – and his well-known friendship with the anti-trinitarian Thomas Firmin placed a question-mark against his own orthodoxy.[133] Worse still, few tories had forgotten that in 1661 the young Tillotson had attended the Savoy conference on liturgical reform as a member, albeit a minor one, of the presbyterian delegation.[134] And the Church party was convinced that Tillotson's true sympathies still lay with the friends of his youth. He had, after all, been the principal architect of the ecclesiastical commission's hated comprehension plan.

Far from being 'just the man to bring the Church' through its post-revolution crisis, as Professor Speck has claimed, Tillotson was the worst possible choice for the primacy.[135] Tories were scandalised by his appointment. 'The rage is as high & gall overflowing against this Archbishop', wrote a caustic Edward Harley to his father in June 1691, 'as if Mr Baxter had been made so'.[136] That animus in no way abated during the course of Tillotson's primacy. 'I have not only heard', declaimed a Church party MP in 1694,

> that the present Archbishop of Canterbury was bred up, preached, prayed & exercised the ministeriall Function when there was no Bishops, no Common Prayer Book among us, but I have also heard of his long & great intimacy with Mr Firmin who is so much noted for an industrious Socinian . . . I must confesse I think Orthodox Christianity as well as the Government of Bishops to be in no good plight whilst he is the great Superintendant of both.[137]

Such sentiments apparently echoed those of much of the lower clergy. As Bishop Burnet lamented in 1693, 'the Clergy seemed to have combined in opposition to him [the Archbishop], to decry him in every thing'.[138]

Archbishop Tillotson and his colleagues had earned the lasting suspicion of High Churchmen, largely because of their commitment to Protestant unity. To High Churchmen, comprehension was a cant word for the destruction of the Church. To the new bishops, in contrast, it was a means of strengthening the Church's authority. And to further that end, the new episcopate also sought to improve the quality of pastoral care provided by the parochial clergy. Of the new generation of prelates, none was more deeply committed to higher clerical standards than the Bishop of Salisbury, Gilbert Burnet. In his *Discourse of the Pastoral Care*, published at Tillotson's behest in 1692, Burnet argued that an immediate and general reformation of manners was necessary to ward off imminent divine retribution upon a sinful nation.[139] But such a reformation, the bishop insisted, would be impossible without better standards of clerical behaviour. Musing upon the reverses suffered by the Protestant cause since the Council of Trent, Burnet concluded that the decisive factor was the very high quality of pastoral care which the Counter-Reformation Papacy had demanded of its parochial clergy. 'For the Manners and Labours of the Clergy,' he wrote, 'are real Arguments, which all people do both understand and feel; they have a much more convincing force, they are more visible, and persuade more universally, than Books can do, which are little read, and less considered: And indeed the Bulk of Mankind is so made, that there is no working on them, but by moving their Affections, and commanding their Esteem.'[140]

In England, alas, the quality of much of the clergy left a great deal to be desired, not least in Burnet's own diocese. 'I thank God I have not met with much scandall among my Clergy,' the bishop had written in the Summer of 1691,

> but many of them are too ignorant, they seem to have no great sense of Devotion and none at all of the pastorall care, but imagine they acquit themselves well, when they performe the publick functions; Covetousness, aspiring to preferments and a restless seeking after great livings, which they desire to hold one upon another, has often made my life a burden to me among them, and the foul suspition of Simony in the disposall of most Benefices which by a carnall and secular word are called Livings is a dreadfull thing.[141]

The upshot of this excessive worldlinesss was the visible growth of irreligion and infidelity amongst the people. 'Now this I am forced to declare', he lamented in *The Discourse*,

> That having had much free conversation with many that have been fatally corrupted that way, they have very often owned to me, that nothing promoted this so much in them, as the very bad Opinion which they took up of all Clergy-men of all sides: They did not see in them that strictness of life, that contempt of the World, that Zeal, that Meekness, Humility and Charity; that Diligence and Earnestness, with relation to the great Truths of the Christian Religion, which they reckoned they would most certainly have, if they themselves firmly believed it: Therefore they concluded, that those, whose business it was more strictly to enquire into the truth of their Religion,

knew that it was not so certain, as they themselves, for other ends, endeavoured to make the World believe it was: And that, tho for carrying on of their own Authority or Fortunes, which in one word they call their Trade, they seemed to be very positive in affirming the Truth of their Doctrines; yet in their own hearts they did not believe it, since they lived so little suitable to it, and were so much set on raising themselves by it; and so little in advancing the Honour of their Profession, by an exemplary Piety, and a Shining Conversation.

This, Burnet had found, was 'so strong a prejudice, that nothing but a real Reformation of it, by the eminent Vertues and Labours of many of the Clergy, will ever conquer it'.[142]

In Burnet's opinion, high pastoral standards were not only essential for the reformation of the conformist laity: they were also a prerequisite for winning dissenters back to the Church. 'If', the bishop averred,

we led such Exemplary Lives, as become our Character, if we applied our selves wholly to the Duties of our Profession, if we studied to outlive and outlabour those that divide from us; we might hope by the Blessing of God, so far to overcome their Prejudices, and to gain both upon their Esteem and Affections, that a very small matter might go a great way towards the healing of those Wounds, which have so long weakened and distracted us. Speculative Arguments do not reach the Understandings of the greater part, who are only capable of sensible ones: and the strongest Reasoning will not prevail, till we first force them to think the better of our Church, for what they see in our selves, and make them wish to be of a Communion, in which they see so much Truth, and unaffected Goodness and Worth.

Once the dissenters had been brought thus far, it would be easy enough to bring the bulk of them back to the bosom of the Church. For

If we did generally mind our duties, and discharge them faithfully, this would prepare such as mean well in their Separation from us, to consider better of the Grounds on which they maintain it: And that will best enforce the Arguments that we have to lay before them. And as for such as divide from us with bad Designs, and an unrelenting Spite, they will have a small party and a feeble support if there were no more occasion given to work on the Affections of the People, by our Errours and Disorders.[143]

If all this sounds like a not-so-veiled rebuke to Burnet's bêtes noires, the intolerant lower clergy, then that is precisely what the redoubtable prelate had in mind. Once, he pointedly reminded readers, there had been 'a Generation of men that cried, The Temple of the Lord, the Temple of the Lord, as loud as we can cry, The Church of England, The Church of England: When yet by their sins they were pulling it down and kindling that Fire which consumed it'. Burnet's message to those latter-day zealots, the highflying clergy, was transparently clear: pious actions spoke far louder than intemperate words. 'It will have a better grace to see others boast of our Church, from what they observe in us, than for us to be crying it up with our words, when our deeds do decry it. Our Enemies will make severe Inferences from them; and our Pretensions will be thought vain and impudent things, as long as our Lives contradict them.'[144]

What standard of pastoral care was necessary to shut the mouths of the Church's critics? For Burnet's colleague, Bishop Kidder, the paradigm was Anthony Horneck, lecturer at the Savoy Chapel and founder of London's lay religious societies. 'He well understood', wrote Kidder in his *Life of Horneck*,

> not only the Dignity, but the Duty and Charge of his Holy Function. He had a mighty sense of the worth of Souls, and of the great care that is to be had of them. Hence it proceeded that he was irreconcilable to Pluralities, and Non-residence: Hence it was that he was so very painfull a Preacher, so very hard a Student: Hence it was that he was so very diligent in Catechizing the youth, in visiting the sick, and in all the parts of his holy Office. His heart was wholly set upon gaining Souls to God. In this work he labour'd incessantly. And those who were thus disposed among the Clergy, he honoured greatly, and served them to his power.[145]

Here, then, was the exalted standard of pastoral care required of the new model cleric.

The episcopal campaign to raise the quality of pastoral care was not a purely post-revolution phenomenon: Archbishop Sancroft had worked tirelessly for the improvement of clerical standards during his primacy.[146] Nevertheless, the Williamite bishops were convinced that the revolution had given a massive boost to the cause of clerical reform. Indeed, Tillotson and Burnet believed that William and Mary had been chosen by God to perfect the Reformation.[147] Burnet was particularly taken with the Queen: 'as I thank God', he mused in 1693,

> that I do still feel the sense of the Christian Religion and of the Reformation of it from Popery, to be that which lies nearer my heart than all the things of this world put together, so I cannot without a particular joy see that Person, whose present Circumstances mark her out to be both the defender and perfecter of that blessed work, to be such in all the parts both of her private Deportment and the publick administration of the Government that she seemeth to be in all points fitted for the work for which she seems to have been born.[148]

The Queen, for her part, held Archbishop Tillotson in the highest regard. King William left ecclesiastical preferment largely in the Queen's hands, and she in turn relied upon the judgment of the primate, favouring and supporting him 'in a most particular manner'.[149] So it was entirely natural that the Archbishop should himself seek the encouragement and advice of the Queen when he was drawing up a scheme for clerical reform in 1694.[150]

That scheme had its origins in a series of regulations for the clergy agreed by the bishops at Lambeth Palace in August 1694.[151] It was originally intended to issue the regulations by episcopal authority. But the Archbishop, wary perhaps of the hostility of the parochial clergy, opted for an alternative mode of issue, first suggested by Bishop Burnet: 'a letter from their Majesties, requiring me and the Archbishop of York to communicate their Majesties pleasure to our suffragan Bishops by way of injunctions from their Majesties'. A royal imprimatur was presumably felt necessary to buttress the authority of the bishops in the face of potential rebellion by their presbyters. But Tillotson 'had also another reason, which moved me herein, that their Majesties concernment for religion and the church might appear to the nation'.[152]

It was one of the Archbishop's final decisions. He died in November 1694, hurried to his end, according to Burnet, by 'the perpetuall ill usage with which he had been persecuted for many years, but more particularly since he had accepted that see [of Canterbury]'.[153] Before the year was out, the Queen too was dead. Thus it was left to King William to issue the *Injunctions* in February 1695.[154] Among other things, they required the bishops to suppress 'the great abuses occasioned by Pluralities & restrain them as much as you can, except where the parishes lie neare one another & the livings are small' (Injunction 9); to 'look to the Lives & manners of their Clergy, that they may be in all things regular & exemplary, according to the 75th Canon' (Injunction 10); to 'use their utmost endeavour to oblige their Clergy to have publick Prayers in the Church, not merely on Holy days & Litanie-days, but as often as may be, and to celebrate the Holy Sacrament frequently' (Injunction 11); to insist that the clergy, who were to 'sett a good example to their People & exhort them frequently to their duty herein', use 'their utmost endeavours that the Lord's day be religiously observed' (Injunction 12); to remind the clergy of their duty to visit the sick (Injunction 13); and to ensure that catechising was duly performed according to the 59th Canon (Injunction 14).[155]

The deaths of Archbishop Tillotson and Queen Mary stymied the episcopal campaign for higher clerical standards. There were no further initiatives from Lambeth Palace until April 1699 when Tillotson's successor at Canterbury, Thomas Tenison, produced a Circular Letter for the bishops of his province. In this, he lamented the 'sensible growth of vice and profaneness in the nation: which, to the great affliction of all good men, appears not only in the corrupt practices of particular persons, but also in the endeavours that are used to subvert the general principles of our holy religion'. To stem the flood-tide, Tenison urged parochial clergymen to co-operate more closely with each other. 'It were to be wished', he wrote to his suffragans, 'that the clergy of every neighbourhood would agree upon frequent meetings, to consult for the good of religion in general, and to advise with one another about any difficulties that may happen in their particular cures. By what methods any evil custom may most easily be broken: how a sinner may be most effectually reclaimed: and (in general) how each of them in their several circumstances may contribute to the advancement of religion.' Such meetings could be made still more useful if the clergy invited the churchwardens and 'other pious persons among the laity, to join with them in the execution of the most probable methods that can be suggested for those good ends'.[156]

The Circular Letter was Tenison's response to the interdenominational societies for reformation of manners which had sprung up since 1691. These godly associations, dedicated to enforcing the laws against vice and profanity, had won the support of a number of bishops. The Archbishop, however, disliked them because they gave the lead to the civil magistrate, not the clergy, in the war against sin.[157] In any event, their work would be unnecessary if the populace were imbued with the principles of Christianity. So Tenison, like Tillotson before him, stressed the duty of clerics to catechise their parishioners. 'And whereas the foundation of piety and morality are best laid at the beginning, in the religious education of children', averred the primate,

> I cannot but wish that every one of the parochial clergy would be very dili-gent in catechising the children under their care; and not only so, but in calling upon them afterwards, as they grow up, to give such further accounts of their religion, as may be expected from a riper age. That being thus care-fully instructed in the faith and duty of a Christian, they also may teach their children the same; and so piety, virtue, and goodness may for ever flourish in our church and nation.[158]

The Archbishop's sentiments were doubtless music to the ears of the Warwickshire clergyman, Thomas Bray. Not only was Bray the nation's most eloquent advocate of catechetical education, he was also an indefatig-able 'projector' of schemes to strengthen the Church's discipline. These included a plan to establish meeting places for the local clergy. But Bray's principal objective was the establishment of a central body to promote the influence of the Church of England at home and abroad. To that end, in March 1699 he set up the Society for Promoting Christian Knowledge (SPCK) with the aid of four like-minded laymen.[159] It soon got to work distributing godly tracts to its correspondents, publicising the catechetical charity schools then being established in the metropolis, and advising their governors. The Society also encouraged the clergy to meet together in accordance with Archbishop Tenison's letter to his bishops.[160]

To judge from the Society's correspondence, efforts to persuade clergy-men to form themselves into associations achieved mixed results. In some places, there was an enthusiastic response. Writing from Caernarvon in April 1700, Robert Wynne reported that 'ye Clergy of each Deanery meet by themselves & make it their constant endeavour to stir up each other to a strict & conscientious discharge of the Ministerial Functions.'[161] That same month, another correspondent informed the SPCK that the 'Clergy in Denbighshire, Flintshire, and Mountgomeryshire, are united in Societies', and that 'they had agreed to rectifie some abuses contrary to the Rubrick & Canons, and had put their agreement in execution with such success that they were encouraged to go on & rectifie others.'[162] In February 1701 a Northumbrian correspondent reported that 'in August last, about nine of the Clergy of Alnwick Deanery, at the request of their Arch-Deacon did agree upon Monthly Meetings to Discourse together & Engage themselves mutually and solemnly to prosecute their Duties.'[163] But in many parts of the country, the clergy proved less eager to form themselves into associations. Writing from Huntingdon in October 1700, a correspondent expressed 'his fears that few of the Clergy will be prevailed with to joyn with them'. On the contrary, 'about a Year Since . . . many had declared against it, most were cold in it, & but one man signified his readiness to joyn in it.'[164] In March 1700 Bishop Fowler of Gloucester had given the Reverend Willett of Stratton 'special direction and encouragem[en]t to invite ye Clergy of the Deanery wherein he lives to meet & consult together'. Three months later, however, a disappointed Willett reported that he found in the clergy 'not ye warmth he expected'.[165] In February John Lewis, the minister of Acryse in Kent, had complained that he could 'find but two Clergymen within ten miles round him whom he can confide in as favourers of the Design, that ye Clergy exposed it as a reviving of Presbyterian Classes encouraging Fanaticism contrary to the 25th of Hen. 8, cap. 19, a breach of ye 12th Canon [against conventicles], an Usurpation on the Rights of the Convocation & an inlet to division and separation'.[166]

All this, needless to say, was a far cry from what the SPCK had intended. As its secretary John Chamberlayne explained in December 1700,

> they apprehended in this they do no more than Revive the Antient Discipline of our Church according to its Primitive Constitution, by w[hi]ch it is divided into Bishopricks, subdivided into A[rch] Deaconries, and these again into Smaller Districts called Rural Deaneries, wherein, when the Clergy shall be brought to meet and consent, matt[e]rs of consequence to the Good of Souls and within their proper spheres, and the Inferior Meetings be always accountable to the Superior, and these to their Diocesans.[167]

Nevertheless the SPCK's timing was singularly unfortunate. Even as Chamberlayne penned his defence of clerical societies, the High Church campaign for the reconvening of convocation was reaching its climax. And it seems that some of the supporters of that campaign saw the SPCK's plans as a 'Contrivance to render a Convocation useless'.[168] Looked at from this point of view, Archbishop Tenison's support for clerical associations probably did them more harm than good. For in the previous three years the primate had shown himself to be an implacable opponent of a sitting convocation.

6. The Convocation Controversy

After the unhappy experience of 1689, King William resolved to dispense
with a sitting convocation. Such an assembly, he concluded, would merely
provide a platform for the many critics of his ecclesiastical policies among
the clergy. Thus convocation, while not actually dissolved, was repeatedly
prorogued before it had the opportunity to sit.[169] But by refusing to allow
convocation to sit, King William stoked in clerical hearts the fires of resentment first kindled by the Toleration Act and the deprivation of the
nonjuring bishops. Those fires were eventually fanned out of control by a
former Oxford don called Francis Atterbury.

In his *Letter to a Convocation-Man*, published in 1696, Atterbury insisted
that the shocking rise of anti-clericalism and freethinking demanded the
reconvening of convocation: 'if ever', he wrote,

> there was need of a convocation since Christianity was established in this
> kingdom, there is need of one now, when such an open looseness in men's
> principles and practices, and such a settled contempt of religion and the
> priesthood have prevailed every where; when heresies of all kinds, when
> scepticism, deism, and atheism itself have overrun us like a deluge . . . when
> the Trinity has been openly denied by some, as the unity of the godhead
> sophistically opposed by others; when all mysteries in religion have been
> decried as impositions on men's understandings, and nothing is admitted as
> an article of faith but what we can fully and perfectly comprehend; nay, when
> the power of the magistrate and the church is struck at, and the indifference
> of all religions is endeavoured to be established by pleas for the justice and
> necessity of an universal, unlimited toleration, even against the sense of the
> whole legislature; at such a time, and in such an age, you and I, sir, and all
> men that wish well to the interests of religion and the state, cannot but think
> that there is great need of a convocation.[170]

Nor would such a body be a mere talking shop. Atterbury contended,
contrary to general belief, that Henry VIII's Act of Submission had left the
powers of convocation largely untouched. Thus convocation's canons,
once given the royal assent, were as much part of the law of the land as
parliamentary statutes.[171] Indeed, Atterbury averred that the wording of
the *praemunientes* writ, by which the bishops were summoned to attend
parliament, showed that convocation was nothing less than the ecclesiastical estate of the legislature. That being so, it followed that convocation
must automatically sit whenever parliament was in session.[172]

The thesis that convocation was part of parliament – developed with the
help of the tory lawyer, Bartholomew Shower – was novel. Less original
was Atterbury's exaltation of the powers of convocation. This drew heavily
upon the ideas of the nonjuring theologian, Henry Dodwell.[173] In
Dodwell's hands, such highflying notions, first broached to show the ille-
gality of lay deprivation, eventually became a device for undermining the

theological foundations of the Henrician royal supremacy. Atterbury's *Letter to a Convocation-Man,* by way of contrast, was not an attack upon the royal supremacy per se. Nevertheless, it was a deeply subversive tract. For one thing, if convocation was indeed the ecclesiastical arm of the legislature, King William's refusal to reconvene convocation was clearly unconstitutional.[174] More boldly still, Atterbury all but challenged Archbishop Tenison to persuade the King to reconvene convocation:

> as a convocation, regularly meeting and acting freely, is the greatest fence against these mischiefs [anti-clericalism and heresy], and the most proper instrument to apply a remedy, so you cannot allow yourselves to doubt but that my Lord of Canterbury's piety and zeal will move his grace to represent it so, and incline his majesty (who has run so many hazards abroad for securing our most holy religion pure and uncorrupted) to think there is now a proper and needful occasion of using this means to preserve it at home.[175]

Implicit in this passage was the charge that King William had hitherto done little to secure 'our most holy religion' at home. Not for the first time, a pointed contrast was drawn between the King's apparent favour to the presbyterian Church of Scotland and his alleged neglect of the episcopal Church of England. Since King William had so often convened presbyterian general assemblies in Scotland, averred the mischievous Atterbury, the Church of England, 'which pays as much regard at least to crowned heads as an assembly does, may justly expect from him as tender a concern for her welfare and interests'.[176]

Atterbury concluded his polemic with an impassioned plea for the lower clergy to be allowed its voice. The bishops, he mused,

> by reason of their high station in the house of peers, and the great business, which, on that account, their hands are full of, may not miss their seat in a convocation-house: But the inferior clergy, the priests, who are in no other capacity of serving the church and kingdom to purpose, but as assembled in synod, are at leisure to reflect often on the neglect with which they are used, and the methods that are taking of making them useless. They are, though under the bishops, a considerable member of the ecclesiastical state. No canon can be made without their assent; and if the canons are not observed as they should be, they have a right to complain of the default, and to move for a redress, and not to be suffered to do this at a time when there is so much need of it, and when the rights of all other bodies are so tenderly preserved, they think to be a very great and designed hardship upon them.[177]

Atterbury's message was clear enough: a convocation was essential since the bishops could not be trusted to uphold the Church's canons and redress the grievances of the disenfranchised lower clergy.

The explosive implications of *A Letter to a Convocation-Man* were all too apparent to Archbishop Tenison, and he was determined that its impudent author would not go unanswered. The man he chose to put Atterbury in his place was William Wake, minister of St James Westminster, and a rising star in the latitudinarian firmament. As a work of scholarship, Wake's *Authority of Christian Princes over their Ecclesiastical Synods Asserted* (1697) was an undeniable success. It showed that Atterbury had hopelessly confused the ecclesiastical synod, which convocation had become, with parliamentary convocations, defunct in their true form since the fourteenth century and wholly anachronistic since the end of clerical self-taxation in 1664.[178] But as polemic, Wake's book misfired badly. In the first place, the central plank of Wake's argument – that it was for the King alone to determine whether convocation should sit – was excessively erastian in tone. Secondly, Wake completely misjudged clerical opinion by insisting that a sitting convocation was simply unnecessary.[179] The upshot was a general outburst of indignation among the clergy. 'I have scarce observ'd of late Years', wrote Wake's old Oxford tutor in 1701, 'any books entertain'd with such a Generall disgust as Yours upon the Prerogative of the King as to Synods.'[180] Not that Wake needed much reminding of the opprobrium which he had brought upon himself. 'I never had any Opinion either of your Learning or Sincerity', an anonymous correspondent had told him in March 1700,

> & by a Late excellent Book I am fully satisfy'd that the Judgment I made of you many years since was not wrong. I will not deny if you were like the Shepherd of St Hermas of an honest & upright Disposition, but that you might make a good Parish-Preist; but since I find such horrid Insincerity & Prevarications in your Writings, I cannot think you fit even for that low Station in the Church; You are a Perfidious Wretch, & deserve all the Reproaches that Honest men can load you with.

By tackling Atterbury's arguments head-on, Wake had inadvertently helped to further his adversary's purposes. All clerical opponents of convocation, from Archbishop Tenison down, could now be stigmatised as traitors. 'Judas betrayed his Lord', concluded Wake's irate correspondent, '& you the Rights of your Mother the Church.'[181]

The scholarly controversy over the nature and rights of convocation, which rumbled on into Anne's reign, was ultimately won by William Wake.[182] It was, however, a distinctly pyrrhic victory. In the late Summer of 1700, the administration of the Junto whigs having collapsed, King William reluctantly asked the Earl of Rochester, younger brother of the Earl of Clarendon, to form a new ministry.[183] High priest of the Cavalier creed, Rochester was an inveterate foe of both the Toleration Act and King William's bishops: 'he talks against Tolleration,' Burnet had complained in 1693, 'and for setting up the high notions of Persecutions, and all the other violent things of King Charles's time, and professes himself a great Enemy to the present Bishops, and to all the methods they are in.'[184] Small wonder, then, that Rochester became a fervent supporter of the campaign to reconvene convocation. And when the King sought his aid in 1700, Rochester insisted upon a sitting convocation as part of his price for re-entering government.[185] King William had been well and truly trumped.

When convocation at last sat in the Spring of 1701, it fulfilled the Archbishop's worst fears. The Lower House of convocation immediately launched proceedings for heresy against John Toland, the most notorious of the freethinking writers. Given King William's well-known aversion to the forcing of conscience, these proceedings were clearly intended to be a shot across his bows. But when in early March the Lower House turned its attention to Bishop Burnet's allegedly unorthodox *Exposition of the Thirty-Nine Articles*, Atterbury and his crew fired a double-shotted broadside into the belly of the Williamite ecclesiastical establishment. Worse still, the Lower House, acting upon Atterbury's contention that it was not subject to the authority of the primate, repeatedly ignored Archbishop Tenison's schedules of prorogation. Never before had the authority of a primate been so slighted.[186]

As Tenison had anticipated, convocation had become an arena in which the High Church lions, long deprived of a hearty meal, were falling over themselves in their eagerness to devour the post-revolution episcopate. But it was not just in convocation that the bishops found themselves savaged. In March 1701 Sir John Packington, a rabid tory, introduced into the House of Commons legislation to prohibit the translation of bishops from one diocese to another. Designed to eliminate the allegedly corrupting effect upon the poorer bishops of the prospect of advancement to richer dioceses, the bill evinced the growing conviction of tory politicians that King William's bishops were putting self-interest before the good of the Church as a whole. Although it did not reach the statute book, Packington's measure had significant political consequences. For it helped persuade the harried 'latitudinarian' bishops to make common cause with their enemies' enemies, the Junto whigs. This much became clear when the tories attempted to impeach Lord Somers in June 1701. Of the fourteen bishops who cast a vote on the issue, eleven – all of them appointed since 1689 – voted to acquit the leader of the Junto.[187]

So it was that Archbishop Tenison and his allies on the episcopal bench, despised and harried by the self-proclaimed Church party, came at last to throw in their lot with whiggery, supposedly the deadly enemy of the Established Church.[188] The irony of the situation was not lost upon the anti-whig writer, Charles Davenant. In Davenant's famous dialogue, *The True Picture of a Modern Whig*, written near the end of the 1701 parliament, Whiglove, a dyed-in-the-wool anti-clerical, asks the Junto mouthpiece Tom Double how he should carry himself in relation to the Church. 'I don't see', replies Double, 'why you should not still continue your wonted Practice of Ridiculing the Church and all Reveal'd Religion, the Heads of our Party do it, nor have the great Ones as yet given out any Orders to the contrary.' Yet, Double acknowledges, 'we have been lately very much oblig'd to some of my L[or]ds the B[isho]ps.' He shows his companion 'a List of Twelve of 'em who help'd us mightily last Sessions, without them we had been thrown upon our Backs.' These bishops, Double observes, 'join'd with us, who always have, and ever shall hate their Hierarchy, against the very Persons that so long have Fought their Battle. Of these truly I think you ought to Speak as well as a Whig can bring himself to Speak of any Church-Man.' This perturbs Whiglove. 'I shall act this Part very awkwardly', says he, 'and shall never be able to mention that Order with any Decency, which my Tongue has been us'd to Explode so many years.' But Double, the true voice of 'modern' whiggery, is troubled not a jot. 'Revile the Order as much as you please,' he retorts, 'but let me beg you Speak well of our Friends the Reverend P[rela]tes.'[189]

6

Godly Reformation

1. Divine Judgment

On 7 June 1692 a massive earthquake struck Port Royal in Jamaica. 'The day when all this befell,' wrote a local clergyman,

> it was very clear, afforded not the suspition of the least evill, but in the space of three minutes, about half-an-hour after eleven in the morning, Port Royall, the fairest town of all the English Plantations, [and] best emporium and mart of that part of the world, exceeding in its riches, plentifull in all good things, was shaken and shattered to pieces, sunk into and covered, for the greatest part by the sea, and will in a short time, be wholly eaten up by it, for few of those houses that yet stand, are left whole, and every day we hear them fall, and the sea daily encroaches upon it.

Fifteen hundred souls, he believed, had perished in the disaster, either drowned in the sea, buried beneath falling buildings or swallowed up by fissures in the earth.[1]

By early August, news of the catastrophe had reached London. On the 10th Charles Hatton informed his brother Lord Hatton of the 'very terrible news from Jamaica, where an earthquake and hurrican hath been and in less than 2 minuits destroy'd and sank ye greatest part of Port Royall with all ye factories, storehouses, and magazines.'[2] Only a month later, Hatton had another earthquake to report, but this time on his own London doorstep. 'We had here, my L[or]d, last Thursday [8 September] . . . an earth-quake, ye effects of w[hi]ch were more or less felt, not only all over London and Westminster but, it is reported, as far as Canterbury and Cambridge.'[3] Another correspondent of Lord Hatton, the physician Edmund King, had been

> at dinour in my dineing room . . . on a suddaine the table and room shakt, put us all into a strange confusion. My wife said: 'Mr King, w[ha]ts this?' Her woman [that] was at dinner w[i]th us started from the table, as pale as death,

and cri'd: 'Oh! an earthquake!' I rise from the table too in the universall motion I saw and felt; it lasted about a minute and halfe. Whilst we was talking of it, a neighbour cam in and ask't if we perceivd anything of an earthquake, for a great many gentlemen came running into the coffee house, pale and frighted, out of their houses, and the women and children in great numbers cam running out of theire houses too into the street in great amazement; and it's the wholl talke now all the towne over; much more frightfull than w[ha]t we felt.[4]

The Jamaica quake and the London tremor gave Englishmen much food for thought. The devastation of Jamaica, affirmed our clerical eyewitness, was an unmistakable sign of the wrath of God. The citizens of Port Royal were 'a most ungodly and debauched people', and on more than one occasion the cleric had 'set before them what would be the issue of their impenitence and wickednes.' Alas, his warnings had gone unheeded, and now Port Royal had suffered 'this terrible judgment of God.'[5] The Scots presbyterian Robert Fleming believed that the Jamaica quake was a 'publick Beacon and Monument of Judgment in this respect, to shew how terrible a thing it is to fall immediately into the Hands of the Living God.' The London tremor had been a second divine shot across the nation's bows.[6] Fleming was not alone in believing that the London tremor bore the portentous imprint of the finger of God: 'o that now Gods judgments are in the earth', wrote Abigail Harley from London on the day of the tremor, 'the inhabitants may learn righteousness & not go on presumptuously in sin, which will be bitterness in the end.'[7]

No family in England was more given to view the world through providentialist lenses than the Harleys of Brampton Bryan. In contrast, the veteran MP Sir Thomas Clarges liked to think himself 'not in these things very superstitious'. Yet he remembered that similar tremors had preceded the outbreak of the Civil War and the death of Charles II, and so 'cannot but observe they have been in some places esteem'd ominous'.[8] Like the Jamaica quake, then, the London tremor was seen as a warning of worse things to come. The tremor had done little damage, observed a pamphleteer. But 'who can tell, this is not the last Warning; and that the next time he shall visit us, he will not in his Fiery Indignation utterly consume us, and swallow us up quick?'[9]

Reverses in the war against France were also read as signs of God's anger with England. When the French captured much of the Turkey merchant fleet in July 1693, Robert Harley wrote to his father that 'God is pleas'd further to express his displeasure against us in cutting us short by sea.'[10] The presbyterian minister Matthew Henry similarly believed that the loss of the Turkey fleet was 'a great token of Gods displeasure'.[11] In August 1693 Thomas Jolly, a Lancashire dissenting minister, groaned that 'the publique discouragements press sore, the Lord rebuking us, emptying us, bringing us low into straits.' God was 'rebuking us severall wayes', he continued, 'not only as to desolation by men's hand in the warr, but by his own immediate hand in the fruits of the earth'.[12] That same month, John Evelyn confided to his diary that 'every thing [was] sadly declining; & all this for our late Injustice and disobedience, & the still reigning of sin among us.'[13]

What did Evelyn mean by 'our late Injustice and disobedience'? As a veteran royalist, he may have been thinking back to the Great Rebellion and the regicide. But it is equally plausible that Evelyn was alluding to the revolution of 1688. Certainly, in July 1693 he had attributed the 'ill successe in all our Concernes' to 'our folly & precipitous Change'.[14] If Evelyn did indeed attribute God's controversy with England to the unrighteous deposition of King James, then his views had something in common with those of unambiguous Jacobites. They saw the miseries of King William's war as divine punishment for the revolution. In a Jacobite allegory of 1694, Jupiter, King of the Gods, curses the faithless people of Utopia (England) for rebelling against their rightful monarch, Eugenius (King James). 'Now,' thunders Jupiter,

> let Nasonius [King William], their Scourge, still harass, impoverish, and bring 'em to the very brink of Ruin. Let the War they maintain to keep him [Eugenius] out, take their Ships, spoil their Traffick, make dear their Foreign Commodities, and all their Provisions too: Let it empty their Purses, and lose the lives of some hundred Thousands of the Utopians; for, till they repent, and heartily desire to restore their King, the Justice of the Goddess Nemesis cannot be satisfied, nor my dread Anger appeased, nor they deserve the mighty Blessing of good Eugenius's Restauration.[15]

According to another Jacobite writer, the clergy were drawing down God's curse upon the nation by exhorting the people to support the revolution:

> What a dishonour is this to God and religion! What a curse to the World! What an injury to men's souls ! And what can it portend but vengeance, and (without a timely and extraordinary repentance) inevitable ruin? Neither can I omit putting my fellow subjects in mind of . . . the never-to-be-forgotten earthquake in Jamaica, and those late monitory shakings which ran through all this island, as well as a great part of the territories of our wicked confederates. I shall not pretend to divine what may be the consequence of them; but we never heard of an earthquake in this island but did certainly forerun some very remarkable calamity.

Unless the revolution was reversed, England would be consumed by God's righteous anger.[16]

Needless to say, Williamites viewed matters from a rather different perspective. The revolution was a 'sudden and seasonable deliverance', preached George Halley at York Minster in February 1689. 'A deliverance which argues the vigilant Eye of Providence, and the powerful Hand of God.'[17] Indeed, the revolution showed the English people to be the 'peculiar care of Heaven, to be the only Blessed Children of the Lord'. But Halley coupled this comforting thought with a caveat:

> if we live not as highly sensible of God's reiterated mercies, (which sense we must demonstrate by a life conformable to his Divine Laws) then, though our Sky at the present is beautified with an Evening Redness, which speaks the Clouds thin, and the Air pure; tho' our Firmament now looks bright and serene; yet God, if provok'd by our ingratitude and impiety, can, in the twinkling of an Eye, change it from an Evening to a Morning Redness; can in a moment make the Firmament lowring, by condensing the Clouds, and veiling the Sky with darkness; will certainly bring us into worse circumstances than before, and pour upon us fiercer instances of his anger and heavy discipline.[18]

A pamphleteer in 1690 gave a similar warning. 'God can create Destruction upon a People, which he hath created Salvation and Deliverance for, that will not accept of it, nor be saved nor delivered by him.'[19]

The military reverses of the early 1690s, together with the seismic shocks of 1692, convinced some Williamites that God was about to forsake the backsliding English people. But to supporters of the revolution, the most ominous event of all was the premature death of Queen Mary on 28 December 1694. 'When God deprives a People of a Wise, Good, and Pious King or Queen,' averred the dissenting minister Thomas Goodwin, 'we should tremble at such a dreadful and portentous Sign of his Displeasure, as foreboding Ruin to us, if we will yet be obstinately resolv'd to continue in Sin, and refuse to be reform'd.'[20]

Thirty-six years earlier, on Cromwell's death, preachers had compared the late Lord Protector to Josiah, the godly prince whose death had marked the beginning of the end of the first Jewish Commonwealth.[21] Queen Mary's eulogists drew a similar analogy. In a sermon on the text of 2 Chronicles, xxxv. 24 – 'And all Judah and Jerusalem Mourned for Josiah' – the conformist divine Thomas Bowber suggested that Queen Mary 'was quickly snatcht away by Death, and no doubt in Mercy, as good Josiah was, that her eyes might not see the Evil, which (we know not how soon) may befall us, without a speedy Reformation.'[22] Bowber returned to this theme later in the sermon. The Queen's death, he warned,

> may strike Dread into our Hearts, and chill our Spirits! For tho She was gathered to Her Grave in Peace, yet for ought we know, it may be a sad Presage of many Miseries and Calamities ready to betide us: Mercies and Deliverances, when abused, turn into Judgments. In Josiah's day God offered the Jews Mercy, but whatever ties and Obligations lay upon them to reform and amend, they would not hearken to the voice of God, nor turn from their Evil ways, which proved their utter Ruin and Destruction.[23]

Bishop Burnet likewise saw a parallel between Queen Mary and the pious King of Judah, reminding readers that after Josiah's death 'Jerusalem was laid in Heaps, their Temple was rased down to the Ground, and Zion became a ploughed field.'[24] The inference was devastatingly clear. Just as King Josiah's death was the harbinger of the fall of ancient Israel, so Queen Mary's demise presaged the destruction of that latterday Zion, Protestant England.

Who was responsible for England's dire predicament? The jeremiads of the 1690s tended to lay the blame squarely on the shoulders of the people. Typical were the sentiments of the presbyterian minister John Woodhouse in 1697. As 'the Sins of some Kings have had a ruining Influence upon their People; so the Sins of many a wicked People, have had a hand to weaken, disappoint (if not ruine) good Kings; Kings better than their People.' King William was such a king, a virtuous prince whose heroic efforts were undermined by the sins of his subjects.[25] At least one commentator, however, thought that the King himself was far from blameless.

Although he had been an ardent supporter of the revolution, the barrister-turned-priest Edward Stephens soon became an acerbic critic of King William and his regime. In a pamphlet written towards the end of 1689, Stephens claimed that England's fortunes had taken a marked turn for the worse since the King's accession. The revolution itself had been accomplished with an ease so miraculous that it betokened the guiding hand of providence. But in the course of 1689 there had been

> a great and unhappy Change in the Course and Progress of our Affairs, from so smooth and prosperous, that formidable Armies could give no check or interruption, but vanished like Smoke before the Wind, to so rough and disturbed, and that so universal in all, that neither Abroad nor at Home, at Sea or at Land, in Country or in Council, do we find any cheerful Face of Affairs, but everywhere Rubs, Impediments, Failures and Disappointments, and our way fenced up that we cannot pass.

These misfortunes showed unmistakably that 'Israel hath sinned and transgressed, and therefore cannot prosper. Our strength is departed from us, and we are become like other Men: Neither will it return,' Stephens explained, 'unless the Cursed Thing be found out and removed. This therefore is our business, which this change of Success loudly calls us to, to find out the Sin that keeps good things from us, and to dissipate the Cloud that intercepts the benign Influences of Heaven.'[26]

Stephens was convinced that he had located the source of the nation's sin. The ease with which the revolution had been effected signified that King William was the chosen instrument of divine dispensation. However, he had been chosen by God not only to humble popery, but also to turn back the tide of debauchery which had inundated England under the restored monarchy. Tragically, the King had failed to keep his side of the bargain. Instead of pursuing God's work, he had submitted himself to fleshly reasoning by employing the debauched servants of the previous monarchs. In this, King William was walking in the footsteps of his great-grandfather, James I. It had been King James's 'Unhappiness' that

> after an admirable deliverance from an horrid Popish Conspiracy, ready for execution, he applied himself at first to connivance, and at last to association with Papists for his security; which, contrary to expectation, proved the original of all the mischiefs which have since befallen his family: So likewise this Prince, after as great an experience of the Divine Providence over him, thought to deal wisely with them [the debauched servants of the previous two kings], and (after Hushai's advice) defer this great work [of reformation], first till the kingdom should be settled, and then when he was proclaimed King, till Ireland should be reduced, and he would have sufficient Power (an Arm of the Flesh) to do it effectually, and in the mean time try what effect a good example and kindness, intrusting them with Offices and Employments in State, Army, and Navy, would have upon such vitious People in the end, which in like manner, contrary to his expectation, hath proved the original of all the Impediments and Disappointments in his affairs.[27]

Hence King William was himself the author of the nation's sin. 'As almost all the Wickedness of the former Reigns proceeded originally from those Kings, and Judgment hath been first executed upon them; so hath likewise the Fault, whereby that great Work, whereof this King was called out to be the Glorious Instrument in these Nations, hath been hitherto interrupted, plainly proceeded from himself.'[28]

Edward Stephens was, to put it mildly, a rather eccentric figure.[29] Yet he was not alone in feeling that the revolution had sadly failed of its promise. The London nonconformist Elias Pledger was a man much given to millenarian speculation: in 1693 he was sure that the latter days were imminent.[30] First, however, God would chastise the people of England for their sins. 'I know Sir we in England & especial in this City have very great reason to fear such a Judgment', wrote Pledger to an acquaintance in January 1694,

> For I question whether ever any nation in the world ever enjoyed the like means [of salvation] & yet that we have carried ourselves worse than others I think is out of question. We have been tryed by all means fair & foul (as we use to say) formerly by continued Judgments Sword Plagues fire scarcity of the word when our ministers were driven in to corners, & of late by a mixture of mercy with judgment, a wonderful & miraculous revolution in our government, taking the crown from the head of one that endeavoured to enslave us body & soul & placing another on the throne whome we thought would have promoted a reformation in church & state & all this with very little if any bloud spilt, & yet notwithstanding we have not behavd our selves as we ought, we have not obeyd the call of providence, but there has been too much use made of the same ministers & tools of the last raigne that helpd to

enslave & debash us. We are now engaged in a bloudy war with a potent enemy who we know not but god reserv'd him to be a scorge to this nation, as he has been to many others. We have had strange rebukes of providence. We have gone many steps back to egipt after we thought we had been upon our march out of it.

What had prevented the people of England from attaining the Promised Land? As we have seen, Pledger had expected the revolution to usher in reformation in both church and state. Reformation in the state had been hampered by the grant of office to those associated with the pre-revolution regime. Nor had reformation in the church fared much better. There were 'Great divisions among protestants', Pledger complained. 'Many too much simbolizing with Antichrist, the greatest enemy of Christ & his Church that ever was in the world both in doctrine & worship.'[31]

Pledger's disappointment with the non-reformation of the church was shared by many, both dissenters and conformists. The revolution had raised hopes that the Church of England's liturgy and the terms of its communion would be altered to facilitate the re-entry of moderate dissent into the establishment. But as we saw in the last chapter, these hopes were dashed by convocation in December 1689. Thus as early as February 1690, reformation of the church was coming to be viewed as an impossible dream. 'Some will not build the Church if they could', lamented a correspondent of Richard Baxter. 'Some would, but on many accounts can not.'[32] The sense of disappointment was particularly acute among those who held the union of godly Protestants to be a prerequisite for a national reformation of manners.

2. Reformation and Union

Critics of the Restoration religious settlement complained that its divisiveness had crippled the Church of England's capacity to combat sin. According to Edward Stephens, the 'mischievous' Act of Uniformity had excluded from the Church 'many good and useful men'. In their place had come 'Covetous, Proud, Ambitious, Worldly Men, and Court Flatterers'.[33] Clergymen of that ilk were more concerned with harassing dissenters than waging war on sin. As Jean Gailhard wrote in 1694, such clerics

> are glad when they have the least colour of law to justify any of their unwarrantable practices against those who dissent from them; but they do not regard good laws for the glory of God, as those we have for due observation of the sabbath, and against swearing, drunkeness, and uncleaness, &c; these they look upon as not worth being taken notice by them. That sort of men, far from advising and promoting a necessary reformation of abuses in religion, according to the word of God (the only rule of such things) though it was their duty, they hindered and opposed it, and persecuted them that

were for it, slandering them with the names of fanatics, schismatics, obstinate, factious.[34]

Two years earlier, the militantly whiggish Earl of Warrington had reminded the Chester Grand Jury how, under the restored monarchy,

> more Diligence and Care was employ'd to punish People for Nonconformity, than to reform their Lives and Manners. For if a Man were openly wicked and debauch'd, and very scarce, if ever, saw the inside of a Church; yet if he could talk loud, and swagger bravely for the Church, and storm against, and pull the Dissenters to pieces, he was cry'd up by all means for a good son of the Church, an honest Man, and truly affected to the Government: Whilst those who could not come up to all the Ceremonies enjoined in the Rubrick, tho their Lives in all other respects were upright, and their Conversations unblameable, yet were call'd Villains and Rogues, and Enemies to the Government, as if the outside and ceremonious part of Religion was more to be valu'd than the Substance and Essence of it.[35]

The godly earl, in contrast, placed the emphasis firmly on the substance of religion, urging the jurymen to implement the laws against swearing and profanation of the sabbath.[36]

Warrington's whiggery was painted in the most violent hues. He would doubtless have shared Thomas Papillon's view that the allies and enemies of godly reformation equated exactly with the advocates and adversaries of reform of the Church. 'Under the name of Whigs', wrote Papillon in a memorial on English politics,

> is comprehended most of the sober and religious persons of the Church of England that sincerely embrace the Doctrines of the Church, and put no such stress on the forms and ceremonies, but look on them as human institutions, and not as the Essentials of Religion, and are willing that there might be a Reformation to take away offence, and that desire that all Swearing, Drunkeness, and Ungodliness should be discountenanced and punished . . . As also all dissenters of the several persuasions are included under this title.

The tory party, on the other hand, was made up of all those

> that press the forms and ceremonies more than the Doctrines of the Church, which are sound and Scriptural; and that either in their own practice are Swearers, Drunkards, or loose in their Conversation, or do allow of and are unwilling such should be punished, but give them all countenance, provided they stickle for the forms and ceremonies, and rail against and endeavour to discountenance all those that are otherwise minded.[37]

It is within the context of this whiggish prejudice that we should place Roger Morrice's comment that the Church of England 'hierarchists' had always discouraged 'practical Religion and Godlynesse which their party has an enmity against and can never bear'.[38]

This was not a charge which could be easily levelled against the post-revolution episcopate. We saw in the last chapter that many of King

William's bishops favoured an accommodation with dissent, not least because they believed unanimity among the godly to be a spiritual imperative.[39] Although saddened by the demise of comprehension, the new episcopate retained a strong commitment to godly reformation. In December 1691 thirteen of the bishops petitioned King William to issue a proclamation for the implementation of the laws against vice.[40] Just such a proclamation was published at the end of January 1692.[41] But this was not the first royal move in favour of reformation of manners. Two years earlier, in an open letter to Bishop Compton of London, King William had promised to 'endeavour a general reformation of the lives and manners of all our subjects'.[42]

What are we to make of this court-sponsored campaign for godly reformation? In part, it represented a clever exercise in propaganda. As Tony Claydon has shown, there was a conscious effort, inspired chiefly by Bishop Burnet, to project William and Mary as divinely-appointed instruments of reformation. By clothing itself in the rhetoric of godly reformation, the precarious revolution regime had an effective means of ideological legitimation. Cornerstone of the Williamite propaganda effort was an unprecedented series of monthly national fasts. Called to invoke divine assistance in the war against France, the fast day services also reminded the people that God's cause and King William's were one and the same.[43] The propagandist aspect of the fast days is captured by a ballad of March 1690:

By Brittains true Monarchs, Great William and Mary . . .
Proclamation is Issu'd, whereby to prepare you,
　　by Fasting and Prayer, their Just Cause to Advance.
　　　By which you may see,
　　　That all Kingdoms be,
The Gift of God only, and no Prince's Fee:
And learn, by true Fasting, Devoutly to Pray
Usurpers and Rebels may ne'r get the Day.[44]

Dr Claydon is clearly right to stress the propagandist dimension of 'courtly reformation'. But in doing so, he has obscured an important truth: Burnet believed what he was saying. As we saw in previous chapters, the bishop considered the Queen to be the very epitome of godly magistracy.[45] Rightly so. No one was more desirous of a true reformation of manners than Queen Mary: 'ce que je souhaite principalement', she wrote in August 1691, 'est de voir mon époux en état à pouvoir réformer le siècle en établissant l'Église; et d'avancer par ces moyens le Royaume de Christ et glorifier ainsi le nom de Dieu!'[46] Nor was anyone more certain of the need for reformation. A woman of deep, sometimes morbid piety, the Queen had been shocked by the state of the nation's religious life upon her return to England in 1689. 'The first thing that surprized me at my coming over,' she later recalled, 'was to see so little devotion in a people so lately in such eminent danger.'[47] While she did what she could to promote godliness at court, the Queen remained fearful of divine retribution. There was so 'universal a corruption', she groaned in 1693, 'that we seem only prepared for vengeance'.[48] As Burnet wrote after the Queen's death, 'how good soever she was in Her self, she carried a heavy Load upon her Mind: The deep Sense that she had of the Guilt and Judgments that seemed to be hanging over us.'[49]

The Queen was also remembered for the distinctly latitudinarian tone of her churchmanship. Burnet wrote that she 'had a true regard to Piety where ever She saw it, in what Form or Party soever. Her Judgment tied her to our Communion, but her Charity was extended to all.'[50] The veteran nonconformist minister John Howe agreed. 'Next to her exemplary Piety towards God,' he recollected,

> shone with a second Lustre her most amiable Benignity towards men; and peculiarly towards them whom she judg'd Pious, of whatsoever Persuasion in respect of the Circumstances of Religion . . . She had divers times express'd her Acceptance, Value, and Desire of their Prayers, whom she knew in some Modes of Worship to differ from her; as one that well understood, that the kingdom of God stands not in lesser things, but in righteousness, peace &c and that they who in these things serve Christ, are acceptable to God, and are to be approved of men.[51]

Other eulogists recalled the Queen's commitment to Protestant union. The presbyterian William Bates stressed her

> sincere Zeal for the healing of our unhappy Divisions in Religious Things, and declared her Resolution upon the first Address of some [dissenting] Ministers, that she would use all Means for that Blessed End. She was so wise as to understand the Difference between Matters Doctrinal and Rituals; and so good as to allow a just Liberty for Dissenters in Things of small Moment. She was not fetter'd with Superstitious Scruples, but her clear and free Spirit was for the Union of Christians in Things essential to Christianity.[52]

The royal chaplain William Payne likewise affirmed that Queen Mary had desired to bring 'all Sober Protestants to one Communion, which would have been the greatest Blow to Popery, and Service to Religion in general'.[53] According to Burnet, 'Few things ever grieved her more, than that those Hopes [of comprehension] seemed to languish: And that the prospect of so desired an Union vanished out of sight.'[54] From the Queen's own account, we know that she was mortified by the miscarriage of the comprehension scheme in the 1689 convocation, and that she had little love for High Churchmen.[55] In contrast, Queen Mary warmly applauded the elevation to the primacy of John Tillotson, leader of the comprehensionist wing of the Church, and she worked with him on a plan for clerical reform.[56]

Small wonder, then, that the deaths of Primate and Queen in the final melancholy weeks of 1694 were viewed as a double blow to the causes of godly reformation and Protestant union. Queen Mary's death, coming just five weeks after Tillotson's, revived in William Bates 'the sorrowful Remembrance of the late Excellent Arch-bishop.' Their 'Principles and Temper, their Designs and Endeavours were for Peace: And the hopes of obtaining it are weakened by the fatal Conjuncture of their Funerals.'[57] Had God prolonged the lives of the Queen and the Archbishop, lamented one of Tillotson's old students, 'we might have expected to have seen and experienced greater public benefits by their Conjunction and further concurrence for the establishing of the church, and reformation of the lives and manners both of the clergy and people, and of procuring a greater union and charity among us.'[58] John Howe was

> persuaded, nothing did more recommend our deceased, excellent Archbishop to Her Majesty, than that She knew His Heart to be as Hers, in that Design, viz. Of a General Reformation of Manners, that must have concern'd all Parties; and without which, (leading and preparing us thereto) Union, and the Cessation of Parties, was little to be hoped for . . . And that Two such Persons should be remov'd out of them, is an Awful Umbrage to us of a Divine determination, That less gentle Methods are fitter for us.[59]

Not all, however, was doom and gloom. For a public campaign, linking the causes of reformation and union, was already well under way.

3. The Reformation Societies

'The world with us is very unruly debauched and profane,' wrote the Londoner Richard Lapthorne in November 1690, 'aboundance of Robberies committed and vice very little checked by those in Authority which makes me feare God is yet providing greater scourges for the Nation which God grant our humiliation and sincere repentance may divert.'[60] Nine months later, Lapthorne was more hopeful: 'things here looke with a tendency to Reformation the Queen strictly enjoyning the Laws to bee put in execution against Sabath breakers and swearers and many have since felt the penalties.'[61] This initiative was a letter of July 1691 in which Queen Mary had urged the Middlesex bench to implement the laws against vice. It had been elicited from the Queen by Bishop Stillingfleet of Worcester, although Stillingfleet himself was acting on behalf of five gentlemen who had recently formed themselves into a society based in the Strand. This was the association which later became known as the First Society for Reformation of Manners.[62]

The society's objective was to combat sin by working for the vigorous enforcement of the many laws against immorality and profanity. To this end, it encouraged informers to denounce offenders before the magistrates.[63] In the Autumn of 1691 alleged legal irregularities in the society's use of informers led to a clash with the Middlesex JPs and the Lords Commissioners of the Great Seal. But thanks largely to the backing of the Court, these early difficulties had been weathered by the Summer of 1692.[64] Indeed, by the mid–1690s, a number of subordinate reformation societies had emerged in the metropolis. Like their parent, these societies promoted the use of the informer as a weapon against sin.[65]

The most distinctive characteristic of these reformation societies was their ecumenism. They counted among their members both Churchmen and moderate dissenters. The broad Protestantism of the societies was symbolised by the reformation sermons which took place from 1697. Organised by the First Society, these sermons were preached by conformist clergy at St Mary le Bow and dissenting ministers at Salters Hall. At both venues, the congregations were mixed.[66]

Co-operation between godly Protestants had been a keynote of the reformation societies from very early days. Towards the end of 1691, the First Society asked dissenting ministers to encourage their congregants to act as informers.[67] Such a readiness to work with dissenters is easily understandable when we examine the membership of the First Society. We know something of the religious sensibilities of three of its five founder members: the west-countryman Maynard Colchester, the Irish gentlemen Richard Bulkeley and our old friend Edward Stephens. Although he was a conformist, Maynard Colchester's religious views were strongly informed by the presbyterian traditions of his grandfather, the famous lawyer Sir John Maynard. Colchester later became a whig MP.[68] Richard Bulkeley was a broad churchman who later became enamoured of the French Prophets, a millenarian group.[69] As for Edward Stephens, there is no doubt of his broad Protestant sympathies. In 1689 he had insisted that reformation had 'been greatly disturbed and interrupted by inconsiderate affectation of Uniformity, and improper and preposterous means for that purpose'. He wanted to see the repeal of the Act of Uniformity and the penal laws against dissenters. For charity and unanimity among Protestants were essential to ward off God's judgments.[70]

Such views remained influential within the reformation societies. Writing in 1699, the author of the official *Account of the Societies for Reformation of Manners* highlighted the importance of unity in furthering the cause of reformation:

> nothing, I think, can be reasonably supposed sufficient to remove our Guilt, than some considerable and remarkable Reformation . . . such a one as may be in some measure proportioned to the Leprosie of Vice and Prophaneness that seems to have almost over-spread us. But if we do truly repent of all our Abominations, and turn from our wicked ways; if we lay aside our unnecessary Strifes, and our unchristian Contentions with one another, which we

have so long felt the dismal effects of; if we express our Zeal, and unite our Strength against the Patrons of Vice, who are the Enemies of God and Goodness, more than against those that differ from us in some few things, and those of lesser moment, but agree with us, I conceive, in those that are essential; if we sincerely, and without delay, set about and further all pious and proper Endeavours for a National Reformation, truly pursue the things that belong to our Peace, it still seems with us a Day of Mercy, and the Scriptures give us Encouragement to hope, that we may not perish.[71]

To those who believed that reformation and Protestant union were inextricably linked, the ecumenism of the reformation societies was a wholly natural and laudable phenomenon. 'A General Conflagration', declared the dissenter Edmund Calamy in February 1699, 'calls for every Man's Bucket; And our spreading Immoralities for all Hands to check them. And it is an hopeful Prognostick in the present Case, that those who differ in Rituals but with too much Vehemence, should unanimously join together in forming those Societies for Reformation, who aim at the Checking those Vices which threaten to over-run us, which are heartily detested by Good Men of all Perswasions.'[72] Nine months earlier, Calamy's fellow nonconformist, Daniel Williams, had similarly stressed the role of the societies in breaking down barriers between Churchmen and dissenters. 'How soon', he had asked rhetorically, 'did Divinely inspir'd Minds coalesce in this Undertaking? – And easily made it evident, That there is no such difference between Members of the Established Church, and the Dissenters, that will not be overlook'd by Serious Persons, when the undoubted Concernments of Christ and Practical Godliness are in danger.'[73]

The reformation societies had effected a *de facto* union among godly Protestants, and some hoped that this would pave the way for a more formal union. By 'more Familiar Acquaintance with one another,' suggested the dissenting minister John Shower in 1699, 'you may find Persons, of both sorts, worthy of your Esteem and Love, as will take off many Prejudices, destroy Bitterness and Rancor, and cure the Evilspeaking and Detraction, which hath been complained of on all sides; It may tend to heal the Moroseness, and Reservedness, and Distrust of one another, which has kept us at such a Distance; And let us see, that there was no sufficient reason for such an Estrangement.'[74] According to Daniel Williams, the 'very Meeting together, and joynt Concurrence [of Churchmen and dissenters] in this Laudable Employment, will conciliate your Minds and melt them down into Moderation, which is a Temper so necessary, and upon which our Happiness so much depends, that I dare deliver this Prognostick: England can never be fixedly happy in its Religious, or Civil Concernments, but by an Union between the Moderate Churchmen and the Moderate Dissenters.'[75] In 1700 John Hooke, a founder member of the SPCK, wrote that the societies for reformation 'hath been great use, to remove the Prejudices, which many had taken up, against the Establish'd Church, and against one another; and hath laid a Foundation of that Union, which may be a probable means of putting an end to Schisms and Divisions, of restoring the Primitive Discipline in the Church, and of teaching England to keep the Unity of the Spirit in the bond of Peace.'[76] Samuel Bradford, the rector of St Mary le Bow, was equally sanguine. It was 'a good Omen,' he told the reformation societies in 1697,

> that God hath stir'd up the hearts of so many among us, to express a concern and zeal for the suppressing Impiety and Vice; and that in prosecuting this Excellent Design, many of our Dissenting Brethren are join'd with those of the Establish'd Communion. 'Tis to be hoped, that the frequent conversing upon so good an Occasion as this, may be a means of removing all Unreasonable Prejudices, and by degrees may beget a better Understanding, and a more favourable Opinion of each other. If our Zeal were but once turn'd towards the great things of Religion, in which we all agree, I am persuaded that our Differences about less Matters would soon abate, and we might perhaps come to an agreement about them before we are aware.[77]

Running through this unionist reformation rhetoric is a deep vein of 'antiformalism',[78] perhaps best expressed by the veteran dissenting minister, John Howe, in a reformation sermon of 1698:

> they who are agreed, with sincere minds, upon so great and important an End, as the serving this most comprehensive Interest, are agreed in a greater Thing than they can differ in. To differ about a Ceremony or two, or set of words, is but a Triffle, compar'd with being agreed in absolute devotedness to God, and Christ, and in a design, as far as in them lies, of doing good to all. An Agreement in Substantial Godliness and Christianity, in humility, meekness, self-denial, in singleness of heart, benignity, charity, entire love to sincere Christians, as such, in universal love to Mankind, and in a design of doing all the good we can in the world, notwithstanding such go under different denominations, and do differ in so Minute Things, is the most Valuable Agreement that can be among Christians.[79]

The words of John Howe remind us of an earlier era of godly reformation. Forty years before his sermon to the reformation societies, Howe had been household chaplain to the Lord Protector, Oliver Cromwell. Then, too, he was noted for stressing the insignificance of divisive religious forms when set beside the virtues of substantial godliness.[80] In this, he was by no means a unique figure among Cromwellian clergymen. On the contrary, the rejection of religious formalism and an emphasis instead on fundamental godliness were hallmarks of Cromwellian churchmanship. By highlighting the areas of agreement between the godly of all denominations, Cromwell and his clerical supporters had hoped both to further the work of reformation and to foster greater unity among godly Protestants.[81] It is within this ideological tradition that we should place many of the leading godly reformers of the 1690s. Like their mid-century predecessors, the proponents of reformation in King William's reign subscribed to a belief in the circular relationship between godly reformation and Protestant union. Unanimity among Protestants, they averred, was a prerequisite for the transformation of England into a truly godly common-wealth. At the same time, by highlighting the fundamental godly virtues at the expense of the insignificant but divisive religious forms, reformation of manners would itself help to effect the cherished goal of Protestant union.

All this was plain enough to Archdeacon William Nicolson, avowed enemy of the interdenominational reformation societies established within his own archdeaconry of Carlisle. Such societies, he wrote to a friend in March 1700, smacked of 'the associations of the Presbyterian and Independent Ministers in the days of the Rebellion', notably Richard Baxter's famous Worcestershire Association. 'Now, sir,' he continued, 'such linsey-woolsey associations as those look like the proper manufac-ture of Kidderminster [Baxter's parish during the 1650s], and might be reasonable enough in those days of confusion: but why they should be brought in a fashion under a settled Church government, unless it be upon the principle of comprehension, I cannot imagine.'[82]

7

Scotland and Ireland

1. The Presbyterian Revolution in Scotland

The Scottish revolution of 1688–9 was an altogether more extreme and violent affair than its English counterpart, but then it was not King William's revolution. The English revolution was essentially a military campaign in which the Prince of Orange's Dutch troops secured a bloodless victory over King James's army. In short, the English revolution was effected by Prince William's army. In Scotland the Prince's role was a good deal more tangential. True, the Scottish revolution was wholly contingent upon events in England: even though King James had emptied Scotland of soldiers to meet the Dutch threat in the south, his hold over the Stuarts' ancient kingdom was not challenged until it became clear that Prince William had triumphed in England.[1] Yet when the Scottish revolution at last dawned in December 1688, its sword arm was provided not by the Prince's Dutch professionals but by the militant covenanting presbyterians of south-west Scotland. And the covenanters had their own private agenda, the first item of which was the destruction of episcopacy in Scotland. This they began on Christmas Day 1688 when presbyterian gangs roamed the south-west, driving the detested episcopalian ministers from their manses.[2] So by March 1689, when a Convention of the Estates met at Edinburgh to sanction the toppling of the old regime in the state, the Scottish revolution was already spinning violently out of King William's control.

Nor did the proceedings of the Convention make life any easier for the new King of Scots. In England the tactical expedients of politicians had worked to King William's advantage. The whig leaders – fearful that an assault on the prerogative would drive their 'Deliverer' into the arms of the Church party – watered down the Declaration of Rights.[3] For their part, the tories, though deeply troubled by Prince William's seizure of the throne, were eventually scared into co-operating with the new King by the terrifying prospect of a whig reaction. Since tory leaders like Nottingham and Carmarthen were ready to serve him, King William was able to play one party off against the other, pouring cold water upon the fires of whig extremism.

No such constraints operated upon the revolutionary party in Scotland. In the first place, many moderate episcopalians from the north of Scotland, unnerved by the violent events in the south-west, failed to take their seats in the Convention. Thus we know of some 30 episcopalian members who only took up their seats at Edinburgh in 1690.[4] An English commentator was speaking with pardonable exaggeration when he called the assembly of the Scottish Estates the 'Rump Convencon'.[5] Secondly, those moderates who did attend the Convention swam with the revolutionary tide – a prudent move with over a thousand armed Cameronians, the most extreme of all the covenanters, patrolling the streets of Edinburgh.[6] Freed from the fear of being outflanked by conservative opponents, the committed revolutionaries in the Convention could be as radical as they liked. Indeed, far from moderating their demands in order to win the King's favour, they used them as a stick with which to beat their way into office.

The revolutionary agenda was enshrined in two documents, the Claim of Right and the Articles of Grievances, which were presented to William and Mary upon their acceptance of the Scottish crown in May 1689. Unlike their English counterpart, the Declaration of Rights, both the Claim and the Articles included provisions which King William found intolerable. For example, the Articles of Grievances, which sought to regulate relations between the executive and the legislature, contained a denunciation of the Lords of the Articles, the parliamentary committee by which absentee Stuart kings had controlled the business of the Scottish Estates. For obvious reasons, the King was keen to retain the services of the Lords of the Articles, and accordingly he resisted the Convention's attempts to secure their abolition.[7]

The proposed abolition of the Lords of the Articles was by no means the only area where the Convention was too radical for King William's comfort. From the very beginning of its proceedings – when it voted to exclude the bishops from the committee for settling the government – the Convention of the Estates had shown itself bitterly hostile to episcopacy.[8] It came as no surprise, therefore, when the Estates, having already denounced 'prelacy' as 'a great and insupportable grievance to this Nation', passed legislation to abolish episcopacy in June 1689.[9]

The beginning of the end for episcopacy in Scotland had come with the south-western disturbances of late December 1688 – the so-called 'rabblings' in which some 160 episcopalian clergymen were expelled from

their manses by presbyterian mobs. Not only did the 'rabblings' win back
for presbyterianism its heartland in the south-west, they also had a decisive influence on the subsequent course of events. As T.N. Clarke has
written, the 'rabblings' 'prejudiced the course of the Revolution which
followed by striking a blow against the Church where and when it was at
its most vulnerable, damaging the morale of James's supporters, and
allowing the Presbyterians to reoccupy parish churches'.[10]

Needless to say, the Convention gave no redress to the 'rabbled' clergy
of the south-west. Instead, it turned its attentions to their colleagues in other
parts of the country. Clergymen were ordered, upon pain of deprivation,
to pray publicly for King William and Queen Mary, and read the proclamation of the new monarchs from their pulpits. This paved the way for the
removal of a further 172 clergymen, deprived by the Privy Council for
allegedly failing to comply with the Estates' commands.[11]

The lead in the continuing purge of the episcopalian clergy was taken
by the Earl of Crawford, President of both the Estates and the Privy
Council. A presbyterian of the old school, Crawford overlooked no pecca-
dillo in his drive to 'out' as many episcopalian clergy as possible. By the
end of 1689, when King William was at last able to restrain the earl's zeal,
Crawford's legal 'rabblings' had brought to 400 the number of deprived
episcopalians.[12]

The piecemeal demolition of the Scottish ecclesiastical establishment
was not at all to the King's liking. He had no fixed policy towards the
Church of Scotland. All that mattered was obtaining a settlement which
would guarantee domestic harmony in Scotland and cause no ructions in
England. Accordingly, King William was willing to accept either presbyterian or episcopal church government in Scotland, provided that the
establishment was sufficiently broad to accommodate moderate men on
both sides.[13] Before his arrival in England, it is true, he had been prejudiced against the Scottish bishops by his confidant and principal adviser
on Scottish affairs, William Carstares. A presbyterian exile, Carstares had
sought to persuade the Prince that Scottish episcopacy was maintained
only by force.[14] Following the revolution, Carstares continued to press the
new King to get rid of episcopacy in the northern kingdom: 'the episcopal
clergy in Scotland, particularly the prelates', he insisted in a paper to the
King, 'had been so accustomed to warp their religious tenets with
the political doctrines of regal supremacy, passive obedience, and non-
resistance, that it became inconsistent with the very end of [King
William's] coming, to continue episcopacy upon its present footing in
Scotland.'[15] But once he was safely ensconced in England, the King was
open to other influences. Not only was he made aware of the strength of
episcopalian sentiment in many parts of Scotland, he also came to realise
that the abolition of Scottish episcopacy would further complicate his
uneasy relationship with the Church party in England. The King was, in

fact, prepared to protect the Scottish bishops as long as they were willing to acquiesce in the revolution.[16]

One of the bishops – Alexander Rose of Edinburgh – had been sent south in December 1688 to assure King James of the loyalty of the Scottish prelates. When Rose arrived in London, he found that his mission had been overtaken by events. However, he was still there in February when the Convention offered the Crown to William and Mary. Shortly afterwards, Bishop Compton of London, apparently acting on the new King's behalf, informed Rose that King William would 'throw off the Presbyterians' if the Scottish bishops promised him their support.[17] Rose's subsequent refusal, in a brief meeting with the King, to commit his brethren to the revolution has been held to have sounded the death-knell for episcopacy north of the border.[18] But such a view presupposes that King William was in a position to carry out his promise. Given the lawless state of Scotland in the early months of 1689, it is by no means clear that he was. With the presbyterians having seized the initiative in the south-west and at Edinburgh, the Scottish bishops could hardly have set much store by the King's assurance. As Bishop Burnet of Salisbury – himself a Scot – later commented, the Scottish bishops, 'finding that the Presbeterians were like to carry all before them resolved to make what party they could for King James and to stick to his interest'.[19] To a man, the bishops refused to forswear their allegiance to James VII. Thus in June 1689 King William had no option but to give his assent to legislation abolishing episcopacy in Scotland.[20]

Although he had acquiesced in the abolition of episcopacy, the King continued to resist the abolition of the Lords of the Articles. That refusal provoked the majority faction in the Estates – the Club – to exercise the weapon of last resort. At a time when a Jacobite force was menacing the Lowlands, the Club blocked all efforts to vote supply for the King.[21] It was a desperate expedient, but it worked. In March 1690, with the Jacobite rebellion contained but not crushed, King William sent to the Edinburgh parliament a new commissioner, Lord Melville. He had a brief to make the concessions required to obtain supply. As a result, the Act for abolishing the Lords of the Articles at last reached the statute book. The full impact of that measure, which destroyed the mechanism by which the Scottish parliament had been subordinated to the will of a distant monarchy, was not to be felt until Queen Anne's reign. Of more immediate effect was legislation abolishing the royal supremacy over the Kirk and reestablishing presbyterian church government. To King William's discomfort, the Act restoring presbyterianism confined membership of the Kirk's General Assembly, for the time being, to known presbyterians: the 60 or so survivors of the anti-presbyterian purge of 1661 – the so-called 'antediluvians' – and their nominees. This was crucial since the General Assembly was given the right 'to try and purge out all insufficient, negligent, scandalous and erroneous ministers'.[22] Scotland was about to be made safe for presbyterians.

Not for the last time in his reign, north or south of the border, King William was forced to swallow a bitter pill. As he explained to a distressed Bishop Burnet, 'since the Presbyterians were the only party that he had there, the granting of their desires at that time were unavoidable, but he assured me he would take care to moderate the violence of Presbytery.'[23] To that end, the King urged the Assembly, which met in October 1690, to act with restraint: 'we expect that your management shall be such as we shall have no reason to repent of what we have done.' For 'we never could be of the mind that violence was suited to the advancing of true religion, nor do we intend that our authority shall ever be a tool to the irregular passions of any party. Moderation is what religion enjoins, neighbouring churches expect from you and we recommend to you.'[24]

The King's letter appears to have had the desired effect. Although the Assembly established two commissions to purge 'the insufficient, or scandalous, or erroneous, or supinely negligent', the commissioners were instructed to admit to ministerial communion all those who were 'orthodox in doctrine, of competent abilities, of a godly, peaceable, and loyal conversation, and who shall be judged faithful to God and to this government'.[25] But when the commissions began work, it became clear that conformity to the old ecclesiastical order in itself gave rise to an irrebuttable presumption of insufficiency, scandal, error or supine negligence. The commission which operated north of the Tay made little headway in purging the episcopalian heartland. Most of the northern clergy were secluded, or voluntarily seceded, from the official judicatures of the Kirk. But protected by the local gentry and buttressed by the support of their parishioners, the episcopalian clergy in the north proved impossible to dislodge from their livings. South of the Tay, however, the commission perfected the work of 'cleansing' begun by the 'rabblers' and continued by Crawford in 1688–9.[26]

The cumulative effect of the successive round of purges was staggering. In 1695 it was reported that only 15 or 16 episcopalians still held parishes in the south of Scotland.[27] Even though the north of the country remained largely untouched by the presbyterian reaction, it seems that more than half of the Scottish clergy were ousted, in one way or another, after 1688.[28] It was the greatest upheaval in the history of the Church of Scotland.

The impact of these events upon opinion within the English Church cannot be overstated. The Earl of Crawford's activities, noted Burnet, 'gave a new quickning to the hatred that was generally borne to the Dissenters here, for it was in every mouth, that it was both unseasonable and unsafe for us to shew any favour to a party that acted so severely against all those of our persuasion when they had power'.[29] Such views, as we saw in an earlier chapter, spelt disaster for Tillotson's comprehension proposals in the convocation of 1689. As Carstares reported to Crawford in early December, 'the Convocation here say, they will do nothing till their persecuted brethren in Scotland be considered.'[30]

Nor was the unhappy fate of the Scottish episcopalians a mere pretext for convocation's refusal to consider an accommodation between Church and dissent in England. English Churchmen genuinely feared that the Scots would seek to export their reformation to the southern kingdom. 'I pray God preserve our Church in its Apostolical Episcopal Government, and that there may never want Bishops to add to the second volume [of your work]', wrote the Cumbrian cleric, Hugh Todd, to the ecclesiastical historian, Henry Wharton, in November 1689. 'If you live so near Scotland as I do, you would believe there might be some reason to doubt of the succession.'[31] Todd's anxiety was not baseless. There was, after all, the unhappy precedent of the 1640s to support the nostrum that Scottish presbyterians would rest content only when England too had been wiped clean of the stain of episcopacy. Writing from Suffolk in May 1690, an English clergyman expressed the hope that the recent defeat of the Jacobite rebels at Cromdale would make Scotland quiet: 'but', he ruefully continued,

> I perceive many wise men are of opinion, that the conquerors are of such a restless temper, that if they want work at home they will com & help their dear brethren in England (as they once before did) to pull down our popish establishment, & erect their super-fine protestant discipline in the room of it, for they are of such a generous & communicative disposition, that they will not be content to ingross Anarchy & confusion, or confine it within the bounds of their own church, without making their neighbours happy in partaking the benefits of their new notions & discoveries, which undoubtedly are all made of a republican mettal, & when they have once ruin'd the Church I am afraid will undermine the monarchy.[32]

Similar fears were aired by the Irish nonjuror, Charles Leslie: 'let us remember,' he wrote in 1694, 'that the covenant (now rampant in Scotland) obliges them to carry on the work of that reformation in England as well as in Scotland, as they did before: And they have the impudence to pray publicly for it now in their churches, for our conversion (as they call it) from prelacy, which they call popery; and idolatry, that is, our liturgy.'[33]

By no stretch of the imagination could Charles Leslie be described as a detached observer of events. A dedicated propagandist for the Jacobite cause, Leslie cited the establishment of presbyterianism north of the border as evidence of King William's true sympathies.[34] Indeed, it was a stock theme in Jacobite propaganda that events in Scotland proved the King to be no friend of episcopacy in any of his domains. King William, observed Nathaniel Johnston in 1690, was now busily professing his loyalty to the Church of England, 'but let Scotland speak how far he may be believed in it'.[35] As a Jacobite poetaster so pithily put it, King William

... never cou'd intend
the Church of England to defend
When prelates he left in the lurch
& sett the Kirk above the Church.[36]

Such sentiments doubtless struck a chord with much of the English clergy. Certainly, the suspicions of King William's intentions evident during the 1689 convocation were still apparent in 1701 when one cleric partly attributed the heats of the convocation controversy to 'the jealousy universally conceiv'd against the King, as being no friend to the Church here in England, because of his suffering Episcopacy to sink in Scotland'.[37]

All this was more than a little unfair to King William. The Scottish revolution was the work of a radical minority, largely beyond the King's control, which had pursued its ends ruthlessly. By 1690, when the revolution was becoming more broadly based, the damage had already been done. For the rest of his reign, King William – anxious both to secure domestic peace in Scotland and reassure episcopalian sentiment in England – did his best to restrain presbyterian excesses. In February 1691 he briefly suspended the operation of the Kirk's commissions, and pressed the General Assembly to take into its ranks the remaining episcopalian ministers.[38] Eleven months later, the King renewed his plea for loyal episcopalians to be re-admitted to the Kirk's judicatories (governing assemblies).[39] When the General Assembly failed to give redress to the episcopalian clergy, King William severely damaged his relations with the presbyterian clergy by dissolving the Assembly without setting a date for its successor to meet.[40]

There was, however, precious little that either the King or his ministers could do to curb the excesses of individual presbyteries. 'Our kirk judicatures', complained Lord Tarbat in June 1692, 'slacken nothing of their hott practices, which raises severall tumults, and is the great mean that keeps up division in the nation, and will creat more, if not prevented, nor doe they stop at the Councel's desyre nor command.'[41] While Tarbat, a convinced episcopalian, blamed the presbyterians for undermining efforts at conciliation, the Scottish Secretary of State, James Johnston, saw fault on both sides. 'As for our clergyes,' he told his English counterpart, the Earl of Nottingham, 'I doe not find that the generality of either of them have an inclination to a union, whatever they pretend.' A presbyterian of erastian views, Johnston despised inflexible episcopalians and highflying presbyterians in equal measure. Left to their own devices, he warned Nottingham, the rival clerics would never be reconciled. Johnston looked instead to the secular arm to 'moderate the pretensions of both parties', for they 'will submit to many things which they will not consent to'.[42]

The upshot was Johnston's Act for 'settling the quiet and peace' of the Kirk, passed by the Estates, now a full parliament, in 1693. This offered security to episcopalian incumbents who were ready to swear allegiance to William and Mary as *de jure* monarchs – the Oath of Assurance – and recognise presbyterian church government.[43] Designed to reconcile the two traditions within the Scottish Church, the scheme united them only in opposition to its provisions. Presbyterians hated the idea that parliament could set the terms of admission to the Kirk. They particularly abhorred the provision which made the holding of any benefice dependent upon swearing the Oath of Assurance – an oath established without the prior approval of the Kirk. When the King sought to impose the oath on the members of the General Assembly, the presbyterians were beside themselves. Only the intervention of William Carstares, who succeeded in persuading King William to back down, prevented a complete rupture between King and Assembly.[44]

The episcopalian ministers were scarcely more enthusiastic about the Act. A mere 30 or so complied with its terms.[45] The rest could not stomach the clauses which required them to 'own and acknowledge' presbyterian church government, and apply for admission to the Kirk's judicatories upon taking the Oaths of Allegiance and Assurance. Those provisions, they feared, would ultimately place them at the tender mercy of their presbyterian 'brethren'.[46] As Alexander Monro, the deprived Principal of Edinburgh University, had written in 1692, 'if I should do all that may possibly be required of me, yet still I am to have no legal Title but by the Presbytery and then you cannot but see that my settlement in that place to be very precarious or rather none at all when ever the [Privy] Council changes their members or their measures.'[47]

Although Monro professed himself to 'love peace and submission with all my heart', he was, in fact, set against any accommodation with the presbyterians. During his exile in England he became convinced that 'unless the fanaticks of Scotland pull down the Church of England', it was inevitable that the English Church, scared of the 'fanaticks' in its own backyard, 'must some time or other blow up the foundations of Presbyterie in Scotland'. Accordingly in December 1694 Monro urged the episcopalian clergy to resist talk of compromise, and pressed them instead to 'adhere to their Orthodox Principals, to assert Episcopacy'.[48] But in the new year the rug was pulled from under the feet of the rejectionists by another piece of Johnstonian legislation.

The Act of 1695 showed that Johnston had learnt from the mistakes of 1693. The episcopalian minsters were still offered protection if they took the Oaths of Allegiance and Assurance. But gone was the requirement that they seek admission to the Kirk's judicatories. Instead, the episcopalian clergy could decide for themselves whether to apply for admission to the General Assembly and the presbyteries. At the same time, the Kirk was left at liberty to refuse admission to the episcopalian clergy.[49]

By dropping attempts to force presbyterians and episcopalians into each other's arms, Johnston's 1695 Act proved an altogether more successful piece of legislation than its predecessor. Whereas they had, for the most part, cold-shouldered the 1693 Act, the episcopalian clergy of northern Scotland now generally swore the oaths to King William. In return, they received statutory confirmation in their livings. Yet the episcopalian incumbents remained, largely through volition, outside the judicatories of the Kirk.[50] The 1695 Act had done nothing to heal the division between presbyterians and episcopalians. But it created a *modus vivendi* between the two traditions which was to survive until the great Jacobite rising of 1715.

2. The Revolution Settlement in Ireland

In the Summer of 1689, as a Jacobite force threatened to penetrate the Scottish Lowlands, King James's Irish army lay entrenched before the walls of Londonderry. The reverse it suffered there at the end of July proved to be the turning point of the British war of succession. Bereft of promised reinforcements from Ireland and leaderless after the death of Dundee, the Scottish Jacobites were eventually penned into their Highland fastnesses. And within a year, a Williamite army, led by King William himself, had broken out of its Ulster bridgehead to begin the reconquest of Catholic Ireland.[51]

The reconquest of Ireland was completed by the Dutch general Ginkel in 1691. But the Williamite victory in Ireland, like the pacification of the Scottish Highlands, did not result in the unconditional surrender of Jacobite forces. Desperate to release troops for service on the Continent, and under pressure from the Emperor Leopold to show lenience towards the Irish Catholics, King William authorised Ginkel to reach a negotiated settlement in the Spring of 1691. The crushing nature of Ginkel's victory at Aughrim in July did not persuade the King to change his policy. Thus when the remnant of the Jacobite army surrendered at Limerick in October, it did so upon honourable terms.[52]

The Treaty of Limerick, whose terms owed much to those agreed upon the surrender of Galway in July 1691, provided for the transportation to France of that major element of the Jacobite army which would not submit to King William. As for those officers and men who chose to remain, they were to be pardoned and guaranteed in the possession of their lands, provided they swore allegiance to the new monarchs. A similar term extended the King's clemency to the civilian population in areas under the control of the Irish army. The Catholic community as a whole was promised the same religious freedoms it had enjoyed under Charles II. That promise, which reflected both King William's well-known aversion to the forcing of conscience and his eagerness to appease the Emperor, was tantamount to granting liberty of worship to the majority population.[53]

These were, on the whole, generous terms. Far too generous in the eyes of most Irish Protestants. The events of King James's reign, when Catholics had gained control of the Irish civil and military administrations, had been a terrible shock to the Protestant gentry. They had particularly painful memories of the Catholic-dominated parliament which had sat at Dublin in the Summer of 1689. Ignoring King James's pleas for moderation, it had torn up the pro-Protestant Restoration land settlement, and attainted hundreds of Protestant gentlemen.[54] This was seen by Protestants as nothing less than an attempt to extirpate them from the face of Ireland. In victory, they were in no mood to be magnanimous. On the contrary, they saw the Catholic defeat as an opportunity to make Ireland safe for Protestantism, once and for all. That opportunity, they believed, was being wasted. 'Tis plain the Irish are in a much better condition, then we hopd they woud be in the end of this war, & by consequence, the conditions of the Protestants so much worse', complained James Bonnell, the Accountant-General of Ireland, to Robert Harley in November 1691. 'Good part of the Irish have their estates, by the Articles of Limerick, & some advantages even above Protestants.' In Bonnell's view, the Treaty of Limerick had thrown away a great opportunity for the Protestant cause. 'Nothing', he explained to Harley,

can secure against the Irish, but increasing the number & the power of the English. Had the Irish bin now totaly reducd & brought low by the loss of all their estates, this country would have bin lookd on by the English as a secure place, & many would have flockt over hither, for advantages to be had, which would have greatly increast our numbers; But as it is, & if it be let go on this foot, we shall be so far from having new ones come to us, that few of the old ones, who can get away, will stay: the consequence of which, neerley touches the interest of England.[55]

Small wonder, then, that Bonnell was so disappointed by the outcome of the war.

James Bonnell's unhappiness with the peace settlement was representative of Protestant opinion as a whole. And in the face of general Protestant hostility towards the Treaty of Limerick, the Irish civil administration – re-established by King William after the Boyne – was soon finding difficulty in implementing its terms. Despite using 'our utmost endeavours' to enforce the peace settlement, wrote the Irish Lords Justices to the Earl of Nottingham at the end of November 1691,

yet wee meete with many difficulties in the performance, as well from the violence and prejudice which the common people have contracted against them [the Catholics] from the ill treatment they received from the Irish dureing the late rebellion as from the heates of those of better quality who ought to understand their Majesties' and the interest of the countrey better.

One such member of the quality who ought to have known better was the Bishop of Meath, Anthony Dopping. Preaching an official thanksgiving sermon in November 1691, Bishop Dopping had denounced as worthless any treaty reached with the treacherous Irish papists. 'This discourse', reported the embarrassed Lords Justices,

> upon so solemne an occasion in so greate an audience, before the government and by a bishopp and one of the Privy Councel, has soe wonderfully dissatisfyed the Irish gentlemen who are now in towne in order to be restored according to the articles, that wee are humbly of opinion it is necessary for his Majestie to show some marke of his displeasure against him, and the least wee thinke can be done is to suspend him from his attendance at Councel.[56]

The King agreed, and Bishop Dopping was duly struck off the Irish Privy Council.[57]

The lenience of the terms granted to the Catholic rebels was not the only grievance of Irish Protestants. Although the English parliament had voted supply for the reconquest of Ireland, the sums provided fell well short of meeting the army's needs. The ultimate victims of the soldiers' penury were the wretched people of Ireland. With a conquered country at its mercy, the army helped itself to the good things of the land, plundering Protestants and papists alike with cheerful impartiality. As Lord Sidney, the senior Lord Justice, wearily commented in October 1690, hardly an hour went by without some new complaint against the army.[58] Nor had matters improved much by December 1691 when an agent of the Duke of Ormonde penned an account of the army's depredations at Kilkenny. 'Our Circumstances here are worse this last yeare', he wrote to an English friend,

> the Soldiers will not suffer us to make distresses for Rent, the tenants pays the foot 1s 9d and 3s 6d to the horse for weekly subsistance besides hay & Oates, the tenants beleeve they'l never be repaid because they cannot gett the last yeares bills paid by the Commissioners in whose hands they are. The tenants are in a Miserable Condicon as the Mayor of Kilkenny declares that the Soldiers are not content with ye Subsistance above said, but Robb theire Landlords, and upon the Markett days they goe to the Citty Gates and take away by force what they please from the Countrey people, soe that the Markett is quite spoyld, and the Dukes tenants are forced to Quitt theire Houses, not being able to live in them by reason aforesaid & without some speedy redress there is no money for Rent to be expected.[59]

This, then, was not the most propitious of times to call a meeting of the Irish parliament. But that was exactly the course upon which King William was set, a parliament being summoned to meet at Dublin on 5 October 1692. It was a momentous decision. Apart from the Jacobite assembly of 1689, no Irish parliament had sat since 1666. A parliament was now thought essential to tie up the many legal loose ends left by the Jacobite parliament and the war. Nevertheless, the calling of the Irish parliament was a potentially risky business. Far from doing the Court's business, parliament might instead provide a forum for airing the grievances of the Protestant gentry. Had the parliament been called earlier, as the Lords Justices had urged, things might have been different. The soldiery, it was believed, would then have been able to bully voters into electing army officers. But by the time the writs were issued, the army's political influence, if not its unpopularity, had diminished greatly. Thus the Protestant propertied elite was more or less free to elect a parliament in its own image.[60] The upshot was a militantly Protestant parliament, bristling with indignation against the Dublin Castle administration, and determined not to be the lapdog of the Court.

When parliament met in October 1692, the Court's legislative program soon began to go awry.[61] Under Poynings' Law of 1494, all Irish legislation, with the exception of money bills, was to be drafted by the Irish Privy Council, dispatched to the English Privy Council for approval, and then sent back to Dublin where the Irish parliament could accept or reject the proposed legislation, but not amend it. In the past, when Irish parliaments had been under the Court's thumb, that final incapacity had mattered little. But in 1692 it proved disastrous. For the newly assertive Irish parliament, bereft of the power to amend, rejected outright a stream of necessary but ill-drafted legislation. Instead, MPs embarked upon a series of investigations into alleged government maladministration and corruption. Worse was still to come for the Court. The Jacobite war had wrecked the finances of the government of Ireland. Although he had not been authorised to do so, Sidney – now Lord Lieutenant – sought supply from parliament to ameliorate the financial difficulties of the civil and military administrations. The Commons were willing to grant supply, but insisted that they had 'the sole right' to formulate the heads of money bills. This was the last straw. Rather than surrender the Crown's right to initiate money bills, an apoplectic Lord Lieutenant prorogued parliament on 3 November, 'with such a Speech as never was Spoke to a house of Commons by any Kings of England Except Charles the 2nd once when he dissolved the [Oxford] Parliament in 81'.[62] Parliament was not to meet again for another three years.

Deprived of a domestic forum of protest, the opponents of the Dublin Castle administration, like the enemies of the Earl of Strafford in 1640, took their grievances to Westminster. There, in February 1693, MPs universally berated the Irish administration. 'I hear the papists speak very well of the government there', averred Jack Howe, 'but no Protestant I can meet with that does, which is very strange to me.' Henry Boyle informed the Commons that he had 'spoke with some [Irish] gentlemen, and if what they tell me be true you will need neither an invasion nor a rebellion but the people will leave that kingdom – they are used so ill.'[63] When one of those gentlemen, James Sloane, was called before the House, he crisply summarised the complaints of Irish Protestants. 'The grievances of the kingdom of Ireland', he told MPs, 'are the quartering of soldiers, which continues to this time, then the embezzling of the revenue, which has been the occasion of the first; then the greatest of all is the encouragement that is given to papists and the Protestants are discouraged.'[64] Two days later, the Commons resolved to address King William for redress of Irish grievances.[65]

The clamour against the Irish administration eventually told. In June 1693 the King recalled Lord Lieutenant Sidney, and sent to Ireland three new Lords Justices: Cyril Wyche, William Duncombe and Henry, Lord Capel, whose late brother, the Earl of Essex, had been a popular Lord Lieutenant – with Protestants at least – in the 1670s. Of these three, only the strongly whiggish Capel was a militant anti-papist. But the growing pre-eminence of whiggery within the English administration soon made Capel the dominant figure at Dublin Castle, and in the Spring of 1695 he was elevated to the dignity of Lord Deputy.[66]

The remodelling of the Dublin administration had not solved its principal conundrum: how to obtain supply from a new parliament without surrendering the Crown's position on 'the sole right'. Wyche and Duncombe deemed the problem to be insoluble. A parliament, they acknowledged in July 1694, was essential to ease the financial pressure on the administration. Yet, they sadly continued, 'we cannot in duty but informe their Majesties that we generally find men as stiff as ever, and as resolved, if not to pursue the point and maintain it, yet not to retract and give it up.'[67] Lord Capel, on the other hand, was convinced that the issue of 'the sole right' could be settled to the Crown's satisfaction. From his own consultations with 'all the Eminent Lawyers, and leading Men', the Lord Deputy had come to the conclusion that

> all heats will be laid aside, and that another Parliament will meet in a temper, and resolution to doe their Majesties, and their Country, all the service that can be expected from good English Men and Protestants, and will contribute to their utmost towards the support of the Government; being sensible they have been burthensome enough already to England, and cannot reasonably expect any further supplies from thence.[68]

In fact, Capel planned to smooth away the Court's difficulties by seeking rapprochement with the leaders of the opposition in the 1692 parliament. To this end, he brought into the administration such outspoken proponents of 'the sole right' as Alan Brodrick and his brother Thomas, Robert Rochfort, Robert Molesworth and Francis Brewster, all of whom were also noted for their militant protestantism.[69] At the same time, Capel planned only a symbolic assertion of the Crown's right to initiate money bills. The

Court would propose an excise bill worth a mere £7000. But it would be left to the Commons to draw up the heads of the more important supply bills.[70]

With his plans carefully laid, Capel called a parliament to meet in August 1695. The conduct of the 1695 parliament completely vindicated Capel's strategy. 'Our sessions opend with what broke the last: the bringing in a money Bill contrary to our vote of Sole Right', reported Richard Warburton from Dublin in September,

> but the House was soe unanimous in resolving to doe nothing that may give the Kings and our Enemyes hopes of a Fraction; that tho it was so opposite to the opinion the House was last [of] and perhaps that most of the partic- ular members still continue to be of, yet rather than the Publick businesse should be interrupted, it was admitted without dividing upon it.[71]

The new mood of harmony continued when the Commons considered the substantive supply bills: 'among all', wrote Warburton in October, 'the Kings business meets with least obstruction, all sides joyning in that therein soe that . . . we are come within 23000 of our promist supply, and that we are goeing to make up by some further Excise on Tobacco.'[72]

A major cause of the transformation in relations between Court and parliament was Capel's readiness to pander to the prejudices of the most intemperate Protestants. The Lord Deputy had already gladdened Protestant hearts by suspending the adjudication of claims under the Treaty of Limerick.[73] In the parliament of 1695 Capel further established his anti-popish credentials by introducing measures to disarm Catholics, make it illegal for them to own horses worth more than £5 and prohibit them from sending their children overseas to be educated.[74] The first breaches had been opened in the spirit of the 1691 settlement.

The anti-popish zeal of Lord Capel and his allies left the Lord Chancellor, Sir Charles Porter, as the odd-man-out at Dublin Castle. A former Lord Justice, Porter had long been a hate-figure to militant Protestants. It was bad enough that he had been a signatory of the detested Treaty of Limerick. But the Lord Chancellor had subsequently com- pounded the felony by construing the treaty in a manner favourable to Catholics claiming the benefit of its terms.[75] For his part, Porter – English- born and a committed Churchman – viewed with suspicion the pan-Protestant sympathies of his colleagues. He was aghast, above all, at the support shown by the new Privy Councillors for the presbyterian Scots of Ulster. Whereas the Brodricks and their friends sought to foster a united 'British Interest' against the Irish papists, the Lord Chancellor looked upon the Catholics as a counterpoise to the Ulster Scots. 'The English Interest in this Kingdome is not sufficient to oppose those of the Irish and Scots should they unite', he explained to Sir William Trumbull, the junior English Secretary of State, in July 1695. 'But', he continued, their mutuall hatred to each other will allways prevent a good understanding, they are each of them tho not in the same Degree at present willing to be rid of us, and to have the intire power. But that which is our security is this that when ever the Irish take Armes against us the Scotts will assist against them, And so when ever the Irish find the Scots against us they will joyn with us for tho they doe not love us, yet they hate the Scotts much more.[76]

Views such as these were anathema to a hot whig like Lord Capel, and he shed no tears when the Lord Chancellor's enemies sought to impeach him in the parliament of 1695. On the contrary, as the impeachment proceedings began, the Lord Deputy was doing his utmost to throw dirt on Porter. 'My Lord Chancellor's party', he wrote to Secretary of State Shrewsbury on 6 October,

consists chiefly in lawyers, attorneys, and solicitors, who make the considerable part of the House. The Commissioners of the Revenue and their collectors are all on his side; many gentlemen likewise that have suits depending in his Court, and all the Irish and Jacobite interest are entirely at his devotion; but the most considerable gentlemen of the House, both as to estates and credit, in the country, vote against him, looking upon him as a man of no integrity, being verily persuaded he is not true to the King's interest, and that should any occasion happen (which God forbid), he would do his utmost for the service of the late King; so that I verily believe they are become irreconcilable to him, and will never think themselves safe under his administration.[77]

To the chagrin of his 'colleagues' at Dublin Castle, the Lord Chancellor escaped impeachment. The proceedings had served only to highlight the English-style party divisions which were beginning to emerge among Irish Protestants.[78] 'Besides the advantages my Lord Chancellor had in the House of Commons by relations, dependences, &c,' reported a bitter Thomas Brodrick to Secretary Shrewsbury,

our Bishops espoused his cause heartily and made it the subject of several sermons, even before my Lord Deputy, and the inferior clergy failed not following the example of their diocesans. From the pulpit, the dangerous consequences of this matter got into the coffee-houses, and became the subject of table talk, that the Church was struck at in this great churchman, and that nobody could tell where this might end.[79]

In other words, some Churchmen, though ready enough to support the administration's anti-popish measures, viewed with suspicion the whiggery of the new men at Dublin Castle.

The chief of those new men, Lord Capel, disingenuously claimed to have played no part in the attack upon Sir Charles Porter. But he made no secret of his loathing for the Lord Chancellor. 'And now, my Lord,' he admitted to Shrewsbury in January 1696,

if I cannot profess so sincere a friendship to Sir Charles Porter as I find may be expected from me, I must humbly crave leave to say that 'tis not from any resentment I retain of his behaviour towards me, but purely in duty to the King, and with regard to the allegiance I augh him, without any other consideration whatever. For, by what I have observed of the Chancellor since my coming into this kingdom, and of his acting here, I have good reason to believe he is not so hearty as he should be to the present Government, and that he has given occasion enough to others to suspect him as one that without much difficulty might be reconciled to the late King's interest.[80]

The tensions between the Lord Deputy and the Lord Chancellor would doubtless have intensified had it not been for Lord Capel's unexpected death in May 1696. Before the year was out, Sir Charles Porter had followed his bitter rival to the grave. The new men at the top in Ireland were the English whig, John Methuen, appointed Lord Chancellor in February 1697, and the Huguenot soldier, Lord Galway, principal Lord Justice from May of the same year. And their immediate task was to secure parliamentary ratification of the Treaty of Limerick.

Although a clause of the Treaty of Limerick had required King William to use his 'utmost endeavours' to have the treaty ratified by the Dublin parliament, he had hitherto baulked at the prospect of bringing the treaty before Irish MPs. His decision to press for ratification in 1697 apparently owed much to the personal interests of English ministers: many senior politicians had received grants of forfeited estates in Ireland, and they hoped that ratification would copper-bottom their titles to the land. But the King may also have hoped that incorporating the treaty into Irish law would stymie further anti-Catholic legislation. If so, he made a sorry miscalculation. For the treaty ratified by the Irish parliament in 1697 was a far cry from the agreement negotiated by Ginkel six years earlier. Due to a clerical error, the copy of the treaty signed by King William had omitted the article granting protection to the civilian population of areas controlled by the Irish army in October 1691. That inadvertent omission was now seized upon by Dublin parliamentarians who refused to include the 'missing clause' in the ratified version of the treaty. Gone also, without even the hint of an excuse, was the clause promising Catholics the same religious freedoms they had enjoyed under Charles II.[81]

Parliament's refusal to include the 'missing clause' in the ratified version of the treaty was not as disastrous for Catholic landowners as at first seemed likely. There was no attempt to review the claims to protection adjudicated by Sir Charles Porter and other judges between 1692 and 1694. In fact, a second batch of claims, predicated upon the assumption that the 'missing clause' remained valid, was heard in the two years following ratification. The scrupulousness with which both batches of claims were adjudicated is fully evinced by the figures: of the 1,283 claims to protection made under the Treaty of Limerick between 1692 and 1699, only 16 were rejected.[82] In effect, the forfeitures had been confined to the estates of those rebels who had been killed in the war or had refused to submit to King William in 1691. As a result, the Catholic gentry, which had held 22 per cent of Irish land in 1688, remained in possession of some 14 per cent of the land at the end of King William's reign.[83]

Although the parliamentary mutilation of the Treaty of Limerick had little immediate impact upon the Irish land settlement, it showed that the anti-popish ardour of the Dublin parliament remained undimmed. That ardour produced two new penal laws in 1697. The first sought to entrench Protestant hold over the land by disinheriting Protestant heiresses who married Catholics. The second struck at the Catholic Church by banishing its bishops and regular clergy from the Kingdom of Ireland. A similar measure, which had applied only to the regular clergy, had been rejected by the English Privy Council in 1695 following the intercession of the Emperor Leopold. Its failure to block the more draconian legislation of 1697 showed that, with the end of the European war, King William now deemed it more more expedient to propitiate the Irish parliament than the Habsburg Emperor.[84]

In the last years of King William's reign, as we shall see later, Irish Protestants became preoccupied with asserting the rights of the Dublin parliament against the pretensions of its Westminster counterpart. The result was a short period of respite for the Catholics of Ireland. But the penal laws of 1697 were portents of things to come. In the next reign the Irish parliament hit the majority population with a series of statutes designed to reduce it to a landless and leaderless underclass. One such measure, which reached the statute book in 1704, helped to achieve a goal long-cherished by Irish Protestants: the virtual extinction of the Catholic landed class.[85]

3. The Church of Ireland and the Ulster Scots

On 7 July 1690 Queen Mary received news of her husband's victory at the Boyne. Those glad tidings broke weeks of tension for the Queen, and she immediately penned a missive of congratulation to the King. As one might expect, the Queen's letter is imbued with the joy which had overcome her on hearing of King William's triumph. But it also provides further testimony of Queen Mary's unremitting piety. 'I must put you in mind', wrote the Queen, 'of one thing, believing it now the season, which is that you wou'd take care of the church in Ireland. Every body agrees it is the worst in Christendom.'[86]

Whether or not the episcopal Church of Ireland was indeed 'the worst in Christendom' is a question well beyond the scope of this study. There is little doubt, however, that in numerical terms at least it was the most beleaguered established church in Europe. Its strongholds in Dublin and the other towns were islands in a Catholic sea. And in the north there was another threat: the Scots presbyterians of Ulster, a cohesive and fast-growing community which outnumbered the province's episcopalians by the 1690s.[87]

Nor is there much reason to doubt that the Church of Ireland was in a generally deplorable condition. 'The state and condition of the Church of Ireland was never very good, nor ever fix'd and regulated as it ought to', lamented Bishop Dopping of Meath in 1697. 'But however the great number of ruinous churches which we every where see, shew that it hath been formerly in a more flourishing condition than now, both as to the number of its Clergy, and houses dedicated to Gods worship and service.' This sorry state of affairs, he attributed to four causes: '1 Want of Ministers. 2 Want of Protestants. 3 The great Pluralitys and non residence of the Clergy who are there. 4 The ruinous condition and want of churches in that kingdome.' He then provided some figures to support his thesis. In his own diocese of Meath there were no fewer than 197 parish churches and 106 chapels of ease. But of the churches, only 43 were in repair, and in the whole of the diocese there were no more than 40 resident clergy and 15 curates. As for the diocese of Kilmore, its 70 parishes were served by a mere 11 resident clergy and 7 curates. As if this were not bad enough, 'many of those who are here reckoned into the number of Curates are also beneficed Clergymen who are forced many times to neglect their own Cures whilst they supply that of others: And yet the state and condition of these two Dioceses as well in this particular as in others is better than others in that kingdome.' The chronic shortage of clergymen, averred the bishop, itself had three causes: the inability of Trinity College, Dublin to turn out sufficient clerics; the poverty of many livings; and the 'frequent wars in that Kingdome, which have occasioned the English Clergymen rather to sit down content with a small maintenance in their own countrey, than transplant themselves into Ireland where they could not secure to themselves any safety or fixed abode.'[88] And who could blame them? After all, during the last of those wars, most of the Irish clergy had themselves decamped for England.[89] Among them were many of the bishops.

The episcopate itself was one of the weakest links in the fragile Irish ecclesiastical chain. A preserve of aristocrats and their clients, the Irish episcopal bench, in marked contrast to its English counterpart, contained few prelates of real distinction or merit in the early 1690s. As a result, the Church was sorely wanting in both moral and political leadership. 'It is certaine that the Church of Ireland is under very unhappy circumstances at this criticall juncture,' wrote an Irish correspondent of Archbishop Tenison of Canterbury in 1695. 'The Lord Primate [the 85 year-old Archbishop Boyle of Armagh] is withdrawne from business, & the others that should are little mindefull of the Churches interest, so that except your Grace be kinde as well as vigilant in relation to her wellfare she will probably suffer more in a litle time then many ages will be able to retrieve.'[90]

In the early 1690s the Church of Ireland was seen at its worst in the Ulster diocese of Down and Connor. Its bishop, the octogenarian Thomas Hacket, had been absent from the diocese for many years, preferring to keep house in the distant but comfortable London suburb of Hammersmith. During that time, claimed a critic, Bishop Hacket 'never cam to visit it, nor took care to have any thing don therin for the Good of the Church, and theire majesties service, but what tended to gett money to himselfe'. Because of the bishop's absence, there had been

> noe confirmation in the diocese, notwithstanding the people have greatly desired it, especially in the beginning of the late troubles, [when] popery was very like to be countenanced, and introduced among us in this kingdom. Neither was there any to ordaine ministers to serve in the Church, by reason whereof, Deacons were curats in many places, and that for 6, 7 or ten yeares together, dureing which time the Sacrament of the Lords supper could not be administered in those parishes nor absolution given to sick and dieing people, if another minister could not be found to doe it.

In fact, the episcopal jurisidiction had been

> wholly neglected at least that part of it which tends to promote pieties, religion and unitie among the people, the churches in many places becom ruinous, many of them not served at all, and others but very meanly served, and that either by unfitt and unable curats, or such as were displeasing to the people, by reason of their irregular liveing. And noe care taken either to reform or punish them, by which neglect many have deserted the church, and gon to conventicles, which much weakens the churches interest, and strengthens theire adversaries in that Country.[91]

As that final observation suggests, Irish Churchmen were deeply alarmed by the strength of Protestant nonconformity. In the early 1690s there were real fears that King William would establish presbyterianism in Ireland, or at least in the province of Ulster, just as he had already done in Scotland. During the Irish campaign of 1690, it had seemed to many that the King was more favourably disposed to the presbyterian ministers than their episcopalian rivals. He had, for example, provided the presbyterian clergy with an annual grant of £1200 (the *regium donum*). This greatly encouraged the Ulster presbyterians. Writing in June 1691, Viscount Fitzharding, an Ulster peer, reported that the King's grant 'gives them occasione to thinke he must rely on them, and they will use all meanes to make him believe it is his interest to do so'. The presbyterians of Scotland, he continued, 'have settled a correspondence with theire friends here, and will mutually assist each other, and theire greate aim is to gett presbitry established in this province'.[92] Although the presbyterians did not achieve their objective, the fate of the episcopal Church of Scotland cast a shadow over its sister church in Ireland throughout the 1690s. 'It is said of the Church of Scotland that it destroyed it self', wrote a critic of the Irish episcopate in 1695,

> & that the late King James so disposed of the Government of it, as might give an easie passage for the introduction of Popery, & though it answered not his end in bringing in the Pope, yet Episcopacy was ruined by it & Presbytery establisht. God grant that the Church of Ireland may not follow the same fate, & that England may not stand alone deprived of both her sisters, nor be surrounded with enemies instead of friends labouring to reduce & not support her.[93]

The response of the Church of Ireland to the very real presbyterian menace was two-pronged. On the one hand, the Church fiercely resisted the grant of any one-sided concessions to Irish dissenters. In particular, it set itself against the passage of an Irish version of the Toleration Act unless it was accompanied by the introduction of the sacramental qualification for office.[94] As the Duke of Shrewsbury, the English Secretary of State, explained to his Scottish counterpart, James Johnston, in August 1695, it was

> objected by several of the Bishops and Church party in Ireland, that a toleration there at present is not so reasonable as it was here, until the Dissenters will agree to pass an Act for qualifying themselves by the Test, which is not in force there as it is here; so that if the toleration passed without the other, the Nonconformists in Ireland would be in a better condition than those in England, which many think not reasonable, but dangerous to the Established Church, they being so numerous in that kingdom.[95]

In the event, the sacramental test was not introduced into Ireland during King William's reign. But there was no Toleration Act either.

Successful though the Church was in resisting pressure for a Toleration Act, some of the Irish bishops were well aware that obduracy was not enough. Energetic prelates such as Narcissus Marsh, Archbishop of Dublin from 1694, and William King, Bishop of Derry from 1691, also sought to breathe new life into the moribund Church of Ireland.[96] In April 1695 Archbishop Marsh regaled Archbishop Tenison with an account of his endeavours. He had visited every parish in his diocese and confirmed almost 5000 young people; was labouring to have weekly catechising introduced throughout his diocese; had ordered monthly communions in rural parishes, fortnightly ones in Dublin's smaller parishes and weekly communions in the capital's larger parishes; had tested the preaching skills of all the clergy of his diocese; and had instructed his clergy to visit their parishioners, no matter their persuasions, and exhort them to family devotion. He was also meeting regularly with half a dozen of the bishops who were in Dublin, and they had resolved, among other things, to 'make the persons to be ordain'd undergo publick Examinations in the Church before the Congregation for several daies, by the Bishop & his Clergy assembled for that purpose, before they be put into Orders'.[97]

The dedication which Archbishop Marsh expected of clergymen is highlighted by the dim view he took of a favour sought by Dr Edward Walkington, a candidate for the episcopal bench: 'about a year ago', Marsh wrote in June 1695,

> he desir'd me to intercede to my Lord Primate for him that he might be excus'd from residing in a parish that he had in the North of Ireland. I demanded his reason for it. He reply'd, because he had not above 6 people come to hear him preach; & understanding that he had many more Parishioners but they all went to the Meetings, I told him that for that very reason he ought to reside, & be more than ordinarily diligent in preaching, Catechising & Exhortations, that he might reclaim them & bring them to Church.[98]

In 1701 Bishop King of Derry delivered a still more stinging rebuke to a non-resident pluralist in his diocese of Derry. 'I must profess to believe it', he wrote to the hapless cleric, 'that Robbing on the high way to maintain ones family is not more unlawfull than pinching or starving a Cure for that End, and if there be any such thing as sacrilege, this is certainly a high Degree of it.' The onslaught went on remorselessly. 'I understand, that there were no sacraments either at Newtown or Colerain last Easter that no Curate resides at Colrain at present no daily prayers as has bin usuall and all this to save £10 per annum.' This, warned the bishop, was a situation 'I cannot bear any longer & therefore I pray interpret it not Displeasure but sense of Duty, if I take the Course the Law prescribes'.[99] Not that Bishop King confined his crusade against non-residence to small fry. In 1694 he led the commission which deprived that most notorious of non-residents, Thomas Hacket, the so-called 'Bishop of Hammersmith', of his diocese of Down and Connor.[100]

In a memorandum written shortly after his elevation to Derry, Bishop King had sought to explain the non-residence of much of the Ulster clergy. This he attributed not to the value of their livings – these were the most profitable in the kingdom – but to the fact that 'there are so many dissenters there, whose daily objections in relation to the differences between them & us they know they must be obliged to answer.' However much it might 'tend to the reconciling of them to the Communion of our Church', daily confrontations with the presbyterians 'dos not quadrate with the Easie way of life such men have proposed to themselves'.[101] Seeking a quiet life was a charge which could never be levelled against William King. A man of combative temperament, he was convinced that relentless attack was the best means of defending the Church from the presbyterians: 'we must not desist,' he instructed his clergy, 'though People seem obstinate but in season, and out of season, by all Means of Importunity and Industry, we must press them to their Duty, and endeavour to bring them back to the Purity of God's Worship, as he has instituted it.'[102]

Bishop King's exhortation to the clergy of the Derry diocese was appended to his book, *A Discourse Concerning The Inventions of Men in the Worship of God.* In that book, the bishop had turned on its head the familiar presbyterian charge that the episcopalian mode of worship was a mere human invention. On the contrary, he averred, the Church of Ireland's form of prayer was ordained by God, and it was the presbyterians who

> not only add to the Gospel a new Command, by teaching that to be Unlawful, which Christ has nowhere Condemned; but they teach that to be Unlawful, which he has positively Commanded. Whoever therefore do Teach Forms of Prayer to be Unlawful, or Countenance those that do Teach this Doctrine of Men, cannot acquit themselves from the Imputation of Resisting the Holy Ghost, by whose Inspiration the Word of God is penn'd.[103]

This bold attack, claimed King, had produced dramatic results: 'when I came to this diocess', he wrote in 1696,

> I found the dissenters mighty insolent, & one of our Communion cou'd no sooner get into their company but they imediatly fell upon him, some times scoffing & sometimes arguing with him, & our own people had little to say for themselves, but that they had an establishment by law, & it did not contradict scripture but since my book came out they are mute, no perswasions will prevale with them to dispute or talk of religion & the members of our church insult over them.[104]

Needless to say, Bishop King's aggressive defence of the Church enamoured him to the Ulster presbyterians not a jot – a state of affairs which induced in this fractious prelate a certain perverse satisfaction. 'I thank God I cannot say my endeavours have bin ineffectual,' he wrote to James Bonnell in January 1695, 'yet you see how much hatred I have incurred by them which I confess pleases me very well, whilst I see the work prosper in my hand.'[105]

But just how effectual were Bishop King's endeavours? It appears that a good deal of effort produced precious little wool. For one thing, the bishop could do nothing to restrain the political activism of the Ulster presbyterians. In February 1693 Lord Lieutenant Sidney reported that the 'Scotch faction' in Londonderry, erstwhile stronghold of episcopalianism in King's diocese, had secured the office of mayor for one 'who has never been at church in his life'.[106] And what the 'Scotch faction' had, it held. In November 1697 a distraught Churchman reported that the Londonderry corporation had passed over the episcopalian candidates for both the mayoralty and the shrievalty, and that the dissenters had resolved 'to continue the magistracy of this place in their own hands & to Crush all those of the Establisht Church to the utmost of their power, unless they meet with a cheque from the Government.'[107] Nor was King able to retard the rapid development of presbyterian church organisation following the first meeting of the synod of Ulster in 1690.[108] Worst of all, presbyterian numbers were swelled after 1691 by a massive influx of migrants from the famine-stricken south-west of Scotland. Was it true, asked an incredulous Englishman at some point in the late 1690s, that 'the last yeares want of corne in Scotland brought over not lesse than 20 thousand poore, & not lesse than 30 thousand before, since the Revolution'?[109] Although the precise figures remain unclear, the scale of the migration was more than enough to disturb the authorities at Dublin Castle. 'The Scotch interest doth grow extreamly & requires a great deal of care', observed an alarmed Lord Chancellor Methuen in September 1697, 'because they are closely united to one another & to their freinds in Scotland & the difference of Religion divides them from the English.'[110]

When Methuen registered his disquiet at the growth of the 'Scotch interest', the security of the state probably loomed a good deal larger in his thoughts than the welfare of the Church. Certainly, Bishop King was convinced that the men in power at Dublin were indifferent, if not downright hostile, to the interests of the Church of Ireland. It 'has been the busyness of most of our governours since the revolution to make an interest for Dissenters,' he complained to an English bishop in December 1696. 'My Lord Capell did it above board, and professed that he had the Kings comands to do it, which intimation did them more service than all other wayes he cou'd have invented, for every body has a mighty deference to his Majesties pleasure.' As an instance of Capel's 'byas that way', King cited the previous year's list of sheriffs: 'it will appear that if he cou'd find a dissenter in the whole County, tho the meanest contemptible fellow in it, he was sure to be named sherif, tho the gentlemen of the County looked on it as an affront & remonstrated from their quarter sessions against it'. If, concluded the bishop glumly,

> we have such governours still put on us 'twill be impossible what ever reason or scriptures be against schismaticks to hinder their multiplying for most people value their interest above their religion, & if dissenters be pitched out for places of honour trust & profitt whilest their equals are past by, many will dayly qualify themselves as they see their neighbours do.[111]

As if this were not bad enough, King was certain that many in high places were only too happy to give succour to dangerous free-thinkers such as the young Irishman, John Toland. 'I am most sensible of the ill aspect that the generality of men cast on the church & churchmen', he wrote to Bishop Foy of Waterford in October 1697,

> the faith of Religion is very weak amongst all and the sense of it almost lost, and the matter is laid deeper than most are aware of, 'Tis come to a formed

conspiracy & agents & emissarys are imployed to cry down the credit of religion in generall & instill profane maxims & principles into youth, My Lord it is not credible what pains are taken this way & how dilligent some persons of great quality are to propagate irreligion.[112]

Since it could expect no support from Dublin Castle, Bishop King believed that the Church must have recourse to its own institutions in order to throw back the onslaught of its enemies, schismatics and freethinkers alike. The bishop looked forward, in particular, to a meeting of the Church of Ireland's long-defunct convocation. He followed the English convocation controversy with interest, and, as one might expect, viewed with distaste the erastian arguments of the anti-convocation camp. William Wake's book on convocation, he complained in December 1697, had 'intirely betray'd the church & was against the Kings oath, for the first article in Magna charta is that the Church of England shall be free, & that freedom can consist in nothing but in choosing the Ecclesiasticall constitutions by which she is governed in convocations'. Like Wake's enemy, Francis Atterbury, the bishop was convinced that convocation was 'the Kings Councell for Ecclesiasticall affairs, but such a Councell as the parlement was for the civill, & consequently part of the legislative power'.[113]

So, as 1697 drew to a close, Bishop King seemed intent upon launching an Irish convocation controversy. Instead, in the next few years he would become a leading player in a much wider dispute: the Irish segment of a crisis which threatened to destroy the very fabric of the British triple monarchy.

4. The Company of Scotland and the Anglo-Scottish Crisis

By the late seventeenth century, Scotland's trade with the Continent, once the basis of its national prosperity, had long been in decline. The formerly privileged trade with France had been languishing ever since the Union of Crowns, while trade with the Dutch was virtually confined to the insignificant port of Veere.[114] The terminal decline in Scotland's continental trade – accelerated both by Charles II's Dutch wars and King William's war with France – meant that the kingdom's few exports (chiefly cattle, linen and wool) were fast becoming dependent upon English markets. This was not a happy state of affairs. For the Westminster parliament, ever ruthless in its defence of England's commercial interests, was rarely slow to protect domestic traders from Scottish competition. In the 1660s, for example, tariffs and marketing restrictions had been imposed upon imports of Scottish linen and cattle.[115] Still more galling for the Scots, the English Navigation Acts made no distinction between Scotland and other

European states. Accordingly the Scots, with no colonies of their own, were barred from trading with the English plantations in America and the Caribbean. There was, it is true, some illegal trade between Scotland and the English colonies, but its clandestine nature severely restricted its scale.[116]

In short, Scotland had become an economic backwater, increasingly dependent upon the goodwill of an overbearing neighbour. And in the early 1690s, England – its own trade devastated by the French war – was less inclined to be generous than ever. In 1689 an English Royal Navy vessel, sent into Scottish waters to deal with potential French incursions, added insult to injury by spending much of its time enforcing the Navigation Acts against the Scots.[117]

Excluded from England's colonial markets, the Scots sought to develop a long-haul trade of their own. This aspiration had first become apparent in 1681 when the Duke of York – the future James VII and II – had established a Council of Trade at Edinburgh.[118] After the revolution, it gave impetus to a campaign for the establishment of a joint stock company which would rival the great English and Dutch trading companies. In 1695 that campaign met with success. Assured by his Scottish ministers that the foundation of such a trading company would propitiate his fractious northern subjects, King William authorised them to approve the requisite legislation. The upshot was the Scottish parliament's Act for a Company Trading with Africa and the Indies, touched with the royal sceptre by King William's Commissioner, the Marquis of Tweeddale, in June 1695. The Act granted the new Company of Scotland a 31 year monopoly over Scottish trade with the Americas, and a perpetual monopoly over the kingdom's trade with Africa and Asia. In addition, its ships and goods were to be exempt from Scottish customs and other duties for 21 years. The Company was also granted the right to plant colonies in any part of the Indies where there was no existing European settlement, as long as the native population consented. Another clause provided that at least half of the Company's capital was to be reserved for Scots dwelling north of the Tweed.[119]

That final provision evinced the determination of Edinburgh parliamentarians to prevent Scotland's bold new venture from falling under English control. But it also betokened a lack of confidence on the part of the Company's projectors in their capacity to raise sufficient capital within the borders of Scotland. It is no surprise, therefore, that the Company opened its first subscription books not in Edinburgh but in the English capital. The London subscription proved a great success. Within a fortnight of its launch in November 1695, some £300,000 had been subscribed by English and Anglo-Scottish merchants who saw the Company of Scotland as an opportunity to break the power of the East India and Africa Companies.[120]

The motivation of investors south of the Tweed was readily apparent to a group of Bristol merchants, led by John Cary, which detested the old English joint stock companies and their new Scottish rival in equal measure. 'Wee have seen the Act of the Scotch Parliament for encouragement of Trade,' they informed their city's MPs in December 1695,

> & judge it will be best to quench that Nations falling thereon in the beginning, which we apprehend cannot be done more effectually then by discouraging their dependence on English Stocks to manage it; & here we think it not amiss to put you in mind that we conceive the foundation of this Act to proceed from the restraint put on the Merchants of England from trading to the East Indies & the Coast of Africa by those two Companys or Monopolies, which hath made them seek protection from Scotland, that they may trade thither under the shelter of this Act.

That being so, it was inevitable that the breaking of the old monopolies would also sink the Company of Scotland: 'no question if this were done', concluded the Bristolians, 'none would choose to trade thither from Edinburgh who could be permitted to do it from London, by which means this great Leviathan would fall of its self.'[121]

The East India Company, for its part, was just as eager as the Bristol merchants to thwart the Scottish Company. But it did not intend to commit suicide in order to do so. Instead, the East India Company began to flex its political muscle at Westminster, lobbying parliamentarians to condemn its dangerous new competitor. The Company's complaints, which dwelt upon the threat posed to English commerce by the Scots, were echoed by those of the Customs Commissioners. As the Commissioners explained to the House of Lords in early December 1695, the privileges showered upon the Scots 'must necessarily draw the trade to themselves from England, especially where the duty is higher than the value of the commodity as in many East India goods and in the West Indies in that of tobacco'.[122]

The efforts of the East India Company and the Customs Commissioners produced a stinging parliamentary denunciation of the Company of Scotland. In a joint address to the King on 14 December 1695, the two houses complained that the Scottish Company's customs exemption would turn Scotland into

> a free port for all East India commodities; and consequently those several places in Europe, which were supplied from England, would be furnished from Scotland much cheaper than could be done by the English; and therefore this nation would lose the benefit of supplying foreign parts with those commodities, which had always been a great article in the balance of their foreign trade.

What was more, 'the said commodities would unavoidably be brought by the Scots into England by stealth, both by sea and land, to the great prejudice of the English trade and navigation, and to his majesty in his customs.' As if that were not bad enough, once the Scots had settled themselves in plantations in America the English commerce in tobacco, sugar, cotton, wool, skins, masts, &c would be utterly lost, because the privileges of that nation, granted to them by this act, were such, that that kingdom must be the magazine for all commodities, and the English plantations, and the traffic there, lost to this nation, and their exportation of their own manufactures yearly decreased.

The Lords and Commons also took exception to a clause of the Scottish Trade Act which apparently committed King William 'to interpose his authority to have restitution, reparation, and satisfaction made for any damage, that might be done to any one of the ships, goods, merchandize, persons, or other effects whatsoever belonging to the said company, and that upon the public charge'. For that clause, parliament not unreasonably concluded, 'did seem to engage his majesty to employ the shipping and strength at sea of this nation, to support this new company, to the great detriment even of this kingdom'.[123]

If the aim of the address was to scare off English investment in the Company of Scotland, it was a resounding success. All but four of the Company's 200 or so London-based subscribers took fright and withdrew their investments.[124] But if parliament also sought to strangle the Scottish Company at birth, then its address proved entirely counter-productive. For the antagonism of the Westminster parliament helped to turn the Scottish Company into a truly national cause north of the border. 'Scots' humours', observed Lord Justice Clerk Cockburn,

seem no less warme in prosecuting the bussines then the Inglish are in opposing it, and if the Inglish do persist, I know not a more effectual way for that company being brought to some good account. 'Twas the notice the parliament of England first took of it made the whole nation throng in to have some share, and I'm of the opinion the resentments people are acted by are the greatest supplyes that furnishes life to that affaire.[125]

In the Spring and Summer of 1696 the Company's offices in Edinburgh and Glasgow were thronged with patriotic investors. The subscription eventually brought in £400,000, an astonishing sum for a country as poor as Scotland.[126]

Fortified by the response of their countrymen to the Company's hour of need, the directors looked to the future with confidence. It seems that they swiftly abandoned their original plan to concentrate the Company's resources upon the East Indies trade, and instead turned their attentions towards the Caribbean. In particular, the directors adopted an ambitious plan to establish a great trading colony at Darien on the Isthmus of Panama. The scheme was the brainchild of William Paterson, the celebrated Anglo-Scottish merchant and financial innovator, who had long dreamt of turning Darien into the entrepot of the world. If a colony were established at Darien, he wrote some years later,

The time and expense of the navigation to China, Japan, the Spice Islands, and the far greatest part of the trade of the East Indies, will be lessened more than half and the consumption of European commodities and manufactories will soon be more than doubled. Trade will increase trade, and money will beget money, and the trading world shall need no more to want work for their hands, but will rather want hands for their work. Thus, this door of the seas and the key of the universe, with anything of a sort of reasonable management, will of course enable the proprietors to give laws to both oceans and to become arbitrators of the commercial world, without being liable to the fatigues, expenses and dangers, or contracting the guilt and blood of Alexander and Caesar.[127]

Such was the Utopian vision which animated the Darien venture.

After months of preparation, a squadron of five Company vessels, carrying some 1200 colonists, set sail for Panama in July 1698. The expedition made landfall at Darien on 1 November, and immediately set about establishing the colony of Caledonia.[128] Over the next two years, the Darien colony would become a national obsession in Scotland. 'The stock and expense is indeed considerable; and they are many who are concerned as interested in the project', wrote the Scottish Chancellor, Lord Marchmont, to William Carstares in November 1699. 'Yet', he continued,

that is but a small thing in respect of the concern which appears of persons of all ranks, and even of the meaner people, who are not particularly interested, and have no shares in the stock for supporting and prosecuting that undertaking. It is a thing scarcely to be imagined. I will assure you, any that would pretend here to persuade any body, that the following out that design may prove a prejudice to this nation, would prevail nothing, but lose himself, and carry the ill-will and disesteem almost of every one. What the matter will turn to, the Lord knows: But, from the first, till now, and still on so, there is such an earnestness and disposition towards the matter, without any sparing, either of their persons or purses, that every observer must think it wonderful.[129]

Quite why the Scots should have become so enamoured of the Darien venture is, in fact, not too difficult to discern. In the mid–1690s Scotland suffered a series of disastrous crop failures. The result was widespread famine.[130] Visitors from England, where the experience of dearth was fast passing out of living memory, were shocked by the scenes which greeted them north of the border. 'Mr Archdeacon Nicolson [of Carlisle] sends us a most melancholy account of their sufferings in Scotland, for want of common necessaries', wrote the English clergyman, Edmund Gibson, in June 1699, 'to such a degree, that at Glasgow they saw a poor Creature die upon a dunghill, in one of the most publick places of the City; and yet noe notice was taken of it by any but themselves. Which convinc'd them of the truth of what the Inhabitants said, That it was noe more than what hapn'd daily: and [he] adds, that they lay naked and starving in every corner of the Streets'.[131] At a time when the poor were dying in the streets, the colony of Caledonia came to arouse among the Scots messianic visions of national redemption – 'the only means', in the words of the political thinker Andrew Fletcher, 'to recover us from our miserable and despicable condition'.[132] But, alas, as is the wont of messianic movements, 'Darienism' was to prove the bane of its followers.

There was just one small catch in Paterson's grand vision: the site of the Scottish colony lay within the American dominions of the King of Spain. It was not that the Scots had failed to take this little detail into account. On the contrary, the Scots fully anticipated Spanish resistance to their colony, but were confident of their capacity to deal with it. After all, had not the English buccaneer, Henry Morgan, captured Panama City itself with a mere 1200 men in 1669?[133] What the Scots had not reckoned with, however, was the determination of their own King to snuff out the Darien colony.

The Company of Scotland had proved a massive embarrassment to King William from its very inception. With so many other pressing demands on his time, he had not paid a great deal of attention to the Scottish Trade Act of 1695, and had certainly failed to appreciate its full implications. He was thus taken aback by the furore it aroused at Westminster, and rounded on his Scottish ministers for giving him bad advice. 'I have been ill-served in Scotland', he muttered, when the English parliament denounced the Scottish Trade Act.[134] From that point on, King William set out his stall to thwart the enterprises of the Company of Scotland. In particular, he sabotaged the Company's efforts to raise capital on the Continent. Since the Dutch trading companies were no more ecstatic than their English counterparts at the prospect of a new competitor, the Scottish Company's attempts to raise capital in the Netherlands were doomed from the start.[135] But its chances were much better at Hamburg, where the city's merchants viewed the enterprises of the Scottish Company as an opportunity to rekindle the fading glory of the Hanseatic ports.[136] In April 1697, however, the Company's hopes were shattered by the intervention of Sir Paul Rycaut, the King's resident at Hamburg: 'his Majesty', Rycaut informed the shocked city burghers, 'would regard such proceedings as an Affront to his Royal Authority and . . . he would not fail to resent it.'[137] Virtually overnight, Hamburg's enthusiasm for the Scottish Company waned to the point of extinction.[138]

At the time of Rycaut's intervention at Hamburg, it was not yet known that the Scots had set their sights upon Panama. From King William's point of view, it was bad enough that the foundation of the Scottish Company had caused ructions at Westminster, and had upset both the English and Dutch trading companies. But when the Scottish Company turned its attentions towards Darien, an acute domestic irritant was transformed into a potential diplomatic catastrophe. Even as the Scots were en route to

America, King William was finalising the first Partition Treaty with King Louis of France. That treaty, and its successor, were not at all to the liking of the Spanish court.[139] So King William already had his work cut out to smooth the ruffled feathers of his ally, the King of Spain. Not surprisingly, then, the King was beside himself when he received news that his Scottish subjects, acting under statutory authority, had 'invaded' Spanish territory. And in his fury, King William issued an extraordinary order to the governors of all the English colonies in America and the Caribbean. In the words of the proclamation subsequently issued by Governor Beeston of Jamaica, the King's governors were

> strictly to command His Majesty's subjects, whatsoever, that they do not presume, on any pretence whatsoever, to hold any correspondence with the said Scots [at Darien], nor to give them any assistance of arms, ammunition, provisions, or any other necessaries whatsoever, either by themselves or any other for them, or by any of their vessels, or of the English nation, as they will answer the contempt of His Majesty's command, at their utmost peril.[140]

King William had resolved to starve the Scots out of Darien.

When news of the King's command reached Darien in May 1699, it found a colony whose morale was already at a low ebb. Due to an astonishing oversight on the part of the Company's directors, no credit facilities had been arranged for the colonists. As a result, the Scots had already found extreme difficulty in obtaining supplies from the English colonies in the New World. Nor had the colonists received any news of anticipated reinforcements from Scotland. The royal proclamations proved to be the last straw. In June 1699, just seven months after they had landed so hopefully at Darien, the Scots abandoned the colony of Caledonia.[141]

No tears were shed in England at the fate of Caledonia. The Scottish colony had crossed not only King William's foreign policy interests but also the commercial interests of the English nation. 'It is to be wished that the Spaniard could beat out the Scotch at Darien,' wrote the Earl of Jersey in July 1699, 'for that colony gives a good deal of trouble here; the English are apprehensive that the Scotch settling in those parts (with the advantages granted them by Act of Parliament) will be a prejudice to trade here.'[142] Six months later, the English Board of Trade, in a report to the House of Lords, concluded that the planting of a colony at Darien 'would inevitably involve his Majesty in such Differences with Spain as may prove fatal to the Peace and good Accord between the two Crowns; And consequently be destructive of our Trade, and highly prejudicial to our Plantations in America. But supposing', the report went on,

> no such War should ensue for the settling of a Colony of Scotch as has been lately attempted, It would nevertheless be highly mischievous to our said Plantations, and principally to the island of Jamaica (the most important of any of them) by alluring away their Inhabitants with the hopes of Mines and

Treasure, and diverting the present course of Trade which is of the greatest advantage to England.[143]

That prospect appalled the English Secretary of State, James Vernon. 'It is in the interest of England to take all the fair ways they can to defeat that settlement of Darien,' he had written to King William's ambassador at Madrid in March 1699, 'the consequence whereof would be the draining of all our Colonies of the young and vigorous men, by whom the plantations should be improved and secured.'[144] So Vernon was speaking both as a patriotic Englishman and a loyal servant of the King when he wrote in December 1699 that the evacuation of Darien was 'a thorn drawn out of our side'.[145] But unbeknown to Vernon, the thorn had not yet been fully drawn.

In August 1699, a month before word reached Scotland of the abandonment of the colony, the Scottish Company had at last despatched reinforcements to Caledonia.[146] When the second expedition landed at Darien in November 1699, it was astonished to find the colony deserted. Unperturbed, the new colonists speedily re-established the outpost and, with the assistance of the local Indian tribes, even managed to win a skirmish against advancing Spanish forces in February 1700. But the victory at Toubacanti proved to be the last hurrah for the Scots in Panama. By March the Spaniards had succeeded in blockading Caledonia by both sea and land. Cut off from their water supply, running short of other provisions, and riddled with disease, the colonists sought terms. In April 1700 the Scots abandoned Caledonia for a second and final time.[147]

With the sorry demise of the second colony, the iridescent hopes of 1698 were reduced to ashes. 'Our Colony', lamented the young Robert Wodrow in July 1700, 'is broke and that (as it seems) for ever, our money & quhich is worse, our credite & reputation lost, and after all we knou [not] quher to or hou to help our selvs.'[148] What had gone wrong? To Englishmen, the disaster which had befallen the Scots was the entirely predictable outcome of a madcap escapade: 'when I consider that Caledonian undertaking', wrote a scornful English observer in August 1700,

> I am sometimes perswaded it was at first but a matter calculated to stirr up that waspish Nation into discontents that out of it a Rebellion might be easier formed there never being a rationall prospect of the successe of such an Adventure unless we would have lent our own hands to our own Destruction and the Spaniards would have tyed theirs behinde them to have their throatts cutt.[149]

Nor were such views entirely confined to Englishmen. One survivor of the first Darien expedition dismissed that venture as an 'Airy Project' in which '1050 Men were sent by the Scotch Company on a blind Project, of getting Riches for them with five or six months Allowance at most, no Credit, and a ridiculous Cargo, neglected by them, and expos'd to Famine Death and Spanish Mines.'[150] But that was a view which few Scots wished to hear. Instead, as despair turned to anger, they sought out scapegoats south of the border.

Representative of the anglophobia generated by the Darien affair were two inflammatory pamphlets, *A Defence of the Scots Settlement at Darien*,

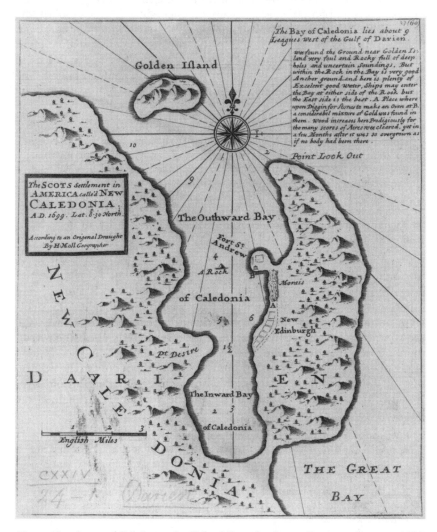

Figure 13   A map of Caledonia, the ill-fated Scottish colony at Darien in Panama, 1699. The failure of the colony increased King William's unpopularity in Scotland and led to a crisis in Anglo-Scottish relations.

written after the evacuation of the first colony, and *An Enquiry into the Causes of the Miscarriage of the Scots Colony at Darien*, published in 1700. The author of the former piece contended, not without reason, that England had set out to obstruct the endeavours of the Scottish Company.[151] This itself, he insisted, was but the latest instance of a nefarious and long-standing English policy: to sabotage Scotland's efforts at self-help while at the same time excluding the Scots from a share in England's many good things. As the pamphleteer explained, ever since the Union of the Crowns, the 'Honour and Substance' of the Scottish kingdom had been 'swallow'd up by the kingdom of England; and yet they will neither admit us to the privileges of Fellow-Subjects with themselves, nor suffer us to stand on our own bottom'.[152] But that was a most misguided policy. The Scots, warned the pamphleteer, would not remain passive forever, and the English

> must not think that we have so far degenerated from the Courage and Honour of our Ancestors, as tamely to submit to become their Vassals, when for 2000 years we have maintain'd our Freedom; and therefore it is not their Interest to oppress us too much. If they consult their Histories, they will find that we always broke their Yoke at long-run, if at any time we were brought under it by Force or Fraud. The best way to assure themselves of us is to treat us in a friendly manner: Tho we be not so great and powerful as they, it is not impossible for us to find such Allies as may enable us to defend our selves now as well as formerly.[153]

Exactly where those allies might be found was readily discernible. As the author of *An Enquiry* wrote, no one could blame the Scots if their ill-usage by England forced them into a French alliance.[154] But there were other reasons why England should have pause for thought. The Scots were not alone in complaining of English high-handedness. As we shall see later, Irish Protestants were protesting just as bitterly about their treatment at the hands of the Westminster parliament. In this fraught atmosphere, an Anglo-Scottish rupture would lead not only to the restoration of the 'auld alliance'. It might also endanger England's hold over Ireland. 'If the State of Affairs in Ireland be consider'd,' explained the pamphleteer,

> it will appear to be such, as may make it dangerous to suffer the Scots to be oppressed and provok'd in this manner. It is well enough known that the People of Ireland are not very well pleas'd with their Treatment by some in England. This, together with the great number of Scots in the North of that Kingdom, who bear a natural Affection to their Country, and would be very uneasy to see its Ruin, may prove of dangerous consequence, in case of a Rupture with Scotland.[155]

The Darien affair had exposed the fragility of the Anglo-Scottish relationship under the Union of Crowns. It also brought into question the role of King William himself. According to the author of *A Defence*, the King had acted in flagrant breach of his own laws. It was to have been wished, he wrote, 'that his Majesty of England had not in the least concurr'd, or giv'n his countenance to that [English] Opposition [to the Scottish Company]; for as King of Scots it is plain he could not do it: he hath confirm'd what we have done by the Touch of his Scepter, which no private Order or Instructions can revoke.'[156] As for the author of *An Enquiry*, he all but accused King William of betraying the Scottish people to their English enemies. The King's well-reported comment that he had been 'ill-served in Scotland' would have been thought by 'our Ancestors' to be 'inconsistent with the Trust reposed in a King of Scots, a manifest Reflection upon the Justice and Fidelity of the Nation, and a discovery of their *Arcana Imperii* to those that were quarrelling with them'.[157]

Both writers, following the usual convention, attributed the King's misconduct to the machinations of English evil councillors – rogues who would do well to 'remember that Strafford and Laud lost their heads for giving K[ing] Charles I that fatal Advice of oppressing and opposing the Scots'.[158] But if the King continued to act against the interests of his ancient kingdom, warned the author of *An Enquiry*, the Scots would have no option but

> either sue for a Divorce, as in the case of a wilful Desertion, and denying conjugal Duty, or withdraw from under his roof, and remove to another Family, as God and Man will allow one Sister to do that is oppressed, and denied the Privileges of paternal Love and Protection, whilst another is caressed and dandled, and has her Fortune raised by diminishing that of her neglected Sister.[159]

There was no tradition of non-resistance in Scotland, averred the author of *A Defence*. On the contrary, the Scots had never been afraid to disobey the orders of their kings. He reminded readers, in particular, of an episode in the fifteenth century: 'we refused Obedience to K[ing] James I when detain'd Prisoner in England contrary to the Law of Nations, and carried over into France, to command his Subjects there not to bear Arms against the English Army, where he was in Person. We told him we knew how to distinguish betwixt the Commands of a King and those of a Captive.'[160] It was an apposite precedent. As the Darien affair had so clearly shown, William II, King of Scots, lay a forlorn prisoner at the court of William III, King of England. 'The King of England', lamented the pamphleteer, 'he is our Enemy, and emitted those Proclamations [against the colony of Caledonia]; the King of Scots is detain'd in England, and not Master of himself, but is forc'd to act thus contrary to the Interest of his own antient Crown and Kingdom.'[161] That sorry state of affairs was itself directly attributable to the Union of Crowns which had made the Scots 'the most unhappy People in the World'. For if England oppose us, we have no King to appeal to, but one that is either an Alien and Enemy to us, as being King of a greater People who are such, or if he be inclinable to protect and do us Justice as King of Scots, he is a Prisoner in England, and cannot do it: If they question him in the Parliament of England for any thing relating to his Government of Scotland, as in the case of our late Act for an East-India and African Trade, his Interest as King of England obliges him to submit himself as King of Scotland; by which means our Crown, which we defended so gallantly for so many ages, and which the English could never make subject to theirs by force, is now intirely subjected by a false step of our own, in suffering our King to take their Crown upon him without making better terms for our selves: So that instead of having a King to fight our Battels, we have made a surrender of our Prince to the Enemy, who arm him against us.[162]

While the pamphleteers laid bare Scotland's predicament under the Union of Crowns, the whirlwind of discontent blowing in from the Caribbean threatened to overwhelm King William's ministers on the chilly banks of the Forth. Despite the abolition of the Lords of the Articles in 1690, the Edinburgh parliament, dominated by various magnate factions, had been a largely docile creature in the following years.[163] All that was about to change. The determination of King William's Commissioner, the Duke of Queensberry, to win for his family and friends all positions of power and profit in Scotland had already created a potentially powerful parliamentary opposition to the Scottish administration. The Darien disaster now gave Queensberry's many enemies a stick with which to beat the Duke and his royal master. It also provided them with a means to detach from the court MPs of a more disinterested bent. When in May 1700 a bill was introduced asserting the Scottish Company's right to Darien, Queensberry averted a court defeat only by the expedient of a peremptory adjournment.[164]

The unrest now spread to the streets of Edinburgh. In June the capital's celebrations of the victory at Toubacanti turned into a full-scale riot. By singing a ditty called 'Willful Willy, wilt thou be willful still', the rioters left no doubt as to whom they considered responsible for the misfortunes of Caledonia.[165] A petitioning campaign, calling upon the King to recall parliament and assert 'the nation's right and title to Caledonia', won widespread support. When 'Willful Willy' failed to respond, the opposition threatened to call an extraordinary Convention of the Estates.[166] 'All the blame is laid upon the King', lamented Robert Wodrow in mid-July, 'and peaple turning to very bigg words on the head.'[167] Such indeed was the ferment in Scotland that some observers feared a national uprising against the King. 'God help us, we are ripening for destruction', wrote a correspondent of William Carstares in June 1700. 'It looks very like Forty-one.'[168] He was wrong. Although the need for supply compelled King William to recall parliament in December 1700, skilful political management on the part of Lord Seafield, the Scottish Secretary of State, largely succeeded in extinguishing the fires of the previous session. The court bowed to parliamentary demands for a variety of 'good laws', including an Act confirming the privileges of the Scottish Company. But there was no attempt to revive the bill asserting the Company's right to Darien.[169]

Although Seafield's managerial skills had helped to lower the political temperature, King William knew they could provide no long-term answer to the Anglo-Scottish crisis. He sought for that instead in the union of the two kingdoms. It was not the first time that the King had espoused the cause of union. In 1689, desperate to bring the free-wheeling northern kingdom under more effective control, he had urged the Scottish parliament to seek a union with England. But in the years which followed the King had judged a union of the kingdoms to be more trouble than it was worth.[170] It took the Anglo-Scottish crisis of the late 1690s to convince him that it was no longer feasible to rule England and Scotland as two separate kingdoms. Only an Anglo-Scottish union could prevent the kind of misunderstanding between King William and his distant Scottish ministers which had resulted in such extravagant privileges being granted to the Scottish Company. Only a union could guarantee that Scotland would never again pursue policies which crossed the interests of both the King and the parliament of England. But could King William persuade his subjects of the necessity of union?

In England, whose citizens could see little benefit in closer ties with 'the beggarly Scots', the notion of a union of the kingdoms had long been viewed with scorn. The unionist ideal had, however, attracted some support in Scotland where an Anglo-Scottish union was seen as a means of boosting national prosperity and neutralising the colossus to the south.[171] Unionist sentiment in Scotland was particularly apparent during the revolution of 1689. Andrew Fletcher of Saltoun was to become the most celebrated Scottish opponent of the Act of Union of 1707. But in January 1689 he had thought 'we can never come to any true settlement but by uniting with England in Parliaments and Trade.'[172] Such a union would make it impossible for a future king to use the resources of one kingdom to impose his will upon the other, as Charles I had attempted to do in the 1640s. Thus an address from East Lothian, promoted by the unionist Marquis of Tweeddale, urged the Prince of Orange to promote an Anglo-Scottish union, so that

> we be not hereafter left open by the advantage may be taken of our distinct and different laws and customs and exercise of government whereby methods are taken by the enemies of our peace and tranquility to raise standing armies in either kingdom by which the other may be threatened or enforced to submit to alterations in their religion or diminution of their liberty or foreign forces be brought in either for the subversion of the religion and liberty of both.[173]

But while the Scottish parliament appointed commissioners to negotiate a union, the parliament of England was sublimely indifferent.[174]

The Scottish revolution had, in fact, made the prospect of an Anglo-Scottish union less likely than ever. For the triumph of presbyterianism in Scotland had revived ancient religious distinctions between the two kingdoms. In 1689 that zealous old puritan, Lord Wharton, still dreamed of a great pan-Protestant union between England, Scotland and the Netherlands.[175] But as Bishop Burnet wrote two years later, it had been 'visible [in 1689] that since the Presbiterian Party was like to prevaile [in Scotland], those in England that were for the Church and were jealous of the Interest that the Dissenters had gained with the present Government would never consent to have a great many more Presbiterian Members sent from Scotland'.[176]

In the years following the revolution, England and its King had ridden roughshod over the interests of Scotland. But far from diminishing the allure of closer ties with England, the events of the late 1690s had given added lustre, at least in the eyes of the pamphleteers, to the case for some sort of union or federal arrangement between the two kingdoms. Even as he fulminated against the iniquity of the Union of Crowns, the author of *A Defence of the Scots Settlement* pleaded for closer Anglo-Scottish ties. A 'stricter Union', he contended, 'is absolutely necessary, that both Nations may have but one Interest, which will render us less liable to Convulsions and intestine Commotions at home, and put us out of danger of being attack'd by Enemies from abroad'.[177] According to the author of *An Enquiry into the Causes of the Miscarriage of the Scots Colony*, a full and equal partnership with England was the only way to avert a complete rupture between the two kingdoms. For the treatment meted out to the Scots in recent years had shown that 'our Disasters are no way to be remedied, but either by a total Separation, or a closer Union of the two kingdoms'.[178]

This was all very well, but how was the haughty Westminster parliament to be persuaded of the merits of a stricter or closer union with Scotland? The author of *A Defence of the Scots Settlement* pressed English fears of monarchical despotism into the service of the unionist cause. The English, he observed, were seeking to preserve their liberties by ridding themselves of King William's army. But their efforts would avail them little 'so long as we remain divided', for 'any King that is so minded, may make use of us to inslave one another; and any envious Neighbour, whose Interest it is to keep this Island low, will be sure to blow the Coals'. That being so, 'it is not the interest of England to slight an Union with us so much as they have don'.[179] Similar views had been aired in 1697 in *The Argument against a Standing Army Rectified*, a pamphlet purportedly written by an English whig. It was 'our interest', insisted the pamphleteer, 'to Cultivate a Good Correspondence with Scotland, in order to which an Union of the Nations should be much more effectual than the Union of the Crowns; for that leaves room for Princes of Arbitrary Tempers to clash us one against another, and to make us the Instrument of their Tyranny by turns'. A union with Scotland

> would also secure this Nation very much in case of any future War with France, or others; whereas if the Scotch be always treated with contempt, or this Nation govern'd by the Councils of a Party that hates them, on the account of their Civil and Religious Principles, it may have ill Consequences at some time or other. The Royal Line which cements them at present, is not very numerous in Off-spring, and that failing, they have Princes of their own Blood at home, who if they strengthen themselves by powerful foreign Alliances, may prove troublesome Neighbours, when we are engaged in a foreign War, especially considering the great Plantation of their Countrymen of the same Principles with themselves in Ireland.[180]

Despite this chilling prospect, Englishmen of all persuasions continued to treat calls for an Anglo-Scottish union with derision. When the whiggish Earl of Peterborough pleaded the case for union before his fellow peers in the parliamentary session of 1699–1700, he was very much living up to his reputation as a mischief-making maverick. More typical was the reaction of the whig leader in the Commons, Charles Montagu. There 'was a Lord who, in another place, had moved for an union betwixt ye two nations', he was reported to have told the lower house, 'but certainly he did it only in jest, for in truth it was only a jest'. Although at the opposite end of the political spectrum from Montagu, the true-blue tory Sir Edward Seymour shared the whig leader's contempt for the notion of a union with the Scots. According to the same report, Seymour suggested that

> it was not now a proper time . . . to debate ye union betwixt Engl[an]d and Scotl[an]d, but, if ever it shou'd be debated, he shou'd oppose it for this reason: that a woman being proposed to a neighbour of his in ye country for a wife, he said he wou'd never marry her, for she was a beggar, and whoever married a beggar cou'd only expect a louse for her portion; w[hi]ch hath most wonderfully exasperated all ye Scotchmen in town.[181]

Not even the death in July 1700 of the young Duke of Gloucester, an event which once more placed the Protestant succession in jeopardy, managed to convince Englishmen of the merits of a union with Scotland. Such, indeed, was the disdain in which the Scots were held that the Westminster parliament did not even deign to consult the Scottish Estates when in 1701 it settled the succession to the English throne in the Hanoverian family. The beggarly Scots, it was presumed, would meekly follow England's lead, just as they had in 1689. This proved to be a sorry miscalculation. By failing to secure the prior agreement of its Scottish counterpart to the Hanoverian succession, the Westminster parliament gave the Scots a weapon which, in the next reign, they would gleefully put to England's head. After King William's death, the antics of an increasingly unmanageable Scottish parliament brought England face to face with the apparition seen in 1697 by the author of *The Argument against a Standing Army Rectified* : a hostile and fully-independent Scotland, once again with a king of its own to fight the nation's battles, forging anew the 'auld alliance' with France against England. That was a spectre which, Englishmen grudgingly came to concede, could be exorcised only by the union of the two kingdoms.[182]

5.   The Case of Ireland and the Interest of England

The calamity which befell English trade during King William's war brought matters mercantile to the top of the political agenda in England. The growing importance of commercial issues at Westminster is evinced most clearly by the agitation which led to the establishment of the Board of Trade in 1696.[183] But it can also be seen in the ruthless determination of the Westminster parliament to stamp out the commercial enterprises of the neighbouring kingdoms. The temerity of the Scots in setting up a trading company of their own was denounced by both houses of parliament in December 1695. Nor did the threat posed to English commerce by the Kingdom of Ireland escape the attention of Westminster parliamentarians. Thus in December 1698, even as the Scots were struggling to establish their colony at Darien, Sir Edward Seymour introduced a bill prohibiting the export of Irish woollens to any territory beyond the confines of England and Wales. It was the third such bill moved in as many parliamentary sessions. The second of these had actually passed the Commons in the session of 1697–8, only to meet defeat in the Lords. At the third time of asking, however, the Irish Woollen Bill passed all its stages in both houses, receiving the Royal Assent in May 1699.[184]

The passage of the Irish Woollen Act represented the culmination of a long campaign by a group of west-country merchants, led inevitably by John Cary of Bristol, to restrict Irish trade. In December 1695, together with another merchant, Cary had urged Bristol's MPs to consider 'the affairs of Ireland, whose Trade will in a short time eat up ours, except some stop be put to it'.[185] Earlier that year, in a book on the advancement of English trade, Cary had similarly complained that 'Ireland is now destructive to the Interest of England'. For 'as long as that People enjoy so free and open a Trade to Foreign Parts, and thereby are encouraged to advance in their Woollen Manufactures, they must consequently lessen ours, than which they cannot do us a greater Mischief, being the Tools whereon we Trade, when they sink our Navigation sinks with them.'[186]

The publication of Cary's book led to a correspondence between the Bristolian and Edmund Bohun, the former licensor of the press. While he generally admired Cary's work, Bohun took issue with his contention that restrictions should be placed on Ireland's foreign trade. It was not in England's power, he argued, to suppress the manufactures of Ireland. Even if it were, it would not be in England's interests to do so. For Bohun believed that the English Protestant settlers – the Anglo-Irish, as they were later dubbed – 'will never stay in Ireland if it [trade] be denied them . . . and if they leave Ireland it will be lost from us because the Natives and old Planted Popish English hate us most mortally'.[187]

Bohun's views cut little ice with Cary: 'ple[ase] to note', he had asked Bohun in January 1696,

> that all Plantations settled abroad out o[f] our own People must needs be a loss to this Kingdome except they are imployed to serv[e] its Interest, nor do they answer the ends of their fir[st] settlement, which were rather to provide Materialls for the increasing our Trade at home, & keepin[g] our people at work here, then by those Conduits let it slide away; This is as opening a Vein in [a] Mans body, & letting him bleed to death, which migh[t] be of good use to his health if no more Blood we[re] taken from him then he could well spare; The hea[rt] of the Common Wealth is to be preferred before that of any part when it sets up a distinct Interest.

As for the English Protestant settlers in Ireland, they were under a special duty to serve the interests of the mother country. 'I will not repeat the obligations laid on Ireland above our other Plantations,' concluded Cary,

> the charge of its reduction twice in 40 years is not a small Article, but if we consider that they are all of them defended & secured at the Expence of England, who alone bears the charge of Warrs & Revolutions, certainly at least the same respect is due it as from a Tenant to his Landlord, who pays him a Pepper Corn in acknowledgment, we only desire for its full value to have the product they raise.[188]

And at Westminster in 1698–9, it was Cary's narrow conception of England's interests, rather than Bohun's broader vision, which prevailed.

While it no doubt delighted Cary and his fellow west-country merchants, Seymour's measure was greeted with consternation across the Irish Sea. The Woollen Act, complained Anglo-Irishmen, would reduce them to penury, and profit only those inveterate enemies of the English interest in Ireland, the papists and the Scots. 'I have this day the honour of yours of the 25th past', wrote a Cork alderman to a friend in June 1699, 'with an Abstract of the Dreadfull Act against poor Ireland, which will in the End, be the Ruine of England; for it will make this an Irish-strong Nation. Many poor English Familys are going away.' In these circumstances, the Westminster parliament was wasting its breath in complaining about the allegedly profligate disposal of forfeited rebel land in Ireland. The 'Parliament in England need not begrudge the Purchasers their Bargains of the forfeited Estates,' the alderman observed, 'for in two Years time, land will be soe cheap, that they will have but sorry bargains.'[189] A Dublin letter-writer was just as bewildered. If it were in England's interests to prevent Ireland falling into the hands of the Scots and the native Irish, those interests could be 'promoted & supported' only by 'Encouraging the English to settle here'. And 'if Denying them to eat the Fruit of their Labour is encourageing I know not how to find out its opposite'. The true beneficiaries of the Act would not be the merchants of England, but the Scots whose strength in recent years had been boosted by a massive influx of migrants from the famine-stricken western Lowlands. 'That nation', the same writer alleged,

> has in great measure engrossed the whole Trade of this Kingdom and a good part of our lands and I doubt not but in time they will swallow downe all the English Interest here, for they are so nationale that from the nobleman to the Pedlar with his Pack they are all Brothers for one another and all the wit they have could never have procured them a better handle than the late English act, for Rooting out the English here, for one English man we have 6 Scots in his Roome.[190]

The Woollen Act, Irish Protestants repeatedly warned, spelt disaster for the English interest in Ireland. It was also said to have alarming implications for the established constitutional relationship between Ireland and England. Anglo-Irishmen did not dispute Ireland's status as an appurtenance of the English Crown. Nor, for the most part, did they challenge the validity of Poynings' Law, the Irish statute of 1494 by which the legislation of the Dublin parliament was made subject to the approval of the English Privy Council.[191] But when it came to the question of Westminster's role in Irish affairs, the views of Anglo-Irishmen were a good deal more ambivalent. On the one hand, as they had shown in 1693, Irish parliamentarians were not averse to taking their grievances to Westminster in order to undermine the authority of an unpopular administration at Dublin Castle. On the other hand, those self-same champions of liberty and Protestantism would not countenance the notion that the English legislature had jurisdiction over Ireland and her parliament. As Sir Charles Porter, the English-born Lord Chancellor of Ireland, wrote in 1695, 'it is no uncomon thing to have some of their Leading Men in the Lawe say that it is an Erroneous opinion to meinteyn that an Act of the parliament in England should binde them here, for they have Parliaments of their Own and those and onely those Lawes are oblidgeing here.'[192] To such men, therefore, the Woollen Act was not merely a threat to Ireland's prosperity: it was also an infringement of the fundamental constitutional rights of Irishmen. 'If I can be taxed & bound by laws to which I am no party', wrote Bishop King of Derry in May 1698, 'I shall reckon my self as much a slave, as one of the grand Seigniours Mutes.'[193]

A spiky character at the best of times, Bishop King had every right to feel personally aggrieved by the increasingly high-handed behaviour of the

Westminster parliament. For years, he had been litigating with the City of London's Irish Society, the body responsible for managing the Londonderry plantation. When the Irish House of Lords ruled in King's favour, the Society took its case to Westminster. As the bishop explained in December 1697, this move had implications extending far beyond his rather arcane dispute with the Irish Society: 'it concerns every Man that has an estate in Ireland as well as me', for 'if their design to appeal to the House of Lords there from the parlement here be admitted, I suppose there is an end of parlements here, at least of the house of Lords.'[194] The appeal was admitted, and so Bishop King emerged as one of the leaders of Anglo-Irish resistance to the English parliament.[195]

In April 1698 Bishop King had been shown the manuscript of a book on the constitutional crisis by the Dublin political thinker, William Molyneux.[196] When it was published soon afterwards, Molyneux's *The Case of Ireland's Being Bound by Acts of Parliament in England Stated* provided a vigorous rebuttal of the pretensions of the Westminster parliament. Like virtually all Anglo-Irishmen, Molyneux had no difficulty in accepting that Ireland was an appurtenance of the English Crown. But drawing upon history, natural rights theory, and the common law, Molyneux contended that, in all other ways, Ireland was as sovereign a state as the Kingdom of Scotland. Ireland was no mere colony of England, and only the Dublin parliament had the right to legislate for the King's Irish subjects. Thus the legislative imperialism of the Westminster parliament was an unlawful assault upon the liberties of Irishmen. Just as Irish Catholics had done in 1641, and the American colonists were to do in the 1760s, Molyneux appealed to the Crown to curb the excesses of the English parliament. 'Your most Excellent Majesty', he wrote in the dedication to King William, 'is the Common Indulgent Father of your Countries and have an Equal Regard to the Birth-Rights of all Your Children; and will not permit the Eldest, because the Strongest, to Encroach on the Possessions of the Younger.'[197]

Molyneux's book caused a sensation on both sides of the Irish Sea. Its target, the Westminster parliament, was both swift and vehement in its denunciation: 'the said Book', resolved the House of Commons in June 1698, 'was of dangerous consequence to the crown and people of England, by denying the authority of the king and parliament of England, to bind the kingdom and people of Ireland, and the subordination and dependence that Ireland has, and ought to have upon England, as being united and annexed to the imperial crown of this realm.'[198] The book came under equally fierce attack in the English press. As its author freely acknowledged, *The Case of Ireland* was something of a rushed job, and Molyneux's critics found it easy to impugn his scholarship.[199] They also lost no opportunity to point out some painful home truths. It was, after all, a strange sort of national sovereignty which rested entirely upon the arms and treasure

Figure 14   A portrait of the Anglo-Irish patriot, William Molyneux. In his book The Case of Ireland, *Molyneux argued that Ireland was a sovereign kingdom, tied to the English Crown but independent of the Westminster parliament. English MPs denounced the book, claiming that it was 'of dangerous consequence to the crown and people of England'.*

of a neighbouring kingdom. 'You know that you are not able to protect and defend your selves against the Rebellions of the Irish,' wrote an English pamphleteer,

> and that the Kings of England cannot raise Money upon the People to help you, without their Consent in Parliament; would you have them then only to have Authority to raise Money, and appropriate it to your Service, without having any more to do with you? Or can you think, that the Parliament of England will ever more assist you upon those terms?

Rather than go down the perilous road to independence, Irish Protestants should know their place and be happy with it.[200] As for the much-vaunted powers of the Irish parliament, these, sneered John Cary, were in reality 'no more then our Foreign Plantations, and great Corporations in England have'.[201] Another pamphleteer, Simon Clement, was more blunt still in asserting the inferior status of the Irish legislature. He recommended that the following inscription be erected in the Dublin parliament and in 'the Houses of Assembly in all other Colonies':

> Let us always remember that this Island (or Province) is a Colony; that England is our Mother Countrey; that we are ever to expect Protection from her in the Possession of our Lands; which we are to cultivate and improve for our own Subsistence and Advantage, but not to Trade to or with any other Nation without her Permission; and that 'tis our incumbent Duty to pay Obedience to all such Laws as she shall Enact concerning Us.

This was to be recited 'the first thing every Day of their sessions'.[202]

The message, then, was stark: the Kingdom of Ireland was no more than a colony of England, its parliament on a par with the assemblies of New York or Barbados. The 'imperial' Westminster parliament thus had every right to legislate for England's Irish colony. As if to ram home that point, in April 1700 the Westminster parliament passed an Act resuming to the Crown all of King William's grants of forfeited land in Ireland.[203] Since much of the land in question had subsequently been purchased by Anglo-Irish gentlemen, the Act of Resumptions was the cause of yet more gnashing of teeth in Ireland: 'what can be more Arbitrary, Disobligeing or Unjust', asked the Irish judge Sir Richard Cox, 'than to Exercise a Judiciall Authority over our freeholds by Resuming the Forfeitures and depriving very many English Protestant purchasers bona fide & for valuable Consideration of their Legall Titles.' Cox was just as critical of the Woollen Act. Unlike Molyneux, however, he implicitly accepted Ireland's colonial status. Rather than challenge the right of the English parliament to legis-late for Ireland, Cox stressed instead the iniquity of Westminster's measures and their wholly counter-productive effect: 'as to the Woollen Bill', he told the English MP Robert Harley in October 1699,

> I should be for it, if I were convinc'd England would reap the benefit of It They expected, which I believe They would not and I fear'd the

> Consequences here would be the Diminution of the Number of the English, which were already fewer than either the Scots or Irish, & the alienation of our affections, which in time would render the disaffected in the Interests of the Scots, and oblige the well affected to return to England as I should doe for one.

Such a sorry state of affairs could hardly be in England's interests, for it 'would follow that whenever England has few Freinds here, it would be difficult to Reteine this Kingdome, & perhaps impossible to Recover it'.[204]

The year before, in a pamphlet addressed to the English House of Lords, Francis Annesley – a member of Bishop King's circle – had painted a similarly doleful picture. After 500 years of war and toil, the English settlers in Ireland had at last gained full control of that troublesome kingdom. But if England

> should lay such difficulties upon them, that they should think it their Interest to leave the Country, or not be very solicitous for the English Interest there, I submit it to your Lordships great wisdom, whether that kingdom may not hereafter give us fresh trouble. France is but a new Friend, and Scotland for late reasons is not much in humour with us; and we know the whole North of Ireland is inhabited by that Nation, and multitudes of them go over every other day, and will do so notwithstanding this [the Woollen Bill] or any other Law that can be made.

In short, the myopic measures of the Westminster parliament would serve merely to place Ireland in the hands of England's once and no doubt future enemies, the Irish papists and the Scots. Worse still, Westminster's oppression of Ireland, together with its contempt for Scottish interests, might have fatal consequences for English liberty. 'No one knows', mused Annesley, 'what unhappy occasions may arise in ages to come of difference between our Kings and People, and therefore we ought to be tender how we make it the Interest of a whole Kingdom to be subservient to the designs of a corrupt Court, who will offer them advantages.' Discord between the British kingdoms had, after all, served the purposes of evil counsellors in the not-so-distant past. 'Most of us have read, and some of us have seen with our Eyes,' wrote Annesley with a view to the reigns of both Charles I and James II, 'those times that Courts have plaid England against Scotland, Scotland against England, and Ireland against both; and we have heard of the time, that an Irish Parliament hath been called to give money to reduce an English one.'[205]

Annesley's jeremiad, heartfelt though it was, would have done little to allay English suspicions of Anglo-Irish aspirations. Those were long-standing. In May 1695 an English official in Ireland had complained that

> there is now a party setting up here which endeavour to join the old English [Protestants] that have been settled here for some time and the Scotch by the name of the British Interest and to set up for that which they call the

interest of this country without regard to England, and indeed in opposition to it; they desire to have this an Independant kingdom, and complain perpetually of being opprest by England, that they are being hindered by it in their growth and trade, that they are dealt with by her as by a step-mother.[206]

Two years later similar views were expressed by James Vernon, the English Undersecretary of State, to his patron, the Duke of Shrewsbury. 'If the Protestants in Ireland were not under some apprehension from the papists there', he wrote, 'their thoughts would be then employed how they might get rid of their dependence on England, as being that which stunts their growth.'[207] In June 1698 the English parliament accused its Irish counterpart – which in the previous year had had the temerity to re-enact and amend an English statute for preserving the King's person – of having encouraged the ideas promulgated by Molyneux in *The Case of Ireland.*[208]

Among those Englishmen wary of the aspirations of Irish parliamentarians was John Methuen, Lord Chancellor of Ireland since 1697. Although 'the several parties differ amongst themselves,' he wrote to Shrewsbury in February 1698, 'yet they agree in desiring to be independent of England, and believing themselves so in right.'[209] In order to avert an open breach between the Dublin and Westminster parliaments, Methuen had persuaded leading English peers to block Seymour's second Woollen Bill in 1698. As a quid pro quo, he had promised to push a similar measure through the Irish legislature. The subsequent failure of the Dublin parliament to impose sufficiently tough restrictions made inevitable the passage of the Woollen Act in the English parliamentary session of 1698–99.[210]

In fact, Westminster parliamentarians may well have seen the Woollen Act as a response to growing truculence on the part of the Anglo-Irish. Thus Sir Robert Southwell, doyen of the Anglo-Irish ruling elite, attributed the anti-Irish legislation of the English parliament to its belief that 'the People of Ireland have a Mind to shake off all Dependence.' Such sentiments distressed Southwell deeply. 'But alas!' he wrote to Bishop King in April 1699, 'how has this Dependence been hitherto preserv'd, or can ever be in the future, but by Cherishing & not Crushing those English Protestants, who have nothing on this side paradise to adhere to, but old England.'[211]

To men such as Southwell, Cox and Annesley, the discord between the Anglo-Irish and their mother country was a tragedy. They were convinced that England's true interest lay in nurturing her sons in Ireland. 'Few have escaped this general destruction [wrought by the Irish Catholics under King James]', wrote Annesley in 1698,

and 'tis hoped you will not let those few be in the condition of poor ship-wract men on some Coasts, who when they were thrown half dead ashore, meet their ruin from those of whom they did expect relief. They are

Englishmen sent over to conquer Ireland, your Countrymen, your Brothers, your Sons, your Relations, your Acquaintances; governed by the same King, the same Laws, of the same Religion, and in the same Interest, and equally engaged in the same common cause of Liberty.[212]

But the very existence of the Dublin parliament meant that there was a profound dissonance between rhetoric and reality. 'It has ruind us in this Kingdom from time to time to have had a Parliament of our own', wrote James Bonnell as early as 1691. 'For this has bred all the jealousy of England toward us, & made us seem to have had a separate interest from them.' Better by far to unite 'this Kingdom to England, as it was in Cromwell's time by our sending over about 30 Comoners, & some representatives of the Lords Spiritual & Temporal to your Parliament. This alone', he concluded, 'would take this Kingdom out of the hands of the Irish, & would take away all Jealousy of it, from the English, since it would seem then to be but a part of themselves, as much as Wales.'[213]

James Bonnell was not alone in advocating union between England and Ireland. In 1690, when English-controlled Ireland was suffering the depredations of its 'liberators', an anonymous writer had seen union as the only sure safeguard against the re-emergence of 'Straffordianism': the deployment, threatened or actual, of the Irish army to impose despotic rule in England. What, he asked, 'will secure England from the force it now lies open to from Ireland? The question is resolved in a few words: unite them and then there can be no more danger than of Wales; make them one body, and then they will be actuated by one spirit.' As he went on to explain, there was 'a double mischief by the different administration of England and Ireland: it naturally leads to an alteration of affections between the English of both kingdoms; those of Ireland cannot but have resentments that they should be used as a slavish, conquered people by their brethren. On the other hand, England is in danger that these men, under arbitrary power, may be instruments to bring them so too.'[214]

In the event, it was England which proved to be a threat to the liberties of Ireland, not the other way round. Yet while they repeatedly denounced Westminster's infringements of their rights, Irish Protestants were only too well aware that, in the final analysis, their pre-eminence in Ireland rested upon the power of England. Trapped on the horns of this particularly uncomfortable dilemma, Anglo-Irish patriots, like their Scottish counterparts, came to see union with England as the solution to their segment of the 'British Problem'.[215] 'For my owne part,' wrote an Irish opponent of the Woollen Bill in 1697, 'I see noe good can come by any other Expedient in the World, than by uniting of the 2 kingdomes, which may comprehend us in the Trade of England, as well as in Taxes & other things.'[216] That same year, Bishop King had written that the union of the kingdoms was 'assuredly the only means to make both flourish effectually'.[217] Writing to

Robert Harley in October 1699, Sir Richard Cox waxed lyrical about the benefits of union. 'And perhaps', mused Cox,

> a few yeares will convince you that you must not only take as much care of our properties as your owne, but also that it is your Interest to unite and Incorporate us with England. For by that meanes the English Interest will be always prevalent here, and this Kingdome as secure to you as Wales or any county in England. Your Taxes will be lessened when we beare part of the Burden. Your force will be augmented, especially at Sea. Your Fleet when one Squadron of it hath its station at Kinsale, will have double the Effect upon any Enemy it has now, all our Money will still center at London, & our Trade and Communication with England will be soe considerable, that we shall think our selves at home when there; & where one goes thither now, Ten will goe, when all our business is transacted in your Parliament to which if we send 64 Knights of our 32 Counties, & 10 Lords and 6 Bishops, they may spend our Money, but cannot Influence your Councills to your Disadvantage.[218]

Even that most celebrated champion of Irish liberty, William Molyneux, saw the union of the two kingdoms as a wholly desirable objective. In his *Case of Ireland*, Molyneux contended that the only English statutes which bound Ireland were those made in certain fourteenth-century parliaments to which Ireland had sent representatives. The conclusion to be drawn from this was clear. 'If from these last mention'd Records, it be concluded that the Parliament of England may Bind Ireland', wrote Molyneux, 'it must also be Allow'd that the People of Ireland ought to have their Representatives in the Parliament of England. And this, I believe we should be willing enough to embrace; but this is an Happiness we can hardly hope for.'[219]

As Molyneux had anticipated, Irish calls for a union of the kingdoms fell on deaf ears. If Englishmen tended to blanch at the prospect of Anglo-Scottish union, they were more scornful still of the case for a union with Ireland. For all their justifiable resentment of English hegemony, the Scots remained an independent people, fully capable, if they so chose, of inflicting real damage upon England's foreign policy and security interests. When, after 1702, the Edinburgh parliament decided to do just that, the case for an Anglo-Scottish union became compelling to English politicians. In contrast, the Protestants of Ireland, dependent upon English arms and money for their very survival, could bring no such pressure to bear in the corridors of Whitehall and the debating chambers of Westminster. Anglo-Irish patriots might huff and puff, but they had neither the inclination nor the capacity to blow the house down. Over the next three decades, the Protestant ruling class would instead come to accept the tutelage of England as the sad but inevitable price of its ascendancy over the Catholic majority.

8

A Remembrance of Times Past

In October 1690, three months after King William's famous victory at the Boyne, an enterprising printer in the metropolis produced a fitting tribute to England's warrior king. The centre-piece of *The Embleme of Englands Distractions* is a splendid full-length portrait of King William. Clad in armour, he treads underfoot the 'Whore of Babilon' and the 'Hydra of Faction and Error'. In his left hand, the King holds an open book – presumably a Bible – displaying the motto 'Tollo Perlego Protego' ('This I exalt, study and protect'). In his right hand, he brandishes a sword. The blade is thrust through the crowns of the three British kingdoms. Behind King William, the angel of 'Fame' sounds a salute. To the King's left, a group of soldiers carry flags of St George. By the soldiery are the words 'Vis unita fortior' ('Greater strength in unity'). On either side of the King rise two mounds, each topped by a column. The hill to the King's right is labelled Mount Sion. Its column – surmounted by a roundel containing a portrait of Queen Mary – bears a variety of legends, including 'Salus Populi Suprema Lex' ('The good of the people is the supreme law') and 'Magna Charta'. The second column is topped by the parliament house. On the column's panels are three female figures, personifications of the British kingdoms. They kneel and present laurel wreaths to their victorious monarch. At the foot of Mount Sion is a peaceful bucolic scene. A shepherd tends his flock. Another man cuts grapes from a vine with a pruning-hook which was once a spear. Elsewhere, a ploughman turns the soil with a sword beaten into a plough-share. Not all, however, wish to see the realisation of Isaiah's prophetic vision of peace. On the mound of parliament and the three kingdoms, husbandmen are planting trees. But their wholesome work is endangered by conspirators who assault the hill with pickaxes. They have dug a mine and crammed it with barrels of gunpowder. One of the fiendish crew is already attempting to ignite the mine's deadly contents. Lurking nearby, no doubt hatching some further devilry, is a brace of Jesuits. But we need not fear. Just as God delivered

Noah on Mount Ararat and Isaac on Mount Moriah – episodes illustrated at the top of the print – so will He also deliver King William from his enemies. For upon the King shines down the radiant light of divine providence, bearing the reassuring promise, 'I will never faile thee, nor forsake thee.'[1]

The Embleme was, and remains, an eye-catching piece of Williamite propaganda. But it was not an original work, having first appeared in 1658 as a tribute to the Lord Protector, Oliver Cromwell. Thirty-two years later, our printer, not averse to a little creative recycling, simply scraped Cromwell's head off the original block and replaced it with King William's. Add a few other minor modifications, and, hey presto, *The Embleme* was ready for a belated second print run, doubtless leaving our printer to congratulate himself on his sleight of hand. His ingenuity, however, made *The Embleme* something of a two-edged sword in propaganda terms. For the scam was spotted by a Jacobite with a long memory and a taste for verse. The result was the wittiest Jacobite poem of the 1690s, *On the Late Metamorphosis*. 'Whether', mused its author,

> . . . the graver did by this intend
> Oliver's shape with King William's head to mend,
> Or grace King William's head with Cromwell's body,
> If I can guess his meaning I'm a noddy.
> Howe'er I pity Cromwell. Thirty year
> And more are past since he did disappear.
> Now, after all this time, 'tis hard to be
> Thus executed in effigie -
> This is a punishment he never dreaded;
> What did his Highness thus to be beheaded?
> Perhaps the artist thinks to get a name
> By showing us how two may be the same.
> If so, he's gained his point, for he's a witch
> That suddenly can tell one which is which![2]

As we saw in chapter 2, the supposed correspondence between the Lord Protector and King William was a mainstay of Jacobite propaganda.[3] But that does not mean that the Oliver/William parallel was entirely without foundation. After all, the ease with which Cromwellian propaganda could be adapted to deliver a Williamite message reminds us that the apotheosis of the two rulers was built on startlingly similar foundations. It was a point emphasised by the author of *On the Late Metamorphosis*. In that verse, a crowd, which has gathered at the printer's shop to gawp at the two versions of *The Embleme*, instantly recognises the scowling figure of the Lord Protector. But it initally mistakes Oliver's bewigged companion for his hapless son, Richard. The error is soon corrected by one of the throng:

Figures 15 & 16 'The Embleme of Englands Distractions As also of her attained, and further expected Freedome, & Happines': the original Cromwellian print of 1658 (left) and the Williamite adaptation of 1690. Protected by divine providence, the two great Protestant heroes tread underfoot the popish whore. Jacobites insisted that King William was a second Cromwell. These prints suggest they had a point.

'You all shoot wide, my masters' says another.
'He in the wig is neither son nor brother,
But a late conqueror of different fame.
Sirs, pull off all your hats, and hear his name!
'Tis good King William. See Rome trampled down.
See his victorious sword thrust through the crown.
See his triumphant foot on papists' necks.
See Salus Populi Suprema Lex.
See Magna Charta. Can all this agree
With any man but Oliver and he? . . .'[4]

Who else indeed? Certainly not King William's two immediate predecessors. True, devotion to Magna Charta and the good of the people was attributed to both Charles II and James II by their partisans. But even their most ardent supporters would have blushed to see the two Stuart brothers depicted as Protestant knights errant, stamping upon the popish whore. So *The Embleme* reminds us that, after the crypto-popery of Charles II and the outright popery of his younger brother, the accession of William III signified a reversion, in the public mind at least, to the unambiguous and militant Protestantism of the Protectorate. Upon the shoulders of King William, saviour of British Protestantism and enemy of popish 'Universal Monarchy', had fallen the mantle of Oliver Cromwell.

Intriguingly, it seems that Oliver did hold some fascination for King William. In his biography of John Howe – one-time chaplain to the Lord Protector – Edmund Calamy remembered that Howe had 'once inform'd me, of some very private Conversation he had with [King William], upon his sending for him, not long before his Death. Among other things,' Calamy continued, 'the King then ask'd him a great many Questions, about his old Master Oliver, as he call'd him, and seem'd not a little pleas'd with the Answers that were return'd to some of his Questions.'[5] Alas, Howe appears to have kept the contents of the King's questions to himself, and it would be fanciful to suggest that King William saw himself treading in Oliver's footsteps. But it is by no means fanciful to see a real correspondence between the fates of Cromwell – the godly champion who had failed to bring about the new Jerusalem – and King William.

In 1689 some of King William's subjects had seen his accession as a glorious new beginning for the Protestant cause. The revolution, such folk believed, would usher in both civil and religious reformation, and ultimately pave the way for the millennium itself. It was surely that wondrous prospect, above all, which had brought Edmund Ludlow, the last of the regicides, home from his long Swiss exile in September 1689.[6] And it was in anticipation of the latter days that a less celebrated veteran of the parliamentary army, one Richard Younge, had written to Postmaster-General John Wildman in May 1689. Taking inspiration from the memory of Naseby, where 'many of us . . . came off with garments washd in blood',

Younge urged Wildman – the living embodiment of the 'old cause' – to press ahead with God's work. 'The eies of most of the good people of the Land are upon yow', he declared:

> the Lord spiritt yow for this greate worke that yow may know what Israell ought to do: & that yow may rule with god & be faithfull to his saints: yow have the prayers of many of the good people of the land for yow . . . feare not tho your work is greate, yett know it, yow & all the good zerubabbells in the house are upon the wings of many prayers: & tis impossible such prayers shall go unanswered.

More than forty years after the providential victory at Naseby, God's people had at last come to the banks of the Jordan. 'Yow have bin an old souldier & desiple for Christ', Younge reminded the Postmaster,

> & have had large experience of gods dealeing both in adversity & in Prosperity. The divell & Antichrist will storm when his kingdom is going down: & who knowes butt that god has spun out the thred of your life & that yow are to be as a Caleb & Joshua to do som speciall work for god & to declare what god did for poore England on the other side of the Red Sea & in the wildernes.[7]

Nor had millenarian excitement been confined to old sectarian radicals like Ludlow and Younge. 'It is from You', Gilbert Burnet had informed the King and Queen at their coronation, 'that we expect the Glorious Reverse of all cloudy days. You have been hitherto our Hope and our Desire: You must now become our Glory and Crown of Rejoycing: Ordinary Vertues in You, will fall so far short of our hopes, that we shall be tempted almost to think them Vices. It is in Your Persons, and under Your Reign, that we hope to see an opening to a Glorious Scene, which seems approaching.'[8] Burnet had explained the nature of that 'Glorious Scene' earlier in his sermon: 'the true Notion of ruling in the fear of the Lord,' he had averred,

> is when Princes make that Religion which God has revealed, the chief mark and measure of their whole Government: When the encouraging and promoting of a vigorous Piety, and sublime Vertue, and the maintaining and propagating of True Religion, by ways and means suitable to it, is the chief design of their Rule: When Impiety and Vice are punished, and Error is repressed, but without the ruine of such as are involved in it: When the decency of the Worship of God is kept up, without adulterating it with Superstition: When Order is carried on in the Church of God, without Tyranny: And above all, when Princes are in their own deportment, Examples of the Fear of God, but without Affectation; and when it is visible that they honour those that fear the Lord, and that vile men are despised by them, then do they truly Rule in the Fear of God. When we see Kings become thus truly Christian Philosophers, then we may expect to see the City of God, the New Jerusalem, quickly come down from Heaven to settle among us: and if we may look for a glorious Thousand Years on Earth, we

may reckon that it is not too far from us, when we see Kings fall down before him that is the King of Kings, and offer up their Crowns to him by whom they Reign.[9]

The death of Queen Mary in 1694 shattered Burnet's dreams. 'I must confess', wrote the bishop, 'my hopes are so sunk with the Queens death that I do not flatter my self with further expectations; If things can be kept in tollerable order, so that we have peace and quiet in our days I dare look for no more: So black a scene of Providence as is now upon us gives me many dismall Apprehensions.'[10] Yet long before the Queen's death, it had become apparent to whig ultras that the revolution had failed of its promise. Within two months of his return to England, Ludlow had been hounded back into exile by outraged tories.[11] By 1691 Wildman and other whig true believers had been kicked out of the King's administration. The truest whig of them all, John Hampden, had been unseated at the 1690 general election.[12] True, the dissenters had been given their liberty. But unless and until the tory 'Achans' were cast out of the camp of Israel, that liberty would remain precarious. Nor could Protestant union and godly reformation be effected while the Church party remained a force in the land. And with those goals unattained, the latter days once again faded from view. As in the 1650s, the blissful revolutionary dawn had given way to a miserable mid-morning subfusc.

It was not all the King's fault. Like Cromwell before him, King William had aroused expectations which no earthly ruler could fulfil. But whiggery's disenchantment with the Williamite regime in the early 1690s can in large measure be attributed to the internal contradictions of the King's policies. Once again the parallels with the Cromwellian era are striking. By seeking to woo conservatives while at the same time protecting the radical sects, Oliver had succeeded in antagonising the latter without winning the allegiance of the former.[13] A little over 30 years after the Protector's demise, King William similarly fell between two stools. The war against France, as well as his own natural inclinations, led the King to seek a broad measure of union among Protestants. This ought to have drawn him to the whigs, party of pan-Protestantism at home and abroad. But the imperative of national unity made King William just as eager to court the tories, party of Church of England exclusivism. Far from extirpating the Church party, as the whigs had hoped, King William had instead granted office to many of its leaders. As a result, whig true believers came to despise King William every bit as much as die-hard Jacobites, while more moderate whigs were left to lament a monarch who had abandoned his friends for the sake of those who would never own him to be their rightful king. By the mid–1690s, it is true, the King had seen the error of his ways. But the price of rapprochement with the mainstream of whiggery was the alienation of the Church party. And even to his whiggish supporters, the Dutch King remained an aloof and cold figure, easier to respect than to love.

That much became clear, if it were not so already, in March 1702. On 21 February King William suffered a broken collarbone when his horse stumbled on a mole-hill in Richmond Park. At first, he seemed to be making a good recovery. But his constitution, weakened by life-long asthma and further undermined by years of campaigning, had been dealt a mortal blow. By 4 March pneumonia had set in. Four days later, the King was dead.[14]

As one might expect, King William's demise was greeted with joy by Jacobites. Among that fraternity, a legend soon grew up that the King's unlucky horse was none other than Sorrel, once the steed of the Jacobite 'martyr', Sir John Fenwick. So it was that one Jacobite penned a paean in praise of the noble creature which, at a stroke, had both avenged its former master and rid the nation of the tyrannical usurper:

> Illustrious Steed, who should the Zodiac grace,
> To whom the Lion and the Bull give Place,
> Blest be the Duggs that fed thee, blessed the Earth,
> Which first receiv'd thee, and beheld thy Birth.
> Did wrong'd Iërne [Ireland], to revenge her slain,
> Produce thee first, or murder'd Fenwick's Strain?
> Where e'er thou art, be now for ever blest,
> And spend the Remnant of thy Days in rest;
> No servile Use thy Sacred Limbs profane,
> No Weight thy Back, no Curb thy Mouth restrain;
> No more be thou, no more Mankind a Slave,
> But both enjoy that Liberty you gave.[15]

To another Jacobite poetaster, however, Sorrel's intervention had come too late in the day to be the cause of much rejoicing. 'Mourn on, you foolish fashionable things,' he told those 'Beaux and Belles' mourning King William's passing,

> But mourn your own condition, not the King's;
> Mourn for the mighty Summs by him mis-spent,
> Those prodigally given, those idly lent;
> Mourn for the Statues, and the Tapestry too,
> From Windsor, gutted to aggrandize Loo.
> Mourn for the Miter long from Scotland gone,
> And mourn as much the Union coming on.
> Mourn for ten Years of War and dismal Weather,
> For Taxes, strung like Necklaces together,
> On Salt, Malt, Paper, Syder, Lights and Leather . . .
> If matters then, my Friends, you see are so,
> Tho now you mourn, 't had lessen'd much your Wo
> Had Sorrel stumbled thirteen Years ago.[16]

The Jacobite response to the King's death was treated with contempt by that fierce Williamite, Daniel Defoe: 'we have here', he hissed,

> . . . an Ignominious Croud,
> That boast their Native Birth and English Blood,
> Whose Breasts with Envy and Contention burn,
> And now rejoice when all the Nations mourn:
> Their awkward Triumphs openly they Sing;
> Insult the Ashes of their injur'd King;
> Rejoice at the Disasters of his Crown;
> And Drink the Horse's Health that threw him down.[17]

In contrast, Defoe lamented the vacuum of national and international leadership created by King William's death. The 'Civil Sword' had been entrusted to the new Queen with general satisfaction. 'But who', he asked,

> . . . shall for us weild the Military?
> Who shall the jarring Generals unite;
> First teach them to agree, and then to fight?
> Who shall renew'd Alliances contrive,
> And keep the vast confederacies alive?
> Who shall the growing Gallick Force subdue?
> 'Twas more than all the World, but him, cou'd do.[18]

Defoe was not alone in genuinely lamenting King William's death. The whig MP for Gloucestershire, Sir Richard Cocks, mourned the passing of 'the supporter of the protestant religion, of the libertye of Europe and an enemy to France, the only obstacle they had that hindred them from being universal monarch.' The King's life, Cocks added,

> was uneasy between the contending partyes. He now and then endeavoured to oblige them [the tories] by trusting and employing them which was the misfortune and blemish of his reign with the neglecting for some short time his best and faithfullest freinds but that was soon over. He was the greatest, wisest and bravest prince of his age and his faults were as few as any, his virtues more than any King now reigning. Those that opposed him living lamented his death. [Ha]d he lived longer it may bee hee might have lived more to our good then to his own glory and honour.[19]

Perhaps the most heartfelt words of grief emanated from the veteran presbyterian minister, Oliver Heywood. 'God hath herin taken the crown from our head, our defence under god is departed from us', mused Heywood two days after the King's death:

> O what use might he have been of, yea and he was of! how many blows did he shield us from! how seasonably did the Lord bring him in! what a nursing father he had been! what peace have we had in his days! what influence hath his incouragements and Example been! But alas how little can one man doe unlesse he have some to assist him! however it is a matter of lamentation that

such a mans place is vacant . . . Blessed be god that we have had such a one that hath kept sinners in awe, and now it may be feared wickednesse will grow rampant, and hell wil break loose.[20]

Yet for all this, England in March 1702 did not look like a nation plunged into grief. 'I never saw soe few mourners as were att Worcester', noted a correspondent of Robert Harley on the 14th.[21] Nor was there any rending of clothes among the citizens of Bath. 'I never saw so short a sorow as was here,' wrote Abigail Pye, one of Harley's numerous cousins, on 25 March. On the contrary, 'the high church' were 'elevated hereabouts.'[22] That air of triumphalism was not confined to Bath. 'It wou'd move ones indignation against Humane kind, to hear how some Triumph at the death of this Great Prince, whom God made our Deliverer from Popery, and by consequence Slavery', confided the Hertfordshire gentlewoman, Lady Sarah Cowper, to her diary on the day after King William's death.[23] The following month, she was appalled by her son's report of the King's funeral in London. 'The most observable thing to me was, that in an Assembly on such an occasion he saw but two persons [one of them, Lord Somers] appear much moved with any humane Affections . . . Divers others on whom he had heap'd Riches and Honour, put not on so much as an Air of Decency.'[24]

The prevailing public mood was denounced by Defoe in his poem, *The Mock Mourners.* 'With what Contempt', he asked,

> . . . will English Men appear,
> When future Ages read his Character?
> They'll never bear to hear in time to come,
> How he was lov'd abroad, and scorn'd at home.
> The World will scarce believe it cou'd be true,
> And Vengeance must such Insolence pursue.
> Our Nation will by all Men be abhorr'd,
> And William's juster Fame be so restor'd.
>   Posterity, when Histories relate
> His Glorious Deeds, will ask, What Giant's that?
> For common Vertues may Mens Fame advance,
> But an immoderate Glory turns Romance.
> Its real Merit does it self undo,
> Men talk it up so high, it can't be true:
> So William's Life, encreas'd by doubling Fame,
> Will drown his Actions to preserve his Name.
> The annals of his Conduct they'll revise,
> As Legends of Impossibilities.
> 'Twill all a Life of Miracles appear,
> Too great for Him to do, or Them to hear.
> And if some faithful Writer shou'd set down
> With what Uneasiness he wore the Crown;
> What thankless Devil had the Land possest;

> This will be more prodigious than the rest.
> With Indignation 'twill their Minds inspire,
> And raise the Glory of his Actions higher.
> The Records of their Fathers they'll Deface,
> And blush to think they sprung from such a Race.
> They'll be asham'd their Ancestors to own,
> And strive their Father's Follies to atone.
> New Monuments of Gratitude they'll raise,
> And Crown his Memory with Thanks and Praise.[25]

In the long-run, Defoe was proved correct. By the late-eighteenth century, the revolution and its architect had become the objects of veneration across the political spectrum.[26] But in March 1702 High Churchmen especially saw little reason to revere King William's memory. Shortly after the King's death, Charles Allestree, tory pamphleteer and vicar of the Northamptonshire parish of Daventry, wrote a revealing letter to an acquaintance, Dr John Younger. The good doctor was disturbed by reports that the local gentry had publicly celebrated the King's demise. Allestree took umbrage at this suggestion. There had indeed been celebrations, but these had been to mark Queen Anne's accession, not King William's death. 'And yet', Allestree could not resist adding,

> I will not Dissemble my Thoughts to you upon this matter. I can consider the late King in several Views. When I look upon Him as the Restorer of our Libertys, and the great Asserter of the Common Cause of Europe, He Appears in this Aspect, a Glorious Heroe, and worthy of the Highest Honours: But when I take my Thoughts upon him, in his Ecclesiastical Capacity, and consider the Affairs of the Church under his Administration, he not only sinks in my esteem, but is Remember'd with Horror: For the Members of the Church of England were never threaten'd with so much Danger from popery, as They were from a Set of Men that He countenanc'd and abetted in their wicked Contrivance to destroy the Establish'd Church.[27]

Although Allestree's language was unusually forthright, it accurately reflects the deep resentment which King William's policies had generated in adherents of the Church party. The overthrow of episcopacy in Scotland; the emancipation of dissent in England; the 'latitudinarian' control of the episcopal bench; and the political dominance of whiggery in the middle years of the reign, these had all helped to convince tories that the King was no friend to the Church of England. King William's reign, like King James's before it, had placed enormous strains on the tory ideology of Church and Crown. For as the reign progressed, it became painfully clear that the two elements of that creed, wrenched apart by James II, remained sundered. The Church party had not regained the Crown.[28]

Small wonder, then, that tories rejoiced at the accession of that true daughter of the Church, Queen Anne. In her portly frame, the sundered halves of their party's ideology would at last be reunited. This was a prospect which filled Oliver Heywood with dread. King William, he remembered, was

> a faithfull friend to poor dissenters obtained for them a legall liberty dispensing with the law by Act of Parliament, issuing out a proclamation for it, which hath continued 14 yeares, blessed be god, we have prayd for him, he hath oft professed to severall N[on] C[onformist] ministers that occasionally addressed him, or did converse with him, that he would stand our friend as long as he lived, and he hath made his words good, but he's gone and Queen Ann (another of K[ing] James daughters) is to succeed who, they say is an high Episcopall woman, and what shall we now doe?[29]

But in tory breasts, the Queen's accession aroused expectations of a second and more glorious Restoration, a golden new dawn for the 'Cavalier' cause after the wretched Williamite interlude.

This was a fitting conclusion to King William's reign. For in its ideological imperatives and contradictions, its hopes unfulfilled and fears unallayed, the reign of William III had come to resemble nothing so much as the Cromwellian Protectorate.

Notes

PREFACE AND ACKNOWLEDGEMENTS

1   Henry Horwitz, 'The 1690s Revisited: Recent Work on Politics and Political Ideas in the Reign of William III', *Parliamentary History*, 15 (1996), 361–77, at 361 n.1.

2   J.C.D. Clark, *English Society 1688–1832: Ideology, social structure and political practice during the ancien regime* (Cambridge, 1985), pp. 6–7.

CHAPTER ONE   WILLIAM THE CONQUEROR

1   The best modern account of the events of King James's reign and the subsequent revolution settlement is W.A. Speck, *Reluctant Revolutionaries: Englishmen and the Revolution of 1688* (Oxford, 1988).

2   For the crisis of the early 1680s, see Tim Harris, *London Crowds in the Reign of Charles II: Propaganda and Politics from the Restoration to the Exclusion Crisis* (Cambridge, 1987); Jonathan Scott, *Algernon Sidney and the Restoration Crisis, 1677–1683* (Cambridge, 1991); Mark Knights, *Politics and Opinion in Crisis, 1678–1681* (Cambridge, 1994). For a useful summary, see Lionel K.J. Glassey, 'Politics, Finance and Government' in *idem*, ed., *The Reigns of Charles II and James VII & II* (1997), pp. 36–70, esp. 61–9.

3   Mark Goldie, 'John Locke's Circle and James II', *HJ*, 35 (1992), 557–86; *idem*, 'James II and the Dissenters' Revenge: the Commission of Enquiry of 1688', *Historical Research*, 66 (1993), 53–88.

4   Tim Harris, *Politics Under the Later Stuarts: Party Conflict in a Divided Society 1660–1715* (Harlow, 1993), pp. 123–8.

5   The standard English-language biography is Stephen Baxter, *William III* (1966). For the Dutch background, see Jonathan I. Israel, *The Dutch Republic: Its Rise, Greatness, and Fall 1477–1806* (Oxford, 1995), pp. 796–841.

6   Dale Hoak, 'The Anglo-Dutch Revolution of 1688–89' in Dale Hoak and Mordechai Feingold, eds, *The World of William and Mary: Anglo-Dutch Perspectives on the Revolution of 1688–89* (Stanford, 1996), pp. 1–26, at 22–4; Simon Groenveld, ' "J'equippe une flotte tres considerable": The Dutch Side of the Glorious Revolution' in Robert Beddard, ed., *The Revolutions of*

1688 (Oxford, 1991), pp. 213–45, at 239.

7   Jonathan I. Israel, 'The Dutch role in the Glorious Revolution' in *idem*, ed., *The Anglo-Dutch Moment: Essays on the Glorious Revolution and its world impact* (Cambridge, 1991), pp. 105–62, esp. 112–15.

8   Ibid., pp. 116–19; K.H.D. Haley, 'The Dutch, the invasion of England, and the alliance of 1689' in Lois G. Schwoerer, ed., *The Revolution of 1688–1689: Changing perspectives* (Cambridge, 1992), pp. 21–34, at 25–6; Groenveld, '"J'equippe une flotte tres considerable"', pp. 240–1.

9   Jonathan I. Israel and Geoffrey Parker, 'Of Providence and Protestant Winds: the Spanish Armada of 1588 and the Dutch armada of 1688' in Israel, ed., *Anglo-Dutch Moment*, pp. 335–63, at 337–8; Israel, 'Dutch role', p. 106.

10 For a more optimistic view of the impact of King James's concessions, see Tony Claydon, 'William III's Declaration of Reasons and the Glorious Revolution', *HJ*, 39 (1996), 87–108, at 95–7.

11 BL Add MS 63057B, fol. 128.

12 Jonathan Israel suggests that no more than half of King James's 40,000 soldiers were mustered at Salisbury; see Israel, 'Dutch role', pp. 124–5.

13 Robert Beddard, *A Kingdom without a King: The Journal of the Provisional Government in the Revolution of 1688* (Phaidon, Oxford, 1988), pp. 34–5.

14 Robert Beddard, 'The Unexpected Whig Revolution of 1688' in *idem*, ed., *Revolutions of 1688*, pp. 11–101, at 16.

15 Ibid., pp. 23–42.

16 Claydon, 'William III's Declaration of Reasons', pp. 101–3.

17 A more radical first draft was watered down by whig leaders in order to ingratiate themselves with Prince William; see Beddard, 'Unexpected Whig Revolution', pp. 97–9.

18 For the Irish war, see J.G. Simms, *Jacobite Ireland 1685–91* (1969); Harman Murtagh, 'The War in Ireland 1689–91' in W.A. Maguire, ed., *Kings in Conflict: The Revolutionary War in Ireland and its Aftermath 1689–1750* (Belfast, 1990), pp. 61–91; David Hayton, 'The Williamite Revolution in Ireland, 1688–91' in Israel, ed., *Anglo-Dutch Moment*, pp. 185–213.

19 Paul Hopkins, *Glencoe and the End of the Highland War* (Edinburgh, 1986), p. 126.

20 J.G. Simms, *Jacobite Ireland 1685–91* (1969), p. 65; Hopkins, *Glencoe*, pp. 140, 154–5.

21 The Jacobite rising in Scotland and its aftermath are exhaustively described in Hopkins, *Glencoe*.

CHAPTER TWO   KING WILLIAM AND HIS CONTEMPORARIES

1   *The Rev. Oliver Heywood, B.A. 1630–1702; His Autobiography, Diaries, Anecdote and Event Books*, ed., J. Horsfall Turner (4 vols, Brighouse and Bingley, 1882–5), III, 234–5.

2   John Tanner, *Angelus Britannicus. An Ephemeris for the Year of our Redemption, 1690* (1690), verse headings to the months of January, April and May.

3   *A Sermon Preached upon The Fast-Day, June the 18th 1690. By a Presbyter of the Church of England, that Swore in the Sincerity of his Heart, with a full satisfied Conscience, to King William and Queen Mary* (1690), pp. 12–13.

4   *In Memory of ye Deliverance from Popery & Slavery by King William III in MDCLXXXVIII* (1689).

5   Tony Claydon, *William III and the Godly Revolution* (Cambridge, 1996), esp. chs 1–3.

6   John Morrill, 'Cromwell and his contemporaries' in *idem*, ed., *Oliver Cromwell and the English Revolution* (1990), pp. 259–81, at 271–3.

7   Tanner, *Angelus Britannicus . . . for the Year . . . 1690*, verse at the head of the astrological observations.

8   Henry Meriton, *A Sermon Preacht at the Cathedral Church in Norwich, Upon the 11th of April, 1696. The Day of His Majesties Coronation* (1696), p. 26.

9   For the analogy between Moses and Cromwell, see Morrill, 'Cromwell and his contemporaries', pp. 271–2.

10   [Richard Blackmore], *A Short History of the Last Parliament* (1699), p. 11.

11   *The Murmurers. A Poem* (1689), pp. 2–3.

12   Ibid., p. 3.

13   Ibid., p. 4.

14   Blackmore, *Short History*, p. 11.

15   *Mercurius Reformatus: Or the New Observator*, 9 July 1690.

16   *A Sermon Preach'd at the Chappel Royal in the Tower Upon the Death of her Sacred Majesty, Our late Gracious Queen Mary* (1695), p. 27.

17   Blackmore, *Short History*, p. 3.

18   John Petter, *A Sermon Preached before Their Majesties, K. William and Q. Mary's Forces, At Gant in Flanders, The Sunday before they marched into the Camp, 1694* (1694), p. 28.

19   John Partridge, *Merlinus Liberatus. Being an Almanack for the Year of Our Redemption, 1692* (1692), verse beneath the regal table.

20   William Lawrence to Sir Michael Hicks, 29 March 1693, *The Pyramid and the Urn. The Life in Letters of a Restoration Squire: William Lawrence of Shurdington, 1636–1697*, ed. Iona Sinclair (Stroud, 1994), pp. 101–2.

21   See below, pp. 124, 126.

22   William Lawrence to William Powlett, 27 Oct 1693, *The Pyramid and the Urn*, p. 104.

23   *Pepys Ballads*, VII, 106–7.

24   Thomas Yalden, *On the Conquest of Namur. A Pindarique Ode* (1695), pp. 9–10.

25   Meriton, *Sermon Preacht*, p. 26.

26   Petter, *Sermon Preached*, pp. 28–9.

27   *Pepys Ballads*, VI, 68.

28   *To the most Illustrious and Serene Prince, His Royal Highness, William Henry Prince of Orange and Nassau* (1688).

29   Jonathan I. Israel, 'The Dutch role in the Glorious Revolution' in *idem*, ed., *The Anglo-Dutch Moment: Essays on the Glorious Revolution and its world impact* (Cambridge, 1991), pp. 105–62, esp. 136–9; *idem*, 'William III and Toleration' in Ole Peter Grell, Jonathan I. Israel and Nicholas Tyacke, eds, *From Persecution to Toleration: The Glorious Revolution and Religion in England* (Oxford, 1991), pp. 129–70, esp. 139–41, 146–50.

30   Ibid., pp. 155–7; Nicholas Tyacke, 'The "Rise of Puritanism" and the Legalizing of Dissent, 1571–1719' in Grell, Israel and Tyacke, eds, *From Persecution to Toleration*, pp. 17–49, at 42; John Bossy, 'English Catholics after

1688' in ibid., pp. 369–87, esp. 369–78.

31 BL Add MS 63057B, fol. 138.

32 Stephen B. Baxter, 'William III as Hercules: the political implications of court culture' in Lois G. Schwoerer, ed., *The Revolution of 1688–1689* (Cambridge, 1992), pp. 95–106; Robert P. Macubbin and Martha Hamilton-Philips, eds, *The Age of William III and Mary II: Power, Politics, and Patronage 1688–1702* (Williamsburg, Virginia, 1989), pp. 8–10; Claydon, *William III and the Godly Revolution*, pp. 72–3 and dust-jacket illustration.

33 *Pepys Ballads*, V, 256.

34 Samuel Barton, *A Sermon Preached at St Mary le Bow before the Right Honourable the Lord Mayor and Court of Aldermen on Wednesday the 16th of July, being the Fast Day* (1690), pp. 26–7.

35 *Idem, A Sermon Preach'd before the Honourable House of Commons, at St Margaret's Westminster, Upon the 16th of April 1696* (1696), p. 22.

36 *A Word to the Wise* (1701), p. 3.

37 [John Sergeant], *An Historical Romance of the Wars, Between the Mighty Giant Gallieno, And the Great Knight Nasonius, And His Associates* (Dublin, 1694), pp. 23–7.

38 *A Letter from the King of Great Britain to the Earl of Portland* (1690/1?), *Somers Tracts*, X, 559–67, at 566.

39 *POAS*, V, 488.

40 Ibid., p. 453.

41 *POAS*, VI, 15.

42 [Nathaniel Johnston], *The Dear Bargain; or, a true Representation of the State of the English Nation under the Dutch* (1690?), *Somers Tracts*, X, 349–77, at 356.

43 Ibid., p. 371.

44 *A Modest Apology for the loyal Protestant Subjects of King James, who desire his Restoration, without Prejudice to our Religion, Laws or Liberties* (1692), *Somers Tracts*, X, 401–29, at 412.

45 Ibid., pp. 408–9.

46 *The Belgick Boar* (1695).

47 [Charlwood Lawton], *A Letter formerly sent to Dr Tillotson, and for Want of an Answer made publick, and now reprinted, with the said Doctor's Letter to the Lord Russel, a little before his Execution* (1691?), *Somers Tracts*, IX, 367–72, at 369.

48 *Observations upon the late Revolution in England* (1690), *Somers Tracts*, X, 336–48, at 340.

49 *POAS*, V, 51–2 .

50 The description is that of Nasonius in [Sergeant], *Historical Romance*, p. 5.

51 [Robert Ferguson], *Whether the preserving the Protestant Religion was the Motive unto, or the End that was designed in, the late Revolution? In a Letter to a Country Gentleman, as an Answer to his first Query* (1695), *Somers Tracts*, IX, 543–69, at 564.

52 *POAS*, V, 38.

53 Ibid., p. 42. See also [Sergeant], *Historical Romance*, where Bentinck appears in the guise of Nasonius's favourite, Sodomicus.

54 *POAS*, VI, 17–18.

55 *Modest Apology*, pp. 418, 428.

56	[Johnston], *Dear Bargain*, p. 369.
57	[Ferguson], *Whether the preserving*, p. 563.
58	*POAS*, V, 47–8. See also *The Belgick Boar*, where King William is described as 'The stubborn Tarquin void of Grace'.
59	*POAS*, V, 250.
60	Ibid., p. 424. For the elder Somers, see William L. Sachse, *Lord Somers: A Political Portrait* (Manchester, 1975), p. 2.
61	*POAS*, V, p. 43.
62	[Charles Leslie], *Querela Temporum; or, the Danger of the Church of England. In a Letter from the Dean of* ——— *to* ——— *Prebend of* ——— (1694), *Somers Tracts*, IX, 509–27, at 519.
63	See below, pp. 212–16.
64	[Johnston], *Dear Bargain*, pp. 367–8.
65	[Leslie], *Querela Temporum*, p. 520.
66	[Sergeant], *Historical Romance*, p. 29.
67	*A Modest Apology*, p. 418.
68	[Sergeant], *Historical Romance*, pp. 32–3.
69	*Observations upon the late Revolution*, p. 344.
70	[Johnston], *Dear Bargain*, p. 374.
71	*Min Heer T. Van C's Answer to Min Heer H. Van L's Letter of the 15th March 1689; representing the true Interest of Holland, and what they have already gained by our Losses* (1690), *Somers Tracts*, X, 314–18, at 318.
72	Ferguson, *Whether the preserving*, p. 555.
73	Israel, 'Dutch role', pp. 128, 145–6.
74	*Letter from the King of Great Britain*, p. 567.
75	[Johnston], *Dear Bargain*, p. 375.
76	*The Price of the Abdication* (1693?), *Somers Tracts*, IX, 451–63, at 456.
77	*A modest Apology*, p. 428.
78	[Johnston], *Dear Bargain*, p. 377.
79	*Belgick Boar*.
80	[James Montgomery], *Great Britain's just Complaint for her late Measures, present Sufferings, and the future Miseries she is exposed to* (1692), *Somers Tracts*, X, 429–71, at 454.
81	BL Add MS 63057B, fol. 103.
82	BL Add MS 20007, II, 58.
83	Gilbert Burnet, *History of His Own Time* (6 vols, Oxford, 1823), IV, 146–7.
84	John Childs, *The British Army of William III, 1689–1702* (Manchester, 1987), pp. 73–4;
85	*The Parliamentary Diary of Narcissus Luttrell 1691–1693*, ed. Henry Horwitz (Oxford, 1972), p. 109.
86	Ibid., p. 243.
87	Ibid., p. 252.
88	*Gloria Cambria: Or, The Speech of a Bold Briton in Parliament, against a Dutch Prince of Wales* (1702), *Somers Tracts*, XI, 387–93, at 391.
89	*POAS*, V, 142.
90	BL Add MS 70014, fol. 353. For King William's troubled relations with the whig party in the early 1690s, see below, pp. 73–6, 78–81.
91	Claydon, *William III and the Godly Revolution*, pp. 164–77.

92 See below, pp. 88–9, 168, 191, 216, 268.
93 See below, p. 72.
94 Thomas Bowber, *A Sermon Preached in the Parish-Church of St Swithin, London, March 10th 1694/5 Upon the Much Lamented Death Of our Most Gracious Queen* (1695), p. 24.
95 William Payne, *A Sermon Upon the Death of the Queen, Preached in the Parish-Church of St Mary White-Chappel* (1695, 3rd edn), p. 16.
96 See below, pp. 186–7, 203–4.
97 Edward Fowler, *A Discourse Of the Great Disingenuity & Unreasonableness Of Repining at Afflicting Providences* (1695), preface, p. 17.
98 BL Add MS 63057B, fol. 158.
99 *The Diary of Abraham de la Pryme*, ed. Charles Jackson (Durham, Surtees Soc 54, 1870), p. 48.
100 BL Add MS 63057B, fol. 162.
101 William Lawrence to Sir Michael Hicks, 5 Jan. 1695, *The Pyramid and the Urn*, p. 111.
102 *The Diary and Letter Book of the Rev Thomas Brockbank 1671–1709*, ed. Richard Trappes-Lomax (Chetham Soc, 1930), pp. 76–7.
103 A[bigail] Pye to Abigail Harley, 13 March 1695, BL Add MS 70018, fol. 7.
104 *POAS*, V, 157. The author of this piece has confused Tarquin, the usurping son-in-law, with Tullius, the murdered King of Rome. See also ibid., p. 52; [Johnston], *Dear Bargain*, p. 371.
105 *Memoirs of Mary Queen of England*, ed. R. Doebner (1886), p. 11.
106 Lawton, *Letter formerly sent to Dr Tillotson*, pp. 369–70.
107 [Thomas Ken], *A Letter to the Author of a Sermon Entituled, A Sermon Preach'd At the Funeral Of Her late Majesty Queen Mary, Of ever Blessed Memory* (1695), pp. 6–7.
108 BL Add MS 5540, fol. 26.
109 [Leslie], *Querela Temporum*, pp. 515–19.
110 Ibid., p. 526.
111 *The Life of that Incomparable Princess Mary, Our Late Sovereign Lady, Of ever Blessed Memory* (1695), p. 73.
112 *Sermon Preach'd at the Chappel Royal*, p. 26.
113 Ibid., p. 25.
114 *Life of that Incomparable Princess*, p. 78.
115 William Sherlock, *A Sermon Preached at the Temple-Church, December 30 1694. Upon the Sad Occasion of the Death of our Gracious Queen* (Dublin, 1695), p. 13.
116 Thomas Bowber, *A Sermon Preached in the Parish-Church of St Swithin, London, March 10th 1694/5 Upon the Much Lamented Death Of our Most Gracious Queen* (1695), pp. 27–8.
117 Fowler, *Discourse Of the Great Disingenuity*, preface, p. 42.
118 Paul Hopkins, 'Aspects of Jacobite Conspiracy in England in the Reign of William III' (University of Cambridge Ph.D. dissertation, 1981), pp. 246–64.
119 Ibid., pp. 63–4, 91–2, 285–94; John Ehrman, *The Navy in the War of William III 1689–97: Its State and Direction* (Cambridge, 1953), pp. 384–96; Eveline Cruickshanks, 'Attempts to Restore the Stuarts, 1689–96' in Eveline Cruickshanks and Edward Corp, eds, *The Stuart Court in Exile and the Jacobites* (1995), pp. 1–13, at 4–6.

120 Hopkins, 'Aspects of Jacobite Conspiracy', p. 347; Daniel Szechi, 'The Jacobite Revolution Settlement, 1689–1696', *EHR*, 108 (1993), 610–28, esp. 621–5.

121 Hopkins, 'Aspects of Jacobite Conspiracy', pp. 316–17, 335, 338–9. See also below, p. 81.

122 *POAS*, V, 200.

123 Hopkins, 'Aspects of Jacobite Conspiracy', pp. 277–8.

124 Henry Horwitz, *Parliament, policy and politics in the reign of William III* (Manchester, 1977), p. 103.

125 Hopkins, 'Aspects of Jacobite Conspiracy', p. 201.

126 Childs, *British Army of William III*, pp. 222–6; Hopkins, 'Aspects of Jacobite Conspiracy', pp. 381–3.

127 Childs, *British Army of William III*, pp. 232–4.

128 Hopkins, 'Aspects of Jacobite Conspiracy', p. 481.

129 Ibid., pp. 233–4, 237–8, 482. The most detailed account of the 'Assassination Plot' is Jane Garrett, *The Triumphs of Providence: The Assassination Plot of 1696* (Cambridge, 1980).

130 Horwitz, *Parliament, policy and politics*, p. 168.

131 Hopkins, 'Aspects of Jacobite Conspiracy', p. 238. Barclay himself evaded capture and slipped back to France.

132 Ehrman, *Navy in the War of William III* , p. 574.

133 Sir Edmund King to Lord Hatton, 25 Feb 1696, *Hatton Correspondence*, II, 220.

134 Horwitz, *Parliament, policy and politics*, pp. 175–6.

135 DWL MS 28.4, fols 74–5.

136 Bod MS Eng. Hist. b. 209, fol 39.

137 *The Triumph's of Providence over Hell, France & Rome, In the Defeating & Discovering of the late Hellish and Barbarous PLOTT, for Assassinating his Royall Majesty King William ye III* (1696).

138 Paul Monod, 'The Jacobite Press and English Censorship, 1689–95' in Cruickshanks and Corp, eds, *Stuart Court in Exile*, pp. 125–42, at 138–40. Anderton was convicted of treason for printing the notorious Jacobite tract, *Remarks upon the present Confederacy*.

139 Hopkins, 'Aspects of Jacobite Conspiracy', pp. 102–3, 183–5.

140 Garrett, *Triumphs of Providence*, chs 12–15; David Ogg, *England in the Reigns of James II and William III* (Oxford, 1955), pp. 435–6.

141 Quoted in Daniel Szechi, 'The Jacobite Theatre of Death' in Eveline Cruickshanks and Jeremy Black, eds, *The Jacobite Challenge* (Edinburgh, 1988), pp. 57–73, at 63.

142 *The Diary of John Evelyn*, ed. E.S. de Beer (6 vols, Oxford, 1955), V, 233.

143 See below, p. 92.

144 Ogg, *England in the Reigns*, p. 438.

145 *POAS*, V, 513–14.

146 Burnet, *History of His Own Time*, IV, 390.

147 Horwitz, *Parliament, policy and politics*, pp. 248–55.

148 Burnet, *History of His Own Time*, IV, 431.

149 W.A. Maguire, 'The Land Settlement' in *idem*, ed., *Kings in Conflict: The Revolutionary War in Ireland and its Aftermath 1689–1750* (Belfast, 1990), pp. 139–56, esp. 148–52; Horwitz, *Parliament, policy and politics*,

pp. 63, 255–6, 262–8.

150 *POAS,* VI, 236, 238.

151 Ibid., 235, 241. The last line was presumably an allusion to Portland's role in negotiating the Treaty of Ryswick.

152 Ibid., 299.

153 Ibid., 294.

154 Ibid., 299–300.

155 David Hayton, 'The "Country" interest and the party system, 1689–*c.*1720' in Clyve Jones, ed., *Party and Management in Parliament 1660–1784* (Leicester, 1984), pp. 37–85, at 60–3.

156 *POAS,* VI, 241.

157 As reported by James Vernon to the Duke of Shrewsbury, 9 April 1700, *Vernon Correspondence,* III, 13.

158 Horwitz, *Parliament, policy and politics,* pp. 35, 40.

159 *Memoirs of Mary,* p. 24.

160 Horwitz, *Parliament, policy and politics,* pp. 67, 76; Edward Gregg, *Queen Anne* (1980), pp. 80, 84–8.

161 *Memoirs of Mary,* pp. 45–6.

162 Robert Harley to Sir Edward Harley, 30 July 1700, BL Add MS 70019, fol. 230.

163 BL Add MS 70020, fol. 9.

164 DWL Morrice MS Q, fol. 597; Horwitz, *Parliament, policy and politics,* pp. 30, 34, 36.

165 Vernon to Shrewsbury, 15 Aug. 1700, *Vernon Correspondence,* III, 129.

166 John Ellis to Robert Harley, 3 Sept. 1700, BL Add MS 70019, fol. 230.

167 Vernon to Shrewsbury, 27 Aug. 1700, *Vernon Correspondence,* III, 133–4.

168 Same to the same, 10 Oct. 1700, ibid., 141.

169 Horwitz, *Parliament, policy and politics,* pp. 283–4; W.A. Speck, *The Birth of Britain: A New Nation 1700–1710* (Oxford, Basil Blackwell, 1994), pp. 24–5.

170 'DH' to 'DC', 17 March 1701, BL Add MS 28886, fol. 375. For the background to these ministerial changes, see below, p. 99.

171 'DH' to 'DC', 17 March 1701, BL Add MS 28886, fols 376–7. Only one tory, John Granville, is known to have spoken in favour of the Jacobite option during the debates on the Settlement Bill; *The Parliamentary Diary of Sir Richard Cocks 1698–1702,* ed. David W. Hayton (Oxford, 1996), p. xlvii.

172 The Act of Settlement can be found in E.N. Williams, ed., *The Eighteenth-Century Constitution 1688–1815* (Cambridge, 1960), pp. 56–60.

173 See below, pp. 164–5.

CHAPTER THREE   PARTIES AND POLITICS

1 Printed in A.F.W. Papillon, *Memoirs of Thomas Papillon, of London, Merchant (1623–1702)* (Reading, 1877), p. 374.

2 Jonathan Scott, *Algernon Sidney and the Restoration Crisis, 1677–1683* (Cambridge, 1991), p. 48.

3 Geoffrey Holmes, *British Politics in the Age of Anne* (2nd edn, 1987), ch. 9.

4 Henry Horwitz, *Parliament, policy and politics in the reign of William III* (Manchester, 1977), pp. 298–9. For the confusion surrounding the outcome

of the elections of 1695 and 1698, and the first election of 1701, see ibid., pp. 157–8, 239–40, 280.

5   Ibid., p. 217.
6   For a similar approach, see Tim Harris, *Politics under the Later Stuarts: Party Conflict in a Divided Society 1660–1715* (Harlow, 1993), p. 5.
7   *The State of Parties, and of the Publick, as influenc'd by those Parties in this Conjuncture, offer'd to Englishmen* (1692), *State Tracts*, II, 208–17, at 211–12.
8   Grey, *Debates*, IX, 82.
9   [John Toland], *The Danger of Mercenary parliaments* (1698), pp. 2–3.
10   [Slingsby Bethel], *The Providences of God, observed through Several Ages, Towards this Nation* (1691), p. 11; [Jean Gailhard], *Some Observations upon the Keeping the Thirtieth of January and Twenty-ninth of May* (1694), *Somers Tracts*, IX, 481–509, at 488.
11   *A Dialogue betwixt Whig and Tory, Alias Williamite and Jacobite* (1693), p. 21.
12   *Plain English: Humbly offered to Consideration of His Majesty, And his Great Council, the Lords and Commons In Parliament Assembled* (1690), p. 24.
13   For whig martyrology, see Melinda Zook, ' "The Bloody Assizes": Whig Martyrdom and Memory after the Glorious Revolution', *Albion*, 27 (1995), 373–96.
14   Tim Harris, *London Crowds in the Reign of Charles II: Propaganda and politics from the Restoration until the Exclusion crisis* (Cambridge, 1987), pp. 133–44; idem, *Politics under the Later Stuarts*, pp. 119–23; Scott, *Sidney and the Restoration*, pp. 45–7.
15   *The Diary and Autobiography of Edmund Bohun Esq.*, ed. S. Wilton Rix (Beccles, 1853), p. 127.
16   Grey, *Debates*, X, 55.
17   BL Stowe MS 119, fol. 45. For the nature and dating of this source, see n. 134 below.
18   Ibid., fol. 47.
19   Bod. MS Eng. Hist. b. 209, fol. 73.
20   *The Kentish Men. A Satyr* (1701).
21   Robert Beddard, 'The Unexpected Whig Revolution of 1688' in *idem*, ed, *The Revolutions of 1688* (Oxford, 1991), pp. 11–101, at 81.
22   For whom, see A.B. Worden, 'Introduction' to Edmund Ludlow, *A Voyce from the Watch Tower: Part Five: 1660–1662* (Camden Soc., 4th Series, 21, 1978).
23   Barbara Taft, 'Return of a Regicide: Edmund Ludlow and the Glorious Revolution', *History*, 76 (1991), 197–220, at 219–20.
24   [Gailhard], *Some Observations*, pp. 481–3.
25   Roger Coke, *A Detection of the Court and State of England during the Four last Reigns, And the Inter-Regnum* (2 vols, 1694), I, 205–6.
26   Ibid., pp. 211–12.
27   [John Trenchard], *A Short History of Standing Armies in England* (1698), p. 6.
28   *Plain English*, p. 3.
29   John Partridge, *Merlinus Liberatus: Being an Almanack for the Year of our Redemption, 1692* (1692). Partridge's gloss on Naseby was omitted from some editions of the 1692 almanac. My reference is to the edition preserved in BL PP. 2465 (1692).

30 *Dialogue betwixt Whig and Tory*, p. 3.
31 *A Letter from a Gentleman in the Country to his Representative in Parliament, shewing the expedience of taking away 25 Ca. 2ca.2. as to making the receiving of the Sacrament a Qualification for an Office* (1689?).
32 POAS, V, 131.
33 *A Letter from a Country Gentleman, to an Eminent but Easy Citizen, who was unhappily misguided in the fatal election of Sir John Moore for Lord Mayor of London, at Michaelmas 1681* (1692).
34 J.P. Kenyon, *Revolution Principles: The Politics of Party 1689–1720* (Cambridge, 1977), pp. 32–4.
35 *Dialogue betwixt Whig and Tory*, p. 23.
36 Somerset Records Office DD/SF 3368. I owe this reference to Mark Goldie. See also Richard Ashcraft, *Revolutionary Politics & Locke's Two Treatises of Government* (Princeton, New Jersey, 1986), pp. 597–600.
37 BL Stowe MS 119, fol. 47.
38 W. G[lover] to [Edmun Bohun], 7 March 1690, CUL Sel. 3. 237[34] (rare books).
39 Harris, *Politics under the Later Stuarts*, pp. 123–9; Mark Goldie, 'James II and the Dissenters' Revenge: the Commission of Enquiry of 1688', *Historical Research*, 66 (1993), 53–88; D.N. Marshall, 'Protestant Dissent in England in the Reign of James II' (Hull University Ph.D. dissertation, 1976), pp. 287–94, 377.
40 Grey, *Debates*, IX, 198.
41 Ibid., X, 57.
42 P.A. Hopkins, 'Aspects of Jacobite Conspiracy in England in the Reign of William III' (Cambridge University Ph.D. dissertation, 1981), pp. 128–36.
43 Beddard, 'Unexpected Whig Revolution', pp. 18–94.
44 Bod. MS Ballard 45, fol. 57.
45 Horwitz, *Parliament, policy and politics*, pp. 17–18.
46 *The Diary of John Evelyn*, ed. E.S. de Beer (6 vols, Oxford, 1955), IV, 635.
47 Horwitz, *Parliament, policy and politics*, pp. 18–19; E.L. Ellis, 'William III and the Politicians' in Geoffrey Holmes, ed., *Britain after the Glorious Revolution 1689–1714* (1969), pp. 115–34, esp. 117–21.
48 Henry Horwitz, *Revolution Politicks: The Career of Daniel Finch, Second Earl of Nottingham, 1647–1730* (Cambridge, 1968), pp. 39–41, 75–83; Keith Feiling, *A History of the Tory Party, 1640–1714* (Oxford, 1924), pp. 258–60.
49 BL Add MS 63057B, fol. 138.
50 Horwitz, *Parliament, policy and politics*, pp. 18–19; Beddard, 'Unexpected Whig Revolution', pp. 33–4.
51 BL Add MS 63057B, fol. 138.
52 J.R. Western, *Monarchy and Revolution: The English State in the 1680s* (1972), p. 86; W.A. Speck, *Reluctant Revolutionaries: Englishmen and the Revolution of 1688* (Oxford, 1988), pp. 88; Horwitz, *Parliament, policy and politics*, p. 19.
53 Ibid., pp. 18–19; Western, *Monarchy and Revolution*, pp. 34, 276–7, 329–30; Speck, *Reluctant Revolutionaries*, pp. 32, 85–6, 220.
54 *POAS*, V, 175. See also Grey, *Debates*, X, 143–4.
55 BL Add MS 63057B, fol. 138.
56 DWL Morice MS Q, p. 654.

57 Grey, *Debates*, IX, 487. For an alternative version of this speeech, see DWL Morrice MS R, p. 46.
58 Thomas Wharton to King William, 25 Dec. 1689, BL Add MS 4155, fols. 3–4.
59 Ibid., fol. 7.
60 Grey, *Debates*, IX, 138.
61 Ibid., p. 322.
62 Ibid., p. 255.
63 DWL Morrice MS Q, p. 566. For the establishment of the Committee of Grievances, see Western, *Monarchy and Revolution*, p. 343.
64 Horwitz, *Parliament, policy and politics*, pp. 29–30.
65 Wharton to King William, 25 Dec. 1689, BL Add MS 4155, fol. 3.
66 For the tortuous progress of the Indemnity Bill, see Horwitz, *Parliament, policy and politics*, pp. 30, 37, 43.
67 DWL Morrice MS Q, p. 655.
68 *A Word of Advice unto all those that have a Right to Choose Parliament-Men* (1690), p. 1.
69 Horwitz, *Parliament, policy and politics*, pp. 33–4, 40–1.
70 Ibid., p. 42.
71 DWL Morrice MS R, p. 77.
72 Horwitz, *Parliament, policy and politics*, pp. 43–4.
73 DWL Morrice MS R, p. 113.
74 Horwitz, *Parliament, policy and politics*, p. 50.
75 Ibid., pp. 50–1; *idem*, 'The General Election of 1690', *JBS*, XI (1971–2), 77–91.
76 We lack a comprehensive study of the electoral politics of the 1690s. This should be remedied when the History of Parliament volumes for 1690–1715 are published.
77 *A Letter to a Friend, upon the Dissolving of the late Parliament, and the Calling of a New One* (1690).
78 [Roger L'Estrange], *Some Queries Concerning the Election of Members For the Ensuing Parliament* (1690), p. 3.
79 *A Letter to a Gentleman about the Election of Members for the County of Cambridg, To serve in this present Parliament* (1690).
80 Edward Harley to Sir Edward Harley, 22 Feb. 1690, BL Add MS 70014, fol. 291.
81 *A Word of Advice*, p. 1.
82 Horwitz, 'General Election', p. 88; *idem*, *Parliament, policy and politics*, pp. 51–2.
83 *Pepys Ballads*, V, 94.
84 G.S. De Krey, *A Fractured Society: The Politics of London in the First Age of Party, 1688–1715* (Oxford, 1985), pp. 49, 65.
85 Horwitz, *Parliament, policy and politics*, pp. 52–3.
86 Ibid., p. 57.
87 For whom, see Mark Goldie, 'The Roots of True Whiggism 1688–94', *History of Political Thought*, I (1980), 195–236.
88 John Hampden to Sir Edward Harley, 4 Nov. 1690, BL Add MS 70014, fol. 353.

89   Horwitz, *Parliament, policy and politics*, p. 66.
90   For Wildman's extraordinary career, see Maurice Ashley, *John Wildman: Plotter and Postmaster* (1947).
91   Hampden to Sir Edward Harley, 28 March 1691, BL Add MS 70015, fol. 33.
92   Jonathan Scott, *Algernon Sidney and the English Republic 1623–1677* (Cambridge, 1988), p. 201. Like his mentor, Hampden had been deeply alarmed in 1680 at the threat posed to English liberties by a revived Stuart-Orange alliance; see *idem, Sidney and the Restoration*, pp. 106–7.
93   *State of Parties*, p. 212.
94   Horwitz, *Parliament, policy and politics*, p. 110.
95   *An Inquiry; or a Discourse between a Yeoman of Kent, and a Knight of a Shire, upon the Prorogation of the Parliament to the second of May, 1693* (1693), *State Tracts*, II, 330–41, at 331. This tract is sometimes attributed to Hampden and Wildman.
96   *Dialogue betwixt Whig and Tory*, p. 2.
97   Ibid., pp. ix–x.
98   *The Charge of the Right Honourable Earl of Warrington, to the Grand Jury at the Quarter Sessions held for the County of Chester, on the 25th Day of April, 1693* (1693), *State Tracts*, II, 342–8, at 344.
99   Speck, *Reluctant Revolutionaries*, pp. 228–9; Western, *Monarchy and Revolution*, pp. 275–6.
100 *The Correspondence of Henry Hyde, Earl of Clarendon, and of his Brother, Laurence Hyde, Earl of Rochester; with the Diary of Lord Clarendon from 1687 to 1690*, ed. Samuel Weller Singer (2 vols, 1828), II, 219.
101 The standard biography is James Ferguson, *Robert Ferguson the Plotter* (Edinburgh, 1887). For the Montgomery plot of 1689–90, see Hopkins, 'Aspects of Jacobite Conspiracy', pp. 246–52; Ashley, *Wildman*, pp. 292–4. General discussions of whig Jacobitism can be found in Paul Monod, *Jacobitism and the English people 1688–1788* (Cambridge, 1989), pp. 23–5, and Goldie, 'Roots of True Whiggism', pp. 228–9.
102 Hopkins, 'Aspects of Jacobite Conspiracy', pp. 246–7; Monod, *Jacobitism and the English people*, pp. 23–4.
103 For a full account of the Jacobite intrigues of these four whigs, see Hopkins, 'Aspects of Jacobite Conspiracy', pp. 116–17, 163–4, 270–1, 283, 285–6, 314–17, 335.
104 *DNB*.
105 David Hayton, 'The "Country" interest and the party system, 1689–c.1720' in Clyve Jones, ed., *Party and Management in Parliament 1660–1784* (Leicester, 1984), 37–85, at 46.
106 *The Parliamentary Diary of Narcissus Luttrell 1691–1693*, ed. Henry Horwitz (Oxford, 1972), pp. 236–7. Although Harley appears to be referring to the Declaration of Rights, that document actually had very little to say about treason trials. So he was probably alluding to the original version of the Declaration which was shorn of its more radical 'heads' in February 1689. One of the lost clauses required the regulation of 'Constructions upon the Statutes of Treason, and trials and proceedings and writs of error in cases of treason'. See Western, *Monarchy and Revolution*, p. 332; Lois G. Schwoerer, *The Declaration of Rights, 1689* (Baltimore, 1981), pp. 202, 226.

107 Horwitz, *Parliament, policy and politics*, pp. 69, 98.

108 Ibid., p. 70.

109 [Richard Hill] to Sir William Trumbull, 8 Dec. 1691, BL Add MS 72530, fol. 10. I do not accept Tim Harris's view - *Politics under the Later Stuarts*, p. 164 - that 'it makes sense to talk of a distinctive Country party in Parliament' between 1691 and 1695. In this period, genuine bi-partisanship was confined to the Commission of Accounts, and a Commission of Accounts does not a party make. If there was a 'Country' moment in King William's reign, it occurred between the fall of the whig ministers in 1699–1700 and Robert Harley's election as Speaker in February 1701; see below, pp. 98–100.

110 Luttrell, *Parliamentary Diary*, p. 275.

111 Ibid., p. 274.

112 Kenyon, *Revolution Principles*, p. 33.

113 Horwitz, *Parliament, policy and politics*, pp. 108–9. A similar measure had failed in both Houses in April/May 1690; ibid., pp. 56–7.

114 Luttrell, *Parliamentary Diary*, pp. 330–1.

115 Horwitz, *Parliament, policy and politics*, pp. 109–10.

116 Ibid., pp. 110, 114.

117 Bohun, *Diary and Autobiography*, p. 113.

118 The standard biography, on which the following passage is based, is J.P. Kenyon, *Robert Spencer, Earl of Sunderland 1641–1702* (1958).

119 Horwitz, *Parliament, policy and politics*, p. 67; Kenyon, *Sunderland*, pp. 248–51. The earl's remark was attributed to him years later by Speaker George Onslow, but it smacks of Sunderland through and through.

120 Horwitz, *Parliament, policy and politics*, p. 114.

121 *Dialogue betwixt Whig and Tory*, p. vi.

122 Ibid., p. iv.

123 BL Add MS 63057B, fol. 157.

124 Abraham Stanyan to Sir William Trumbull, 13 Oct. 1693, BL Add MS 72482, fol. 139.

125 Horwitz, *Parliament, policy and politics*, p. 118.

126 *Memoirs of Mary Queen of England*, ed. R. Doebner (1886), p. 61.

127 Horwitz, *Parliament, policy and politics*, p. 132; Kenyon, *Sunderland*, p. 262. The languid Shrewsbury was reluctant to reassume the burdens of executive office, and the King probably had to wield a stick, as well as dangle a carrot, in order to induce his favourite whig to re-enter the ministry. His instrument of coercion was recently-acquired knowledge of Shrewsbury's intrigues with St Germain; see Hopkins, 'Aspects of Jacobite Conspiracy', p. 380.

128 Horwitz, *Parliament, policy and politics*, pp. 132–4.

129 Lord Godolphin, the only non-whig on the cabinet committee responsible for the purges, complained of the partisan motives behind the remodelling of the Excise commission; see [Godolphin] to the King, 15 June 1694, *CSPD, 1694–1695*, pp. 184–5. Contrast his version of the purge with that put to the King, in three separate letters, by the other members of the committee, Lord Keeper Somers, and Secretaries of State Shrewsbury and Trenchard; ibid., pp. 179–82, 185–6.

130 Somers to the King, 15 June 1694, ibid., p. 180.

131 John Brewer, *The Sinews of Power: War, money and the English state, 1688–1783* (1989), p. 74.
132 Lionel K.J. Glassey, *Politics and the Appointments of Justices of the Peace 1675–1720* (Oxford, 1979), pp. 114–18. See also Bohun, *Diary and Autobiography*, pp. 120–2; Richard Rowe to Roger Kenyon, 30 March 1694, *HMC Kenyon MSS*, p. 291.
133 Bohun, *Diary and Autobiography*, p. 125.
134 BL Stowe MS 119, fols. 45–8, contains eight speeches headed 'When the State of the Nation is debated'. Internal evidence dates them to the early days of the 1694–5 session. They were clearly written after the revision of the Excise Commission and the purges of JPs in the Summer of 1694, but before the death of Archbishop Tillotson in late November. Owing to the lack of parliamentary diaries for the 1694–5 session, we cannot be sure that these speeches were actually delivered in the Commons. But at the very least they provide an interesting insight into tory minds at the time.
135 Ibid., fol. 45.
136 Ibid., fol. 48.
137 Ibid., fols. 47–8.
138 Ibid., fol. 45.
139 Ibid., fol. 46.
140 Horwitz, *Parliament, policy and politics*, pp. 213–14.
141 Ibid., p. 217.
142 Ibid., p. 127.
143 Ibid., pp. 138–9. The successful Triennial Bill of 1694, drawn up chiefly by Robert Harley, differed from its predecessor of 1693 by dropping the requirement for annual parliamentary sessions and the prohibition on early dissolutions.
144 Ibid., pp. 156–8.
145 For the careers of Sir Robert and Sir Edward Harley, see *DNB*; B.D. Henning, ed., *The House of Commons 1660–1690* (3 vols, 1983), II, 494–7. The most penetrating analysis of Robert Harley's elusive personality, to which I am deeply indebted, is David Hayton, 'Robert Harley's "Middle Way": The Puritan Heritage in Augustan Politics', *British Library Journal*, 15 (1989), 158–72.
146 Quoted in Ted Rowlands, 'Robert Harley's Parliamentary Apprenticeship: 1690–1695', *British Library Journal*, 15 (1989), 173–86, at 174.
147 Horwitz, *Parliament, policy and politics*, pp. 109, 214.
148 Ibid., p. 214; Rowlands, 'Harley's Parliamentary Apprenticeship', pp. 174, 184.
149 Hayton, 'Harley's "Middle Way"', pp. 162–8, suggests that Robert's hostility towards partisanship may have been informed by the consensual religious traditions of his family, which were themselves rooted in the conviction that Protestant unity was an overriding virtue. Imbued with the Baxterian vision of a 'middle way' in religion, a 'typical Presbyterian, or Presbyterian offshoot like Harley', writes Dr Hayton, would have inherited, *inter alia*, 'a fondness for "moderation", a preference for consensus, and an aversion to faction' (p. 162). This is an insight which merits further investigation. Yet, as Dr Hayton freely acknowledges, it does not in itself provide a sufficient

explanation for Harley's aversion to partisanship, and whig partisanship in particular. One need only consider the careers of John Hampden, Tom Wharton and Henry Booth, or, for that matter, Sir Edward Harley, to realize that a commitment to Protestant union was more often than not the hand-maiden of zealous whiggery. For no matter how much 'men of latitude' might deprecate the fact, terms such as 'Protestant union' and 'moderation' had themselves become charged with partisan meaning.

150 Horwitz, *Parliament, policy and politics*, p. 98.
151 Ibid., pp. 136, 138, 214.
152 Ibid., p. 215.
153 Ibid., p. 149; Kenyon, *Sunderland*, p. 271.
154 Horwitz, *Parliament, policy and politics*, pp. 155–6.
155 Ibid., pp. 164–5. The Court's defeat was on a motion that the members of the Council of Trade be named by parliament rather than the King. For a discussion of the Council of Trade controversy, see below, pp.128–9.
156 For the tendency of young and ambitious MPs to adopt a temporary 'Country' pose in order to make a mark with the established politicians, see Hayton, 'The "Country" interest', p. 53.
157 Horwitz, *Parliament, policy and politics*, pp. 165–6.
158 See above, pp. 50–52.
159 Horwitz, *Parliament, policy and politics*, pp. 175–6. After April 1696, under the pain of legal penalties if they failed to do so, most tories forced themselves to sign the 'Association'. Nevertheless, some 23 MPs were among the 111 tory JPs removed from the Commissions of the Peace for continuing to refuse the Association; Glassey, *Politics and the Appointment*, p. 123.
160 Horwitz, *Parliament, policy and politics*, pp. 182–4. For the Land Bank, see below, pp. 136–7.
161 Vernon to the Duke of Shrewsbury, 29 Oct. 1696, *Vernon Correspondence*, I, 34.
162 Bohun, *Diary and Autobiography*, pp. 122–3.
163 Ibid., pp. 128–9.
164 Kenyon, *Sunderland*, pp. 295–300; Horwitz, *Parliament, policy and politics*, pp. 225–8.
165 In 1695 Wharton, together with Charles Montagu, had helped to engineer the parliamentary disgrace of two of Sunderland's allies, Secretary of the Treasury Henry Guy and Sir John Trevor, the Speaker of the House of Commons; see Kenyon, *Sunderland*, p. 271.
166 Horwitz, *Parliament, policy and politics*, p. 225.
167 Ibid., p. 229.
168 The army totalled some 66,000 men at the end of the war, and there were also several thousand foreign troops in English pay; see John Childs, *The British Army of William III, 1689–1702* (Manchester, 1987), p. 103.
169 Lois G. Schwoerer, *'No Standing Armies!': The Antiarmy Ideology in Seventeenth-Century England* (Baltimore, 1974), p. 157.
170 Ibid., pp. 171–2; Childs, *British Army*, pp. 193, 196–8; Horwitz, *Parliament, policy and politics*, pp. 226–7, 229.
171 The best account of the 'Roman whigs' can be found in Blair Worden's 'Introduction' to his edition of Ludlow's, *A Voyce from the Watchtower*. See also

Hayton, 'The "Country" interest', pp. 53–4.

172 [John Trenchard], *An Argument, Shewing, that a Standing Army Is inconsistent with A Free Government, and absolutely destructive to the Constitution of the English Monarchy* (1697), p. 13. Trenchard should not be confused with his kinsman, Sir John Trenchard, whig Secretary of State in 1693–5. For a report of the parliamentary debates in early December 1697, see Robert Price to the Duke of Beaufort, 11 Dec 1697, Bod. MS Carte 130, fol. 385.

173 Quoted in Worden, 'Introduction', p. 49. For the compelling case for Toland's editorship of the Ludlow manuscript, see ibid., pp. 22–34.

174 [John Toland], *The Danger of Mercenary Parliaments* (1698), p. 4.

175 [Trenchard], *An Argument, Shewing*, p. 5.

176 *Cursory Remarks upon some late Disloyal Proceedings, in several Cabals, composed of an Intermixture of Interests* (1699), *Somers Tracts*, XI, 149–91, at 155.

177 *Some Remarks Upon a late Paper, Entituled . . . An Argument, Shewing that a Standing Army is Inconsistent with . . . the English Monarchy* (1697), p. 7.

178 Ibid., pp. 5–6.

179 Schwoerer, *'No Standing Armies!'*, pp. 159, 172, 178; Horwitz, *Parliament, policy and politics*, pp. 231–2.

180 Lord Somers to the Duke of Shrewsbury, 25 Oct. 1698, printed in Geoffrey Holmes and W.A. Speck, eds, *The Divided Society: Party Conflict in England 1694–1716* (1967), pp. 18–19.

181 See the somewhat conflicting judgments of the tory peers Digby and Nottingham, quoted in Horwitz, *Parliament, policy and politics*, p. 239.

182 Somers to Shrewsbury, 25 Oct. 1698, printed in Holmes and Speck, *The Divided Society*, p. 18. See also Horwitz, *Parliament, policy and politics*, pp. 237–8.

183 Ibid., p. 249. For William Cowper's notes on the debate, see David Hayton, ed., 'Debates in the House of Commons 1697–1699', *Camden Miscellany XXIX* (Camden Soc., 4th series, 34, 1987), p. 364.

184 Childs, *British Army*, pp. 198–200.

185 Vernon to Shrewsbury, 17 Dec. 1698, *Vernon Correspondence*, II, 236.

186 Same to the same, ibid., p. 244.

187 Same to the same, 19 Jan. 1699, ibid., p. 253.

188 Horwitz, *Parliament, policy and politics*, p. 251; Hayton, ed., 'Debates in the House of Commons', pp. 375–6. The exact number of whigs who voted against the Court on 18 January is unknown. Instead of a full division list, we have only a blacklist of the Court supporters. From this, David Hayton has deduced that some eighty or so whigs failed to support the Court on 18 January. But he believes that no more than thirty-six of these actually voted against the Court; see Hayton, 'The "Country" interest', pp. 46–7, 52 and Appendix 1.

189 Horwitz, *Parliament, policy and politics*, p. 253.

190 Ibid., pp. 252–3, 257–8.

191 Ibid., p. 260.

192 Quoted in ibid., p. 263.

193 Ibid., p. 256.

194 Vernon to Shrewsbury, 19 Dec. 1699, *Vernon Correspondence*, II, 393–4.
195 Hayton, 'The "Country" interest', 60–3; Horwitz, *Parliament, policy and politics*, pp. 269–70.
196 For the King's ministerial tinkerings in 1699–1700, see ibid., pp. 258, 275–6.
197 Ibid., pp. 276–80. The dispute between the two East India Companies, the predominantly tory Old Company and the whiggish New Company established in 1698, was the most notable aspect of this election. In London and some other boroughs, the election was effectively a contest between representatives of the rival Companies; see Henry Horwitz, 'The East India Trade, the Politicians, and the Constitution: 1689–1702', *JBS*, 17 (1977–8), 1–18, at 14.
198 Bod. MS Eng. Hist. b. 209, fol. 79.
199 Horwitz, *Parliament, policy and politics*, p. 281.
200 L'Hermitage to the States-General, 11 Feb. 1701, printed in Holmes and Speck, *The Divided Society*, p. 23.
201 Bod. MS Eng. Hist. b. 209, fol. 79.
202 Horwitz, *Parliament, policy and politics*, p. 299.
203 This first attempt to outlaw occasional conformity was tacked to a measure prohibiting the translation of bishops; see ibid., p. 293.
204 Daniel Williams to Robert Harley, 26 March 1701, BL Add MS 70020, fol. 56.
205 Horwitz, *Parliament, policy and politics*, pp. 283–4.
206 Ibid., pp. 282–3, 286–7, 289–90.
207 Shaftesbury to Benjamin Furly, 15 Nov. 1700, PRO 30/24/20, no. 15.
208 Same to the same, 4 March 1701, ibid., no. 19. As early as 11 January, in fact, Shaftesbury had written to Furly that the tories 'hate the Dutch & love France, & the Whiggs the only contrary party that can now save them & England'; see ibid., no. 53.
209 Cobbett, *Parliamentary History*, V, col. 1251.
210 [Daniel Defoe], *Legion's Memorial* (1701), *Somers Tracts*, XI, 255–64, at 256.
211 *Idem, The History of the Kentish Petition* (1701), *Somers Tracts*, XI, 242–54, at 254.
212 Vernon to Shrewsbury, 21 April 1701, *Vernon Correspondence*, III, 144. None of the whig peers had much, if anything, to do with negotiating the Partition Treaty. That had chiefly been the responsibility of King William's Dutch confidant, the Earl of Portland, who also found himself impeached for his pains.
213 Horwitz, *Parliament, policy and politics*, pp. 287–8; Holmes, *British Politics*, pp. 63–4. The reference to the Junto as 'Brother-Whiggs' can be found in a letter dated 30 Jan. 1702 from Shaftesbury to Furly, in which the Earl condemns the maverick Earl of Peterborough (the former Lord Mordaunt) for having betrayed his party by supporting the impeachments; see PRO 30/24/20, no. 55.
214 Horwitz, *Parliament, policy and politics*, p. 292.
215 *Jura Populi Anglicani: or The Subject's Right of Petitioning Set forth* (1701), p. xii.
216 Ibid., p. 51. The author also accused the Commons of infringing the rights of both the King and the House of Lords; ibid., pp. x–xi.
217 [Defoe], *Legion's Memorial*, p. 256.

218 Ibid., p. 258.
219 Quoted in Horwitz, *Parliament, policy and politics*, p. 295.
220 Kenyon, *Sunderland*, p. 322.
221 Horwitz, *Parliament, policy and politics*, pp. 296–7.
222 For the political events of the last months of King William's reign, see ibid., pp. 298–304; W.A. Speck, *The Birth of Britain: A New Nation 1700–1710* (Oxford, Basil Blackwell, 1994), pp. 28–33.

CHAPTER FOUR KING WILLIAM'S WAR

1 Sir Edward Harley to Robert Harley, 16 April 1689, BL Add MS 70014, fol. 215. The vote formed the basis of an address to the King on 25 April; see DWL Morrice MS Q, pp. 546–7.
2 Jonathan I. Israel, 'The Dutch role in the Glorious Revolution' in *idem*, ed., *The Anglo-Dutch moment: Essays on the Glorious Revolution and its world impact* (Cambridge, 1991), pp. 105–62, at 132–5.
3 For discussions of James II's 'foreign policy', see J.R. Jones, *The Revolution of 1688 in England* (1972), pp. 176–83; J.R. Western, *Monarchy and Revolution: The English State in the 1680s* (1972), pp. 243–4; G.C. Gibbs, 'The Revolution in Foreign Policy' in Geoffrey Holmes, ed., *Britain after the Glorious Revolution 1689–1714* (1969), pp. 59–79, at 60; J.D. Davies, 'International Relations, War and the Armed Forces' in Lionel K.J. Glassey, ed., *The Reigns of Charles II and James VII & II* (1997), pp. 211–33, at 230–1.
4 Israel, 'Dutch role', pp. 105–21; Jones, *Revolution of 1688*, p. 329; Gibbs, 'Revolution in Foreign Policy', pp. 60–1; W.A. Speck, *Reluctant Revolutionaries: Englishmen and the Revolution of 1688* (Oxford, 1988), p. 77.
5 Quoted in E.N. Williams, *The Eighteenth Century Constitution 1688–1715* (Cambridge, 1960), p. 62.
6 *The Pepys Ballads*, ed. H.E. Rollins (8 vols, Cambridge, Massachusetts, 1929–32), III, 321.
7 DWL Morrice MS Q, p. 547; Cobbett, *Parliamentary History*, V, col. 235.
8 *CSPD, 1689–90*, p. 93.
9 See, for example, P.G.M. Dixon, *The Financial Revolution in England: A Study in the Development of Public Credit 1688–1756* (1967); John Brewer, *The Sinews of Power: War, money and the English state, 1688–1763* (1989); Jennifer Carter, 'The Revolution and the Constitution' in Holmes, ed., *Britain after the Glorious Revolution*, pp. 39–58; D.W. Jones, *War and Economy in the Age of William III and Marlborough* (Oxford, Basil Blackwell, 1988); Henry Horwitz, *Parliament, policy and politics in the reign of William III* (Manchester, 1977), pp. 87–8.
10 The court's propaganda is reviewed in Tony Claydon, *William III and the Godly Revolution* (Cambridge, 1996). For the controversy over war strategy, see T.J. Denman, 'The Political Debate Over War Strategy 1689–1712' (unpublished Ph.D. dissertation, University of Cambridge, 1985) and Robert D. McJimsey, 'A Country Divided? English Politics and the Nine Years War', *Albion*, 23 (1991), 61–74.
11 John Hampden, *Some short Considerations concerning the State of the Nation* (1692) in *State Tracts*, II, 320–9, at 322.

12   Thomas Comber, *The Reasons of Praying for the Peace of our Jerusalem. In a Sermon Preached before the Queen at Whitehall, on the Fast-Day, being Wednesday, August 29th 1694* (1694), p. 19.

13   *Pepys Ballads,* VII, 130.

14   Ibid., V, 185.

15   Comber, *Reasons of Praying,* p. 16.

16   Samuel Barton, *A Sermon Preached at St Mary le Bow before the Right Honourable the Lord Mayor and Court of Aldermen on Wednesday the 16th of July, being the Fast Day* (1690), pp. 23–4.

17   *A Brief Memoir of Mr Justice Rokeby, comprising his Religious Journal and Correspondence,* ed. James Raine (Surtees Soc., Durham, 1861), p. 35.

18   John Tillotson, *A Sermon Preached before the King and Queen at White-Hall, the 27th of October, Being the Day appointed for a Publick Thanksgiving to Almighty God, For the Signal Victory at Sea: For the Preservation of His Majesty's Sacred Person, And for His Safe Return to His People* (1692), pp. 30–1.

19   *Pepys Ballads,* V, 256.

20   Comber, *Reasons of Praying,* p. 26.

21   DWL Morrice MS Q, p. 521. The six peers were Oxford, Mordaunt, Montagu, Paget, Wharton and Lovelace.

22   [William Stephens], *An Account of the Growth of Deism in England* (1696), p. 8.

23   Memorandum by Thomas Papillon on English politics, early 1690s, printed in A.F.W. Papillon, *Memoirs of Thomas Papillon, of London, Merchant (1623–1702)* (Reading, 1877), p. 375.

24   DWL Morrice MS Q, p. 568.

25   Thomas Shadwell, *The Scowrers. A Comedy, Acted by Their Majesties Servants* (1691), p. 7.

26   This was a product of Dodwell's belief that the ordinary means of salvation were available only in an episcopal church; see J.C. Findon, 'The Nonjurors and the Church of England 1689–1716' (unpublished D.Phil. dissertation, University of Oxford, 1978), pp. 160–1.

27   Robin D. Gwynn, 'Disorder and Innovation: The Reshaping of the French Churches of London after the Glorious Revolution' in Ole Peter Grell, Jonathan I. Israel and Nicholas Tyacke, eds, *From Persecution to Toleration: The Glorious Revolution and Religion in England* (Oxford, 1991), pp. 251–73; G.C. Gibbs, 'The Reception of the Huguenots in England and the Dutch Republic, 1680–1690' in ibid., pp. 275–306, esp. 287, 290.

28   Grey, *Debates,* IX, 197.

29   DWL Morrice MS Q, p. 575.

30   [John Humfrey], *The Healing Attempt* (1689), 'The Author to the Reader' (unpaginated).

31   DWL Morrice MS Q, p. 516.

32   BL Add MS 63057B, fol. 103.

33   See below, pp. 162, 164–5, 166.

34   See above, pp. 26–7.

35   [Thomas Wagstaffe], *His Majesty's most gracious Speech to both Houses of Parliament, with Additions and Explications: Directed to the House of Commons, by the Free-born People of England* (1692), *Somers Tracts,* X, 598–607, at 605.

36   *Some Paradoxes Presented for a New-Years Gift by the Old, to the New Orthodox,*

serving for an Index to the Revolution (1693).

37 *HMC Finch MSS,* III, 285.

38 *An Impartial Inquiry into the Causes of the present Fears and Dangers of the Government* (1692) in *State Tracts,* II, 218–33, at 232.

39 J.F. Bosher, 'The Franco-Catholic Danger, 1660–1715', *History,* 79 (1994), 5–30.

40 *Pepys Ballads,* V, 49.

41 Ibid., pp. 53–4.

42 George Story, *An Impartial History of the Affairs of Ireland* (1691), preface (unpaginated).

43 Bod MS Eng.Hist.b.209, fol. 30.

44 William Lawrence to Sir Michael Hicks, 29 March 1693, *The Pyramid and the Urn. The Life in Letters of a Restoration Squire: William Lawrence of Shurdington, 1636–1697,* ed. Iona Sinclair (Stroud, 1994), p. 102.

45 Hampden, *Some Short Considerations,* p. 321.

46 For the earlier period, see Steven Pincus, 'The English Debate over Universal Monarchy' in John Robertson, ed., *A Union for Empire: Political Thought and the British Union of 1707* (Cambridge, 1995), pp. 37–62. Dr Pincus argues, with characteristic vigour, that fear of Universal Monarchy, not popery, was the dominant element in anti-French sentiment during Charles II's reign - a thesis which, he says, also holds good for the 1690s. Dr Pincus is clearly right to stress the importance of Universal Monarchy during King William's war. It seems to me, however, that he underestimates the extent to which the war was seen in religious terms. True, contemporaries may not have been clamouring for a crusade against Antichrist (though some, including Mr Justice Rokeby and Archbishop Tillotson, apparently saw the war in just such a light). Nevertheless, it is clear that many viewed the war as a struggle for the very survival of European Protestantism.

47 John Petter, *A Sermon Preached before Their Majesties, K. William and Q. Mary's Forces, At Gant in Flanders, The Sunday before they marched into the Camp, 1694* (1694), p. 34.

48 William King, *Europe's Deliverance from France and Slavery: A Sermon, Preached at St Patrick's Church, Dublin, On the 16th November 1690* (1691), pp. 8–9.

49 *Pepys Ballads,* V, 73.

50 Petter, *Sermon Preached,* pp. 30–1.

51 Story, *Impartial History,* preface (unpaginated).

52 John C. Rule, 'France caught between two balances: the dilemma of 1688' in Lois G. Schwoerer, ed., *The Revolution of 1688–1689: Changing Perspectives* (Cambridge, 1992), 35–51, at 43–4; John Stoye, 'Europe and the Revolution' in Robert Beddard, ed., *The Revolutions of 1688* (Oxford, 1991), pp. 191–212, at 208–11.

53 Jonathan Israel, 'General Introduction' in *idem,* ed., *The Anglo-Dutch moment,* pp. 1–43, at 32–3.

54 Ibid., pp. 36–7; Charles Ingrao, *The Habsburg Monarchy 1618–1815* (Cambridge, 1994), pp. 80–1.

55 *Pepys Ballads,* V, 73.

56 James Smalwood, *A Sermon Preached before the King at Mont-St-Andre-Camp, June 29 1694* (1695), p. 31.

57 *The Dutiful Sons Complaint To Their Mother The Church of England, Concerning the Late Elections* (1690), p. 18.

58 Nicholas Rowe, *Tamerlane. A Tragedy* (1702), p. 3. The eponymous hero of the play is an idealized portrayal of King William.

59 *A Congratulatory Poem On His Highness The Prince of Orange, Upon his Arrival to Town* (1688), p. 2.

60 *Pepys Ballads,* VI, 331.

61 *An Honest Commoner's Speech* (1691), *Somers Tracts,* X, 324–31, at 330–1. There is some confusion over the dating of this pamphlet. Although no publication date is given by Sir Walter Scott in his edition of *Somers Tracts,* the Wing short-title catalogue dates the tract to 1694. I date it to late 1691 since the recent King's speech to which the author refers (pp. 324–5) is clearly that delivered at the opening of parliament in October 1691. For the King's speech, see Grey, *Debates,* X, 161.

62 *The State of Parties, and of the Publick, as influenc'd by those Parties in this Conjuncture, offer'd to Englishmen* (1692), *State Tracts,* II, 208–17, at 214.

63 *Impartial Inquiry,* p. 231.

64 *State of Parties,* p. 213.

65 *Impartial Inquiry,* p. 232.

66 *Honest Commoner's Speech,* pp. 327, 329–30.

67 *Impartial Inquiry,* pp. 230–1.

68 See below, pp. 124–5.

69 *Honest Commoner's Speech,* p. 331.

70 Hampden, *Some Short Considerations,* p. 328.

71 *The Parliamentary Diary of Narcissus Luttrell 1691–1693,* ed. Henry Horwitz (Oxford, 1972), p. 262.

72 Ibid., p. 297.

73 Ibid., pp. 288, 304.

74 Grey, *Debates,* X, 340.

75 For Halifax's observation, see *Memoirs of Sir John Reresby,* ed. Andrew Browning (Glasgow, 1936), p. 572.

76 *The Life and Times of Anthony Wood, antiquary, of Oxford, 1632–1695, described by Himself,* ed. Andrew Clark (3 vols, Oxford, 1891–94), III, 316.

77 Francis Hopegood to Thomas Coke, 31 July 1696, BL Add MS 69944. fol. 10.

78 Wagstaffe, *His Majesty's most gracious Speech,* p. 604.

79 [Samuel Grascombe], *New Court-Contrivances, or, More Sham-Plots still, against true-hearted Englishmen* (1693), p. 2.

80 [James Montgomery], *Great Britain's just Complaint for her late Measures, present Sufferings, and the future Miseries she is exposed to* (1693), *Somers Tracts,* X, 429–71 at 455.

81 *The Autobiography of Sir John Bramston, K.B., of Skreens, in the Hundred of Chelmsford,* ed. Lord Braybrooke (Camden Soc., os, 32, 1845), p. 358.

82 *Min Heer T. Van C's Answer to Min Heer H. Van L's Letter of the 15th of March 1689; representing the true Interest of Holland, and what they have already gained by our Losses* (1690), *Somers Tracts,* X, 314–18, at 315. Jonathan Israel, 'England, the Dutch, and the Struggle for the Mastery of World Trade in the Age of the Glorious Revolution (1682–1702)' in Dale Hoak and Mordechai

Feingold, eds, *The World of William and Mary: Anglo-Dutch Perspectives on the Revolution of 1688–89* (Stanford, California, 1996), pp. 75–86 at 81–2, incorrectly dates this tract to the Spring of 1689. In fact, it was written in February 1690, shortly after the dissolution of the Convention Parliament. Professor Israel appears to have been misled by the pamphlet's allegation that King William was planning to form an alliance with the Church, thereby forcing the dissenters to flee to the Netherlands. He takes this to refer to the period before the passage of the Toleration Act in May 1689. In fact, it is an attempt to play on fears aroused by the King's swing to the tories in the first months of 1690.

83 *A modest Apology for the Loyal Protestant Subjects of King James, who desire his Restoration, without Prejudice to our Religion, Laws or Liberties* (1692), *Somers Tracts*, X, 401–29 at 402.

84 [John Sergeant], *An Historical Romance of the Wars, Between the Mighty Giant Gallieno, and the Great Knight Nasonius, And His Associates* (Dublin, 1694), p. 30.

85 Ibid., p. 33.

86 *Min Heer T. Van C's Answer*, p. 315. For parliament's reimbursement of the Dutch, see Horwitz, *Parliament, policy and politics*, p. 34.

87 Bod. MS Tanner 25, fol. 54.

88 [Nathaniel Johnston], *The Dear Bargain; or, a true Representation of the State of the English Nation under the Dutch* (1690?), *Somers Tracts*, X, 349–77, at 356.

89 *Pepys Ballads*, VI, 276.

90 For a brief account of the Irish campaign, see above, pp. 13–17.

91 John Childs, *The Nine Years' War and the British Army 1688–1697: The Operations in the Low Countries* (Manchester, 1991), pp. 144–6.

92 John Ehrman, *The Navy in the War of William III: Its State and Direction* (Cambridge, 1953), pp. 343–51. See also Peter Le Fevre, 'Lord Torrington's Trial - A Rejoinder', *Mariner's Mirror*, 78 (1992), 7–15.

93 David Ogg, *England in the Reigns of James II and William III* (Oxford, 1955), pp. 354–6; Ehrman, *The Navy*, p. 353; A.W.H. Pearsall, 'The War at Sea' in W.A. Maguire, ed., *Kings in Conflict: The Revolutionary War in Ireland and its Aftermath 1689–1750* (Belfast, 1990), pp. 92–105, at 102.

94 Ogg, *England in the Reigns*, pp. 367–9; Ehrman, *The Navy*, pp. 393–7.

95 Ibid., pp. 381–2, 400–11.

96 *Memoirs of Mary, Queen of England (1689–1693)*, ed. R. Doebner (1886), p. 54.

97 John Childs, *The British Army of William III, 1689–1702* (Manchester, 1987), p. 217.

98 Ibid., p. 211.

99 Childs, *Nine Years' War*, pp. 159–62.

100 D.W. Jones, *War and Economy in the Age of William III and Marlborough* (Oxford, Basil Blackwell, 1988), p. 8 and n. 8.

101 Childs, *Nine Years' War*, pp. 194–204.

102 Nottingham to Portland, 14 June 1692, *HMC Finch MSS*, IV, 233.

103 Nottingham to Blathwayt, 26 Aug. 1692, ibid., 418. In September one of Nottingham's colleagues, the Earl of Rochester, told Halifax 'that we must keep a good fleet, but it was impossible to keep so many land men, and to send so much money out of the kingdom': BL Add MS 51511, fol. 68.

104 Carmarthen to the King, 9 Sept. 1692, *CSPD, 1691–2*, pp. 443–4. For the impact of Continental remittances upon the English currency, see below, p. 137

105 Luttrell, *Parliamentary Diary*, p. 242.

106 Ibid., p. 288.

107 Ibid., p. 288.

108 Ibid., p. 242.

109 Ibid., p. 291.

110 Ibid., p. 290.

111 Horwitz, *Parliament, policy and politics*, p. 106.

112 Childs, *Nine Years' War*, pp. 237–41, 245.

113 For the commanding officer's account of this unhappy expedition, see BL Add MS 70017, fols. 60–3 (the campaign journal of Rear-Admiral Sir Francis Wheeler).

114 Ogg, *England in the Reigns*, p. 389; Ehrman, *The Navy*, pp. 501–2.

115 Jones, *War and Economy*, p. 131.

116 Ibid., pp. 158–9.

117 Grey, *Debates*, IX, 421.

118 BL Add MS 63057B, fol. 153.

119 Hampden, *Some Short Considerations*, p. 327.

120 Luttrell, *Parliamentary Diary*, p. 245.

121 BL Add MS 63057B, fol. 153.

122 Jones, *War and Economy*, p. 156.

123 Ibid., p. 158.

124 *The Diary of John Evelyn*, ed. E.S. de Beer (6 vols, Oxford, 1955), V, 218. In 1694–5 the Navy bombarded several towns on the French coast; see Ogg, *England in the Reigns*, p. 395.

125 James Whiston, *The Causes of our Present Calamities In reference to the Trade of the Nation Fully Discovered* (1696), p. 9. This was an updated edition of a pamphlet first published in 1692.

126 John Cary, *An Essay on the State of England, In Relation to its Trade, its Poor, and its Taxes, For carrying on the present War against France* (Bristol, 1695), p. 28.

127 Ibid., pp. 29–30.

128 Ibid., pp. 139–41.

129 Whiston, *Causes of our Present Calamities*, pp. 5–6.

130 Ibid., p. 9.

131 Ibid., p. 10.

132 Horwitz, *Parliament, policy and politics*, pp. 161–2, 164–5, 176, 178–9.

133 Ogg, *England in the Reigns*, pp. 305–6. For a fuller discussion of the controversy surrounding the Council of Trade, see Colin Brooks, 'Taxation, Finance and Public Opinion 1688–1714' (Cambridge University Ph.D. dissertation, 1970), pp. 174–9.

134 Horwitz, *Parliament, policy and politics*, p. 118.

135 Ibid. pp. 123–4.

136 Ibid., p. 136. £2.5m were voted for the army, and just under £2.4m for the navy.

137 See above, pp. 118–19. We should note, however, that at least one hot whig, Sir John Thompson, was an acerbic critic of the Dutch Republic's

role in the war; see, Grey, *Debates*, X, 340. By Anne's reign, perhaps because of his rabidly anti-Dutch views, Thompson had gone over to the Church party.

138 For a similar interpretation of the essentially non-partisan character of the disputes over war strategy, see Robert D. McJimsey, 'A Country Divided? English Politics and the Nine Years War', *Albion*, 23 (1991), 61–74.
139 Evelyn, *Diary*, V, 169.
140 Horwitz, *Parliament, policy and politics*, p. 135; Childs, *Nine Years' War*, pp. 260–1. For the raid on Brest, and the controversy surrounding its failure, see *idem*, *British Army of William III*, pp. 221–34; Ogg, *England in the Reigns*, pp. 393–4.
141 Childs, *Nine Years' War*, p. 296.
142 Ehrman, *The Navy*, pp. 515–16.
143 Ibid., pp. 526–37, 548.
144 *The Diary of Abraham de la Pryme*, ed. Charles Jackson (Durham, Surtees Soc., 54, 1870), p. 64.
145 Dickson, *Financial Revolution*, p. 46; Brewer, *Sinews of Power*, p. 30, table 2.1.
146 Dickson, *Financial Revolution*, p. 10; Brewer, *Sinews of Power*, p. 40.
147 Ibid., p. 89.
148 Brooks, 'Taxation, Finance and Public Opinion', pp. 340–6, 363–7; Brewer, *Sinews of Power*, pp. 145–9.
149 Dickson, *Financial Revolution*, p. 47.
150 Brewer, *Sinews of Power*, p. 95.
151 W.R. Ward, *The English Land Tax in the Eighteenth Century* (Oxford, 1953), p. 3. The abandonment of the assessment made the land tax easier to evade, since local assessors often deliberately underassessed their neighbours' tax liability. The consequent diminution in yields led to a return to the quota system in 1698, but the new county and borough assessments were based on the pound rate figures of 1693.
152 Ogg, *England in the Reigns*, pp. 401–2.
153 Dickson, *Financial Revolution*, p. 10.
154 Ibid., pp. 47, 343.
155 Brewer, *Sinews of Power*, pp. 152–3.
156 Jones, *War and Economy*, p. 11.
157 Ehrman, *The Navy*, p. 488.
158 For the details of which, see Dickson, *Financial Revolution*, pp. 52–4.
159 Jones, *War and Economy*, pp. 12–13; Dickson, *Financial Revolution*, pp. 54–5; Horwitz, *Parliament, policy and politics*, pp. 130–1; Sir John Clapham, *The Bank of England: A History* (2 vols, Cambridge, 1944), I, 14–19.
160 Jones, *War and Economy*, pp. 249–50, 301–6. Merchants in the depressed Iberian wine trade were particularly heavy investors in the Bank of England and the other new stocks which emerged in the 1690s.
161 Clapham, *Bank of England*, I, 19–20.
162 Jones, *War and Economy*, pp. 13–14; Ehrman, *The Navy*, pp. 542–3.
163 Jones, *War and Economy*, p. 276; Dickson, *Financial Revolution*, pp. 486–7.
164 Luttrell, *Parliamentary Diary*, p. 147.
165 Dickson, *Financial Revolution*, pp. 32–3.
166 John Cary, *Essay on the State of England*, p. 36.

167 *Idem, An Essay Towards the Settlement of a National Credit, In the Kingdom of England, Humbly presented to the two Honourable Houses of Parliament* (1696/7), p. 17.

168 John Locke to John Freke and Edward Clarke, 18 Feb. 1695, *Locke Correspondence*, V, 271–2.

169 Sir Francis Brewster, *Essays on Trade and Navigation* (1695), p. 6.

170 Cary, *Essay Towards the Settlement*, p. 2.

171 Ibid., p. 13. See also Cary to John Locke, 28 Nov. 1696, *Locke Correspondence*, V, 725–6. For the Bank's problems in 1696, see below, p. 141.

172 Cary, *Essay Towards the Settlement*, p. 2.

173 Ibid., pp. 7, 9–10.

174 Ibid., pp. 11–12.

175 J[ohn] B[riscoe], *A Discourse on the late Funds of the Million-Act, Lottery-Act, and Bank of England* (1694), p. 14.

176 Ibid., pp. 15–16.

177 Ibid., p. 18.

178 Ibid., p. 11.

179 Ibid., pp. 23–30. For Chamberlen's land bank schemes, see J. Keith Horsefield, *British Monetary Experiments 1650–1710* (1960), ch. 14.

180 Briscoe, *Discourse on the late Funds,* pp. 30–2.

181 For the operations of Briscoe's land bank, see Horsefield, *British Monetary Experiments,* pp. 186–93.

182 Ibid., pp. 197–8.

183 Ibid., pp. 201–3.

184 Horwitz, *Parliament, policy and politics,* pp. 166–7, 177–8.

185 Ibid., pp. 180–2; Horsefield, *British Monetary Experiments,* p. 207.

186 Jones, *War and Economy,* pp. 18–20, 228–34, 247–8.

187 Ming-Hsun Li, *The Great Recoinage of 1696 to 1699* (1963), pp. 12, 56–7, 116.

188 Even before the demonetization of the clipped coin, silver money was becoming scarce, since the sound coin, mostly of post-Restoration vintage, was apparently being hoarded in expectation of a sterling devaluation. Despite this, the country experienced something of a hyper-inflationary boom in 1695. Uncertainty over the status of the silver coin stimulated demand for gold guineas which were then used to buy up goods and commodities. But the subsequent increase in the price of gold led in turn to a sharp rise in demand for Continental gold, thereby contributing to a disastrous collapse in the sterling exchange rate. For a fascinating discussion of these aspects of the recoinage crisis, see Jones, *War and Economy,* pp. 20–1, 237–40.

189 Charles Price to Sir William Trumbull, 14 June 1696, BL Add MS 72535, fol. 209.

190 Edmund Bohun to John Cary, 31 July 1696, BL Add MS 5540, fol. 64.

191 Roger Kenyon to Mr Macy, 13 June 1696, *HMC Kenyon MSS,* p. 409.

192 Alan Chambre to Sir Daniel Fleming, 9 June 1696, *HMC Le Fleming MSS,* pp. 343–4. The disturbance had been sparked by the refusal of the excise collectors to accept clipped coin in payment of the tax.

193 Hugh Todd to Arthur Charlett, 10 June 1696, Bod. MS Ballard 18, fols 16–17.

194 Ibid.
195 De la Pryme, *Diary*, p. 97.
196 John Gale to Sir John Lowther, 8 Nov. 1696, *The Correspondence of Sir John Lowther of Whitehaven 1693–1698: A Provincial Community in Wartime*, ed. D.R. Hainsworth (1983), p. 319.
197 De la Pryme, *Diary*, pp. 95–6.
198 Ehrman, *The Navy*, p. 574.
199 Ibid., pp. 586–8.
200 Jones, *War and Economy*, pp. 18, 37.
201 W. Marston Acres, *The Bank of England From Within 1694–1900* (2 vols., 1931), I, 52–3. In April 1695 the Bank established an office at Antwerp to manage the remittances.
202 Jones, *War and Economy*, p. 21; Li, *Great Recoinage*, p. 13; Acres, *Bank of England*, I, 52–5.
203 Jones, *War and Economy*, pp. 23–5.
204 Timothy Banks to James Graham, 3 Sept. 1696, *HMC Bagot MSS*, p. 333.
205 De la Pryme, *Diary*, p. 111.
206 Gale to Lowther, 22 Nov. 1696, *Lowther Correspondence*, pp. 325–6. As this letter shows, the Recoinage Act of January 1696 had left a fog of uncertainty over the legal status of the old coin, both clipped and unclipped.
207 Hopegood to Coke, 18 Sept. 1696, *HMC Cowper MSS*, II, 363.
208 Same to the same, 31 July 1696, BL Add MS 69944, fol. 10.
209 Ogg, *England in the Reigns*, p. 437.
210 Dickson, *Financial Revolution*, pp. 348–52.
211 Ibid., pp. 353–5.
212 Sir George Rooke to the Marquis of Halifax, 14 June 1697, BL Althorp MS C11 (unfoliated papers).
213 James Vernon to the Duke of Shrewsbury, 19 June 1697, *Vernon Correspondence*, I, 274.
214 Rooke to Halifax, 10 Aug. 1697, BL Althorp MS C11 (unfoliated papers).
215 Jones, *War and Economy*, p. 26. The continuing financial pressure on the government was the chief reason why it enthusiastically promoted the establishment of the New East India Company in the Spring of 1698. The New Company's directors had promised to raise £2m for the Crown in exchange for the grant of a charter; see Henry Horwitz, 'The East India Trade, the Politicians, and the Constitution 1689–1702', *JBS*, 17 (1977–8), 1–18, at 10–11.
216 Ogg, *England in the Reigns*, pp. 438–9.
217 'GB' to Robert Harley, 21 Sept. 1697, BL Add MS 70018, fol. 200.
218 ———— to Robert Harley, 21 Sept. 1697, BL Add MS 70018, fol. 202.
219 Vernon to Shrewsbury, 28 Sept. 1697, *Vernon Correspondence*, I, 410.
220 Ibid., p. 411.
221 Charles Hatton to Lord Hatton, 4 Dec. 1697, *Hatton Correspondence*, II, 230.
222 Lord Somers to the King, 28 Aug. 1698, printed in Cobbett, *Parliamentary History*, V, col. 1247. The House of Commons had already shown itself determined to slash the size of the army.
223 For King William's view of the international situation after the peace of Ryswick, see Gibbs, 'Revolution in Foreign Policy', p. 69.

224   Ogg, *England in the Reigns*, pp. 448–9.
225   Ibid., p. 453.
226   Ibid., pp. 454–6.
227   Thomas Johnson to Richard Norris, 14 Nov. 1700, *The Norris Papers*, ed. Thomas Heywood (Manchester, Chetham Soc., 1846), p. 49.
228   Sir William Hodges to John Jackson, 6/17 Jan. 1701, *Private Correspondence and Miscellaneous Papers of Samuel Pepys 1679–1703*, ed. J.R. Tanner (2 vols, 1926), II, 167.
229   Same to the same, 20/31 Jan. 1701, ibid., p. 175.
230   Samuel Pepys to Sir William Hodges, 28 January 1701, ibid., p. 180.
231   J. Brydges to Thomas Coke, 13 July 1700, *HMC Cowper MSS*, II, 401.
232   Samuel Collins to Robert Walpole, 21 Nov. 1700, CUL Cholmondley (Houghton) Correspondence, no. 85. See also Gibbs, 'Revolution in Foreign Policy', p. 70.
233   Ogg, *England in the Reigns*, p. 460.
234   Christopher Haynes to John Jackson, 23 Feb./6 March 1701, *Pepys Correspondence*, II, 197.
235   Sir William Hodges to John Jackson, 23 Feb./6 March 1701, ibid., p. 199.
236   Sir Edward Coke to Thomas Coke, 3 Feb. 1701, *HMC Cowper MSS*, II, 418.
237   Charles Davenant to Thomas Coke, 10 Dec. 1700, *HMC Cowper MSS*, II, 410.
238   PRO 30/24/20, no. 17.
239   Bod MS Eng.Hist.b.209, fols 78–9.
240   Horwitz, *Parliament, policy and politics*, pp. 286–7, 289–90, 294.
241   Cobbett, *Parliamentary History*, V, col. 1295; Horwitz, *Parliament, policy and politics*, p. 291.
242   Daniel Defoe, *Legion's Memorial* (1701), *Somers Tracts*, XI, 255–64, at 257.
243   *An Argument for War, In Answer to the Argument for Peace: Being a Vindication of Two Books, Entituled, the Duke of Anjou's Succession Consider'd* (1701), p. 2.
244   Cobbett, *Parliamentary History*, V, col. 1251.
245   POAS, VI, 321.
246   Evelyn, *Diary*, V, 461.
247   De la Pryme, *Diary*, pp. 242–3.
248   [Charles Davenant], *Essays upon I. The Ballance of Power. II. The Right of Making War, Peace, and Alliances. III. Universal Monarchy* (1701), p. 76.
249   Ibid., pp. 80–1.
250   Ibid., pp. 89–90.
251   [Charles Davenant], *The True Picture of a Modern Whig, Set forth in a Dialogue between Mr Whiglove & Mr Double, Two Under-Spur-Leathers to the late Ministry* (1701, 2nd edn.), p. 11.
252   Ibid., p. 26.
253   Thomas Mansell to Thomas Pitt, 14 April 1701, BL Add MS 22851, fol. 191.
254   Lord De la Warr to Thomas Pitt, 4 July 1701, BL Add MS 22851, fol. 183.
255   Ogg, *England in the Reigns*, pp. 469–72. Although by the Treaty of Ryswick Louis XIV had promised to give no further aid to King William's enemies, the treaty had not required the French King to withdraw his recognition of James II as the legitimate King of England. Thus King Louis was technically correct, though massively disingenuous, in arguing that a mere recognition of James III did not constitute a breach of the peace of 1697.

256 By mid-November, the *London Gazette* had printed well over 100 loyal addresses, and had noticed several more.
257 Robert Jennens to Thomas Coke, 4 Oct. 1701, *HMC Cowper MSS*, II, 436.
258 Henry Whistler to Thomas Pitt, 20 Dec. 1701, BL Add MS 22851, fol. 132.
259 Ibid., fol. 131.
260 Charles Davenant to Marlborough, 30 Sept. 1701, BL Add MS 61363, fol. 30.

CHAPTER FIVE   THE CHURCH OF ENGLAND

1 Robert Beddard, 'The Restoration Church' in J.R. Jones, ed., *The Restored Monarchy* (1979), pp. 155–75, at 172–4. For Sancroft's early career, see *DNB*.
2 Keith Feiling, *A History of the Tory Party, 1640–1714* (Oxford, 1924), p. 231; John Miller, 'Proto-Jacobitism? The Tories and the Revolution of 1688–9' in Eveline Cruickshanks and Jeremy Black, eds, *The Jacobite Challenge* (Edinburgh, 1988), pp. 7–23 at 11.
3 Robert Beddard, *A Kingdom without a King: The Journal of the Provisional Government in the Revolution of 1688* (Phaidon, Oxford, 1988), pp. 39–40, 71–2.
4 For the legislation imposing the new oath, see John Findon, 'The Nonjurors and the Church of England 1689–1716' (University of Oxford D.Phil. Dissertation, 1978), pp. 8–14.
5 The episcopal nonjurors were Turner of Ely, Lloyd of Norwich, Frampton of Gloucester, White of Peterborough and Ken of Bath and Wells. Two other bishops who refused the oath, Thomas of Worcester and Lake of Chichester, died before they could be deprived, as did Cartwright of Chester who had joined King James in Ireland. For a list of all known clerical nonjurors, see Findon, 'Nonjurors', Appendix 2.
6 *Letters on Various Subjects, Literary, Political, and Ecclesiastical, to and from William Nicolson, D.D*, ed. John Nichols (2 vols, 1809), I, 7–8.
7 William Wake to Arthur Charlett, 7 Nov. 1689, Bod. MS Ballard 3, fol. 53.
8 The best analysis of *de facto* theory can be found in J.P. Kenyon, *Revolution Principles: The Politics of Party 1689–1720* (Cambridge, 1977), ch. 3.
9 Henry Horwitz, *Parliament, policy and politics in the Reign of William III* (Manchester, 1977), p. 21.
10 Prideaux to Ellis, 4 Dec. 1693, *Letters of Humphrey Prideaux to John Ellis, 1674–1722*, ed. E.M. Thompson (Camden Soc., ns 15, 1875), p. 158.
11 Bishop Thomas's dying declaration, 23 June 1689, printed in *The Works of John Kettlewell* (2 vols, 1719), I, 85.
12 *The Correspondence of Henry Hyde, Earl of Clarendon, and of his Brother, Laurence Hyde, Earl of Rochester; with the Diary of Lord Clarendon from 1687 to 1690*, ed. Samuel Weller Singer (2 vols, 1828), II, 266. William Lloyd, successively Bishop of St Asaph, Lichfield and Coventry, and Worcester, should not be confused with his namesake, the nonjuring Bishop of Norwich.
13 *Clarendon Correspondence*, II, 300. Bishop Lloyd was one of the chief proponents of the providential right and conquest theory justifications of the revolution; see Kenyon, *Revolution Principles*, pp. 29–30.
14 Charles Leslie, *An Answer to a Book Intituled, The State of the Protestants in*

Ireland Under the late King James's Government (1692), p. 123.

15 [Thomas Wagstaffe], *A Letter out of Suffolk to a Friend in London, giving some Account of the last Sickness and Death of Dr William Sancroft, late Archbishop of Canterbury* (1694), *Somers Tracts*, IX, 527–40, at 531–2.

16 Kettlewell, *Works*, I, 85.

17 [Wagstaffe], *Letter out of Suffolk*, p. 532.

18 Ibid., p. 531.

19 Francis Brokesby, *The Life of Mr Henry Dodwell* (1715), pp. 224–34; Mark Goldie, 'The Nonjurors, Episcopacy, and the Origins of the Convocation Controversy' in Eveline Cruickshanks, ed, *Ideology and Conspiracy: Aspects of Jacobitism 1689–1759* (Edinburgh, 1982), pp. 15–35, at 20. See also [Samuel Grascombe], *A brief Answer to a late Discourse Concerning The Unreasonableness of a New Separation* (1691), pp. 5–6.

20 —— to William Beveridge, 28 May 1691, Bod. MS Tanner 26, fol. 74.

21 Goldie, 'Nonjurors', pp. 19–20.

22 Henry Dodwell to John Tillotson, 12 May 1691, BL Stowe MS 746, fols. 141–2.

23 White Kennett to Mr Blackwell, 29 Jan. 1698, BL Lansdowne MS 1013, fol. 65.

24 Goldie, 'Nonjurors', p. 20; Findon, 'Nonjurors and the Church of England', pp. 155–6, 170–3. Kettlewell differed from the other nonjurors in holding that the perjury of the swearing clergy was sufficient in itself to justify the breaking of communion with the Established Church.

25 [Wagstaffe], *Letter out of Suffolk*, p. 539.

26 Goldie, 'Nonjurors', p. 20; Findon, 'Nonjurors and the Church of England', pp. 177–80. The consecrations of Hickes and Wagstaffe were kept secret from Dodwell.

27 [Henry Maurice], *A Letter to a Member of the House of Commons: concerning the Bishops lately in the Tower, and now under suspension* (1689).

28 *Some Paradoxes Presented for a New-Years Gift by the Old, to the New Orthodox, serving for an Index to the Revolution* (1693).

29 *Remarks upon the present Confederacy, and late Revolution in England* (1693), *Somers Tracts*, X, 491–523, at 504–5.

30 [Charles Leslie], *Querela Temporum; or, the Danger of the Church of England. In a Letter from the Dean of —— to —— Prebend of ——* (1694), *Somers Tracts*, IX, 509–27, at 518.

31 [Wagstaffe], *Letter out of Suffolk*, p. 530. Although Archbishop Sancroft, appreciating the need for a united Protestant front against James II, had himself sought a rapprochement with the presbyterians in 1688, he does not appear to have been prepared to make significant concessions to the dissenters; Timothy J. Fawcett, *The Liturgy of Comprehension in 1689: An abortive attempt to revise The Book of Common Prayer* (Southend, 1973), pp. 18–23. For Tillotson's role in the 1689 comprehension plan, see below p. 167.

32 *The Murmurers. A Poem* (1689), p. 12.

33 [Edward Stephens], *The True English Government, and Misgovernment Of the four last kings* (1689), p. 6.

34 DWL Morrice MS Q, p. 335.

35 Ibid., p. 435.

36 For the contents of the two bills, see Henry Horwitz, *Revolution Politicks: The Career of Daniel Finch, Second Earl of Nottingham 1647–1730* (Cambridge, 1968), pp. 87–91.

37 DWL Morrice MS Q, p. 498; Douglas R. Lacey, *Dissent and Parliamentary Politics in England, 1661–1689: A Study in the Perpetuating and Tempering of Parliamentarianism* (New Brunswick, NJ, 1969), pp. 361–2, n. 92; Roger Thomas, 'Comprehension and Indulgence' in Geoffrey F. Nuttall and Owen Chadwick, eds., *From Uniformity to Unity 1662–1962* (1962), pp. 189–253, esp. 226–7, 245–7.

38 Locke to Philippus van Limborch, 12 March 1689, *Locke Correspondence*, III, 584.

39 John Spurr, 'The Church of England, Comprehension and the Toleration Act of 1689', *EHR*, 104 (1989), 927–46, esp. 940–4.

40 *A Letter from the Member of Parliament, in Answer to the Letter of the Divine, concerning the Bill for Uniting Protestants* (1689), p. 5.

41 Grey, *Debates*, IX, 198.

42 Rupert Browne to Sir William Trumbull, 17 March 1689, BL Add MS 72527, fol. 24. For the King's initial inclination towards whiggery, see above, p. 71.

43 *Memoirs of Sir John Reresby*, ed. Andrew Browning (Glasgow, 1936), p. 557.

44 Cobbett, *Parliamentary History*, V, col. 184.

45 In July 1689 King William told the Marquis of Halifax that 'Hampden Sen[io]r' had 'made the Speech for admitting dissenters into places'; BL Add MS 51511, fol. 19. So unless King William was lying, Jonathan Israel is clearly wrong in asserting that the King consulted only his Dutch advisers before making this speech; see Israel, 'William III and Toleration' in Ole Peter Grell, Jonathan I. Israel and Nicholas Tyacke, eds, *From Persecution to Toleration: The Glorious Revolution and Religion in England* (Oxford, 1991), pp. 129–70, at 152.

46 Edward to Robert Harley, 19 March 1689, BL Add MS 70014, fol. 183.

47 DWL MS Q, p. 505.

48 Grey, *Debates*, IX, 190–8 (my italics).

49 —— to Arthur Charlett, 28 March 1689, Bod. MS Ballard 45, fol. 41; DWL Morrice MS Q, p. 516.

50 Reresby, *Memoirs*, p. 572.

51 Lacey, *Dissent and Parliamentary Politics*, p. 235.

52 —— to Arthur Charlett, 9 April 1689, Bod. MS Ballard 45, fol. 35a.

53 Charles Hatton to Lord Hatton, 9 April 1689, *Hatton Correspondence*, II, 128.

54 DWL Morrice MS Q, p. 534.

55 Horwitz, *Parliament, policy and politics*, p. 25; Israel, 'William III and Toleration', p. 152.

56 Horwitz, *Parliament, policy and politics*, p. 29.

57 The most important provisions of the Toleration Act can be found in E.N. Williams, ed., *The Eighteenth Century Constitution* (Cambridge, 1960), pp. 42–6.

58 DWL Morrice MS Q, p. 558. 'And it's as certain', Morrice added wryly, 'they do now heartily repent they have past it, and if it were not past they would stop it.'

59 *The Note Book of the Rev. Thomas Jolly 1671–1693*, ed. Henry Fishwick (Manchester, Chetham Soc., 1894), p. 94.

60 *The Rev. Oliver Heywood, B.A., 1630–1702; His Autobiography, Diaries, Anecdote and Event Books*, ed. J. Horsfall Turner (4 vols., Brighouse and Bingley, 1882–5), III, 260–1.

61 The terms of the commission can be found in Fawcett, *Liturgy of Comprehension*, pp. 26–7.

62 Tony Claydon, *William III and the Godly Revolution* (Cambridge, 1996), p. 168.

63 These three, together with three other commissioners, failed to attend a single session; see LPL MS 1774, fol. 57.

64 Ibid., fols. 7–8.

65 Ibid., fol. 13.

66 For Jane's comment, see G.V. Bennett, 'Loyalist Oxford and the Revolution' in L.S. Sutherland and L.G. Mitchell, eds, *The History of the University of Oxford: V: The Eighteenth Century* (Oxford, 1986), pp. 9–29, at 27–8. The proposed revisions to the liturgy are set out in Fawcett, *Liturgy of Comprehension*, pp. 49–159. The commission's proposals are conveniently summarised in Thomas Lathbury, *A History of the Convocation of the Church of England* (1842), pp. 266–9. They were closely related to heads of reform drawn up by Tillotson shortly before the commission began its work; see Thomas Birch, *The Life of the Most Reverend Dr John Tillotson, Lord Archbishop of Canterbury* (1752), pp. 182–4. For the controversy over episcopal re-ordination, see below, pp. 170–1.

67 Thomas Comber to Simon Patrick, 19 Oct. 1689, *The Autobiographies and Letters of Thomas Comber*, ed. C.E. Whiting (2 vols., Surtees Soc., 1946–7), II, 182.

68 Lathbury, *History of the Convocation*, p. 271.

69 BL Add MS 63057B, fol. 141.

70 Ibid.

71 Quoted in Donald Maclean, *London at Worship 1689–90* (Presbyterian Hist. Soc. of England, 6th Annual Lecture, 1928), p. 24. I am grateful to Mark Goldie for alerting me to this source.

72 As does Gordon J. Schochet, 'The Act of Toleration and the Failure of Comprehension: Persecution, Nonconformity, and Religious Indifference' in Dale Hoak and Mordechai Feingold, eds, *The World of William and Mary: Anglo-Dutch Perspectives on the Revolution of 1688–9* (Stanford, California, 1996), pp. 165–87, at 185. Professor Schochet's account overlooks both the impact of events in Scotland and the issue of episcopal re-ordination.

73 DWL Morrice MS Q, p. 493.

74 Matthew Henry to Philip Henry, 23 May 1689, Bod. MS Eng. Lett. e. 29, fol. 88.

75 Quoted in Thomas, 'Comprehension and Indulgence', p. 244.

76 DWL Morrice MS Q, pp. 423–4. For the Uxbridge Treaty, see S.R. Gardiner, *History of the Great Civil War 1642–1649* (4 vols., 1901), II, 124–6.

77 DWL Morrice MS Q, p. 648.

78 Wake to Charlett, 7 Nov. [1689], Bod. MS Ballard 3, fol. 53.

79 [John Humfrey], *The Healing Attempt* (1689), 'The Author to the Reader' (unpaginated).
80 LPL MS 1774, fols. 34, 40.
81 See below, pp. 206–9.
82 DWL Morrice MS J (unfoliated historical collections 1625–95), entry for 1694.
83 Tillotson to Frederick Spanheim, 6 Feb. 1691, printed in Birch, *Life of Tillotson*, p. 254.
84 John Hampden to Francis Tallents, 27 May 1693, BL Stowe MS 747, fol. 16.
85 BL Add MS 63057B, fol. 157.
86 *The Diary of Mr Justice Rokeby*, ed. William Boyd (1888?), p. 33.
87 [Leslie], *Querela Temporum*, p. 523.
88 Bishop Lloyd to Bishop Stillingfleet, 13 Nov. 1693, DWL MS 201.38, fol. 66.
89 Edward Bowerman to Thomas Tenison, 17 Dec. 1692, LPL MS 933, no. 9.
90 Humphrey Prideaux to John Ellis, 27 June 1692, *Letters of Prideaux*, p. 154.
91 Same to the same, 18 July 1693, ibid., p. 154.
92 Craig Rose, 'The Origins and Ideals of the SPCK 1699–1716' in John Walsh, Colin Haydon and Stephen Taylor, eds, *The Church of England c.1689–c.1833: From Toleration to Tractarianism* (Cambridge, 1993), pp. 172–90, at 180.
93 Edward Bowerman to Thomas Tenison, 17 Dec. 1692, LPL MS 933, no. 9.
94 Bishop Lloyd to Bishop Stillingfleet, 13 Nov. 1693, DWL MS 201.38, fol. 65. Clause IV of the Toleration Act actually provided that no qualified dissenters were to be 'prosecuted in any ecclesiastical court, for or by reason of their non-conforming to the church of England'; see Williams, *Eighteenth Century Constitution*, p. 43.
95 Bishop Lloyd to Bishop Stillingfleet, 28 Jan. 1694, DWL MS 201.38, fols. 69–70.
96 *The Life and Times of Anthony Wood, antiquary, of Oxford, 1632–1695, described by Himself*, ed. Andrew Clark (5 vols., Oxford, 1891–1900), III, 439.
97 BL Stowe MS 119, fol. 47.
98 *The Diary of Abraham de la Pryme*, ed. Charles Jackson (Durham, Surtees Soc., 54, 1870), pp. 319–20.
99 DWL Morrice MS Q, p. 401.
100 Philip Henry to Matthew Henry, 1 June 1689, *Diaries and Letters of Philip Henry, M.A.*, ed. Matthew Henry Lee (1882), p. 362.
101 *Several Plain and Weighty REASONS for removing The Sacramental Test, Humbly Proposed to Consideration* (1689), p. 2.
102 DWL Morrice MS Q, p. 521.
103 [John Howe], *The Case of the Protestant Dissenters, Represented and Argued* (1689), p. 4.
104 *Several Plain and Weighty REASONS*, p. 1. See also DWL Morrice MS Q, p. 521; [Howe], *Case of the Protestant Dissenters*, p. 4.
105 [Jean Gailhard], *Some Observations upon the keeping the Thirtieth of January and Twenty-ninth of May* (1694), *Somers Tracts*, IX, 481–509, at 508.
106 G.S. De Krey, *A Fractured Society: the Politics of London in the First Age of Party 1688–1715* (Oxford, 1985), pp. 20, 112–14.
107 BL Stowe MS 119, fol. 46.
108 Ibid., fol. 47.

109   De Krey, *Fractured Society*, pp. 114–15.
110   [William Baron], *The Dutch Way of Toleration Most proper for English Dissenters* (1698), p. 3.
111   Ibid., p. 7.
112   Horwitz, *Parliament, policy and politics*, p. 293.
113   [William Stephens], *An Account of the Growth of Deism in England* (1696), p. 10. The themes touched upon in this section are exhaustively discussed in J.A.I. Champion, *The Pillars of Priestcraft Shaken: The Church of England and its Enemies 1660–1730* (Cambridge, 1992).
114   [Stephens], *Account of the Growth of Deism*, pp. 11–12; *Dr Sherlock Vindicated, or Cogent Reasons, Why that Worthy Person hath complied with the Necessity of the Times, and why he at first refused it* (1690), p. 2.
115   [Stephens], *Account of the Growth of Deism*, p. 12.
116   Ibid., pp. 7–8.
117   Ibid., p. 31.
118   Ibid., p. 19.
119   [Sir Robert Howard], *The History of Religion* (1694), pp. 42–3.
120   [Stephens], *Account of the Growth of Deism*, p. 16.
121   Nicholas Rowe, *Tamerlane. A Tragedy* (1702), p. 40.
122   [Stephens], *Account of the Growth of Deism*, pp. 20–1.
123   Champion, *Pillars of Priestcraft*, pp. 109–10.
124   Ibid., pp. 106–7. For Firmin's career and beliefs, see H.W. Stephenson, 'Thomas Firmin, 1632–97' (University of Oxford, D.Phil. dissertation, 1949). The first biography of Firmin was penned by Stephen Nye in 1698, the year after his patron's death.
125   James Lardner, *Of earnestly contending for the Faith. A Sermon Preached at the Cathedral Church of St Paul . . . On Sunday, Sept. the 22th, There Being that Day an Ordination by the Right Reverend the Lord Bishop of London* (1700), preface (unpaginated).
126   Thomas Bray, *A Course of Lectures upon the Church Catechism* (Oxford, 1696), epistle dedicatory (unpaginated).
127   Nine vacancies were created by the deaths of incumbents (some of whom had died before the revolution), six through the deprivation of the nonjurors, and three through the translation of bishops from one see to another. Only two of these vacancies (Ely and Hereford in 1691) were filled by existing bishops, and both these men (Patrick of Chichester and Ironside of Bristol) had been new appointees in 1689. In short, 16 new faces appeared on the bench between 1689 and 1691.
128   Claydon, *William III and the Godly Revolution*, p. 65. The other names on Burnet's list were William Wake, who was offered but refused the diocese of Bath and Wells in 1691, and Anthony Horneck, preacher at the Savoy.
129   G.V. Bennett, 'King William III and the Episcopate' in *idem* and J.D. Walsh, eds, *Essays in Modern English Church History* (1966), pp. 104–32. In marked contrast to his colleagues, Fowler had actively opposed the persecution of dissent during the 'tory reaction' of the early 1680s; see Mark Goldie and John Spurr, 'Politics and the Restoration Parish: Edward Fowler and the Struggle for St Giles Cripplegate', *EHR*, 109 (1994), 572–96.
130   Edward Harley to Sir Edward Harley, 4 March 1690, BL Add MS 70014,

fol. 301. Tenison was close to the Earl of Clarendon at this time.
131 For an interesting discussion of the difference in approach between Sancroft and the 'London clergy', see Fawcett, *Liturgy of Comprehension*, pp. 18–23. Eleven members of the commission (Tillotson, Sharp, Kidder, Hall, Grove, Patrick, Fowler, Tenison, Burnet, Stillingfleet and Stratford) were elevated to the episcopal bench between 1689 and 1691. A twelfth, John Williams, was appointed a bishop later in King William's reign. By the end of the reign, after more than a decade of religious pluralism, Archbishop Sharp's views had diverged markedly from those of his colleagues. He was no longer seen as 'a man of latitude', and had become instead the voice of moderate High Churchmanship on the episcopal bench.
132 See above, p. 160.
133 [Howard], *History of Religion*, p. xix; *POAS*, V, 119–20.
134 Birch, *Life of Tillotson*, p. 18.
135 W.A. Speck, 'William – and Mary?' in Lois G. Schwoerer, ed., *The Revolution of 1688–1689: Changing perspectives* (Cambridge, 1992), pp. 131–46, at 137.
136 Edward Harley to Sir Edward Harley, 6 June 1691, BL Add MS 70015, fol. 96.
137 BL Stowe MS 119, fol. 45.
138 BL Add MS 63057B, fol. 157.
139 Gilbert Burnet, *A Discourse of the Pastoral Care* (1692), pp. x–xi. For Tillotson's role in the production of the *Discourse*, see Claydon, *William III and the Godly Revolution*, p. 175; Mark Goldie, 'John Locke, Jonas Proast and religious toleration 1688–1692' in Walsh, Haydon and Taylor, eds, *The Church of England*, pp. 141–71, at 165.
140 Burnet, *Discourse of the Pastoral Care*, pp. v–vi.
141 BL Add MS 63057B, fol. 141.
142 Burnet, *Discourse of the Pastoral Care*, pp. xii–xiii.
143 Ibid., pp. xv–xvi.
144 Ibid., pp. xvi–xvii (mispaginated as xxxiii). If, as Tony Claydon has claimed (*William III and the Godly Revolution*, p. 175), the *Discourse* 'might have been intended to garner tory support', it was a singularly ham-fisted effort. Such a stinging critique of the clergy would have been all very well had it been penned by a Sancroft or a Ken. Falling from the lips of Burnet, it could only have reinforced the High Church prejudice that King William's bishops were more charitable to the dissenters than to their own brethren.
145 Richard Kidder, *The Life Of the Reverend Anthony Horneck, DD* (1698), pp. 42–3. The religious societies, which first emerged in the late 1670s, were conformist devotional 'clubs' whose goal was the spiritual edification of their own members.
146 John Spurr, *The Restoration Church of England, 1646–1689* (New Haven, Connecticut, 1991), pp. 86–7, 193–4.
147 See, for example, Burnet's epistle dedicatory to his *Discourse of the Pastoral Care*.
148 BL Add MS 63057B, fol. 158.
149 Ibid., fol. 157.
150 Birch, *Life of Tillotson*, pp. 338–9.
151 Ibid., p. 335.

152 Archbishop Tillotson to Bishop Burnet, 31 Aug. 1694, printed in ibid., pp. 336–7.
153 BL Add MS 63057B, fol. 162.
154 It appears that the *Injunctions* had been drafted by Archbishop Tillotson himself. One of the two manuscript copies of the *Injunctions* in the Tenison papers (LPL MS 933, no. 15) has an endorsement by Archbishop Tenison, saying they were prepared by his predecessor.
155 LPL MS 933, no. 15. Although I have used a manuscript copy of the *Injunctions*, they may be more conveniently found in Edward Cardwell, ed., *Documentary Annals of the Reformed Church of England* (2 vols, Oxford, 1839), II, 330–4.
156 Archbishop Tenison's Circular Letter to the bishops of the province of Canterbury, 4 April 1699, printed in Cardwell, *Documentary Annals*, II, 347–52, quotes at 347, 349–50.
157 A.G. Craig, 'The Movement for Reformation of Manners, 1688–1715' (University of Edinburgh Ph.D. dissertation, 1980), pp. 266–8.
158 Cardwell, *Documentary Annals*, II, 352.
159 Craig Rose, 'The origins and ideals of the SPCK 1699–1716' in Walsh, Haydon and Taylor, eds, *Church of England*, pp. 172–90.
160 *Idem*, 'Politics, religion and charity in Augustan London *c.*1680–*c.*1720' (Cambridge University Ph.D. dissertation, 1989), pp. 89–95; W.K. Lowther Clarke, *A History of the SPCK* (1959), ch. 3. For the SPCK's advocacy of clerical associations, see the Society's Second Circular Letter to its clerical correspondents (February 1700), printed in Edmund McClure, ed., *A Chapter in English Church History: SPCK Minutes and Correspondence 1698–1704* (1888), pp. 45–6. The SPCK's interests initially extended to the American colonies, but after 1701 missionary work in America came under the remit of the chartered Society for Propagating the Gospel, another brainchild of Thomas Bray.
161 Robert Wynne to John Chamberlayne, 15 April 1700, McClure, *Chapter in Church History*, p. 287.
162 Mr Price to John Chamberlayne, 29 April 1700, ibid., p. 289.
163 Vincent Edwards to John Chamberlayne, 21 Feb. 1701, ibid., p. 321.
164 Rev Mapletoft to John Chamberlayne, 12 Oct. 1700, ibid., p. 305.
165 Rev Willett to John Chamberlayne, 23 March and 10 June 1700, ibid., pp. 283, 293.
166 John Lewis to John Chamberlayne, 28 Feb. 1700, ibid., p. 281.
167 John Chamberlayne to Mr De Beberinghen, 3 Dec. 1700, ibid., p. 95.
168 The reported view of some members of the Consistory Court of Llandaff; see Mr Harries to John Chamberlayne, 21 June 1700, ibid., p. 295.
169 G.V. Bennett, *The Tory Crisis in Church and State 1688–1730: The Career of Francis Atterbury, Bishop of Rochester* (Oxford, 1975), p. 47.
170 [Francis Atterbury], *A Letter to a Convocation-Man, concerning the Rights, Powers, and Privileges of that Body* (1696), *Somers Tracts*, IX, 411–33, at 412. Sir Walter Scott wrongly attributed this piece to Atterbury's collaborator, Bartholomew Shower.
171 Ibid., pp. 430–1.
172 Ibid., pp. 421–3.

173 Goldie, 'Nonjurors', pp. 26–8.
174 [Atterbury], *Letter to a Convocation-Man*, pp. 422–3.
175 Ibid., pp. 413–14.
176 Ibid., p. 418.
177 Ibid., p. 432.
178 Bennett, *Tory Crisis*, pp. 51–2. Wake proved his point conclusively in his *State of the Church and Clergy of England in their Councils, Synods, Convocations and other Public Assemblies* (1703).
179 Norman Sykes, *William Wake, Archbishop of Canterbury 1657–1737* (2 vols, Cambridge, 1957), I, 88–96.
180 Maurice Wheeler to William Wake, 3 March 1701, CCL Arch.W.Epist. 23, no. 132.
181 ——— to William Wake, 25 March 1700, CCL Arch.W.Epist. 17, fol. 120. The 'Late excellent Book' was probably Atterbury's *Rights, Powers and Privileges of an English Convocation Stated and Vindicated* (1700), which contained a vicious personal attack upon Wake.
182 The best account of the controversy as a whole remains Sykes, *William Wake*, I, 81–116.
183 See above, p. 99.
184 BL Add MS 63057B, fol. 157.
185 Bennett, *Tory Crisis*, p. 55; Sykes, *William Wake*, I, 104.
186 Bennett, *Tory Crisis*, pp. 56–60. The proceedings against Bishop Burnet are discussed in detail in Martin Greig, 'Heresy Hunt: Gilbert Burnet and the Convocation Controversy of 1701', *HJ*, 37 (1994), 569–92.
187 Horwitz, *Parliament, policy and politics*, pp. 293, 312. The three bishops who voted for Lord Somers' impeachment (Compton of London, Sprat of Rochester and Trelawney of Exeter) were survivors of the pre-revolution episcopate.
188 Bennett, *Tory Crisis*, p. 60; *idem*, 'King William III and the Episcopate', pp. 129–30.
189 [Charles Davenant], *The True Picture of a Modern Whig, Set forth in a Dialogue between Mr Whiglove & Mr Double, Two Under-Spur-Leathers to the late Ministry* (1701, 2nd edn), p. 62.

CHAPTER SIX   GODLY REFORMATION

1 *HMC Kenyon MSS*, pp. 268–9.
2 Charles Hatton to Lord Hatton, 10 Aug. 1692, *Hatton Correspondence*, II, 183.
3 Same to the same, 10 Sept. 1692, ibid., pp. 184–5.
4 Sir Edmund King to Lord Hatton, 8 Sept. 1692, ibid., p. 184.
5 *HMC Kenyon MSS*, pp. 266, 268.
6 Robert Fleming, *A Discourse of Earthquakes* (1693), pp. 15–17.
7 Abigail Harley to Sir Edward Harley, 8 Sept. 1692, BL Add MS 70116, unfoliated bundle of Abigail Harley's letters.
8 Sir Thomas Clarges to Robert Harley, 8 Sept. 1692, BL Add MS 70016, fols. 108–9.
9 *A True and Faithfull Account of all the Earthquakes, and the Dreadful Effects thereof,*

That have happened in England since the Norman Conquest, to this Day (1692), pp. 1–2.

10   Robert Harley to Sir Edward Harley, 25 July 1693, BL Add MS 70017, fol. 126.

11   Matthew Henry to Philip Henry, 18 July 1693, DWL MS 90.7, letter 30.

12   *The Note Book of the Rev. Thomas Jolly 1671–1693*, ed. Henry Fishwick (Manchester, Chetham Soc., 1894), p. 118.

13   *The Diary of John Evelyn*, ed. E.S. de Beer (6 vols, Oxford, 1955), V, 152.

14   Ibid., p. 148.

15   [John Sergeant], *An Historical Romance of the Wars, Between the Mighty Giant Gallieno, And the Great Knight Nasonius, And His Associates* (Dublin, 1694), p. 58.

16   *Remarks upon the present Confederacy, and the late Revolution in England* (1693), *Somers Tracts*, X, 491–523, at 522–3.

17   George Halley, *A Sermon Preached in the Cathedral and Metropolitical Church of St Peter in York, On Thursday the Fourteenth of February, 1688/9* (1689), p. 22.

18   Ibid., pp. 27–8.

19   *A Word of Advice unto all those that have a Right to Choose Parliament-Men* (1690), p. 1.

20   Thomas Goodwin, *Of the Happiness of Princes led by Divine Counsel. A Sermon Occasioned by the Death Of that most Excellent Princess, Our late Sovereign Queen Mary* (1695), p. 24.

21   John Morrill, 'Cromwell and his contemporaries' in *idem*, ed., *Oliver Cromwell and the English Revolution* (1990), pp. 259–81, at 272–3.

22   Thomas Bowber, *A Sermon Preached in the Parish-Church of St Swithin, London, March 10th 1694/5 Upon the Much lamented Death Of our Most Gracious Queen* (1695), p. 2.

23   Ibid., pp. 21–2.

24   Gilbert Burnet, *An Essay on the Memory Of the late Queen* (1695), pp. 38–43, at 43.

25   John Woodhouse, *A Sermon Preach'd at Salters-Hall, to the Societies for Reformation of Manners, May 31 1697* (1697), p. 51.

26   Edward Stephens, *Reflections upon the Occurrences of the Last Year from 5 Nov. 1688 to 5 Nov. 1689* (1689), pp. 12–13.

27   Ibid., pp. 19–23, at 22–3.

28   Ibid., p. 32. Soon after the Prince of Orange's landing in England, Stephens had presented him with a draft of a declaration against debauchery. It was William's failure to implement this scheme which lay at the bottom of Stephens's animus; see ibid., pp. 21–2; *idem, The True English Government, and Misgovernment Of the Four last Kings* (1689), pp. 7–8.

29   During the course of the 1690s, perhaps because of disillusion with King William, Stephens came to espouse fiercely anti-erastian views. In fact, he argued that the erastianism of the Reformation had unchurched the Church of England. For a brief review of Stephens's ideas, see Eamon Duffy, 'Primitive Christianity Revived: Religious Renewal in Augustan England' in Derek Baker, ed, *Renaissance and Renewal in Christian History: Studies in Church History 14* (Oxford, Basil Blackwell, 1977), pp. 287–300, at 297–8.

30   DWL MS 28.4, fols. 59–60.

31 Ibid., fols. 61–2.

32 F[rancis] T[allents?] to Richard Baxter, 12 Feb. 1690, DWL MS 59.5, fol. 125.

33 Edward Stephens, *A Caveat against Flattery and Profanation of Sacred things to Secular Ends* (1689), pp. 24–5.

34 J[ean] G[ailhard], *Some Observations upon the Keeping the Thirtieth of January and Twenty-ninth of May* (1694), *Somers Tracts*, IX, 481–509, at 502.

35 *The Speech of the Right Honourable Henry Earl of Warrington, Lord Delamere, to the Grand Jury at Chester, April 13 1692* (1692), *State Tracts*, II, 195–200, at 198–9.

36 Ibid., pp. 199–200.

37 Quoted in A.F.W. Papillon, *Memoirs of Thomas Papillon, of London, Merchant (1623–1702)* (Reading, 1877), pp. 374–5.

38 DWL Morrice MS Q, p. 495.

39 See above, pp. 182–3.

40 BL Add MS 70015, fol. 276.

41 Tony Claydon, *William III and the Godly Revolution* (Cambridge, 1996), p. 115.

42 *His Majesty's Letter to the Right Reverend Father in God Henry Lord Bishop of London, to be communicated to the Two Provinces of Canterbury and York, 13 February 1689/90* (1690), *Somers Tracts*, IX, 588–90, at 589.

43 Claydon, *William III and the Godly Revolution*, pp. 100–10.

44 *The Pepys Ballads*, ed. Hyder Edward Rollins (8 vols, Cambridge, Massachusetts, 1929–32), V, 85.

45 See above, pp. 41–2, 186.

46 *Lettres et Mémoires de Marie Reine D'Angleterre*, ed. Countess Bentinck (The Hague, 1880), p. 94.

47 *Memoirs of Mary Queen of England*, ed. R. Doebner (1886), p. 11.

48 Ibid., p. 59. For the Queen's godliness, see above, pp. 41–2; Claydon, *William III and the Godly Revolution*, pp. 94–9; Mark Goldie, 'John Locke, Jonas Proast and religious toleration 1688–1692' in John Walsh, Colin Haydon and Stephen Taylor, eds, *The Church of England c.1689–c.1833: From Toleration to Tractarianism* (Cambridge, 1993), pp. 143–71, at 163–4.

49 Burnet, *Essay on the Memory*, p. 134.

50 Ibid., p. 102.

51 John Howe, *A Discourse Relating To the Much-lamented Death, And Solemn Funeral Of Our Incomparable and most Gracious Queen Mary, Of most Blessed Memory* (1695), p. 36.

52 William Bates, *A Sermon Preached upon the much Lamented Death Of our Late Gracious Sovereign Queen Mary* (1695), p. 20.

53 William Payne, *A Sermon Upon the Death of the Queen, Preached in the Parish-Church of St Mary White-Chappel* (1695), p. 16.

54 Burnet, *Essay on the Memory*, pp. 102–3.

55 *Memoirs of Mary*, pp. 18, 24, 39.

56 Thomas Birch, *The Life Of the Most Reverend Dr John Tillotson, Lord Archbishop of Canterbury* (1752), pp. 249, 338–9.

57 Bates, *Sermon Preached*, p. 20.

58 Quoted in Birch, *Life of Tillotson*, p. 432.

59 Howe, *Discourse Relating*, p. 38.

60 Richard Lapthorne to Richard Coffin, 8 Nov. 1690, *The Portledge Papers*, ed. Russell J. Kerr and Ida Pine Coffin (1928), p. 90.

61 Same to the same, 1 Aug. 1691, ibid., p. 117.

62 A.G. Craig, 'The Movement for Reformation of Manners, 1688–1715' (University of Edinburgh Ph.D. dissertation, 1980), pp. 25–8.

63 Ibid., pp. 31–2.

64 Ibid., pp. 41–63.

65 Ibid., pp. 72–3; D.W.R. Bahlman, *The Moral Revolution of 1688* (New Haven, Connecticut, 1957), pp. 37–8. A reformation society established by Robert Harley's brother, Edward, in 1693 was independent of the First Society.

66 Craig, 'Movement for Reformation', p. 178.

67 Ibid., p. 95.

68 Draft biography of Maynard Colchester, History of Parliament Trust. I am grateful to David Hayton for permitting me to consult this biography, and for informing me of Colchester's debt to his grandfather.

69 T.C. Barnard, 'Reforming Irish Manners: The Religious Societies in Dublin during the 1690s', *HJ*, 35 (1992), 805–38, at 818–19; Hillel Schwartz, *The French Prophets: The History of a Millenarian Group in Eighteenth-Century England* (Berkeley, California, 1980), pp. 79–80, 232 n. 38.

70 Stephens, *Caveat against Flattery*, pp. 33, 36.

71 *An Account of the Societies for Reformation of Manners, In England and Ireland* (2nd edn, 1699), p. 109.

72 Edmund Calamy, *A Sermon Preach'd before the Societies for Reformation of Manners, in London and Middlesex, upon Monday, Febr. 20 1698/9* (1699), epistle dedicatory (unpaginated).

73 Daniel Williams, *A Sermon Preached at Salters-Hall, To the Societies for Reformation of Manners, May 16 1698* (1698), preface (unpaginated).

74 John Shower, *A Sermon Preach'd to the Societies for Reformation of Manners, in the Cities of London and Westminster, Nov. 15 1697* (1698), pp. 59–60.

75 Williams, *A Sermon Preached*, p. 54.

76 [John Hooke], *A Short Account of the Several Kind of Societies, Set up of late Years, for the promoting of God's Worship, for the Reformation of Manners, and for the Propagation of Christian Knowledge* (1700), p. 2. For Hooke's authorship of this tract, see C.M. Rose, 'Politics, Religion and Charity in Augustan London c.1680–c.1720' (University of Cambridge Ph.D. dissertation, 1989), p. 82.

77 Samuel Bradford, *A Sermon Preach'd at the Church of St Mary le Bow, to the Societies for Reformation of Manners, Octob. 4 1697* (1697), pp. 42–3.

78 This term was coined by Colin Davis to denote a central characteristic of Cromwellian churchmanship; see Colin Davis, 'Cromwell's religion' in John Morrill, ed., *Oliver Cromwell and the English Revolution* (1990), pp. 181–208, at 191.

79 John Howe, *A Sermon Preach'd Febr. 14 1698. And now Publish'd at the Request of the Societies for Reformation of Manners in London and Westminster* (1698), p. 48.

80 Henry Rogers, *The Life and Character of John Howe. With an Analysis of His Writings* (1836), pp. 30–1, 82–4; R.F. Horton, *John Howe* (1895), pp. 37, 49–50.

81 Davis, 'Cromwell's religion', pp. 201–7; *idem*, 'Against Formality: One

Aspect of the English Revolution', *TRHS*, 6th series, 3 (1993), 265–88; Blair Worden, 'Toleration and the Cromwellian Protectorate' in W.J. Sheils, ed., *Persecution and Toleration: Studies in Church History 21* (Oxford, Basil Blackwell, 1984), pp. 199–233, at 210–11.

82   William Nicolson to Mr Yates, 15 March 1700, *Letters on Various Subjects, Literary, Political, and Ecclesiastical, to and from William Nicolson, DD*, ed. John Nichols (2 vols, 1809), I, 153–4.

CHAPTER SEVEN   SCOTLAND AND IRELAND

1   Ian B. Cowan, 'The Reluctant Revolutionaries: Scotland in 1688' in Eveline Cruickshanks, ed., *By Force or by Default? The Revolution of 1688–1689* (Edinburgh, 1989), pp. 65–81.

2   T.N. Clarke, 'The Scottish Episcopalians, 1688–1720' (University of Edinburgh Ph.D. dissertation, 1987), pp. 7–10; William Ferguson, *Scotland 1689 to the Present* (Edinburgh, 1968), pp. 14, 104; Tim Harris, 'Reluctant Revolutionaries? The Scots and the Revolution of 1688–89' in Howard Nenner, ed., *Politics and the Imagination in Later Stuart Britain: Essays Presented to Lois Green Schwoerer* (Rochester, NY, 1997), pp. 97–117, at 107–8.

3   Robert Beddard, 'The Unexpected Whig Revolution of 1688' in *idem*, ed., *The Revolutions of 1688* (Oxford, 1991), pp. 11–101, at 97–9.

4   P.W.J. Riley, *King William and the Scottish Politicians* (Edinburgh, 1979), p. 38.

5   ———— to Arthur Charlett, 17 April 1689, Bod MS Ballard 45, fol. 37.

6   For the presence of the Cameronians in Edinburgh, overlooked by most historians, see Paul Hopkins, *Glencoe and the End of the Highland War* (Edinburgh, 1986), p. 126.

7   Ferguson, *Scotland*, pp. 6, 8–9.

8   Clarke, 'Scottish Episcopalians', p. 13.

9   Ferguson, *Scotland*, pp. 5, 8.

10   Clarke, 'Scottish Episcopalians', pp. 8–9.

11   Ibid., pp. 24–5, 38.

12   Ibid., pp. 49–50, 422; Riley, *King William and the Scottish Politicians*, pp. 35–6; Ferguson, *Scotland*, pp. 104–5.

13   Lionel K.J. Glassey, 'William II and the Settlement of Religion in Scotland, 1688–1690,' *Records of the Scottish Church History Society*, 23 (1987–9), 317–29.

14   Ferguson, *Scotland*, p. 103.

15   Printed in Joseph M'Cormick, ed., *State-papers and Letters addressed to William Carstares* (Edinburgh, 1774), p. 39.

16   Riley, *King William and the Scottish Politicians*, p. 4.

17   Robert Keith, *A Large New Catalogue of the Bishops of the several Sees Within the Kingdom of Scotland Down to the Year 1688* (Edinburgh, 1755), pp. 41–5; Robert Herbert Story, *William Carstares: A Character and Career of the Revolutionary Epoch 1649–1715* (1874), p. 164.

18   Ian B. Cowan, 'Church and State reformed? The Revolution of 1688–9 in Scotland' in Jonathan I. Israel, ed., *The Anglo-Dutch Moment: Essays on the Glorious Revolution and its world impact* (Cambridge, 1991), pp. 163–83, at 175.

19   BL Add MS 63057B, fol. 134.

20   Ferguson, *Scotland*, p. 8.

21   Ibid., pp.8–9; Hopkins, *Glencoe*, p. 180. See also James Halliday, 'The Club and the Revolution in Scotland 1689–90', *SHR*, 45 (1966), 143–59.

22   Ferguson, *Scotland*, pp. 12–13; Riley, *King William and the Scottish Politicians*, pp. 38–9; Clarke, 'Scottish Episcopalians', pp. 57–8.

23   BL Add MS 63057B, fol. 141.

24   Quoted in Riley, *King William and the Scottish Politicians*, p. 62.

25   Story, *William Carstares*, pp. 197–8.

26   Clarke, 'Scottish Episcopalians', pp. 60–1; Ferguson, *Scotland*, pp. 15, 105.

27   LPL MS 806, no. 3, fol. 36.

28   LPL MS 929, no. 18.

29   BL Add MS 63057B, fol. 141.

30   Carstares to Crawford, 7 Dec. 1689, *HMC Hope Johnstone MSS*, p. 144.

31   Todd to Wharton, [Nov.] 1689, *Letters on Various Subjects, Literary, Political, and Ecclesiastical, to and from William Nicolson, D.D.*, ed. John Nichols (2 vols, 1809), I, 17.

32   W. Glover to Edmund Bohun, 16 May 1690, CUL Sel. 3. 237¹⁴³ (rare books).

33   [Charles Leslie], *Querela Temporum; or, the Danger of the Church of England. In a Letter from the Dean of —— to ——, Prebend of —— (1694)* in *Somers Tracts*, IX, 509–27, at 518. In fact, the post-revolution Kirk asserted neither the National Covenant of 1638 nor the Solemn League and Covenant of 1643. The latter had provided for the establishment of presbyterianism on both sides of the border.

34   Ibid., p. 519.

35   [Nathaniel Johnston], *The Dear Bargain; or, a true Representation of the State of the English Nation under the Dutch* (1690?) in *Somers Tracts*, X, 349–77, at 367.

36   BL Sloane MS 1731A, fol. 155.

37   Maurice Wheeler to William Wake, 3 March 1701, CCL Arch. W. Epist. 23, no. 132.

38   King William to the General Assembly, 13 Feb. 1691, *CSPD, May 1690–Oct. 1691*, p. 258.

39   Same to the same, *CSPD, Nov. 1691–Dec. 1692*, pp. 86–8.

40   Ferguson, *Scotland*, p. 108; Riley, *King William and the Scottish Politicians*, pp. 74–5.

41   Tarbat to the Earl of Nottingham, 8 June 1692, *HMC Finch MSS*, IV, 212.

42   Johnston to Nottingham, 13 Aug. 1692, ibid., 388.

43   Clarke, 'Scottish Episcopalians', pp. 114–15; Riley, *King William and the Scottish Politicians*, p. 87.

44   Story, *William Carstares*, pp. 236–42.

45   Tristram Clarke, 'The Williamite Episcopalians and the Glorious Revolution in Scotland', *Records of the Scottish Church History Society*, 24 (1990–92), 33–51 at 49.

46   LPL MS 806, no. 3, fol. 29.

47   Alexander Monro to John Mackenzie, 5 July 1692, *Miscellany of the Scottish Historical Society V* (Edinburgh, 1933), p. 228.

48   Same to the same, 11 Dec. 1694, ibid., p. 266.

49   Clarke, 'Scottish Episcopalians', p. 127.

50   Ibid., p. 130; Riley, *King William and the Scottish Politicians*, p. 95.

51 See above, pp. 16, 122.
52 For the background to the Treaty of Limerick, see D.W. Hayton, 'The Williamite Revolution in Ireland, 1688–91' in Israel, ed., *Anglo-Dutch Moment*, pp. 185–213, at 207–8; Jonathan I. Israel, 'The Dutch role in the Glorious Revolution' in ibid., pp. 105–62, at 158.
53 Harman Murtagh, 'The War in Ireland 1689–91' in W.A. Maguire, ed., *Kings in Conflict: The Revolutionary War in Ireland and its Aftermath 1689–1750* (Belfast, 1990), pp. 61–91 at 90–1; J.G. Simms, *Jacobite Ireland 1685–91* (1969), pp. 249–53; Hayton, 'Williamite Revolution', p. 208; Israel, 'Dutch role', p. 158.
54 Simms, *Jacobite Ireland*, pp. 82–4.
55 Bonnell to Harley, 3 Nov. 1691, BL Add MS 70015, fol. 235.
56 Lords Justices of Ireland to the Earl of Nottingham, 30 Nov. 1695, *HMC Finch MSS*, III, 304.
57 S.J. Connolly, 'The Penal Laws' in Maguire, ed., *Kings in Conflict*, pp. 157–72 at 157.
58 Sidney to the Earl of Portland, 3 Oct. 1690, *CSPD, July–Dec. 1695 and Addenda 1689–95*, pp. 155–6.
59 ——— to John Ellis, 4 Dec. 1691, BL Add MS 28877, fol. 221.
60 Hayton, 'Williamite Revolution', p. 209.
61 This paragraph is based on James I. McGuire, 'The Irish Parliament of 1692' in Thomas Bartlett and D.W. Hayton, eds, *Penal Era and Golden Age: Essays in Irish History 1690–1800* (Belfast, 1979), pp. 1–31.
62 BL Add MS 70017, fol. 36.
63 *The Parliamentary Diary of Narcissus Luttrell 1691–1693*, ed. Henry Horwitz (Oxford, 1972), p. 439.
64 Ibid., p. 441.
65 Ibid., p. 448.
66 McGuire, 'Irish Parliament', pp. 26–8; Horwitz, *Parliament, policy and politics*, p. 154.
67 Wyche and Duncombe to Sir John Trenchard, 14 July 1694, BL Add MS 21136, fol. 25.
68 Lord Capel to Sir John Trenchard, ibid., fol. 27.
69 Hayton, 'Williamite Revolution', p. 209; S.J. Connolly, *Religion, Law and Power: The Making of Protestant Ireland 1660–1760* (Oxford, 1992), p. 76.
70 McGuire, 'Irish Parliament', p. 29. Wyche and Duncombe complained to English ministers that the excise bill was an inadequate assertion of the Crown's right to send money bills to Ireland; see *CSPD, July–Dec. 1695*, p. 4.
71 Richard Warburton to John Ellis, 19 Sept. 1695, BL Add MS 28879, fol. 138.
72 Same to the same, 18 Oct. 1695, ibid., fol. 210.
73 W.A. Maguire, 'The Land Settlement' in *idem*, ed., *Kings in Conflict*, pp. 139–56 at 148.
74 Connolly, 'Penal Laws', p. 161; Hayton, 'Williamite Revolution', p. 209; Charles Ivar McGrath, 'Securing the Protestant interest: the origins and purpose of the penal laws of 1695', *IHS*, 30 (1996–7), 25–46.
75 Maguire, 'Land Settlement', p. 148; Connolly, 'Penal Laws', p. 161.
76 Sir Charles Porter to Sir William Trumbull, 9 July 1695, BL Add MS 72532, fol. 126.

77 Lord Capel to the Earl of Shrewsbury, 6 Oct. 1695, *HMC Buccleugh MSS*, II, 235.

78 Connolly, *Religion, Law and Power*, pp. 77–8; David Hayton, 'The Beginnings of the "Undertaker System"' in Bartlett and Hayton, eds, *Penal Era*, pp. 32–54, at 43–4.

79 Brodrick to Shrewsbury, *HMC Buccleugh MSS*, II, 250.

80 Capel to Shrewsbury, ibid., 288–9.

81 Connolly, 'Penal Laws', p. 162; Hayton, 'Williamite Revolution', p. 210.

82 Maguire, 'Land Settlement', pp. 145–6; Connolly, 'Penal Laws', p. 162.

83 Maguire, 'Land Settlement', p. 156.

84 Connolly, *Religion, Law and Power*, pp. 268–9; *idem*, 'Penal Laws', pp. 161–2; Patrick Kelly, 'Ireland and the Glorious Revolution' in Beddard, ed., *Revolutions of 1688*, pp. 163–90, at 185.

85 Connolly, 'Penal Laws', pp. 162–4, 171–2; Simms, *Jacobite Ireland*, pp. 262–3.

86 Queen Mary to King William, 7 July 1690, printed in Marjorie Bowen, *The Third Mary Stuart: Mary of York, Orange & England: Being a Character Study with Memoirs and Letters of Queen Mary II of England, 1662–1694* (1929), p. 198.

87 Simms, *Jacobite Ireland*, p. 8; Connolly, *Religion, law and power*, pp. 161, 167.

88 'A short view of the present condition of the Church of Ireland, together with some Remedys proposed by B.L., April 1697', LPL MS 929, no. 60, fols. 1–3. This paper is attributed to Bishop Dopping in John Brady, 'Remedies Proposed for the Church of Ireland (1697)', *Archivium Hibernicum*, 22 (1959), 162–73.

89 In August 1690 it was reported from Dublin that Dr William King, one of the few episcopal clergy to remain at his post during the Catholic ascendancy, 'expected a great facon between the Clergy that went to England & that staid here; & that the first being more numerous would defeat all the good that could be proposed to be done for this church': James Bonnell to John Strype, 5 Aug. 1690, CUL Mm.6.49, no. 8.

90 Letter to Archbishop Tenison, endorsed in his hand 'Clergy of Ireland 1695', LPL MS 929, no. 96.

91 'A memorandum concerning ye Diocess of Down and Connor in ye Kingdom of Ireland', LPL MS 929, no. 55.

92 Viscount Fitzharding to John Fitzpatrick, 13 June 1691, *HMC Finch MSS*, III, 110. The *regium donum* had been established by Charles II, but fell into abeyance during his brother's reign.

93 LPL MS 929, no. 96.

94 Phil Kilroy, *Protestant Dissent and Controversy in Ireland 1660–1714* (Cork, 1994), pp. 188–93.

95 Shrewsbury to Johnston, 1 Aug. 1695, *HMC Buccleugh MSS*, II, 210. See also [Anthony Dopping], *The Case of the Dissenters of Ireland Consider'd, in Reference to the Sacramental Test* (Dublin, 1695), pp. 1–2.

96 T.C. Barnard, 'Reforming Irish Manners: the Religious Societies in Dublin during the 1690s', *HJ*, 35 (1992), 805–38, esp. 808–11.

97 Archbishop Marsh to Archbishop Tenison, 27 April 1695, LPL MS 942, no. 96.

98 Same to the same, 18 June 1695, ibid., no. 65.

99 Bishop King to Richard Griffith, 12 Feb. 1701, TCD MS 750/2, fol. 94.

100 James Bonnell to John Strype, 4 Jan. 1695, CUL Add MS 1, no. 79.
101 Memorandum by Bishop King on 'The State of the Church of Ireland', TCD MS 1995–2008, no. 115a, fol. 3.
102 William King, *A Discourse Concerning The Inventions of Men in the Worship of God* (2nd edn., 1694), p. 166.
103 Ibid., p. 58.
104 Bishop King to Bishop Lloyd of Lichfield and Coventry, 15 Dec. 1696, TCD MS 750/1, fol. 48. For a vigorous response to Bishop King's book, see Joseph Boyse, *Remarks On a Late Discourse of William Lord Bishop of Derry; Concerning The Inventions of Men in the Worship of God* (Dublin, 1695).
105 King to Bonnell, 18 January 1695, TCD MS 1995–2008, no. 396.
106 Lord Sidney to the Earl of Nottingham, 20 Feb. 1693, *CSPD, 1693*, p. 39.
107 Henry Ash to Bishop King, 2 November 1697, TCD MS 1995–2008, no. 548.
108 Raymond Gillespie, 'The Presbyterian Revolution in Ulster, 1660–1690' in W.J. Shiels and Diana Wood, eds, *The Churches, Ireland and the Irish: Studies in Church History 25* (Oxford, Basil Blackwell, 1989), 159–70, esp. 168–9; Connolly, *Religion, law and power*, p. 167.
109 BL Sloane MS 2902, fol. 218.
110 John Methuen to Robert Harley, 27 Sept. 1697, BL Add MS 70018, fol. 208.
111 Bishop King to Bishop Lloyd of Lichfield and Coventry, 15 Dec. 1696, TCD MS 750/1, fol. 48.
112 Bishop King to Bishop Samuel Foy of Waterford, 5 Oct. 1697, ibid., fol. 96.
113 Bishop King to Sir Robert Southwell, 21 Dec. 1697, ibid., fol. 149.
114 Ferguson, *Scotland*, p. 82.
115 T.C. Smout, 'The Road to Union' in Geoffrey Holmes, ed., *Britain after the Glorious Revolution, 1689–1714* (1969), pp. 176–96, at 180.
116 Ferguson, *Scotland*, p. 83; Smout, 'Road to Union', p. 178.
117 Eric Graham, 'In Defence of the Scottish Maritime Interest', *SHR*, 71 (1992), pp. 88–109, at 93–4.
118 Ibid., p. 89.
119 Riley, *King William and the Scottish Politicians,* pp. 97–8; George Pratt Insh, *The Company of Scotland Trading to Africa and the Indies* (1932), pp. 20–1.
120 Ibid., pp. 27–8, 47–8; Ferguson, *Scotland*, p. 27.
121 John Cary et al. to the MPs for Bristol, 28 Dec. 1695, BL Add MS 5540, fol. 90.
122 Report of the Customs Commissioners to the House of Lords, 5 Dec. 1695, *HMC Hastings MSS*, IV, 315; Insh, *Company of Scotland*, pp. 54–5.
123 Cobbett, *Parliamentary History*, V, cols 975–6.
124 Insh, *Company of Scotland*, p. 61.
125 Quoted in ibid., pp. 64–5.
126 Ibid., pp. 65–7; John Prebble, *The Darien Disaster* (1968), pp. 56–60.
127 Quoted in Insh, *Company of Scotland*, pp. 72–3. For a fuller discussion of the ideas underpinning the Darien scheme, see David Armitage, 'The Scottish Vision of Empire: Intellectual Origins of the Darien Venture' in John Robertson, ed., *A Union for Empire: Political Thought and the British Union of 1707* (Cambridge, 1995), pp. 97–118.
128 Insh, *Company of Scotland*, pp. 118–19, 127–8.

129 Earl of Marchmont to William Carstares, 25 Nov. 1699, *Carstares State-Papers*, p. 511.

130 Daniel Szechi and David Hayton, 'John Bull's Other Kingdoms: The English Government of Scotland and Ireland' in Clyve Jones, ed, *Britain in the First Age of Party: Essays Presented to Geoffrey Holmes* (1987), pp. 241–80, at 247.

131 Edmund Gibson to Arthur Charlett, Bod MS Ballard 5, fol. 162.

132 Quoted in Armitage, 'Scottish Vision', p. 107.

133 Insh, *Company of Scotland*, p. 77.

134 Ibid., p. 57; Riley, *King William and the Scottish Politicians*, pp. 98–9.

135 Insh, *Company of Scotland*, pp. 86–7.

136 Ibid., pp. 91–2.

137 Quoted in ibid., p. 95.

138 Ibid., p. 96.

139 For the Partition Treaties, see above pp. 144–51.

140 Quoted in Prebble, *Darien Disaster*, p. 197; Insh, *Company of Scotland*, pp. 147–9.

141 Ibid., pp. 161–5.

142 Earl of Jersey to Matthew Prior, 10 July 1699, *HMC Bath MSS*, III, 370.

143 BL Add MS 46542, fol. 36.

144 James Vernon to Alexander Stanhope, 27 March 1699, quoted in Insh, *Company of Scotland*, p. 151.

145 James Vernon to Duke of Shrewsbury, 2 Dec. 1699, *Vernon Correspondence*, II, 374.

146 Insh, *Company of Scotland*, pp. 175–7.

147 Ibid., pp. 185–98.

148 Robert Wodrow to James Wallace, 16 July 1700, *Early Letters of Robert Wodrow 1698–1709*, ed. L.W. Sharp (Edinburgh, 1937), p. 92.

149 John Cherry to John Ellis, 16 Aug. 1700, BL Add MS 28885, fol. 327.

150 [Walter Herries], *A Defence of the Scots Abdicating Darien. Including An Answer to the Defence of the Scots Settlement there* (1700), epistle dedicatory (unpaginated) and p. 150. Herries had been a surgeon in the first expedition.

151 *A Defence of the Scots Settlement at Darien* (Edinburgh, 1699), p. 29.

152 Ibid., p. 47.

153 Ibid., p. 41.

154 *An Enquiry into the Causes of the Miscarriage of the Scots Colony at Darien* (Glasgow, 1700), p. 45.

155 Ibid., p. 46.

156 *A Defence*, pp. 29–30.

157 *An Enquiry*, p. 9.

158 *A Defence*, p. 30. See also, *An Enquiry*, pp. 40–1.

159 Ibid., p. 37.

160 *A Defence*, pp. 45–6.

161 Ibid., p. 59.

162 Ibid., p. 55.

163 The affairs of the Scottish parliament are chronicled in great detail in Riley, *King William and the Scottish Politicians*.

164 Ibid., pp. 129–33, 137–8.

165 Lord Melville to William Carstares, 27 June 1700, *Carstares State-Papers*, p. 546; Insh, *Company of Scotland*, pp. 220–24.
166 Ibid., pp. 227–8; Riley, *King William and the Scottish Politicians*, p. 135.
167 Robert Wodrow to James Wallace, 16 July 1700, *Early Letters of Wodrow*, p. 92.
168 Colonel Ferguson to William Carstares, 15 June 1700, *Carstares State-Papers*, p. 527.
169 Riley, *King William and the Scottish Politicians*, pp. 147–51.
170 Ibid., pp. 52, 160.
171 Smout, 'Road to Union', pp. 182–3.
172 Quoted in ibid., p. 184.
173 Quoted in Riley, *King William and the Scottish Politicians*, pp. 51–2.
174 Ibid., p. 53; William Ferguson, *Scotland's Relations with England: A Survey to 1707* (Edinburgh, 1977), pp. 171–2.
175 Bod. MS Carte 81, fol. 766.
176 BL Add MS 63057B, fol. 140.
177 *A Defence*, pp. 51–2.
178 *An Enquiry*, p. 40.
179 *A Defence*, pp. 57–8.
180 *The Argument against a Standing Army Rectified, and the Reflections and Remarks upon it in Several Pamphlets, Consider'd* (1697), p. 28.
181 Charles Hatton to Lord Hatton, 20 Jan. 1700, *Hatton Correspondence*, II, 246.
182 Smout, 'Road to Union', pp. 181–2. The events leading to the Act of Union of 1707 are described in W.A. Speck, *The Birth of Britain: A New Nation 1700–1710* (Oxford, Basil Blackwell, 1994).
183 See above, pp. 128–9.
184 Horwitz, *Parliament, policy and politics*, pp. 235, 256; H.F. Kearney, 'The Political Background to English Mercantilism, 1695–1700', *Economic History Review*, 2nd series, 11 (1958–9), 484–96; Patrick Kelly, 'The Irish Woollen Export Prohibitions Act of 1699: Kearney Revisited', *Irish Economic and Social History*, 7 (1980), 22–43.
185 John Cary and Edward Hacket to Sir Thomas Day and Major Yate, 2 Dec. 1695, BL Add MS 5540, fol. 78.
186 John Cary, *An Essay on the State of England, In Relation to its Trade, Its Poor, and its Taxes, For carrying on the present War against France* (Bristol, 1695), p. 91.
187 Edmund Bohun to John Cary, 15 Feb. 1696, BL Add MS 5540, fol. 62. Although the term 'Anglo-Irish' is anachronistic, I use it in this section as a convenient way of describing Irish Protestants of English descent. Until the Restoration, at least, they were most commonly referred to as the 'New English' to distinguish them from the 'Old English', the descendants of the pre-Reformation English settlers who had generally remained faithful to the old religion. By the end of the seventeenth-century, the 'Old English', save for the minority which had accepted Protestantism, had been displaced as Ireland's ruling elite by the 'New English'. After the wars of the 1640s and 1689–91, Irish Protestants could no longer see any good reason to distinguish the 'Old English' from the latter's erstwhile enemies, the Gaels. True, Gaels and 'Old English' had different ethnic origins. But as far as most Irish Protestants were concerned, they were both 'Irish' i.e.,

papists; see Connolly, *Religion, Law and Power*, pp. 114–18.

188   John Cary to Edmund Bohun, 31 Jan. 1696, BL Add MS 5540 fol. 61. The letters in square brackets are missing from the edge of the folio.

189   'Extract from Mr Alderman Crofts of Corke, the 2nd June 1699', BL Add MS 21133, fol. 39.

190   'Extract to L[or]d Weymouth in answer to Querys sent touching the high rates of Wool there &c', Dublin, 7 Sept. 1699, BL Add MS 21133, fols. 45–6. For further complaints that the Scots were coming to monopolize the trade of Ireland, see Arthur Bushe to John Ellis, 11 March 1696, BL Add MS 28880, fol. 87; BL Sloane MS 2902, fol. 138.

191   For the operation of Poynings' Law, see above, p. 221. By the late 1690s the Irish parliament had, to some degree, circumvented Poynings' Law through its practice of drawing up the 'heads of bills' which were then formally drafted by the Irish Privy Council; see Szechi and Hayton, 'John Bull's Other Kingdoms', pp. 260–1.

192   Sir Charles Porter to Sir William Trumbull, 9 July 1695, BL Add MS 72532, fol. 127.

193   Bishop King to the Bishop of Killaloe, 13 May 1698, TCD MS 750/1, fol. 229.

194   Bishop King to Sir Robert Southwell, 4 Dec. 1697, TCD MS 750/1, fol. 141.

195   Szechi and Hayton, 'John Bull's Other Kingdoms', pp. 266–7.

196   Bishop King to Francis Annesley, 16 April 1698, ibid., fols. 211–12.

197   William Molyneux, *The Case of Ireland's Being Bound by Acts of Parliament in England Stated* (Dublin, 1698), epistle dedicatory (unpaginated). For a recent analysis of Molyneux's arguments, see Jacqueline Hill, 'Ireland without union: Molyneux and his legacy' in Robertson, ed., *Union for empire*, pp. 271–96.

198   Cobbett, *Parliamentary History*, V, col. 1181.

199   William Molyneux to John Locke, 19 April 1698, *Locke Correspondence*, VI, 337. Comprehensive assaults on Molyneux's scholarship can be found in *An Answer to Mr Molyneux His Case of Ireland's being bound by Acts of Parliament in England, Stated* (1698) and W. Atwood, *The History and Reasons, of the Dependency of Ireland upon the Imperial Crown of the Kingdom of England* (1698).

200   *An Answer to Mr Molyneux*, epistle dedicatory (unpaginated). Much the same argument would be used against the American colonists more than sixty years later.

201   John Cary, *A Vindication of the Parliament of England, In Answer to . . . The Case of Ireland . . .* (1698), p. 2.

202   [Simon Clement], *The Interest of England, As it stands with Relation to the Trade of Ireland Considered* (1698), p. 23.

203   Horwitz, *Parliament, policy and politics*, pp. 266–8; Szechi and Hayton, 'John Bull's Other Kingdoms', p. 267. See also above, p. 54–5.

204   Sir Richard Cox to Robert Harley, 28 Oct. 1699, BL Add MS 70019, fol. 129.

205   [Francis Annesley], *Some Thoughts on the Bill Depending before the Right Honourable the House of Lords, For Prohibiting the Exportation of the Woolen Manufactures of Ireland to Foreign Parts* (1698), pp. 7–8. For Annesley's authorship of this piece, often attributed to Sir Richard Cox, see Kelly, 'Irish Woollen Export Prohibitions Act', p. 35, n. 47.

206 BL Add MS 72532, fol. 14.
207 James Vernon to the Duke of Shrewsbury, 12 Oct. 1697, *Vernon Correspondence*, I, 429.
208 Cobbett, *Parliamentary History*, V, col. 1181. The Irish parliament's bill to 'secure the King's person' never in fact became law; see Connolly, *Religion, Law and Power*, p. 271.
209 John Methuen to the Duke of Shrewsbury, 3 Feb. 1698, *HMC Buccleugh MSS*, II, 600.
210 Horwitz, *Parliament, policy and politics*, pp. 235, 256; Kelly, 'Irish Woollen Export Prohibitions Act', pp. 36–42.
211 Sir Robert Southwell to Bishop King of Derry, 26 April 1699, TCD MS 1995–2008, no. 606.
212 [Annesley], *Some Thoughts*, pp. 17–18.
213 James Bonnell to Robert Harley, 3 Nov. 1691, BL Add MS 70015, fols. 235–6.
214 'Remarks shewing that it is not the interest of England that Ireland should be a separate kingdom', *CSPD, May 1690–Oct. 1691*, pp. 201–6, at 205.
215 James Kelly, 'The origins of the Act of Union: an examination of unionist opinion in Britain and Ireland, 1650–1800', *IHS*, 25 (1986–7), 236–63 at 240–2; Jim Smyth, ' "Like Amphibious Animals": Irish Protestants, Ancient Britons, 1691–1707', *HJ*, 36 (1993), 785–97, at 792–5; *idem*, ' "No remedy more proper": Anglo–Irish unionism before 1707' in Brendan Bradshaw and Peter Roberts, eds, *British consciousness and identity. The making of Britain, 1533–1707* (Cambridge, 1998), pp. 301–20.
216 'Extract of a Letter from Dublin 17 Aprill 1697', BL Sloane MS 2902, fol. 138.
217 Bishop King to Sir Robert Southwell, 19 July 1697, TCD MS 750/1, fol. 79.
218 Sir Richard Cox to Robert Harley, 28 Oct. 1699, BL Add MS 70019, fol. 130.
219 [Molyneux], *The Case of Ireland*, pp. 95–8, at 97–8.

CHAPTER EIGHT   A REMEMBRANCE OF TIMES PAST

1 *The Embleme of Englands Distractions As also of her attained, and further expected Freedome, & Happines* (1690).
2 *POAS*, V, 149.
3 It was a theme also taken up by Louis XIV's propagandists. See Jonathan I. Israel, 'General introduction' in *idem*, ed., *The Anglo-Dutch Moment: Essays on the Glorious Revolution and its world impact* (Cambridge, 1991), pp. 1–43, at 43.
4 *POAS*, V, 150–1.
5 Edmund Calamy, *Memoirs of the Life Of the Late Revd Mr John Howe* (1724), p. 131.
6 For Ludlow's brief return to England, see Barbara Taft, 'Return of a Regicide: Edmund Ludlow and the Glorious Revolution', *History*, 76 (1991), 197–220.
7 Richard Younge to John Wildman, 23 May 1689, BL Add MS 61690, fol. 98.
8 Gilbert Burnet, *A Sermon Preached at the Coronation of William III and Mary II* (1689), pp. 27–8.
9 Ibid., pp. 19–20.

10   BL Add MS 63057B, fol. 162.
11   Taft, 'Return of a Regicide', pp. 219–20.
12   See above, pp. 81–2.
13   John Morrill, 'Introduction' in *idem*, ed., *Oliver Cromwell and the English Revolution* (1990), pp. 1–18, esp. 15–17; Derek Hirst, 'The Lord Protector, 1653–1658' in ibid., pp. 119–48, esp. 125–30.
14   Horwitz, *Parliament, policy and politics*, pp. 303–4.
15   *POAS*, VI, 366.
16   Ibid., pp. 362–3.
17   Ibid., p. 396.
18   Ibid., p. 393.
19   Bod MS Eng. Hist. b. 210, fols 6–7.
20   *The Rev. Oliver Heywood, B.A. 1630–1702; His Autobiography, Diaries, Anecdote and Event Books*, ed. J. Horsfall Turner (4 vols, Brighouse and Bingley, 1882–5), IV, 63.
21   Robert Price to Robert Harley, 14 March 1702, BL Add MS 70020, fol. 162.
22   A[bigail] Pye to Abigail Harley, 25 March 1702, ibid., fol. 164.
23   Hertfordshire Records Office D/EP/F29, fol. 198.
24   Ibid., fol. 209.
25   *POAS*, VI, 394–5.
26   Kathleen Wilson, 'A Dissident Legacy: Eighteenth Century Popular Politics and the Glorious Revolution' in J.R. Jones, ed., *Liberty Secured? Britain before and after 1688* (Stanford, California, 1992), pp. 298–334, esp. 301–12.
27   BL Add MS 27440, fol. 84.
28   For a similar view, see Israel, 'General introduction', pp. 42–3.
29   Heywood, *Diaries*, IV, 61–2.

Index